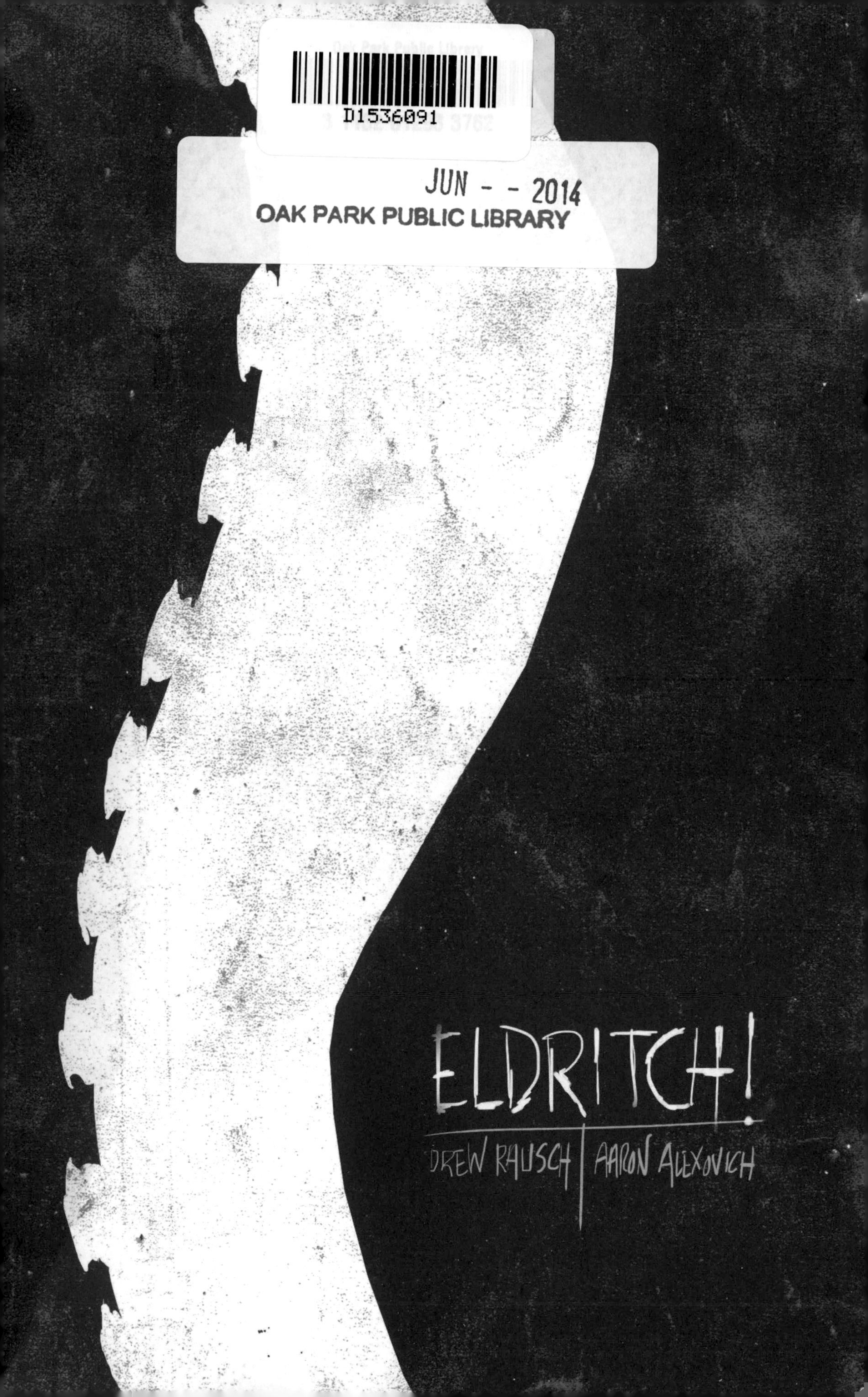
ELDRITCH!
DREW RAUSCH | AARON ALEXOVICH

ELDRITCH!

ART by DREW RAUSCH

WRITTEN by AARON ALEXOVICH

for H.P.

IA! IA!
LOVECRAFT
FHTAGN!

published by SLG PUBLISHING

44 Race Street San Jose, CA 95126
President and Publisher – Dan Vado

July 2013
ISBN – 978-1-59362-249-7

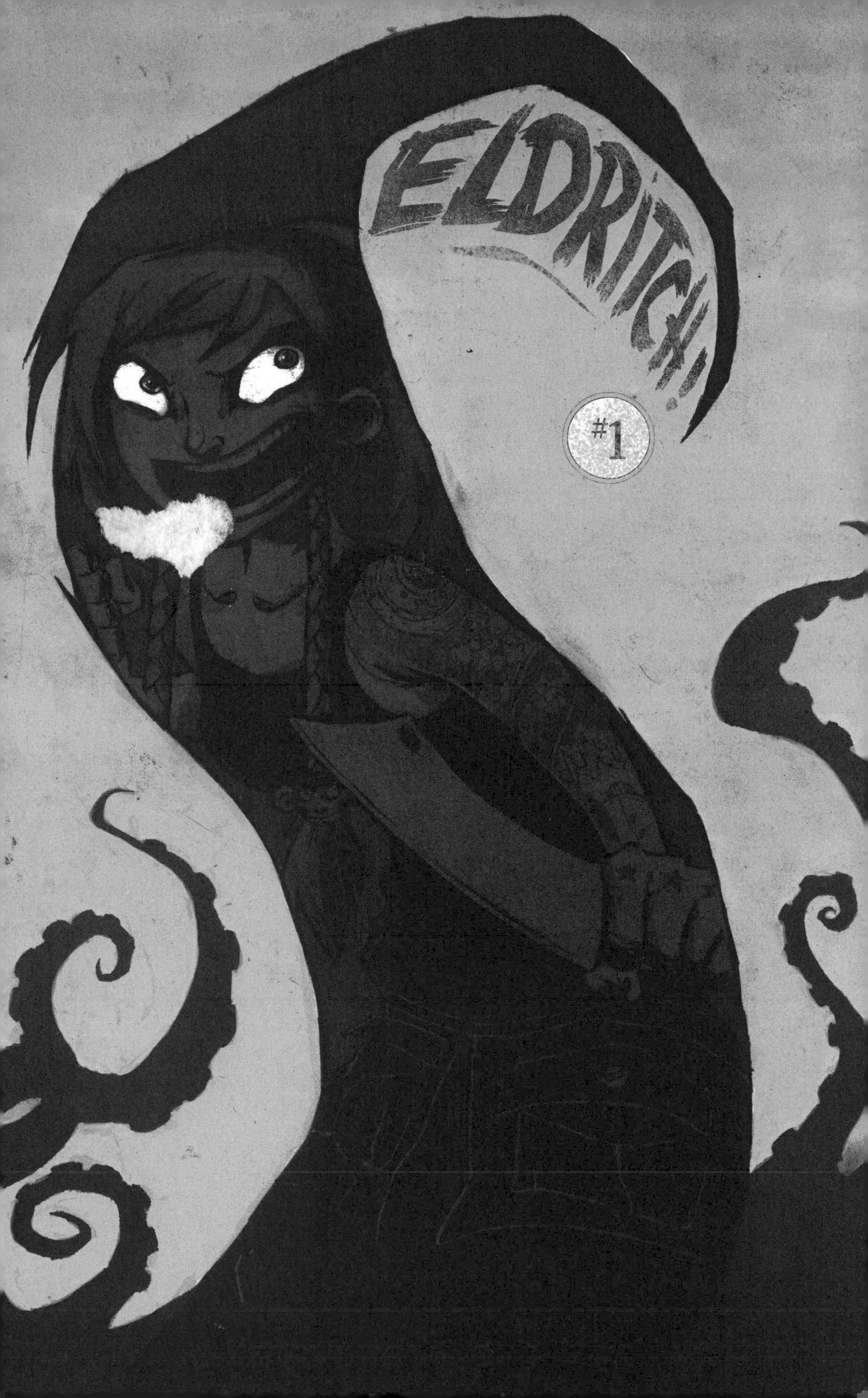
ELDRITCH!
#1

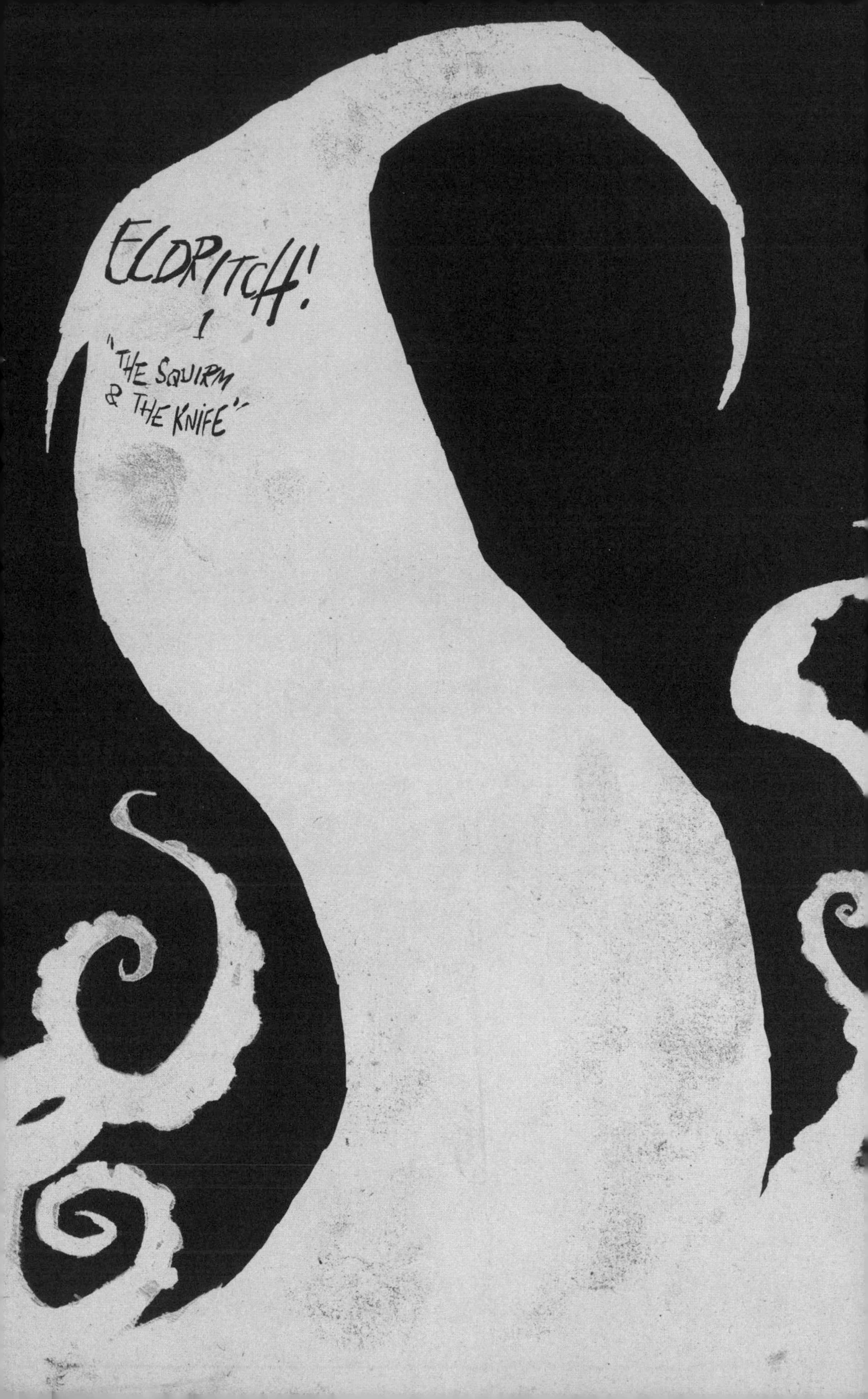
ELDRITCH!
1
"THE SQUIRM
& THE KNIFE"

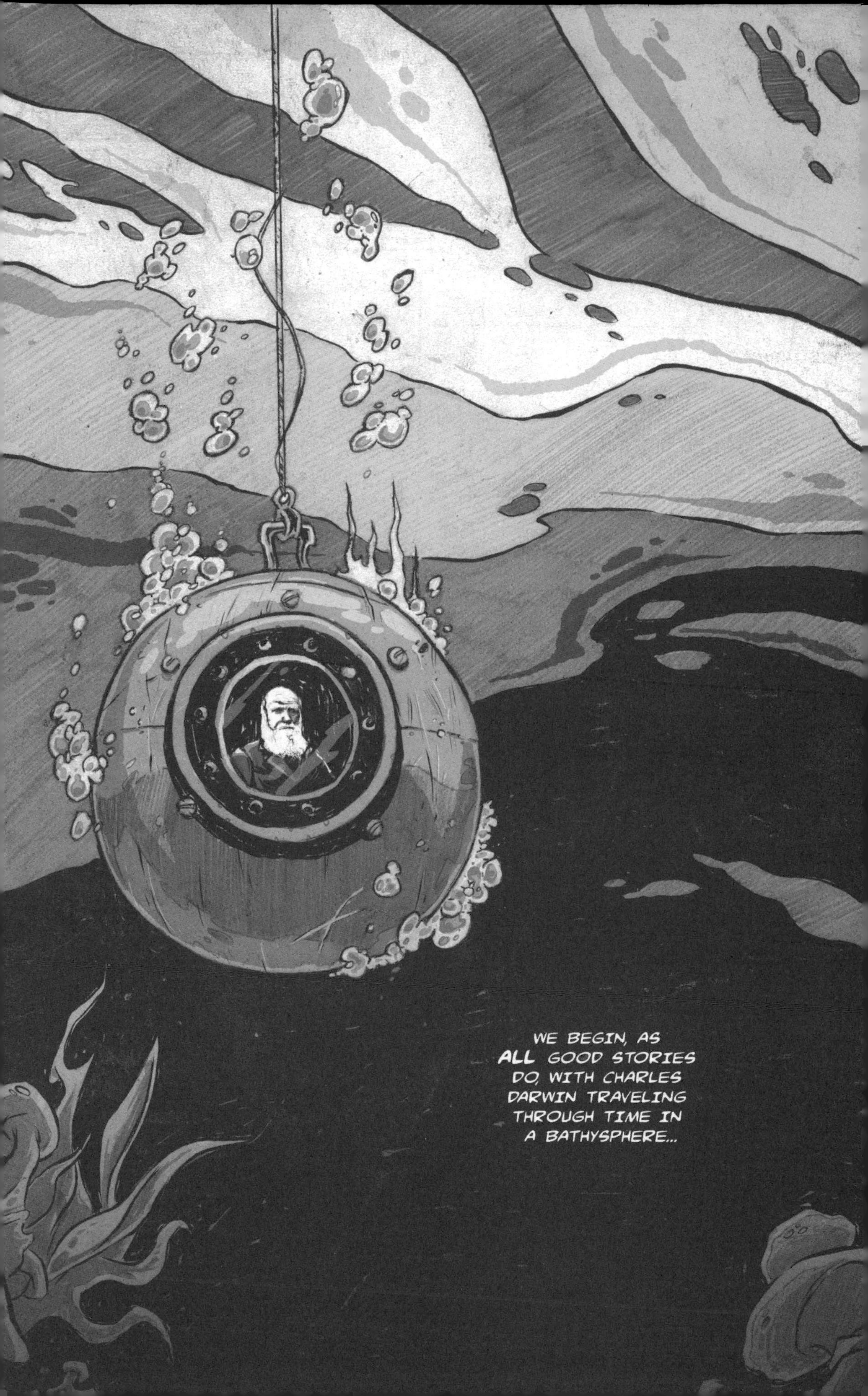
WE BEGIN, AS ALL GOOD STORIES DO, WITH CHARLES DARWIN TRAVELING THROUGH TIME IN A BATHYSPHERE...

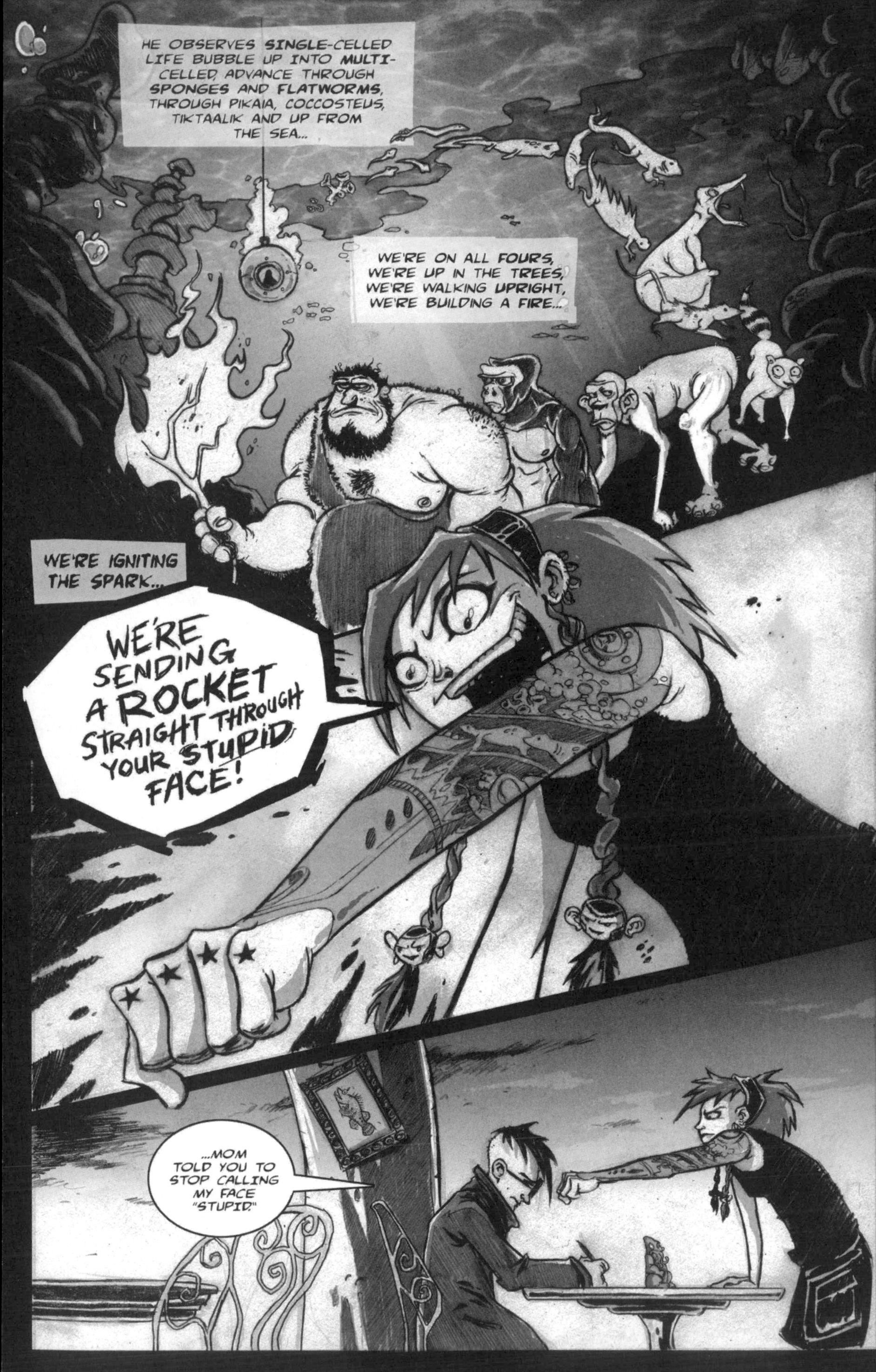
HE OBSERVES SINGLE-CELLED LIFE BUBBLE UP INTO MULTI-CELLED, ADVANCE THROUGH SPONGES AND FLATWORMS, THROUGH PIKAIA, COCCOSTEUS, TIKTAALIK AND UP FROM THE SEA...
WE'RE ON ALL FOURS, WE'RE UP IN THE TREES, WE'RE WALKING UPRIGHT, WE'RE BUILDING A FIRE...
WE'RE IGNITING THE SPARK...
WE'RE SENDING A ROCKET STRAIGHT THROUGH YOUR STUPID FACE!
...MOM TOLD YOU TO STOP CALLING MY FACE "STUPID."

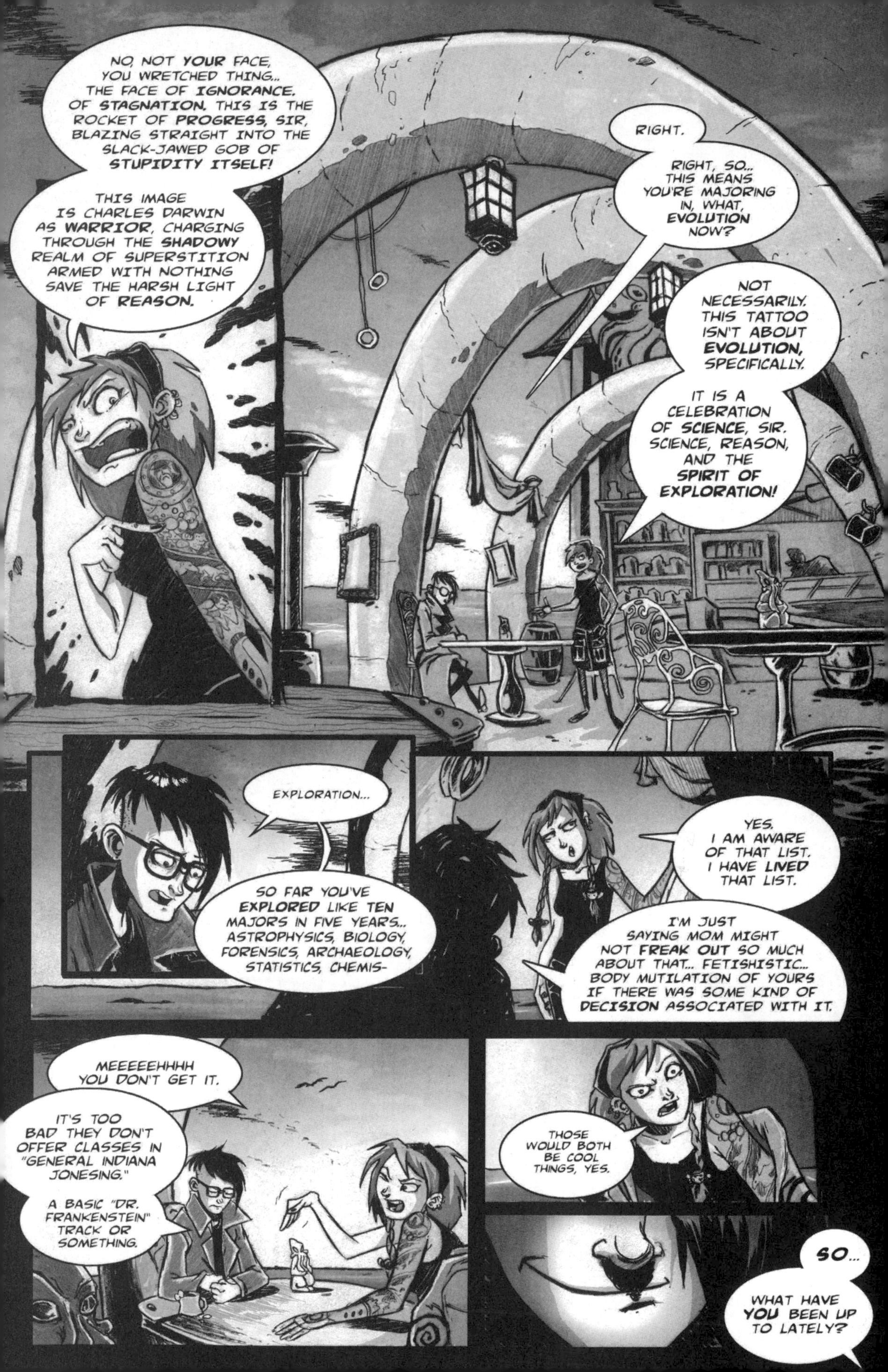
NO, NOT YOUR FACE, YOU WRETCHED THING... THE FACE OF IGNORANCE. OF STAGNATION. THIS IS THE ROCKET OF PROGRESS, SIR, BLAZING STRAIGHT INTO THE SLACK-JAWED GOB OF STUPIDITY ITSELF!
THIS IMAGE IS CHARLES DARWIN AS WARRIOR, CHARGING THROUGH THE SHADOWY REALM OF SUPERSTITION ARMED WITH NOTHING SAVE THE HARSH LIGHT OF REASON.
RIGHT.
RIGHT, SO... THIS MEANS YOU'RE MAJORING IN, WHAT, EVOLUTION NOW?
NOT NECESSARILY. THIS TATTOO ISN'T ABOUT EVOLUTION, SPECIFICALLY.
IT IS A CELEBRATION OF SCIENCE, SIR. SCIENCE, REASON, AND THE SPIRIT OF EXPLORATION!
EXPLORATION...
SO FAR YOU'VE EXPLORED LIKE TEN MAJORS IN FIVE YEARS... ASTROPHYSICS, BIOLOGY, FORENSICS, ARCHAEOLOGY, STATISTICS, CHEMIS-
YES. I AM AWARE OF THAT LIST. I HAVE LIVED THAT LIST.
I'M JUST SAYING MOM MIGHT NOT FREAK OUT SO MUCH ABOUT THAT... FETISHISTIC... BODY MUTILATION OF YOURS IF THERE WAS SOME KIND OF DECISION ASSOCIATED WITH IT.
MEEEEEHHHH YOU DON'T GET IT.
IT'S TOO BAD THEY DON'T OFFER CLASSES IN "GENERAL INDIANA JONESING."
A BASIC "DR. FRANKENSTEIN" TRACK OR SOMETHING.
THOSE WOULD BOTH BE COOL THINGS, YES.
SO...
WHAT HAVE YOU BEEN UP TO LATELY?

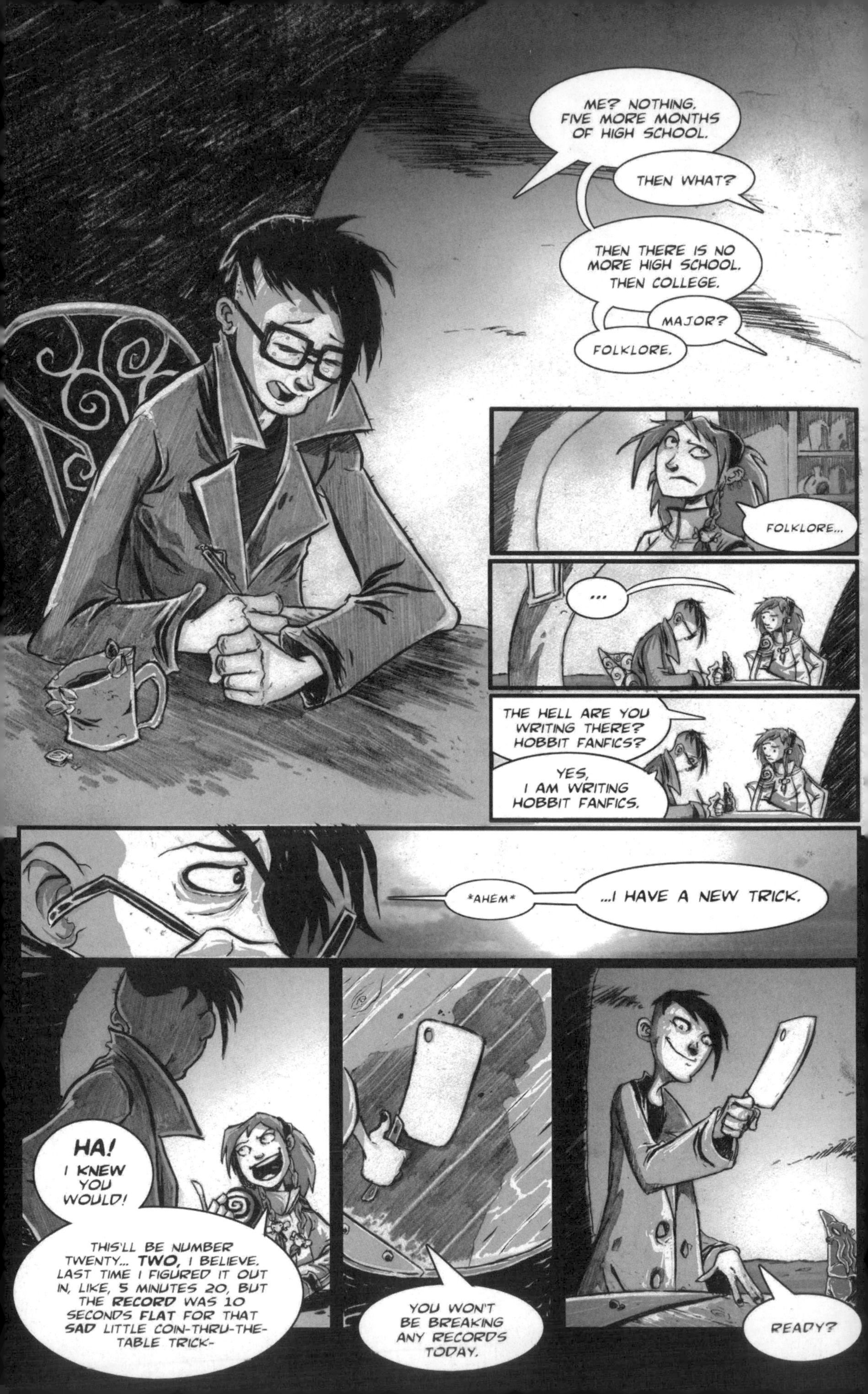
ME? NOTHING. FIVE MORE MONTHS OF HIGH SCHOOL.
THEN WHAT?
THEN THERE IS NO MORE HIGH SCHOOL. THEN COLLEGE.
MAJOR?
FOLKLORE.
FOLKLORE...
...
THE HELL ARE YOU WRITING THERE? HOBBIT FANFICS?
YES, I AM WRITING HOBBIT FANFICS.
AHEM
...I HAVE A NEW TRICK.
HA! I KNEW YOU WOULD!
THIS'LL BE NUMBER TWENTY... TWO, I BELIEVE. LAST TIME I FIGURED IT OUT IN, LIKE, 5 MINUTES 20, BUT THE RECORD WAS 10 SECONDS FLAT FOR THAT SAD LITTLE COIN-THRU-THE-TABLE TRICK-
YOU WON'T BE BREAKING ANY RECORDS TODAY.
READY?

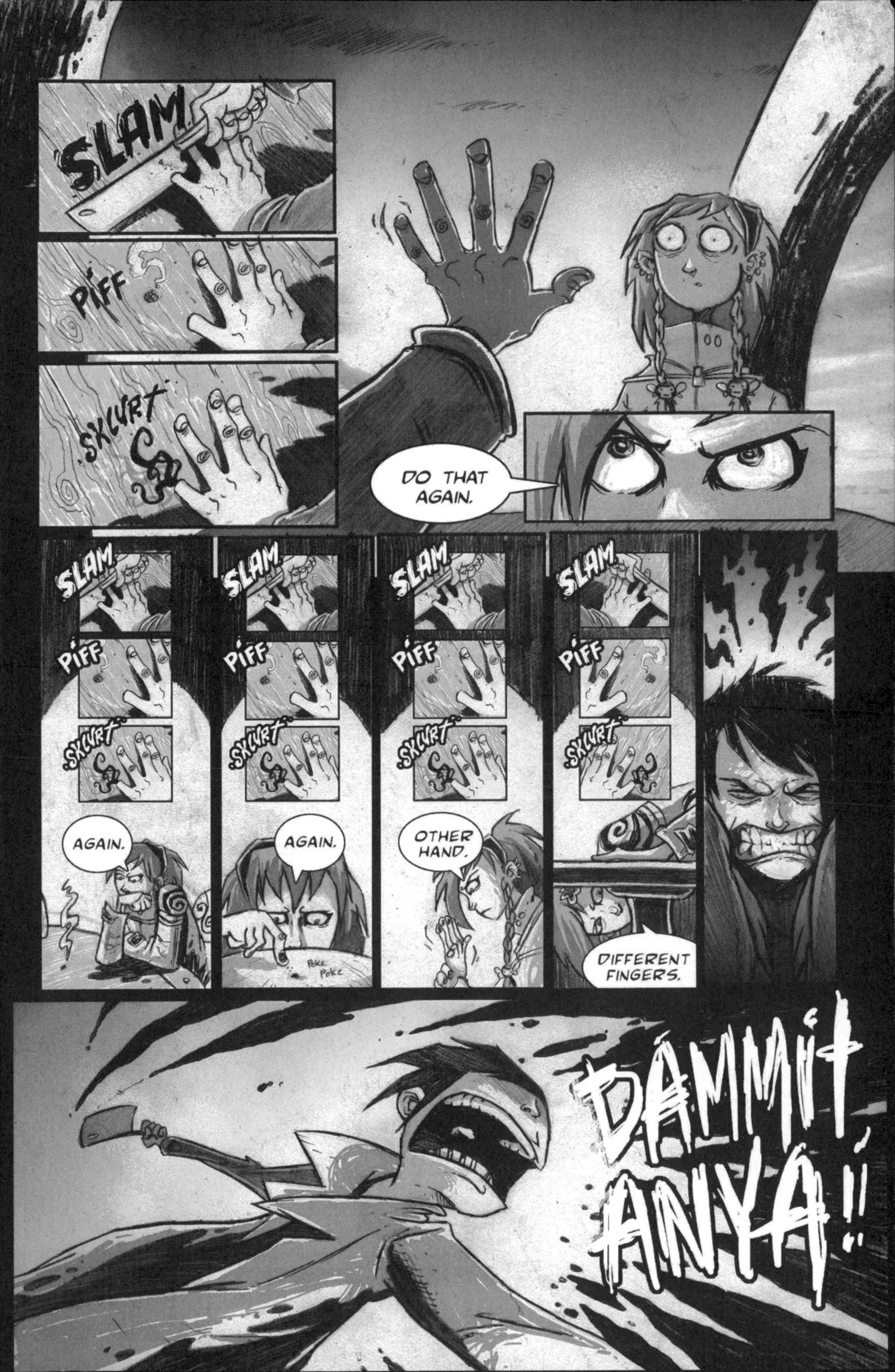
SLAM
PIFF
SKLURT
DO THAT AGAIN.
SLAM
PIFF
SKLURT
AGAIN.
SLAM
PIFF
SKLURT
AGAIN.
POKE POKE
SLAM
PIFF
SKLURT
OTHER HAND.
SLAM
PIFF
SKLURT
DIFFERENT FINGERS.
DAMMIT, ANYA!!

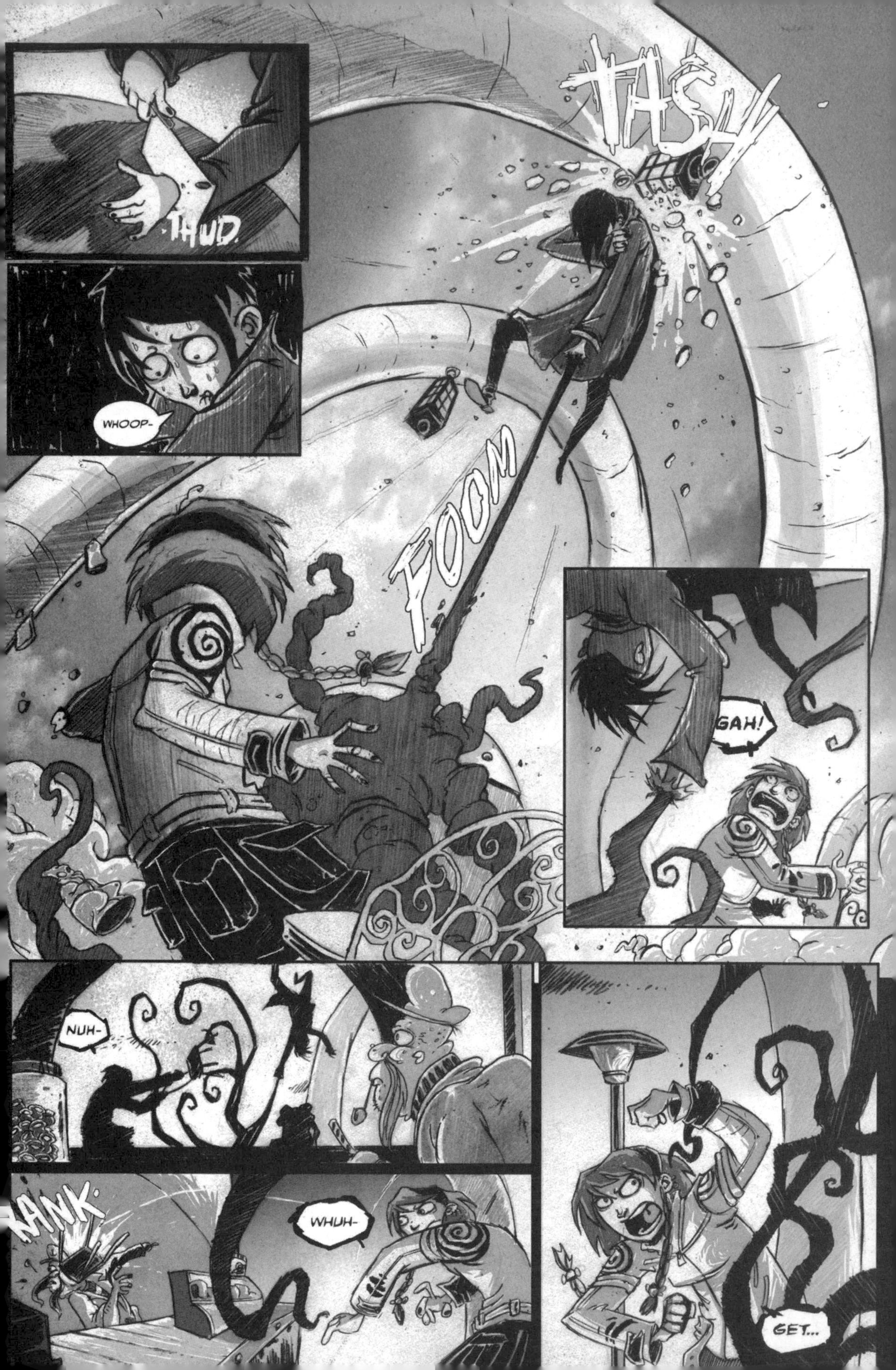
THUD.
WHOOP-
FOOM
GAH!
NUH-
RANK
WHUH-
GET...

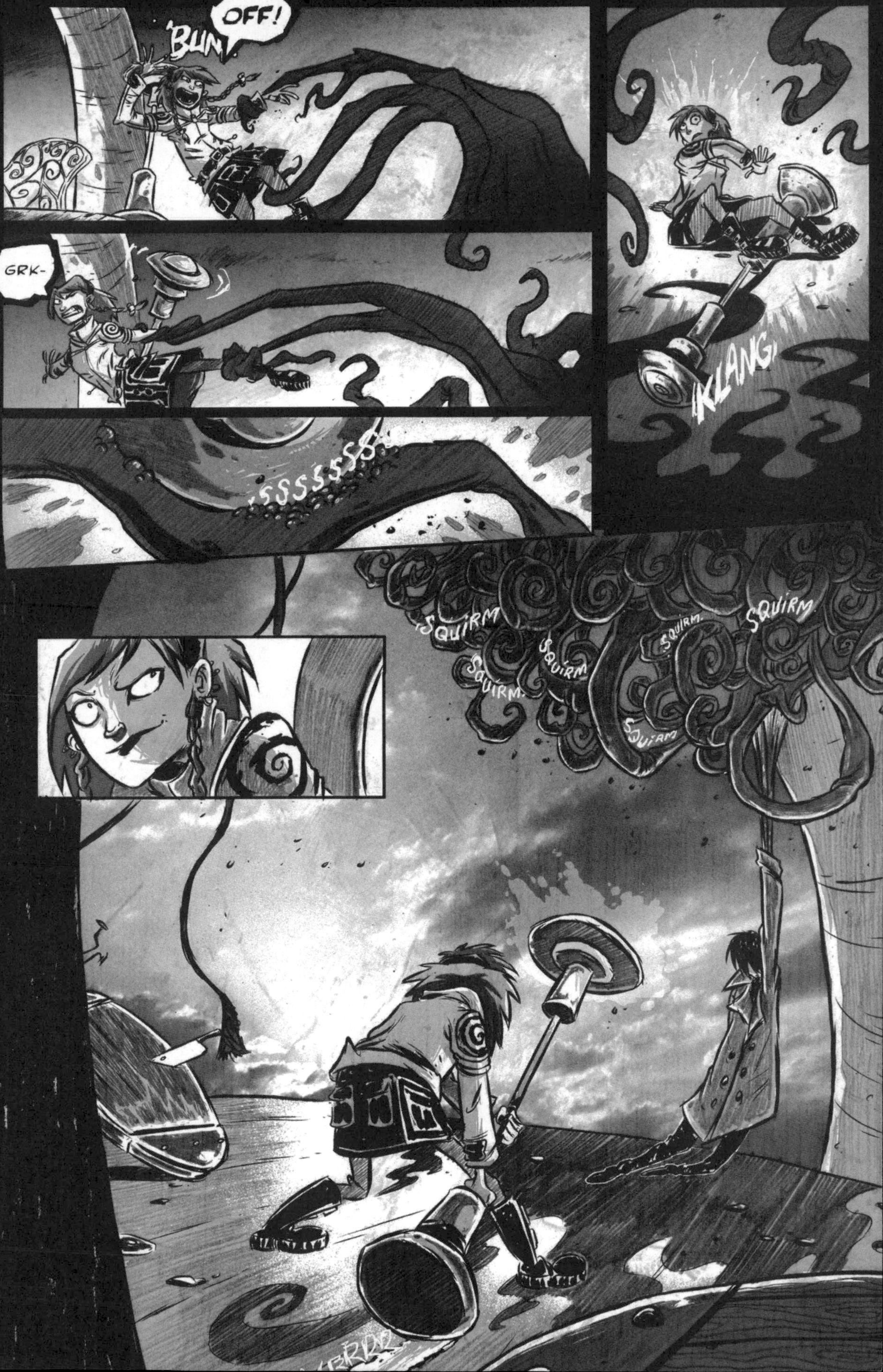
BUN
OFF!
KLANG
GRK-
SSSSSSSS
SQUIRM
SQUIRM
SQUIRM
SQUIRM
SQUIRM
SQUIRM

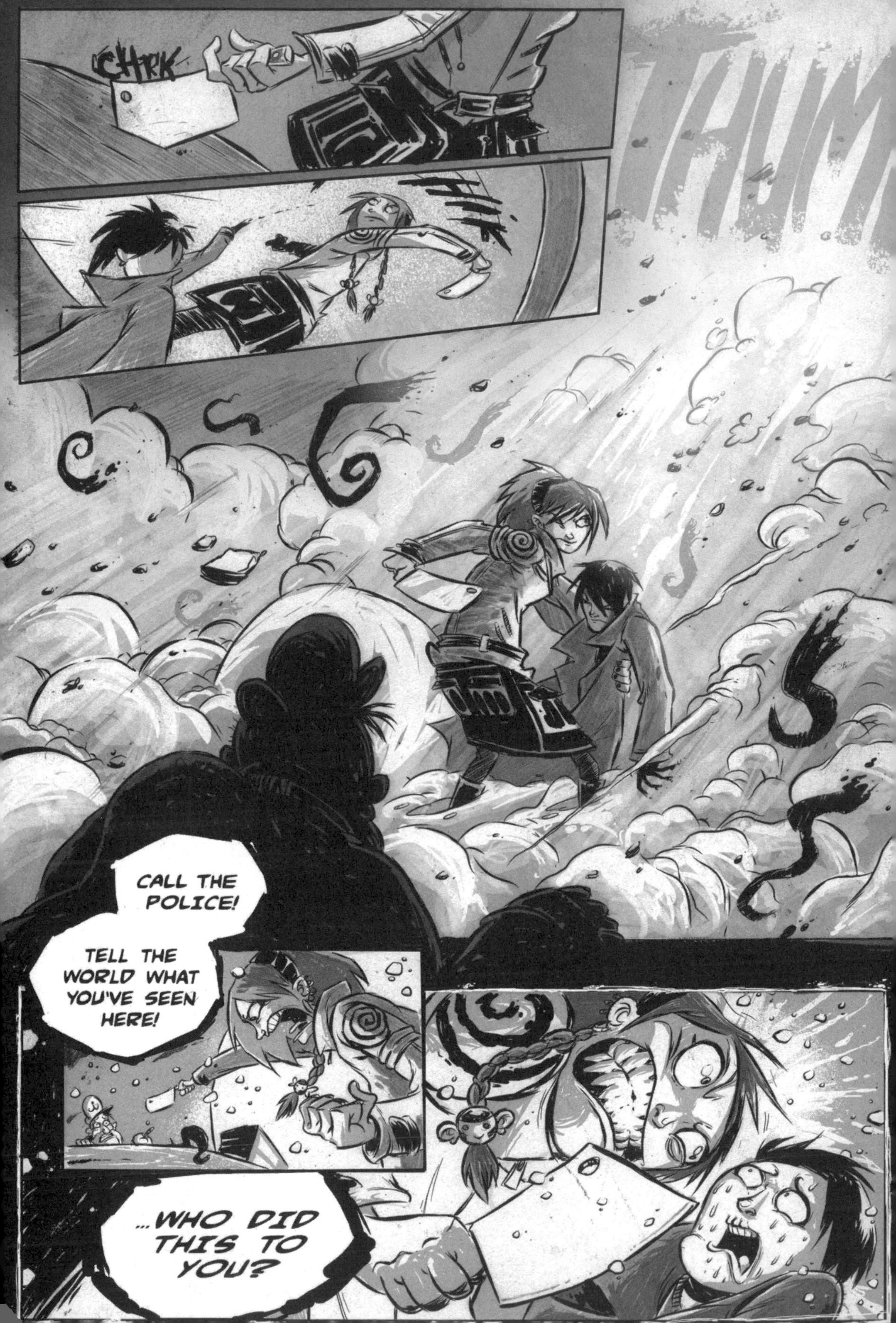
CHRK
THUM
CALL THE POLICE!
TELL THE WORLD WHAT YOU'VE SEEN HERE!
...WHO DID THIS TO YOU?

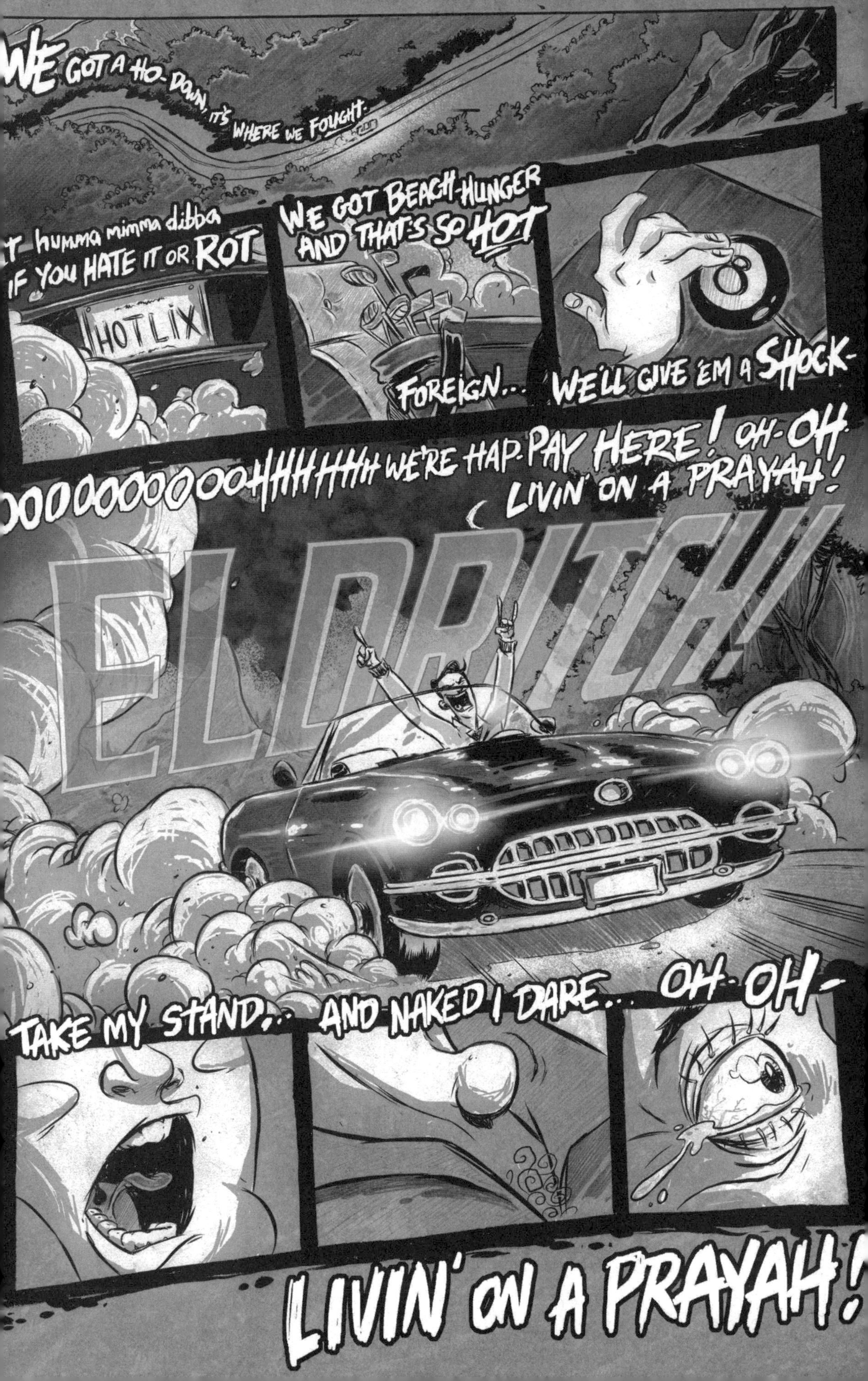
WE GOT A HO-DOWN, IT'S WHERE WE FOUGHT.
T humma mimma dibba IF YOU HATE IT OR ROT
WE GOT BEACH-HUNGER AND THAT'S SO HOT
HOTLIX
FOREIGN... WE'LL GIVE 'EM A SHOCK-
OOOOOOOOOOHHHHHHH WE'RE HAP-PAY HERE! OH-OH LIVIN' ON A PRAYAH!
ELDRITCH!
TAKE MY STAND... AND NAKED I DARE... OH-OH-
LIVIN' ON A PRAYAH!

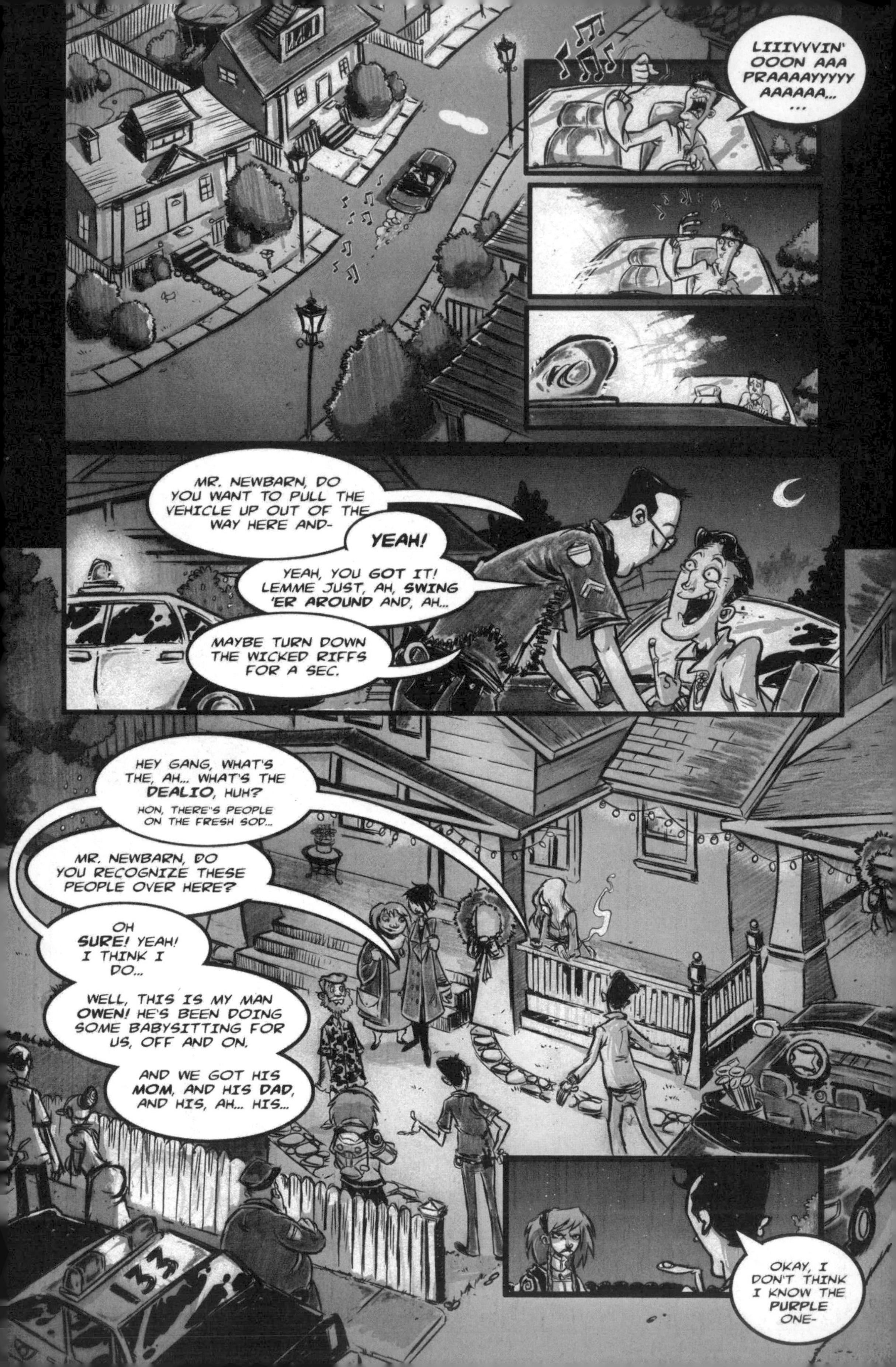

LIIIVVVIN' OOON AAA PRAAAAYYYYY AAAAAA... ...
MR. NEWBARN, DO YOU WANT TO PULL THE VEHICLE UP OUT OF THE WAY HERE AND-
YEAH!
YEAH, YOU GOT IT! LEMME JUST, AH, SWING 'ER AROUND AND, AH...
MAYBE TURN DOWN THE WICKED RIFFS FOR A SEC.
HEY GANG, WHAT'S THE, AH... WHAT'S THE DEALIO, HUH?
HON, THERE'S PEOPLE ON THE FRESH SOD...
MR. NEWBARN, DO YOU RECOGNIZE THESE PEOPLE OVER HERE?
OH SURE! YEAH! I THINK I DO...
WELL, THIS IS MY MAN OWEN! HE'S BEEN DOING SOME BABYSITTING FOR US, OFF AND ON.
AND WE GOT HIS MOM, AND HIS DAD, AND HIS, AH... HIS...
OKAY, I DON'T THINK I KNOW THE PURPLE ONE-

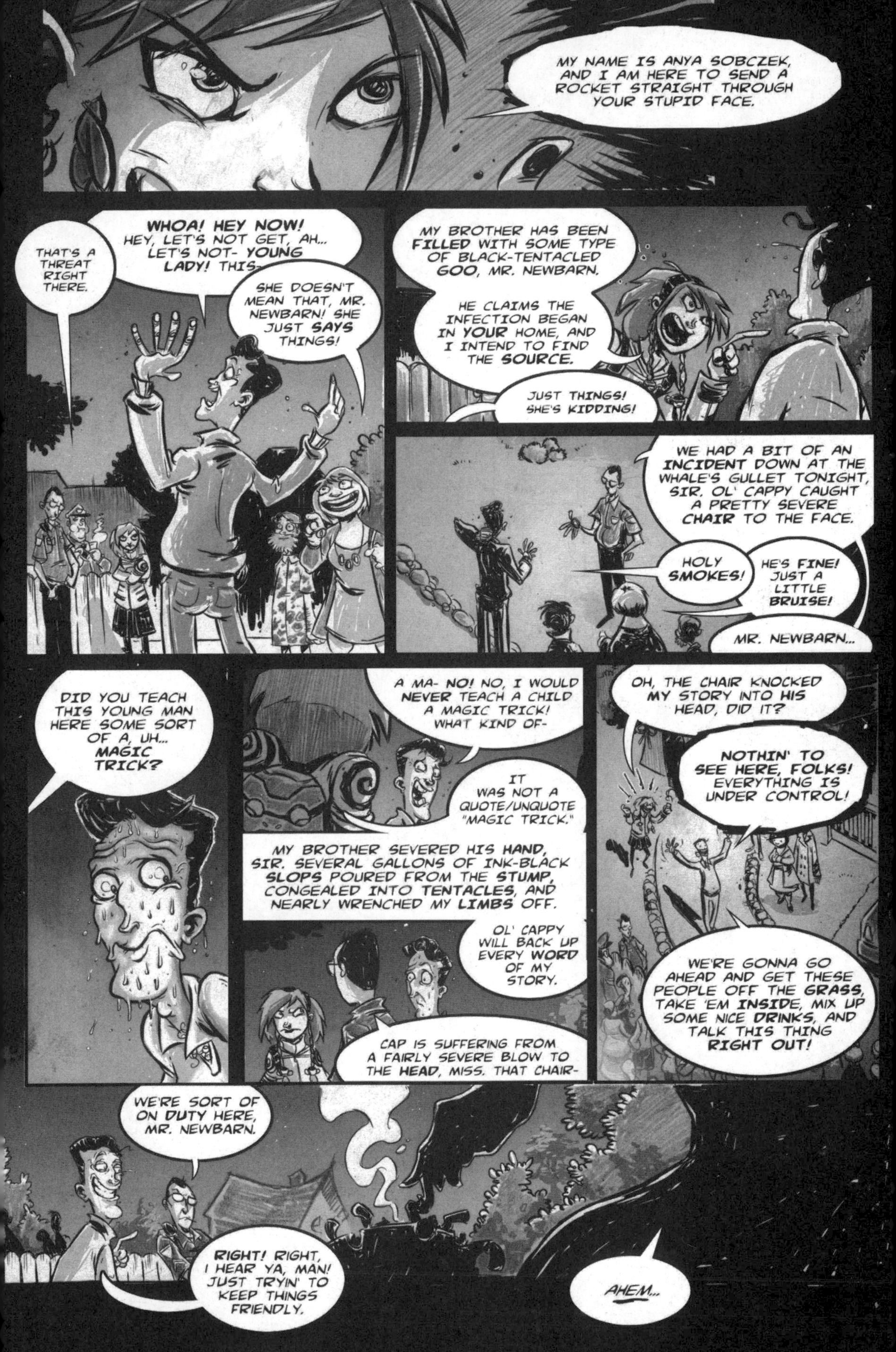

MY NAME IS ANYA SOBCZEK, AND I AM HERE TO SEND A ROCKET STRAIGHT THROUGH YOUR STUPID FACE.
THAT'S A THREAT RIGHT THERE.
WHOA! HEY NOW! HEY, LET'S NOT GET, AH... LET'S NOT- YOUNG LADY! THIS-
SHE DOESN'T MEAN THAT, MR. NEWBARN! SHE JUST SAYS THINGS!
MY BROTHER HAS BEEN FILLED WITH SOME TYPE OF BLACK-TENTACLED GOO, MR. NEWBARN.
HE CLAIMS THE INFECTION BEGAN IN YOUR HOME, AND I INTEND TO FIND THE SOURCE.
JUST THINGS! SHE'S KIDDING!
WE HAD A BIT OF AN INCIDENT DOWN AT THE WHALE'S GULLET TONIGHT, SIR. OL' CAPPY CAUGHT A PRETTY SEVERE CHAIR TO THE FACE.
HOLY SMOKES!
HE'S FINE! JUST A LITTLE BRUISE!
MR. NEWBARN...
DID YOU TEACH THIS YOUNG MAN HERE SOME SORT OF A, UH... MAGIC TRICK?
A MA- NO! NO, I WOULD NEVER TEACH A CHILD A MAGIC TRICK! WHAT KIND OF-
IT WAS NOT A QUOTE/UNQUOTE "MAGIC TRICK."
MY BROTHER SEVERED HIS HAND, SIR. SEVERAL GALLONS OF INK-BLACK SLOPS POURED FROM THE STUMP, CONGEALED INTO TENTACLES, AND NEARLY WRENCHED MY LIMBS OFF.
OL' CAPPY WILL BACK UP EVERY WORD OF MY STORY.
CAP IS SUFFERING FROM A FAIRLY SEVERE BLOW TO THE HEAD, MISS. THAT CHAIR-
OH, THE CHAIR KNOCKED MY STORY INTO HIS HEAD, DID IT?
NOTHIN' TO SEE HERE, FOLKS! EVERYTHING IS UNDER CONTROL!
WE'RE GONNA GO AHEAD AND GET THESE PEOPLE OFF THE GRASS, TAKE 'EM INSIDE, MIX UP SOME NICE DRINKS, AND TALK THIS THING RIGHT OUT!
WE'RE SORT OF ON DUTY HERE, MR. NEWBARN.
RIGHT! RIGHT, I HEAR YA, MAN! JUST TRYIN' TO KEEP THINGS FRIENDLY.
AHEM...

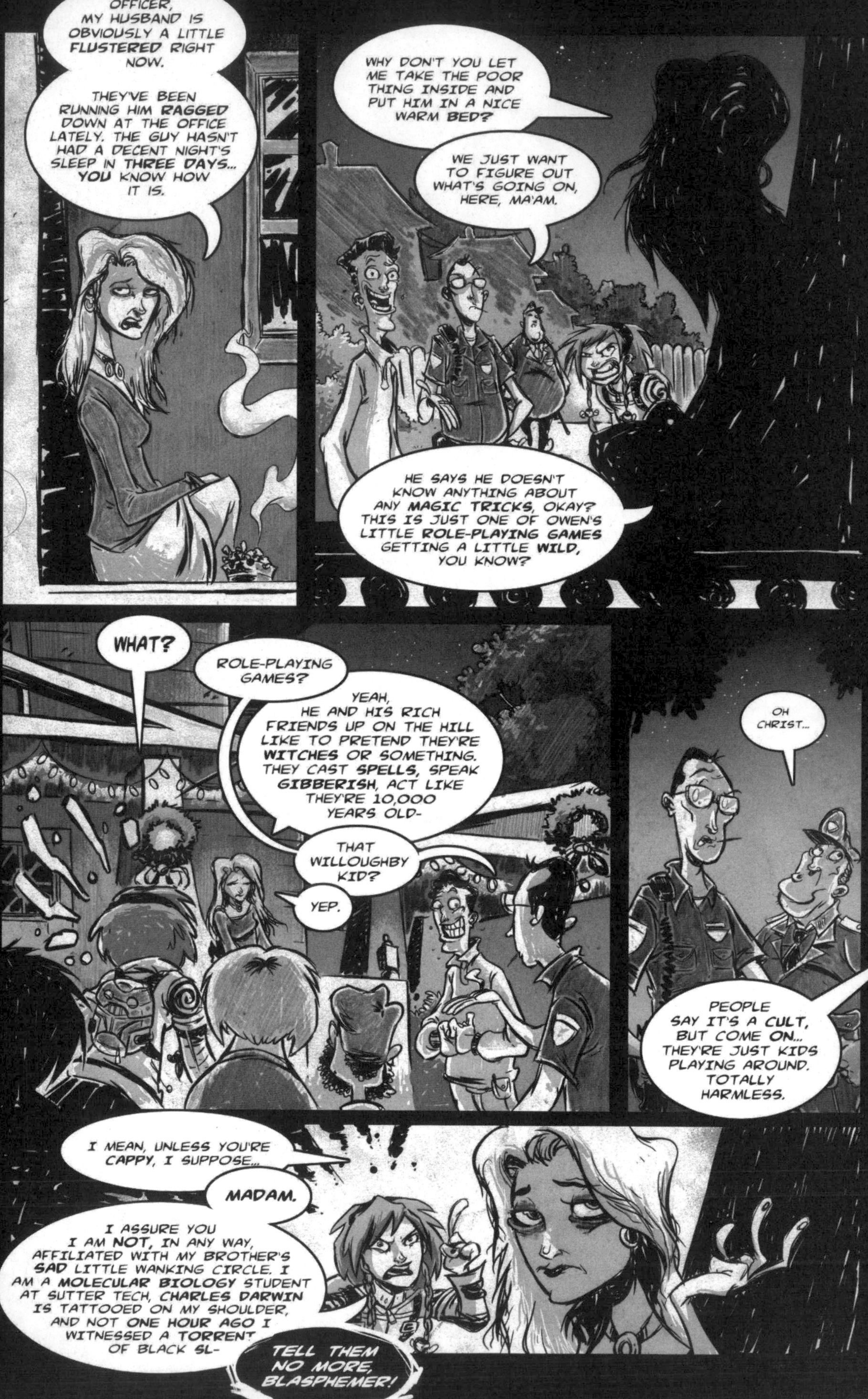
OFFICER, MY HUSBAND IS OBVIOUSLY A LITTLE FLUSTERED RIGHT NOW.
THEY'VE BEEN RUNNING HIM RAGGED DOWN AT THE OFFICE LATELY. THE GUY HASN'T HAD A DECENT NIGHT'S SLEEP IN THREE DAYS... YOU KNOW HOW IT IS.
WHY DON'T YOU LET ME TAKE THE POOR THING INSIDE AND PUT HIM IN A NICE WARM BED?
WE JUST WANT TO FIGURE OUT WHAT'S GOING ON, HERE, MA'AM.
HE SAYS HE DOESN'T KNOW ANYTHING ABOUT ANY MAGIC TRICKS, OKAY? THIS IS JUST ONE OF OWEN'S LITTLE ROLE-PLAYING GAMES GETTING A LITTLE WILD, YOU KNOW?
WHAT?
ROLE-PLAYING GAMES?
YEAH, HE AND HIS RICH FRIENDS UP ON THE HILL LIKE TO PRETEND THEY'RE WITCHES OR SOMETHING. THEY CAST SPELLS, SPEAK GIBBERISH, ACT LIKE THEY'RE 10,000 YEARS OLD-
THAT WILLOUGHBY KID?
YEP.
OH CHRIST...
PEOPLE SAY IT'S A CULT, BUT COME ON... THEY'RE JUST KIDS PLAYING AROUND. TOTALLY HARMLESS.
I MEAN, UNLESS YOU'RE CAPPY, I SUPPOSE...
MADAM.
I ASSURE YOU I AM NOT, IN ANY WAY, AFFILIATED WITH MY BROTHER'S SAD LITTLE WANKING CIRCLE. I AM A MOLECULAR BIOLOGY STUDENT AT SUTTER TECH, CHARLES DARWIN IS TATTOOED ON MY SHOULDER, AND NOT ONE HOUR AGO I WITNESSED A TORRENT OF BLACK SL-
TELL THEM NO MORE, BLASPHEMER!

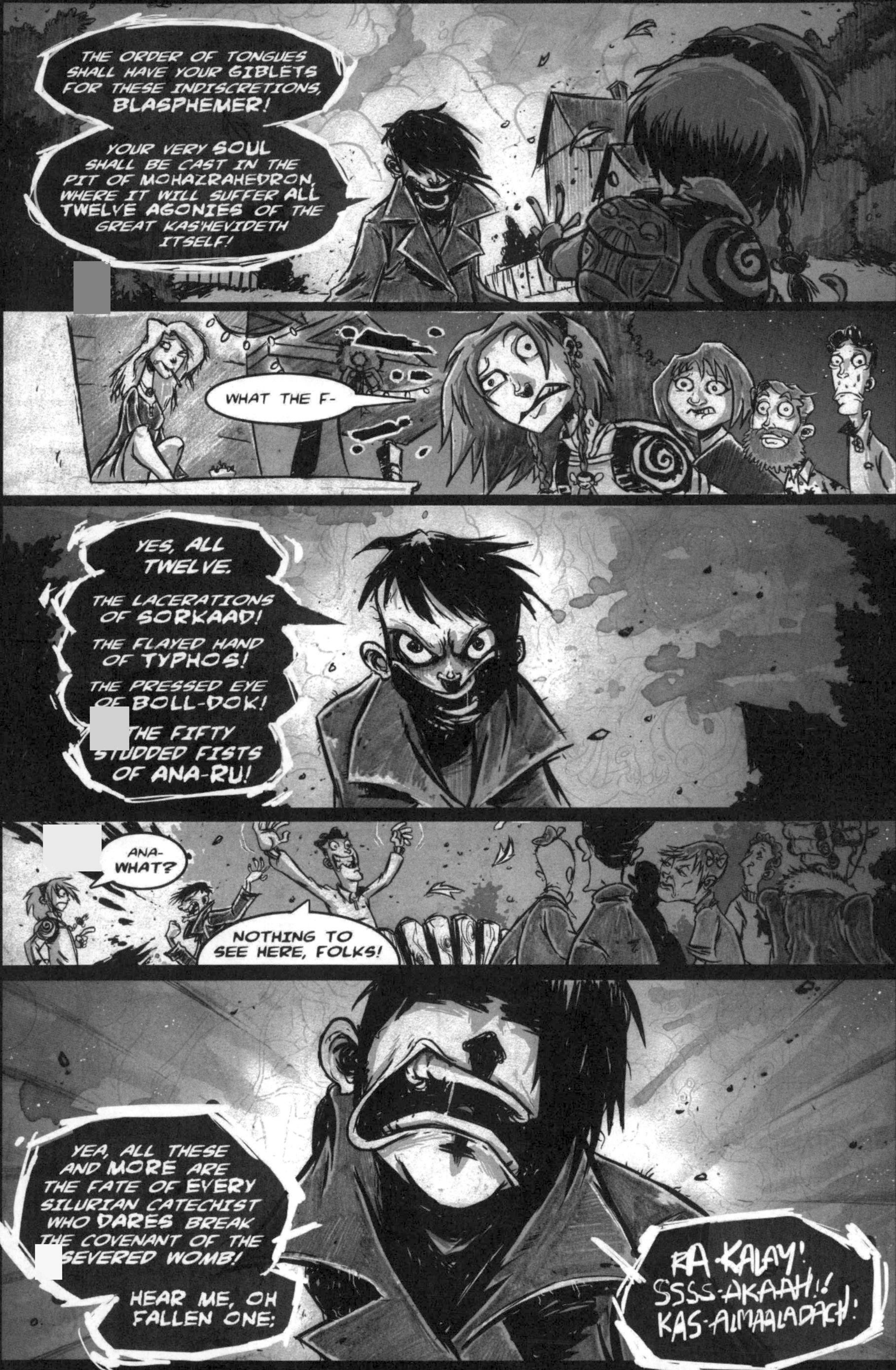
THE ORDER OF TONGUES SHALL HAVE YOUR GIBLETS FOR THESE INDISCRETIONS, BLASPHEMER!
YOUR VERY SOUL SHALL BE CAST IN THE PIT OF MOHAZRAHEDRON, WHERE IT WILL SUFFER ALL TWELVE AGONIES OF THE GREAT KAS'HEVIDETH ITSELF!
WHAT THE F-
YES, ALL TWELVE.
THE LACERATIONS OF SORKAAD!
THE FLAYED HAND OF TYPHOS!
THE PRESSED EYE
BOLL-DOK!
HE FIFTY
TUDDED FISTS OF ANA-RU!
ANA-WHAT?
NOTHING TO SEE HERE, FOLKS!
YEA, ALL THESE AND MORE ARE THE FATE OF EVERY SILURIAN CATECHIST WHO DARES BREAK THE COVENANT OF THE
EVERED WOMB!
HEAR ME, OH FALLEN ONE:
RA-KALAY! SSSS-AKAAH!! KAS-ALMAALADACH!

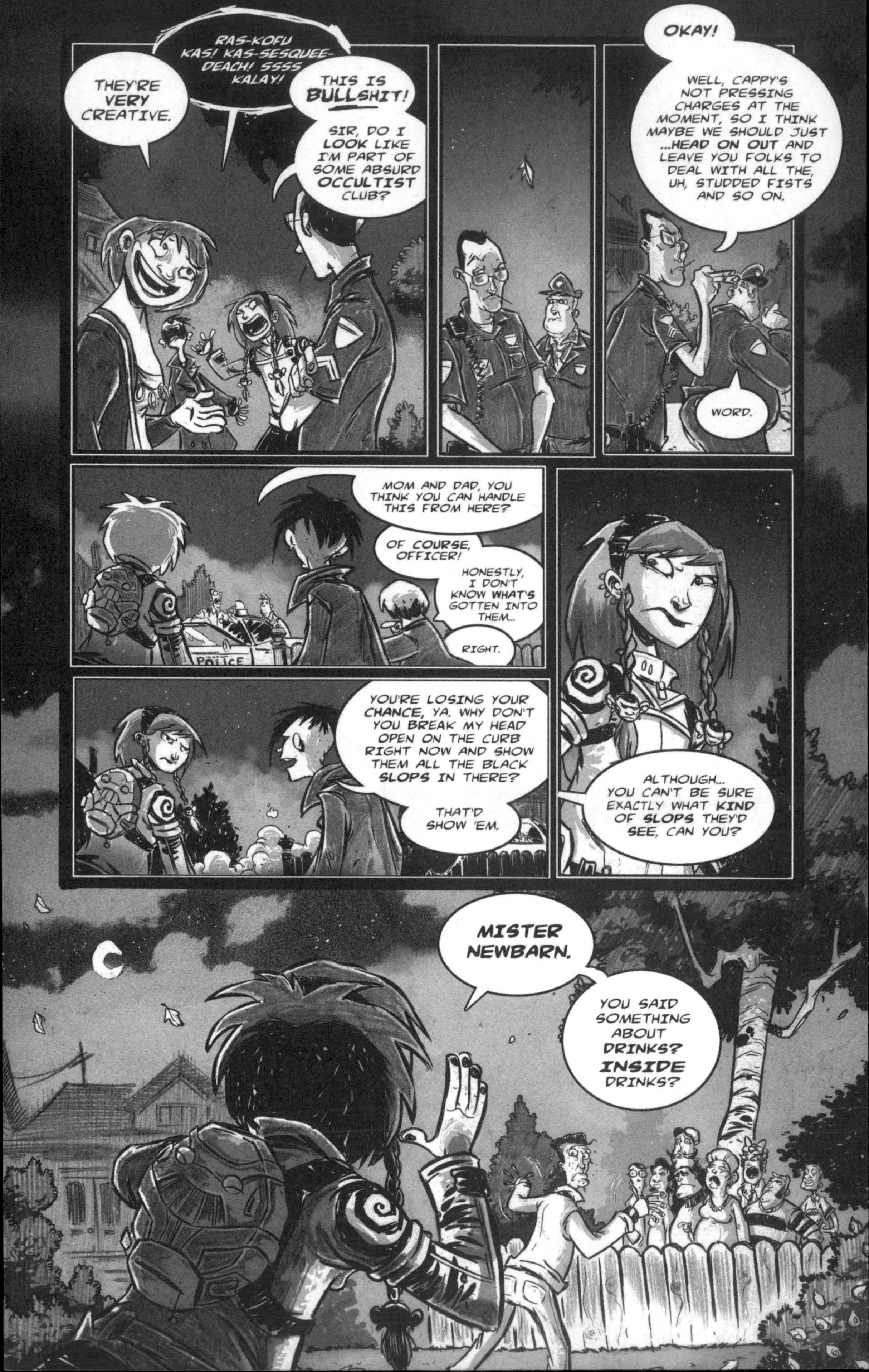
RAS-KOFU KAS! KAS-SESQUEE-DEACH! SSSS KALAY!
THEY'RE VERY CREATIVE.
THIS IS BULLSHIT!
SIR, DO I LOOK LIKE I'M PART OF SOME ABSURD OCCULTIST CLUB?
OKAY!
WELL, CAPPY'S NOT PRESSING CHARGES AT THE MOMENT, SO I THINK MAYBE WE SHOULD JUST ...HEAD ON OUT AND LEAVE YOU FOLKS TO DEAL WITH ALL THE, UH, STUDDED FISTS AND SO ON.
WORD.
MOM AND DAD, YOU THINK YOU CAN HANDLE THIS FROM HERE?
OF COURSE, OFFICER!
HONESTLY, I DON'T KNOW WHAT'S GOTTEN INTO THEM...
RIGHT.
POLICE
YOU'RE LOSING YOUR CHANCE, YA. WHY DON'T YOU BREAK MY HEAD OPEN ON THE CURB RIGHT NOW AND SHOW THEM ALL THE BLACK SLOPS IN THERE?
THAT'D SHOW 'EM.
ALTHOUGH... YOU CAN'T BE SURE EXACTLY WHAT KIND OF SLOPS THEY'D SEE, CAN YOU?
MISTER NEWBARN.
YOU SAID SOMETHING ABOUT DRINKS? INSIDE DRINKS?

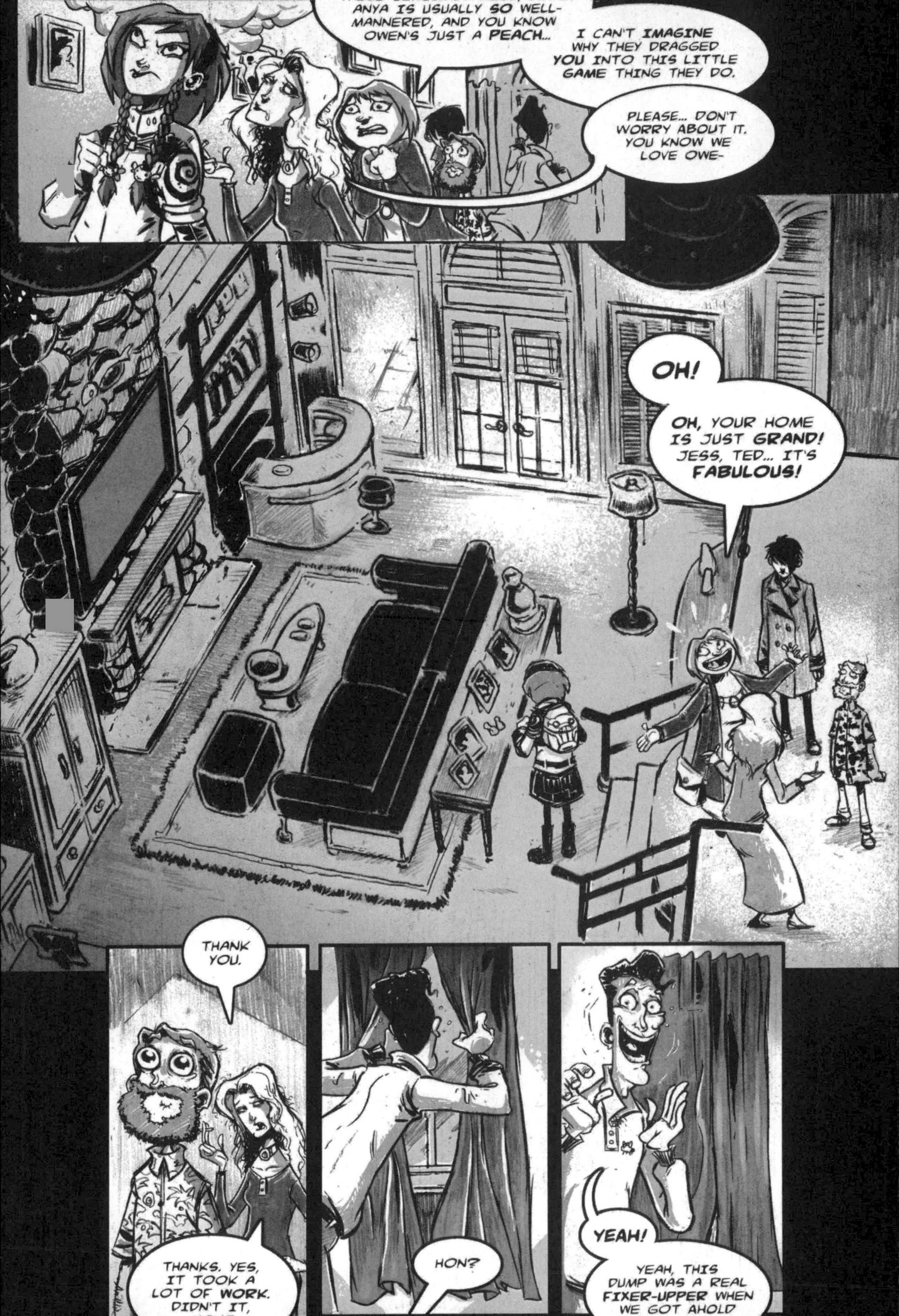
ANYA IS USUALLY SO WELL-MANNERED, AND YOU KNOW OWEN'S JUST A PEACH...
I CAN'T IMAGINE WHY THEY DRAGGED YOU INTO THIS LITTLE GAME THING THEY DO.
PLEASE... DON'T WORRY ABOUT IT. YOU KNOW WE LOVE OWE-
OH!
OH, YOUR HOME IS JUST GRAND! JESS, TED... IT'S FABULOUS!
THANK YOU.
THANKS. YES, IT TOOK A LOT OF WORK. DIDN'T IT,
HON?
YEAH!
YEAH, THIS DUMP WAS A REAL FIXER-UPPER WHEN WE GOT AHOLD

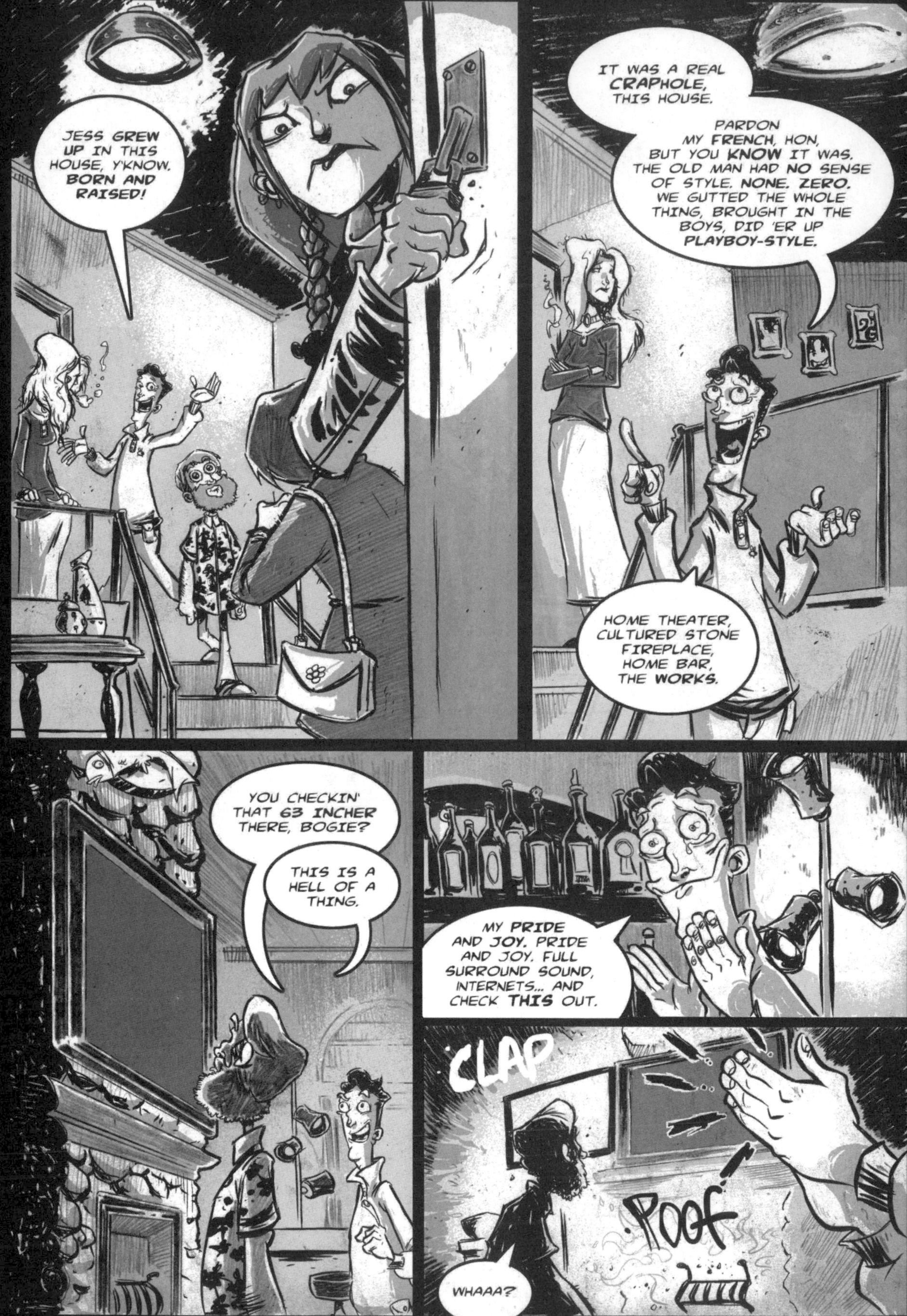
JESS GREW UP IN THIS HOUSE, Y'KNOW. BORN AND RAISED!
IT WAS A REAL CRAPHOLE, THIS HOUSE.
PARDON MY FRENCH, HON, BUT YOU KNOW IT WAS. THE OLD MAN HAD NO SENSE OF STYLE. NONE. ZERO. WE GUTTED THE WHOLE THING, BROUGHT IN THE BOYS, DID 'ER UP PLAYBOY-STYLE.
HOME THEATER, CULTURED STONE FIREPLACE, HOME BAR, THE WORKS.
YOU CHECKIN' THAT 63 INCHER THERE, BOGIE?
THIS IS A HELL OF A THING.
MY PRIDE AND JOY. PRIDE AND JOY. FULL SURROUND SOUND, INTERNETS... AND CHECK THIS OUT.
CLAP
POOF
WHAAA?

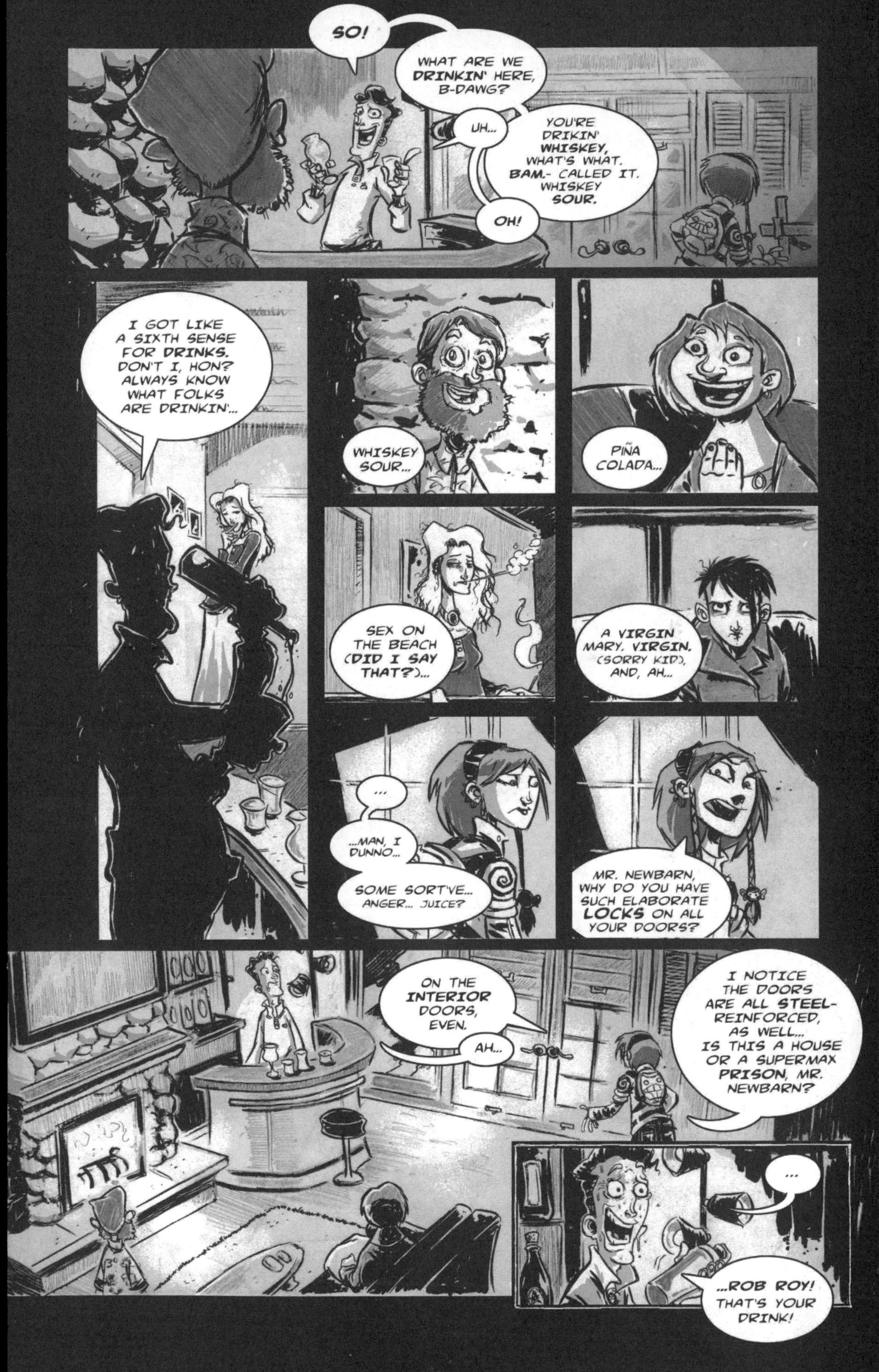
SO!
WHAT ARE WE DRINKIN' HERE, B-DAWG?
UH...
YOU'RE DRIKIN' WHISKEY, WHAT'S WHAT. BAM.- CALLED IT. WHISKEY SOUR.
OH!
I GOT LIKE A SIXTH SENSE FOR DRINKS. DON'T I, HON? ALWAYS KNOW WHAT FOLKS ARE DRINKIN'...
WHISKEY SOUR...
PIÑA COLADA...
SEX ON THE BEACH (DID I SAY THAT?)...
A VIRGIN MARY. VIRGIN. (SORRY KID), AND, AH...
...
...MAN, I DUNNO...
SOME SORT'VE... ANGER... JUICE?
MR. NEWBARN, WHY DO YOU HAVE SUCH ELABORATE LOCKS ON ALL YOUR DOORS?
ON THE INTERIOR DOORS, EVEN.
AH...
I NOTICE THE DOORS ARE ALL STEEL-REINFORCED, AS WELL... IS THIS A HOUSE OR A SUPERMAX PRISON, MR. NEWBARN?
...
...ROB ROY! THAT'S YOUR DRINK!

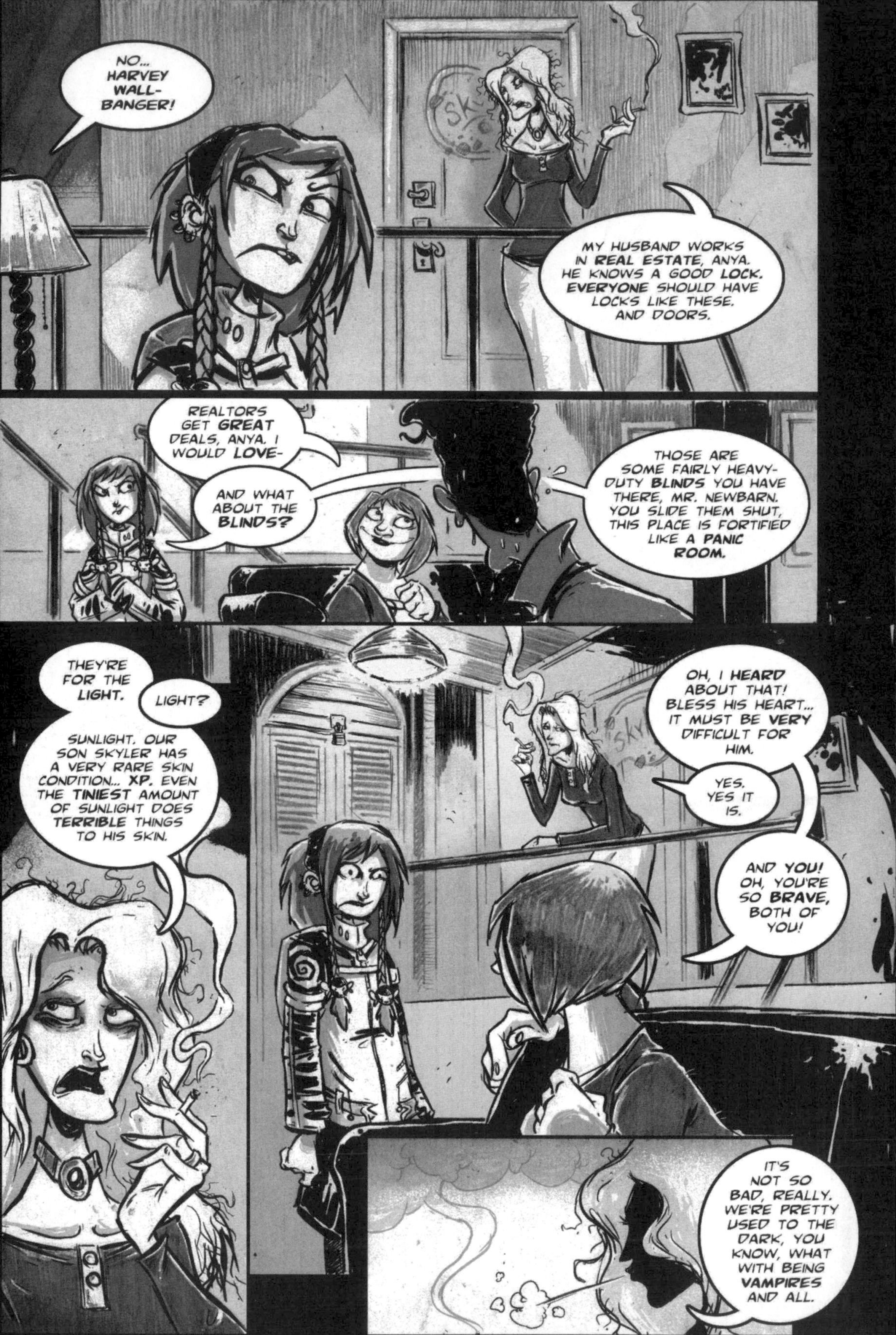
NO... HARVEY WALL-BANGER!
MY HUSBAND WORKS IN REAL ESTATE, ANYA. HE KNOWS A GOOD LOCK. EVERYONE SHOULD HAVE LOCKS LIKE THESE. AND DOORS.
REALTORS GET GREAT DEALS, ANYA. I WOULD LOVE-
AND WHAT ABOUT THE BLINDS?
THOSE ARE SOME FAIRLY HEAVY-DUTY BLINDS YOU HAVE THERE, MR. NEWBARN. YOU SLIDE THEM SHUT, THIS PLACE IS FORTIFIED LIKE A PANIC ROOM.
THEY'RE FOR THE LIGHT.
LIGHT?
SUNLIGHT. OUR SON SKYLER HAS A VERY RARE SKIN CONDITION... XP. EVEN THE TINIEST AMOUNT OF SUNLIGHT DOES TERRIBLE THINGS TO HIS SKIN.
OH, I HEARD ABOUT THAT! BLESS HIS HEART... IT MUST BE VERY DIFFICULT FOR HIM.
YES. YES IT IS.
AND YOU! OH, YOU'RE SO BRAVE, BOTH OF YOU!
IT'S NOT SO BAD, REALLY. WE'RE PRETTY USED TO THE DARK, YOU KNOW, WHAT WITH BEING VAMPIRES AND ALL.

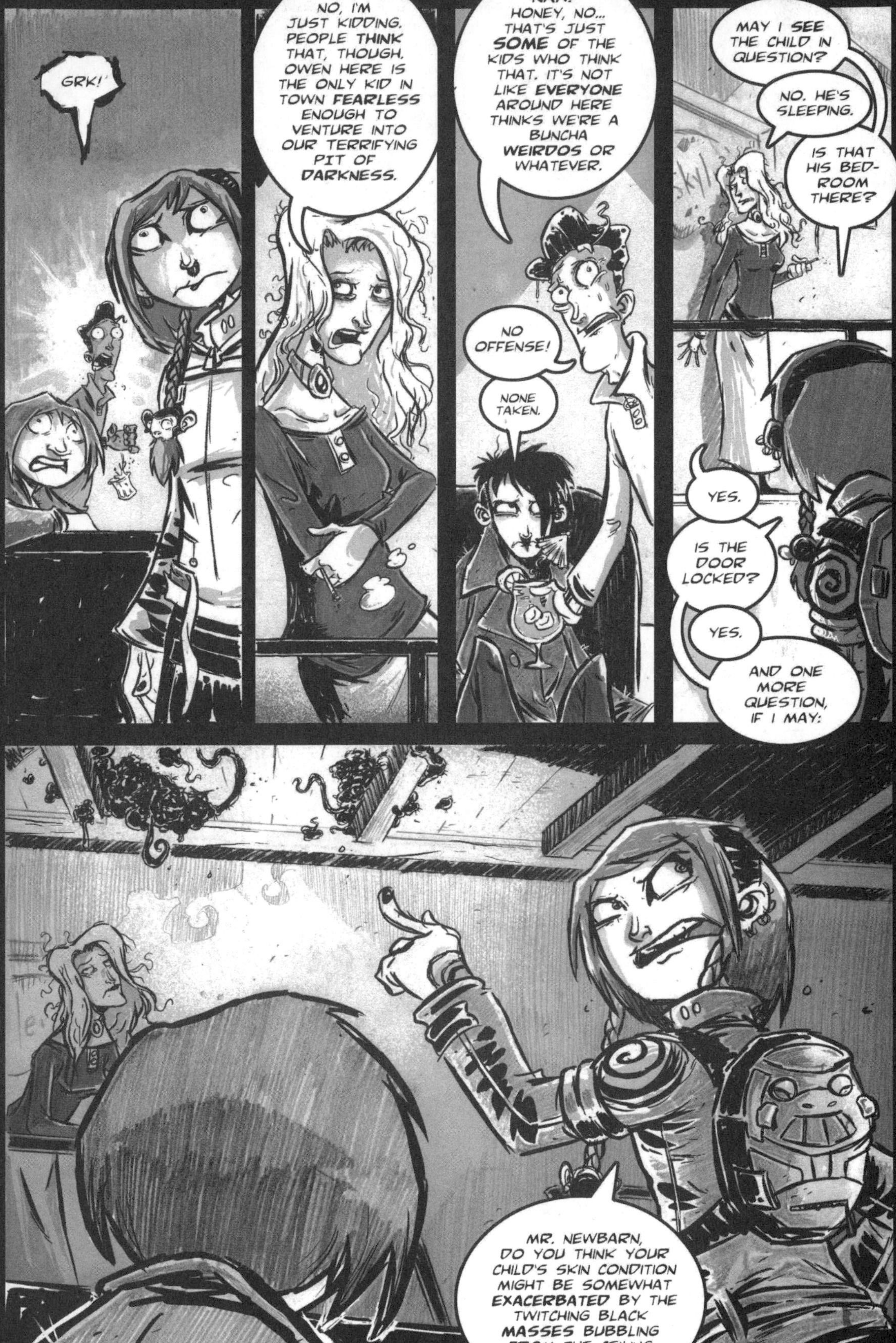
GRK!
NO, I'M JUST KIDDING. PEOPLE THINK THAT, THOUGH. OWEN HERE IS THE ONLY KID IN TOWN FEARLESS ENOUGH TO VENTURE INTO OUR TERRIFYING PIT OF DARKNESS.
NAH! HONEY, NO... THAT'S JUST SOME OF THE KIDS WHO THINK THAT. IT'S NOT LIKE EVERYONE AROUND HERE THINKS WE'RE A BUNCHA WEIRDOS OR WHATEVER.
NO OFFENSE!
NONE TAKEN.
MAY I SEE THE CHILD IN QUESTION?
NO. HE'S SLEEPING.
IS THAT HIS BED-ROOM THERE?
YES.
IS THE DOOR LOCKED?
YES.
AND ONE MORE QUESTION, IF I MAY:
MR. NEWBARN, DO YOU THINK YOUR CHILD'S SKIN CONDITION MIGHT BE SOMEWHAT EXACERBATED BY THE TWITCHING BLACK MASSES BUBBLING FROM THE CEILING OF THIS ROOM?

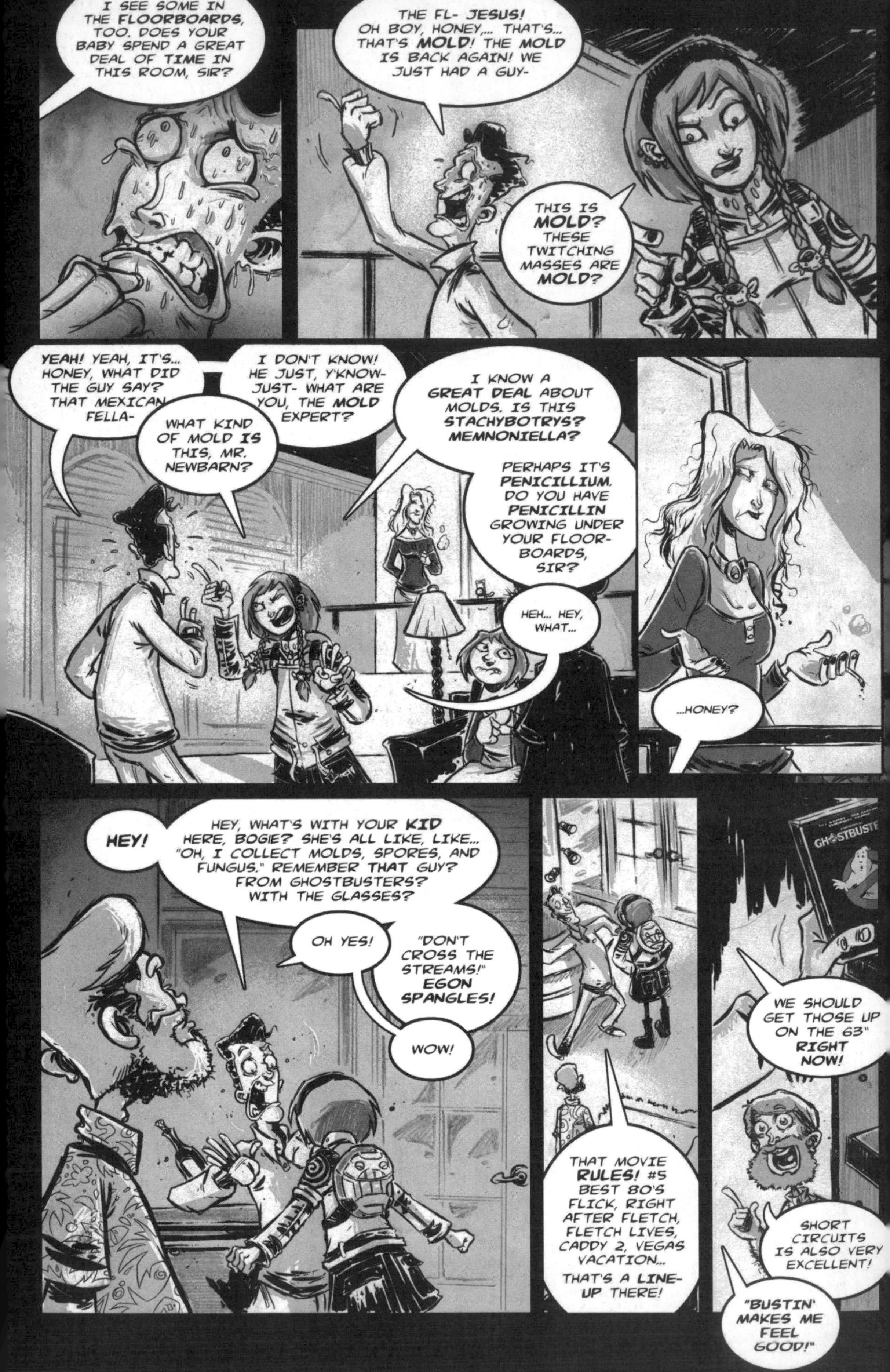

I SEE SOME IN THE FLOORBOARDS, TOO. DOES YOUR BABY SPEND A GREAT DEAL OF TIME IN THIS ROOM, SIR?
THE FL- JESUS! OH BOY, HONEY,... THAT'S... THAT'S MOLD! THE MOLD IS BACK AGAIN! WE JUST HAD A GUY-
THIS IS MOLD? THESE TWITCHING MASSES ARE MOLD?
YEAH! YEAH, IT'S... HONEY, WHAT DID THE GUY SAY? THAT MEXICAN FELLA-
I DON'T KNOW! HE JUST, Y'KNOW- JUST- WHAT ARE YOU, THE MOLD EXPERT?
WHAT KIND OF MOLD IS THIS, MR. NEWBARN?
I KNOW A GREAT DEAL ABOUT MOLDS. IS THIS STACHYBOTRYS? MEMNONIELLA?
PERHAPS IT'S PENICILLIUM. DO YOU HAVE PENICILLIN GROWING UNDER YOUR FLOOR-BOARDS, SIR?
HEH... HEY, WHAT...
...HONEY?
HEY!
HEY, WHAT'S WITH YOUR KID HERE, BOGIE? SHE'S ALL LIKE, LIKE... "OH, I COLLECT MOLDS, SPORES, AND FUNGUS." REMEMBER THAT GUY? FROM GHOSTBUSTERS? WITH THE GLASSES?
OH YES!
"DON'T CROSS THE STREAMS!" EGON SPANGLES!
WOW!
THAT MOVIE RULES! #5 BEST 80'S FLICK, RIGHT AFTER FLETCH, FLETCH LIVES, CADDY 2, VEGAS VACATION...
THAT'S A LINE-UP THERE!
WE SHOULD GET THOSE UP ON THE 63" RIGHT NOW!
SHORT CIRCUITS IS ALSO VERY EXCELLENT!
"BUSTIN' MAKES ME FEEL GOOD!"

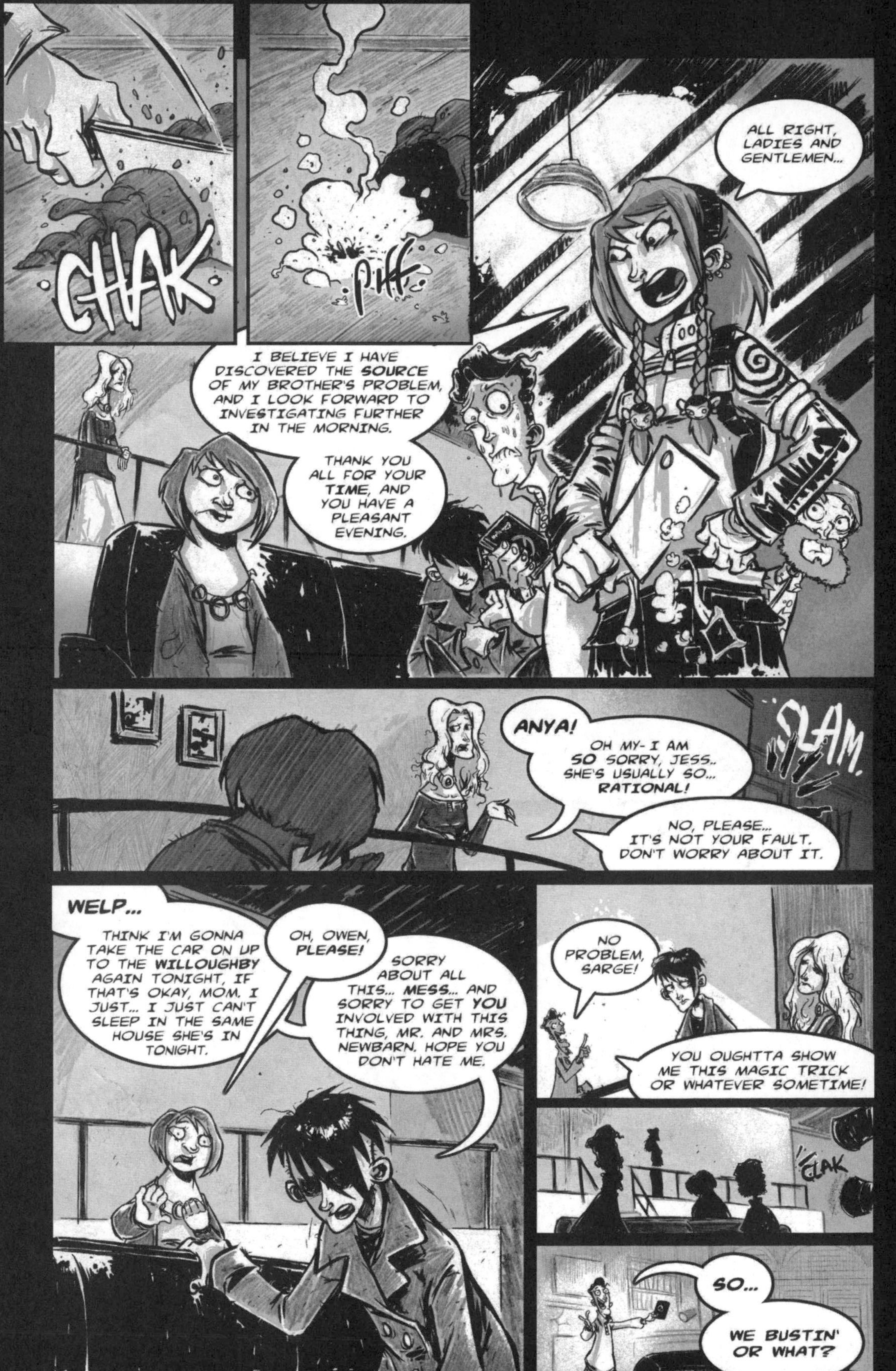

CHAK
PIFF
ALL RIGHT, LADIES AND GENTLEMEN...
I BELIEVE I HAVE DISCOVERED THE SOURCE OF MY BROTHER'S PROBLEM, AND I LOOK FORWARD TO INVESTIGATING FURTHER IN THE MORNING.
THANK YOU ALL FOR YOUR TIME, AND YOU HAVE A PLEASANT EVENING.
ANYA!
OH MY- I AM SO SORRY, JESS.. SHE'S USUALLY SO... RATIONAL!
SLAM
NO, PLEASE... IT'S NOT YOUR FAULT. DON'T WORRY ABOUT IT.
WELP...
THINK I'M GONNA TAKE THE CAR ON UP TO THE WILLOUGHBY AGAIN TONIGHT, IF THAT'S OKAY, MOM. I JUST... I JUST CAN'T SLEEP IN THE SAME HOUSE SHE'S IN TONIGHT.
OH, OWEN, PLEASE!
SORRY ABOUT ALL THIS... MESS... AND SORRY TO GET YOU INVOLVED WITH THIS THING, MR. AND MRS. NEWBARN. HOPE YOU DON'T HATE ME.
NO PROBLEM, SARGE!
YOU OUGHTTA SHOW ME THIS MAGIC TRICK OR WHATEVER SOMETIME!
CLAK
SO...
WE BUSTIN' OR WHAT?

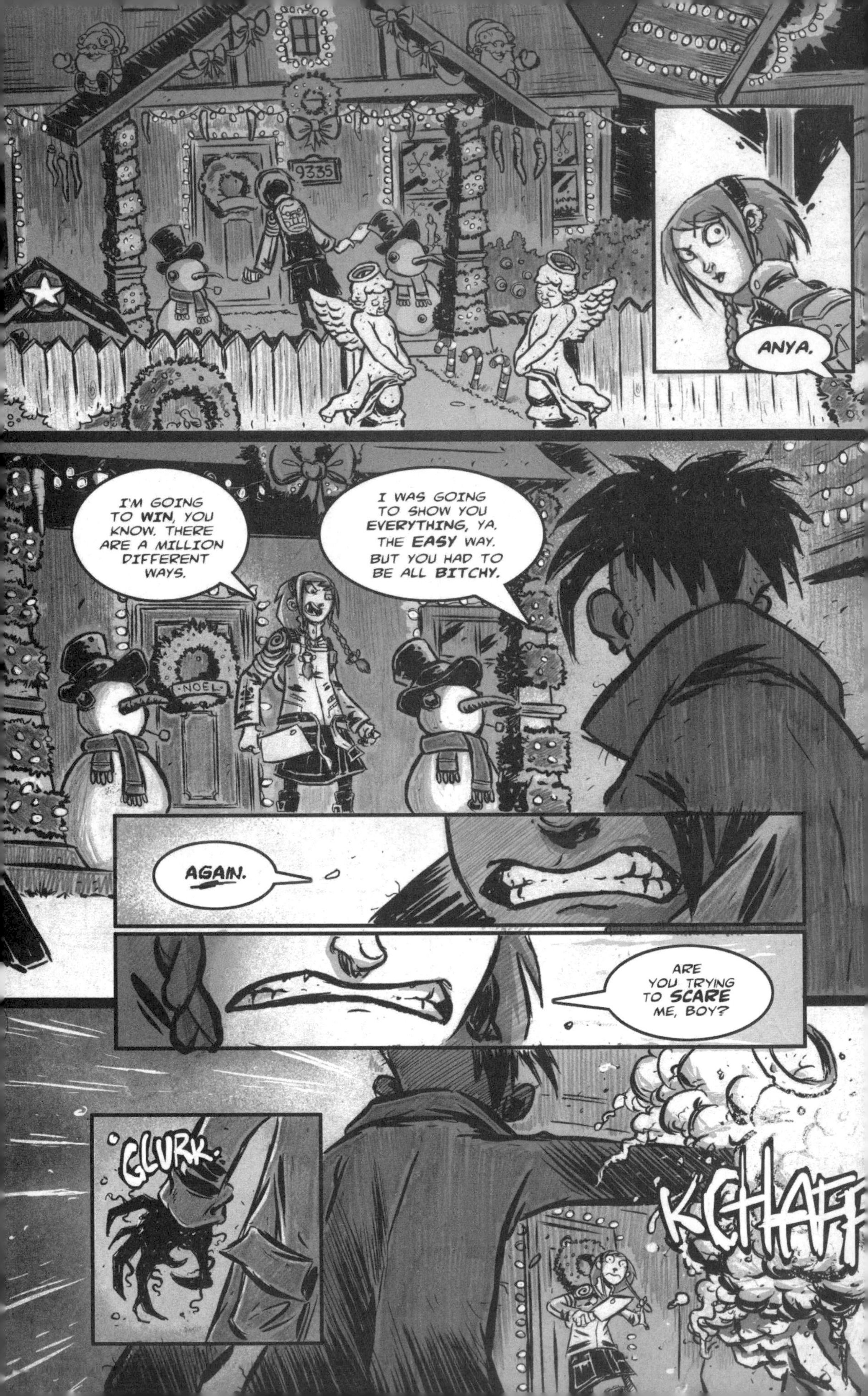
ANYA.
I'M GOING TO WIN, YOU KNOW. THERE ARE A MILLION DIFFERENT WAYS.
I WAS GOING TO SHOW YOU EVERYTHING, YA. THE EASY WAY. BUT YOU HAD TO BE ALL BITCHY.
AGAIN.
ARE YOU TRYING TO SCARE ME, BOY?
GLURK.
KCHAFF

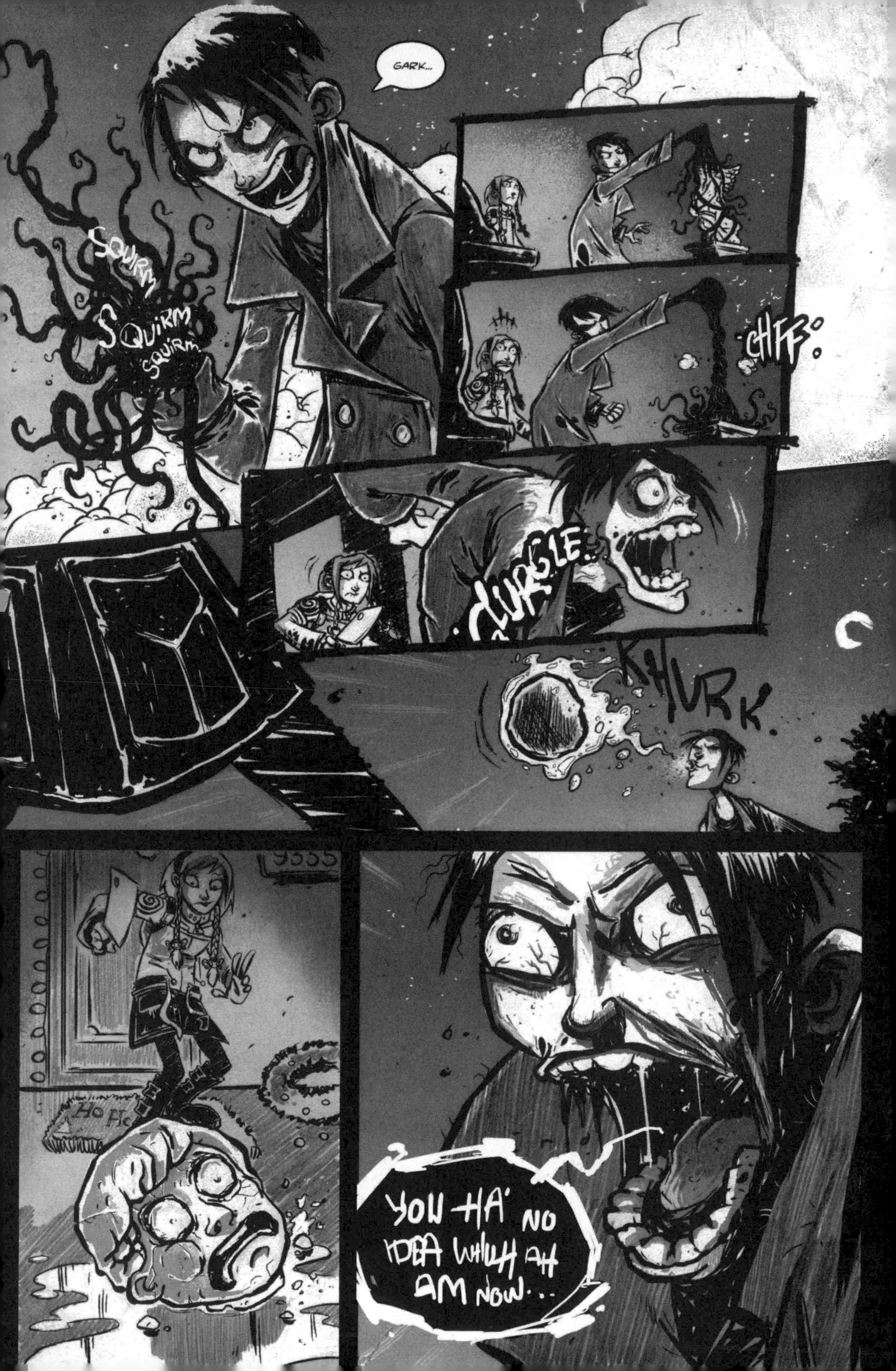
GARK...
SQUIRM
SQUIRM
SQUIRM
CHFF.
LURGLE..
KHURK!
YOU HA' NO IDEA WHUH AH AM NOW...

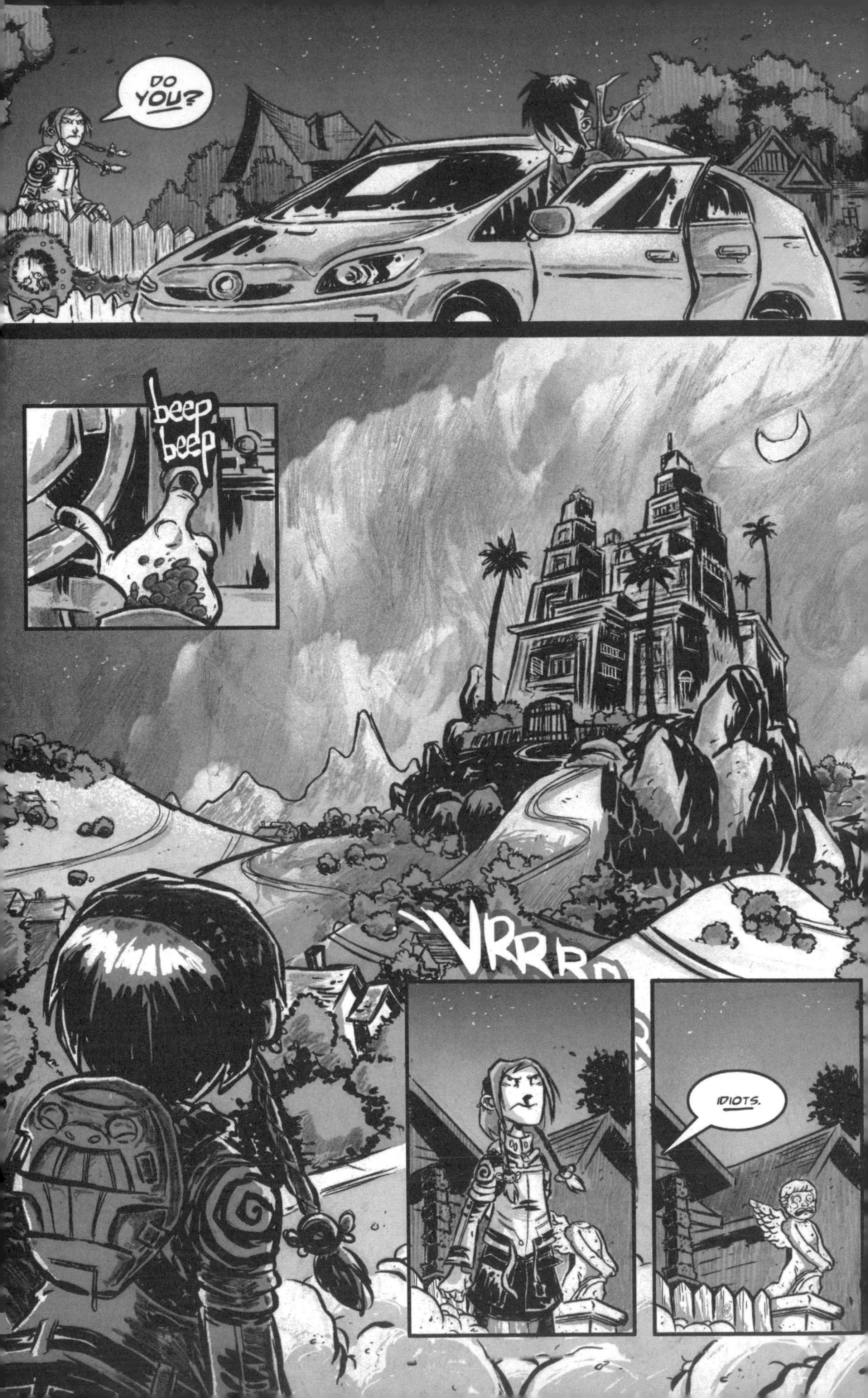
DO YOU?
beep beep
VRRRR
IDIOTS.

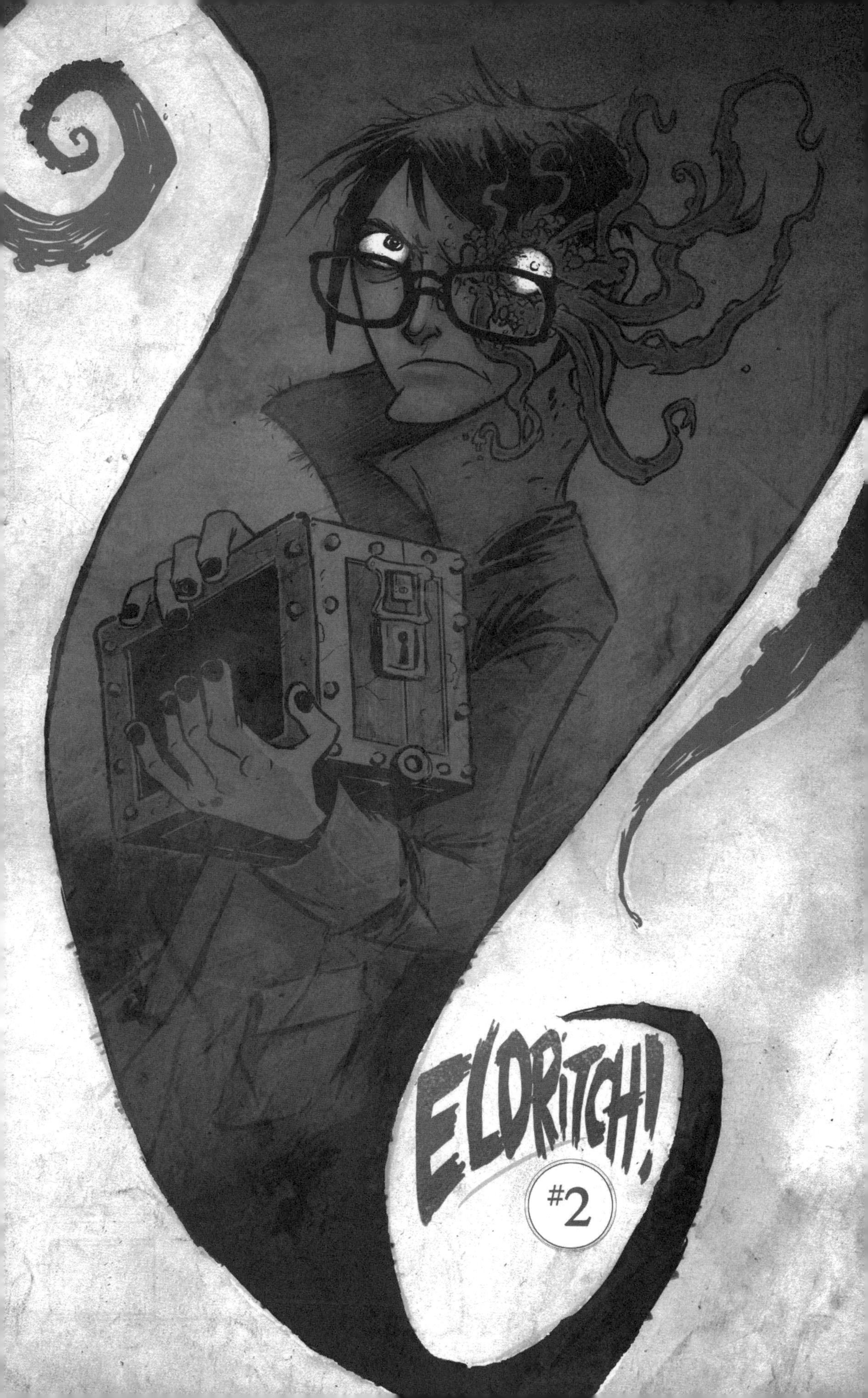
ELDRITCH!
#2

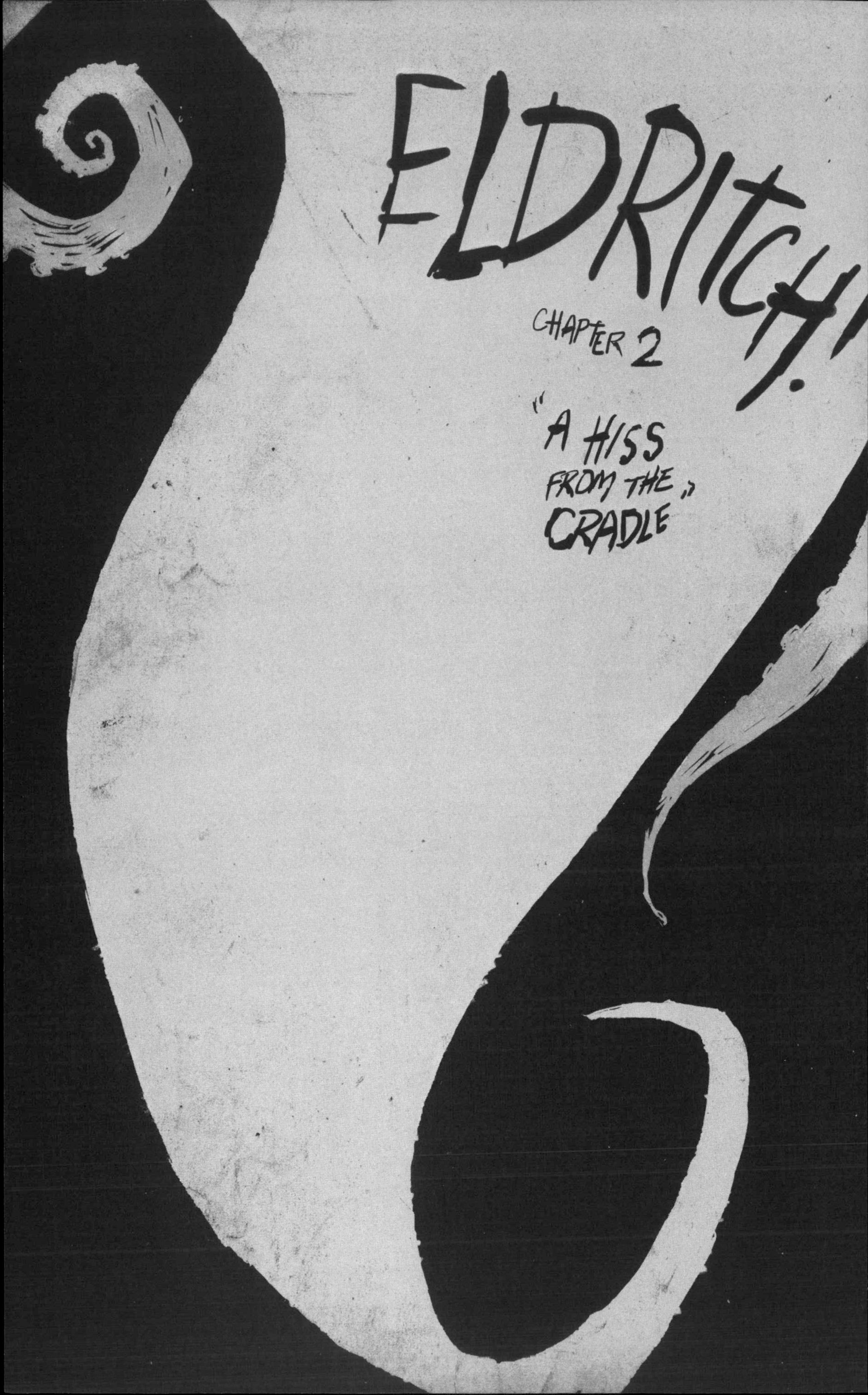
ELDRITCH!
CHAPTER 2
"A HISS FROM THE CRADLE"

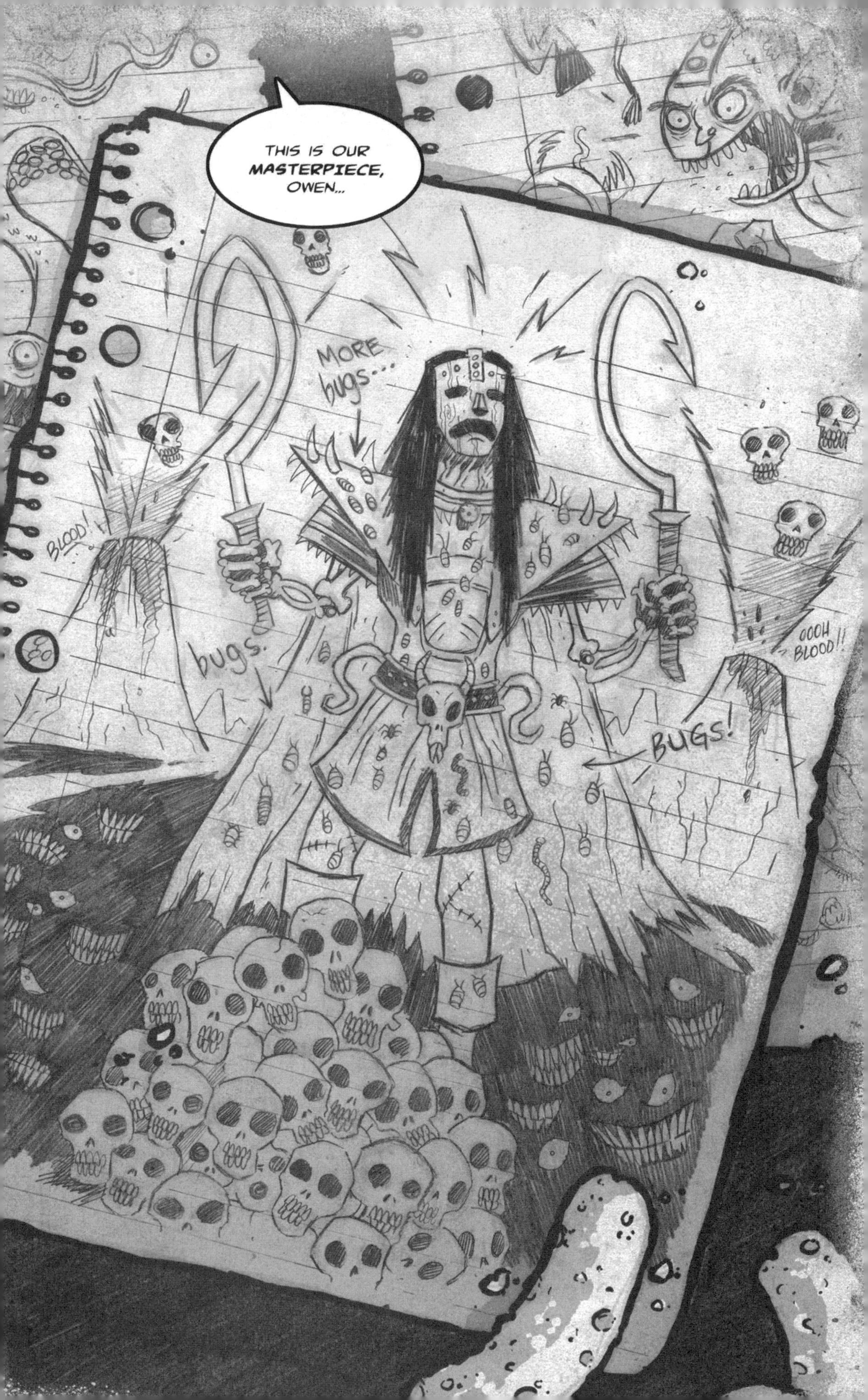
THIS IS OUR MASTERPIECE, OWEN...
MORE bugs....
BLOOD!
bugs.
OOOH BLOOD!!
BUGS!

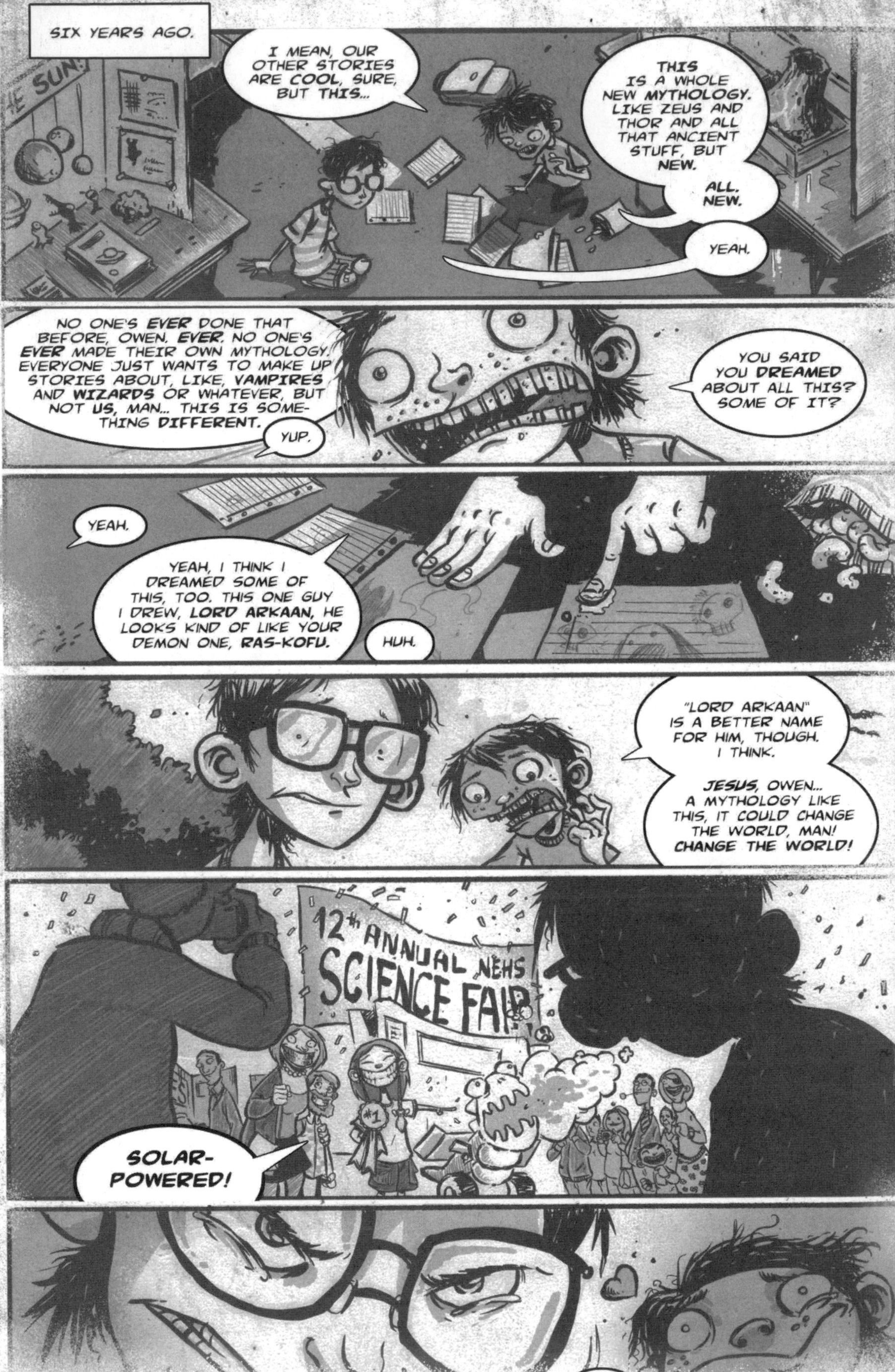
SIX YEARS AGO.
THE SUN!
I MEAN, OUR OTHER STORIES ARE COOL, SURE, BUT THIS...
THIS IS A WHOLE NEW MYTHOLOGY. LIKE ZEUS AND THOR AND ALL THAT ANCIENT STUFF, BUT NEW.
ALL. NEW.
YEAH.
NO ONE'S EVER DONE THAT BEFORE, OWEN. EVER. NO ONE'S EVER MADE THEIR OWN MYTHOLOGY. EVERYONE JUST WANTS TO MAKE UP STORIES ABOUT, LIKE, VAMPIRES AND WIZARDS OR WHATEVER, BUT NOT US, MAN... THIS IS SOMETHING DIFFERENT.
YUP.
YOU SAID YOU DREAMED ABOUT ALL THIS? SOME OF IT?
YEAH.
YEAH, I THINK I DREAMED SOME OF THIS, TOO. THIS ONE GUY I DREW, LORD ARKAAN, HE LOOKS KIND OF LIKE YOUR DEMON ONE, RAS-KOFU.
HUH.
"LORD ARKAAN" IS A BETTER NAME FOR HIM, THOUGH. I THINK.
JESUS, OWEN... A MYTHOLOGY LIKE THIS, IT COULD CHANGE THE WORLD, MAN! CHANGE THE WORLD!
12th ANNUAL NEHS SCIENCE FAIR
#1
SOLAR-POWERED!
YEAH...

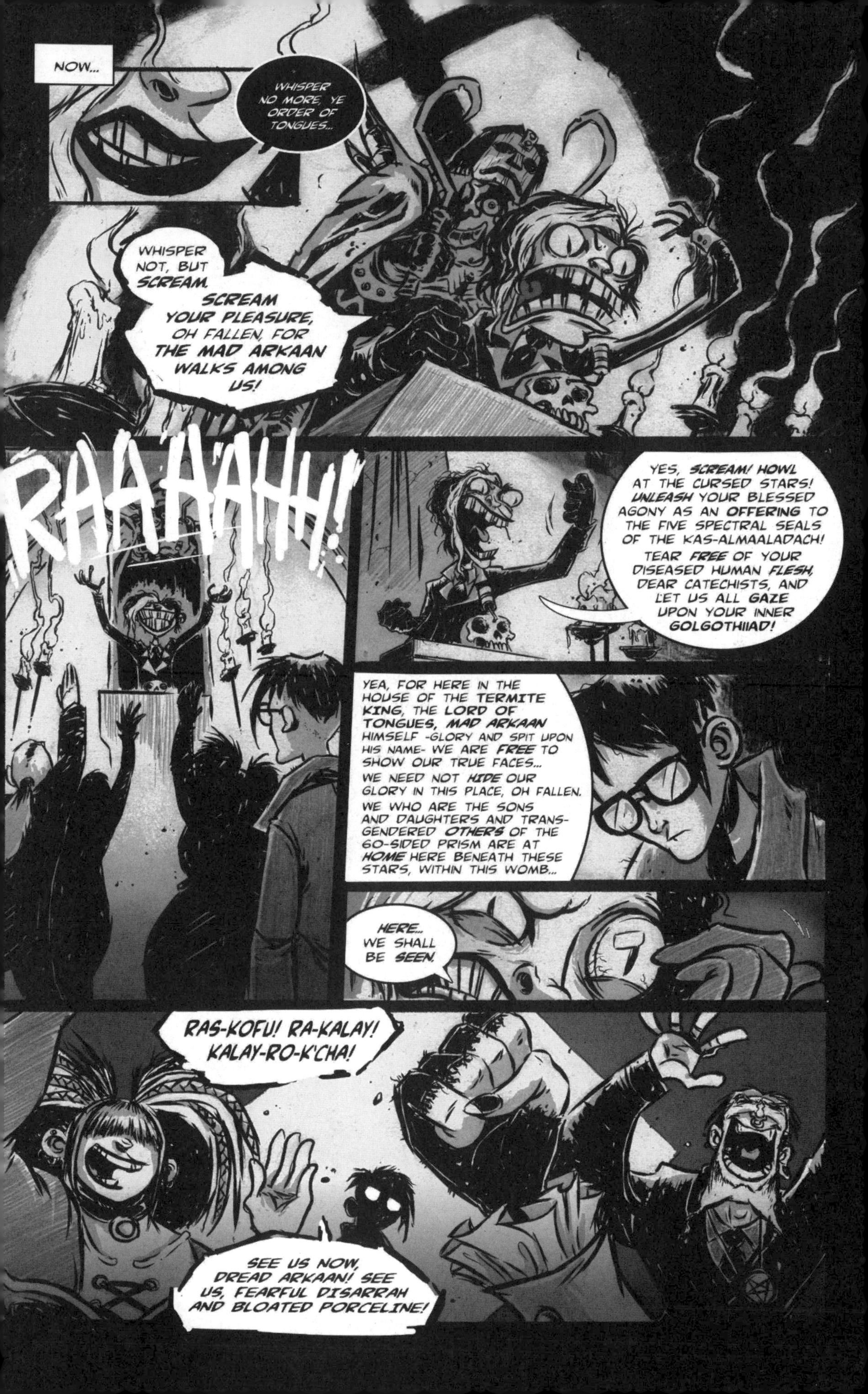
NOW...
WHISPER NO MORE, YE ORDER OF TONGUES...
WHISPER NOT, BUT SCREAM. SCREAM YOUR PLEASURE, OH FALLEN, FOR THE MAD ARKAAN WALKS AMONG US!
RAAAAHH!
YES, SCREAM! HOWL AT THE CURSED STARS! UNLEASH YOUR BLESSED AGONY AS AN OFFERING TO THE FIVE SPECTRAL SEALS OF THE KAS-ALMAALADACH!
TEAR FREE OF YOUR DISEASED HUMAN FLESH, DEAR CATECHISTS, AND LET US ALL GAZE UPON YOUR INNER GOLGOTHIIAD!
YEA, FOR HERE IN THE HOUSE OF THE TERMITE KING, THE LORD OF TONGUES, MAD ARKAAN HIMSELF -GLORY AND SPIT UPON HIS NAME- WE ARE FREE TO SHOW OUR TRUE FACES...
WE NEED NOT HIDE OUR GLORY IN THIS PLACE, OH FALLEN.
WE WHO ARE THE SONS AND DAUGHTERS AND TRANS-GENDERED OTHERS OF THE 60-SIDED PRISM ARE AT HOME HERE BENEATH THESE STARS, WITHIN THIS WOMB...
HERE... WE SHALL BE SEEN.
RAS-KOFU! RA-KALAY! KALAY-RO-K'CHA!
SEE US NOW, DREAD ARKAAN! SEE US, FEARFUL DISARRAH AND BLOATED PORCELINE!

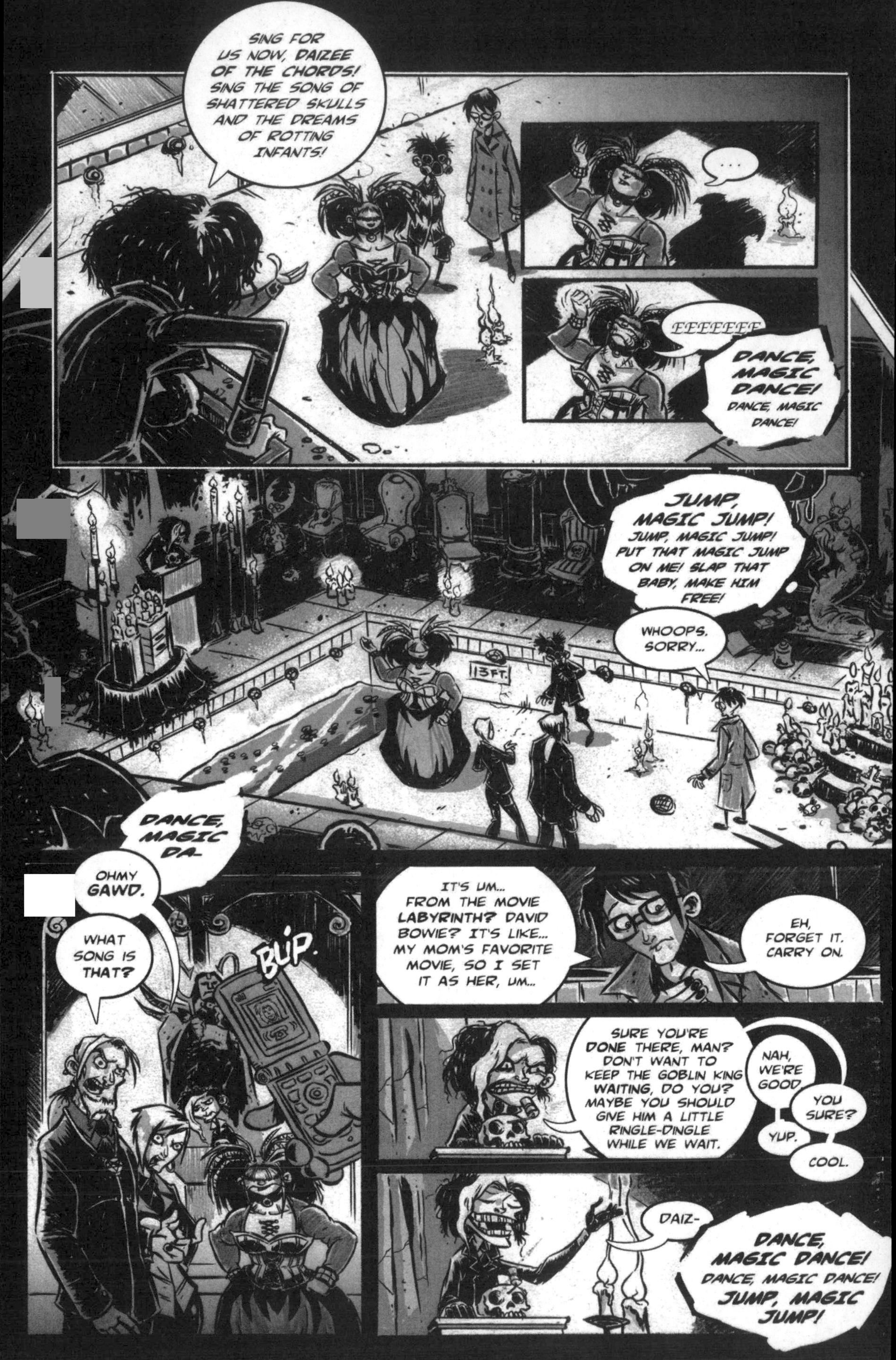
SING FOR US NOW, DAIZEE OF THE CHORDS! SING THE SONG OF SHATTERED SKULLS AND THE DREAMS OF ROTTING INFANTS!
...
EEEEEEE
DANCE, MAGIC DANCE! DANCE, MAGIC DANCE!
JUMP, MAGIC JUMP! JUMP, MAGIC JUMP! PUT THAT MAGIC JUMP ON ME! SLAP THAT BABY, MAKE HIM FREE!
WHOOPS. SORRY...
13FT.
DANCE, MAGIC DA-
OHMY GAWD.
WHAT SONG IS THAT?
BLIP.
IT'S UM... FROM THE MOVIE LABYRINTH? DAVID BOWIE? IT'S LIKE... MY MOM'S FAVORITE MOVIE, SO I SET IT AS HER, UM...
EH, FORGET IT. CARRY ON.
SURE YOU'RE DONE THERE, MAN? DON'T WANT TO KEEP THE GOBLIN KING WAITING, DO YOU? MAYBE YOU SHOULD GIVE HIM A LITTLE RINGLE-DINGLE WHILE WE WAIT.
NAH, WE'RE GOOD.
YOU SURE?
YUP.
COOL.
DAIZ-
DANCE, MAGIC DANCE! DANCE, MAGIC DANCE! JUMP, MAGIC JUMP!

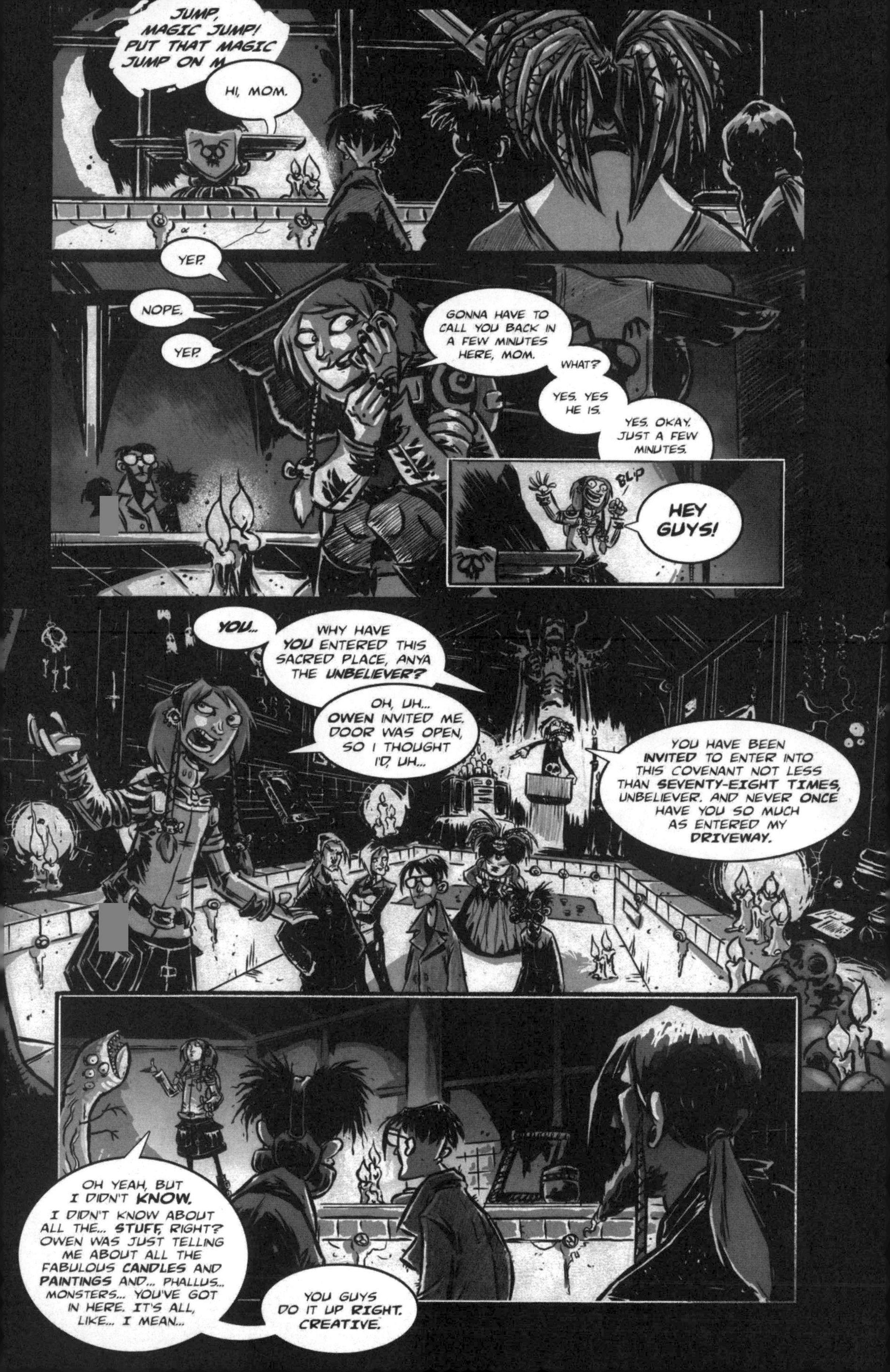
JUMP, MAGIC JUMP! PUT THAT MAGIC JUMP ON M
HI, MOM.
YEP.
NOPE.
YEP.
GONNA HAVE TO CALL YOU BACK IN A FEW MINUTES HERE, MOM.
WHAT?
YES. YES HE IS.
YES. OKAY. JUST A FEW MINUTES.
BLIP
HEY GUYS!
YOU...
WHY HAVE YOU ENTERED THIS SACRED PLACE, ANYA THE UNBELIEVER?
OH, UH... OWEN INVITED ME. DOOR WAS OPEN, SO I THOUGHT I'D, UH...
YOU HAVE BEEN INVITED TO ENTER INTO THIS COVENANT NOT LESS THAN SEVENTY-EIGHT TIMES, UNBELIEVER. AND NEVER ONCE HAVE YOU SO MUCH AS ENTERED MY DRIVEWAY.
OH YEAH, BUT I DIDN'T KNOW. I DIDN'T KNOW ABOUT ALL THE... STUFF, RIGHT? OWEN WAS JUST TELLING ME ABOUT ALL THE FABULOUS CANDLES AND PAINTINGS AND... PHALLUS... MONSTERS... YOU'VE GOT IN HERE. IT'S ALL, LIKE... I MEAN...
YOU GUYS DO IT UP RIGHT. CREATIVE.

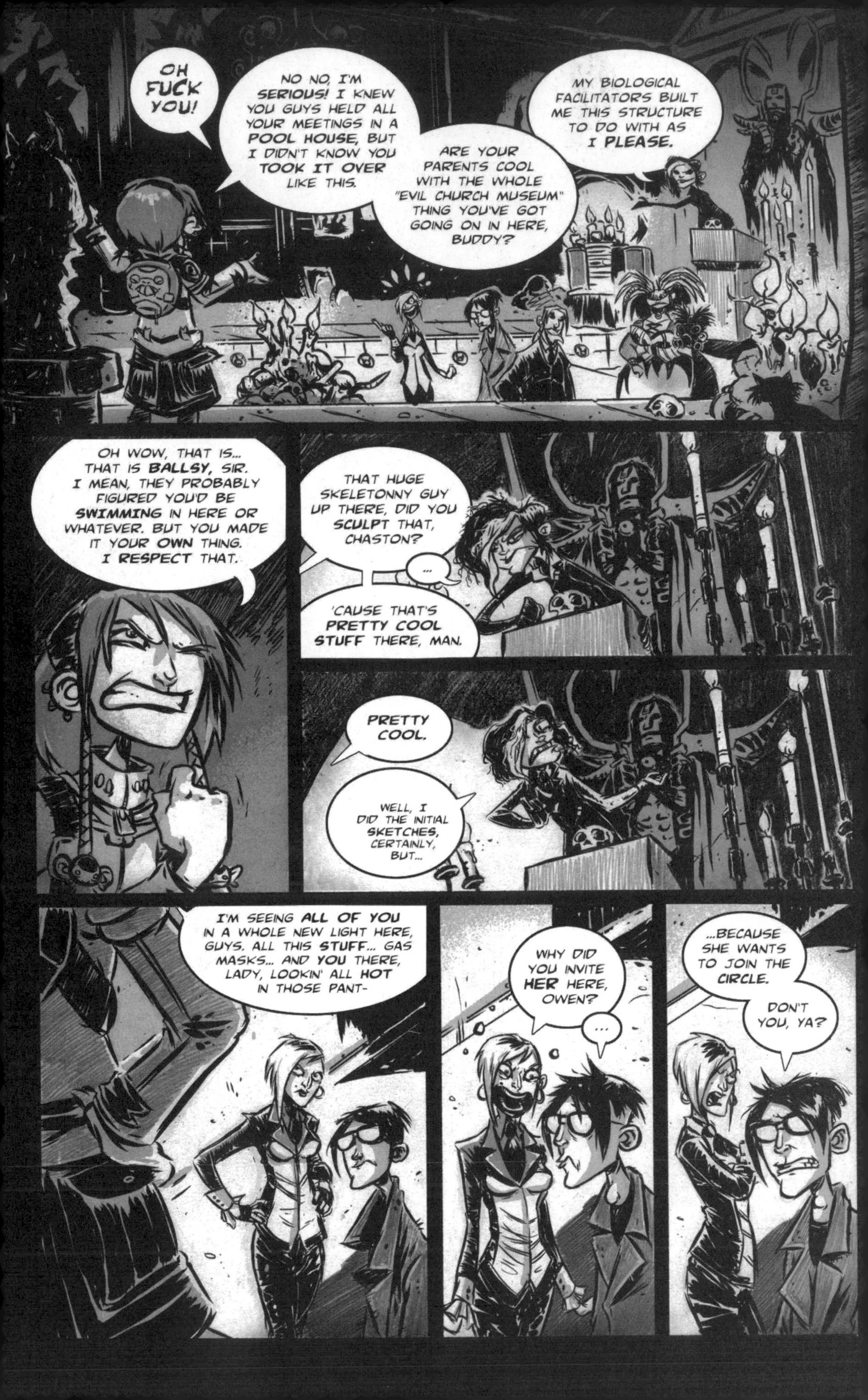
OH FUCK YOU!
NO NO, I'M SERIOUS! I KNEW YOU GUYS HELD ALL YOUR MEETINGS IN A POOL HOUSE, BUT I DIDN'T KNOW YOU TOOK IT OVER LIKE THIS.
ARE YOUR PARENTS COOL WITH THE WHOLE "EVIL CHURCH MUSEUM" THING YOU'VE GOT GOING ON IN HERE, BUDDY?
MY BIOLOGICAL FACILITATORS BUILT ME THIS STRUCTURE TO DO WITH AS I PLEASE.
OH WOW, THAT IS... THAT IS BALLSY, SIR. I MEAN, THEY PROBABLY FIGURED YOU'D BE SWIMMING IN HERE OR WHATEVER. BUT YOU MADE IT YOUR OWN THING. I RESPECT THAT.
THAT HUGE SKELETONNY GUY UP THERE, DID YOU SCULPT THAT, CHASTON?
...
'CAUSE THAT'S PRETTY COOL STUFF THERE, MAN.
PRETTY COOL.
WELL, I DID THE INITIAL SKETCHES, CERTAINLY, BUT...
I'M SEEING ALL OF YOU IN A WHOLE NEW LIGHT HERE, GUYS. ALL THIS STUFF... GAS MASKS... AND YOU THERE, LADY, LOOKIN' ALL HOT IN THOSE PANT-
WHY DID YOU INVITE HER HERE, OWEN?
...
...BECAUSE SHE WANTS TO JOIN THE CIRCLE.
DON'T YOU, YA?

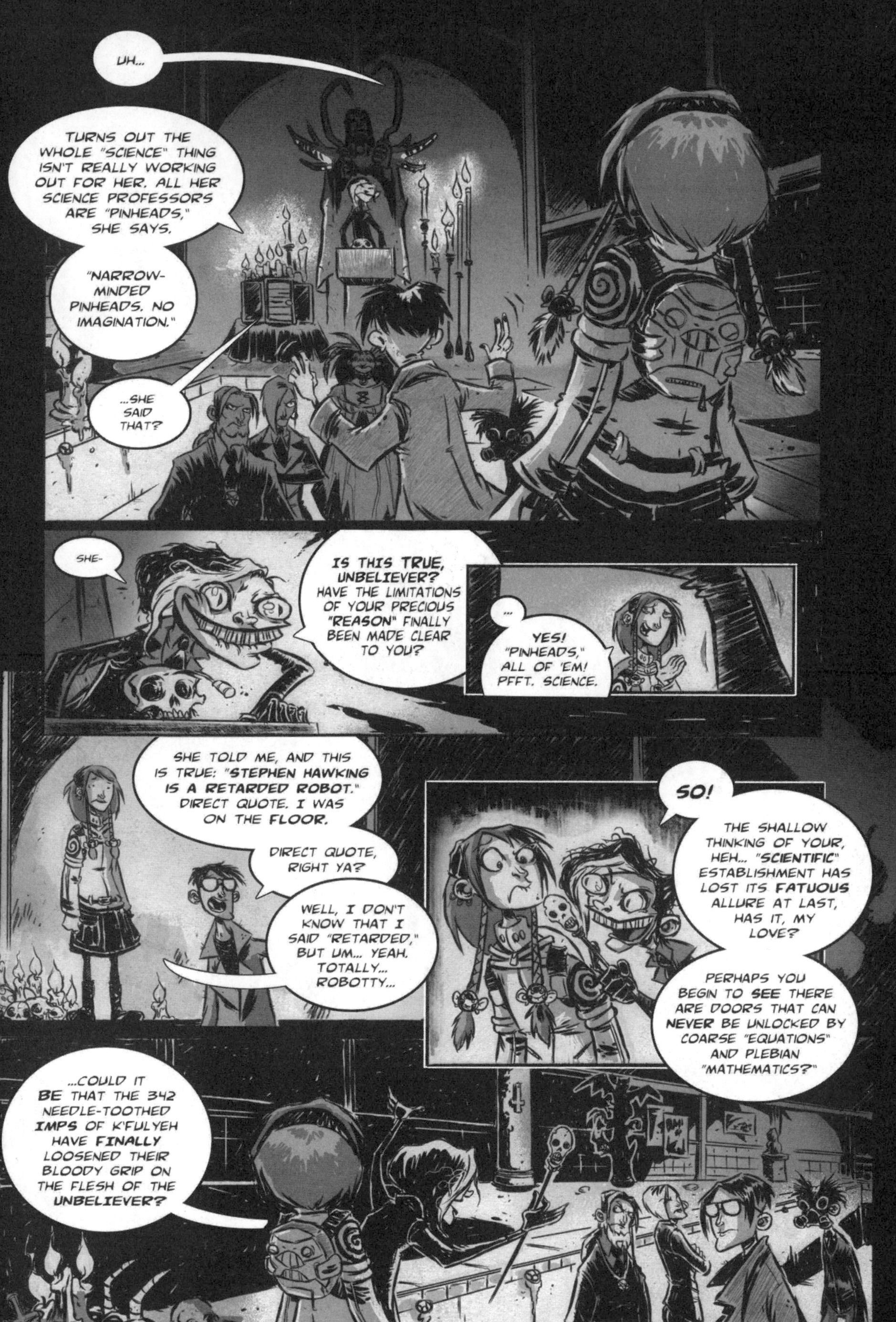
UH...
TURNS OUT THE WHOLE "SCIENCE" THING ISN'T REALLY WORKING OUT FOR HER. ALL HER SCIENCE PROFESSORS ARE "PINHEADS," SHE SAYS.
"NARROW-MINDED PINHEADS. NO IMAGINATION."
...SHE SAID THAT?
SHE-
IS THIS TRUE, UNBELIEVER? HAVE THE LIMITATIONS OF YOUR PRECIOUS "REASON" FINALLY BEEN MADE CLEAR TO YOU?
...
YES! "PINHEADS," ALL OF 'EM! PFFT. SCIENCE.
SHE TOLD ME, AND THIS IS TRUE: "STEPHEN HAWKING IS A RETARDED ROBOT." DIRECT QUOTE. I WAS ON THE FLOOR.
DIRECT QUOTE, RIGHT YA?
WELL, I DON'T KNOW THAT I SAID "RETARDED," BUT UM... YEAH. TOTALLY... ROBOTTY...
SO!
THE SHALLOW THINKING OF YOUR, HEH... "SCIENTIFIC" ESTABLISHMENT HAS LOST ITS FATUOUS ALLURE AT LAST, HAS IT, MY LOVE?
PERHAPS YOU BEGIN TO SEE THERE ARE DOORS THAT CAN NEVER BE UNLOCKED BY COARSE "EQUATIONS" AND PLEBIAN "MATHEMATICS?"
...COULD IT BE THAT THE 342 NEEDLE-TOOTHED IMPS OF K'FULYEH HAVE FINALLY LOOSENED THEIR BLOODY GRIP ON THE FLESH OF THE UNBELIEVER?

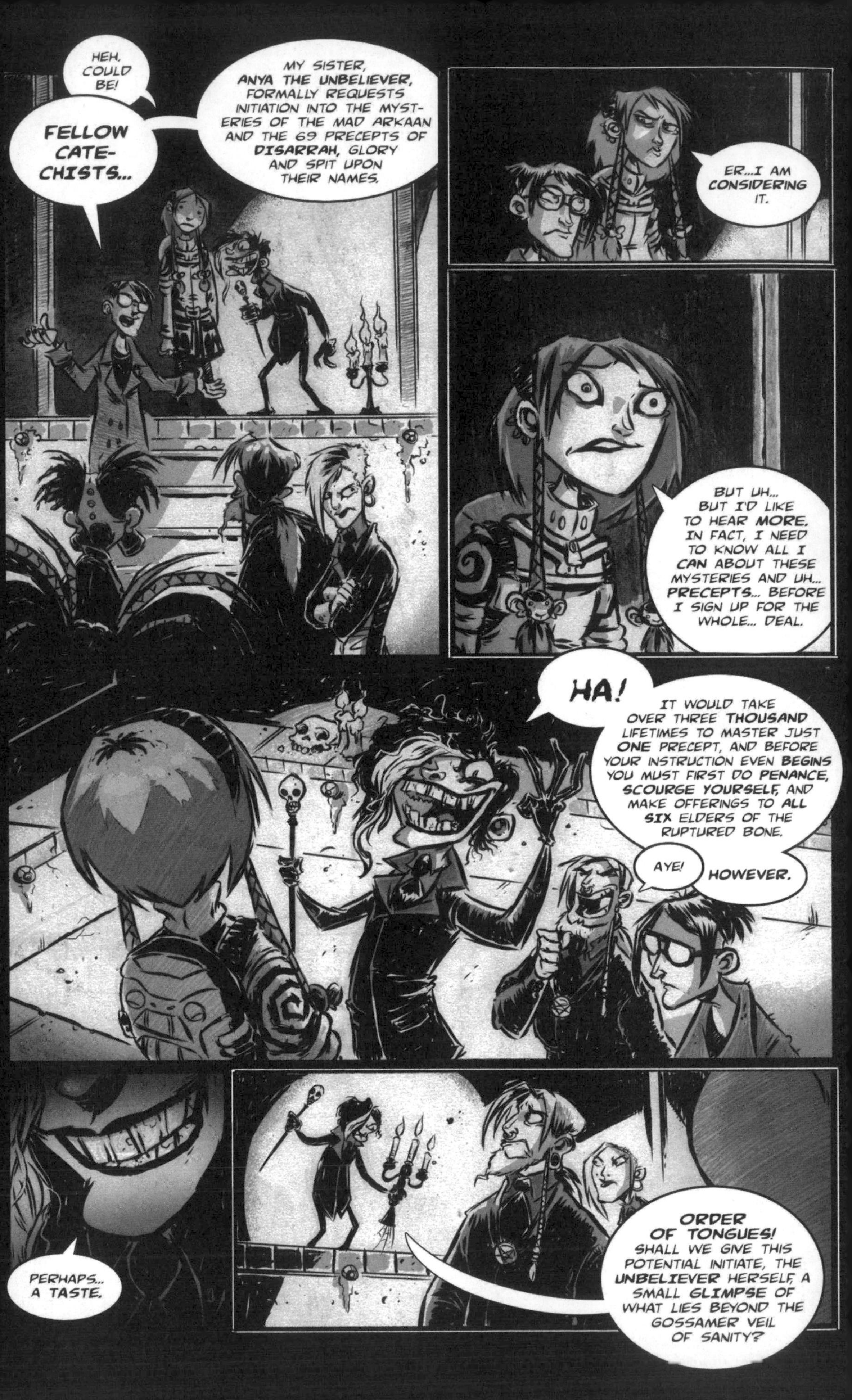
HEH. COULD BE!
FELLOW CATE-CHISTS...
MY SISTER, ANYA THE UNBELIEVER, FORMALLY REQUESTS INITIATION INTO THE MYSTERIES OF THE MAD ARKAAN AND THE 69 PRECEPTS OF DISARRAH, GLORY AND SPIT UPON THEIR NAMES.
ER...I AM CONSIDERING IT.
BUT UH... BUT I'D LIKE TO HEAR MORE. IN FACT, I NEED TO KNOW ALL I CAN ABOUT THESE MYSTERIES AND UH... PRECEPTS... BEFORE I SIGN UP FOR THE WHOLE... DEAL.
HA!
IT WOULD TAKE OVER THREE THOUSAND LIFETIMES TO MASTER JUST ONE PRECEPT, AND BEFORE YOUR INSTRUCTION EVEN BEGINS YOU MUST FIRST DO PENANCE, SCOURGE YOURSELF, AND MAKE OFFERINGS TO ALL SIX ELDERS OF THE RUPTURED BONE.
AYE!
HOWEVER.
PERHAPS... A TASTE.
ORDER OF TONGUES! SHALL WE GIVE THIS POTENTIAL INITIATE, THE UNBELIEVER HERSELF, A SMALL GLIMPSE OF WHAT LIES BEYOND THE GOSSAMER VEIL OF SANITY?

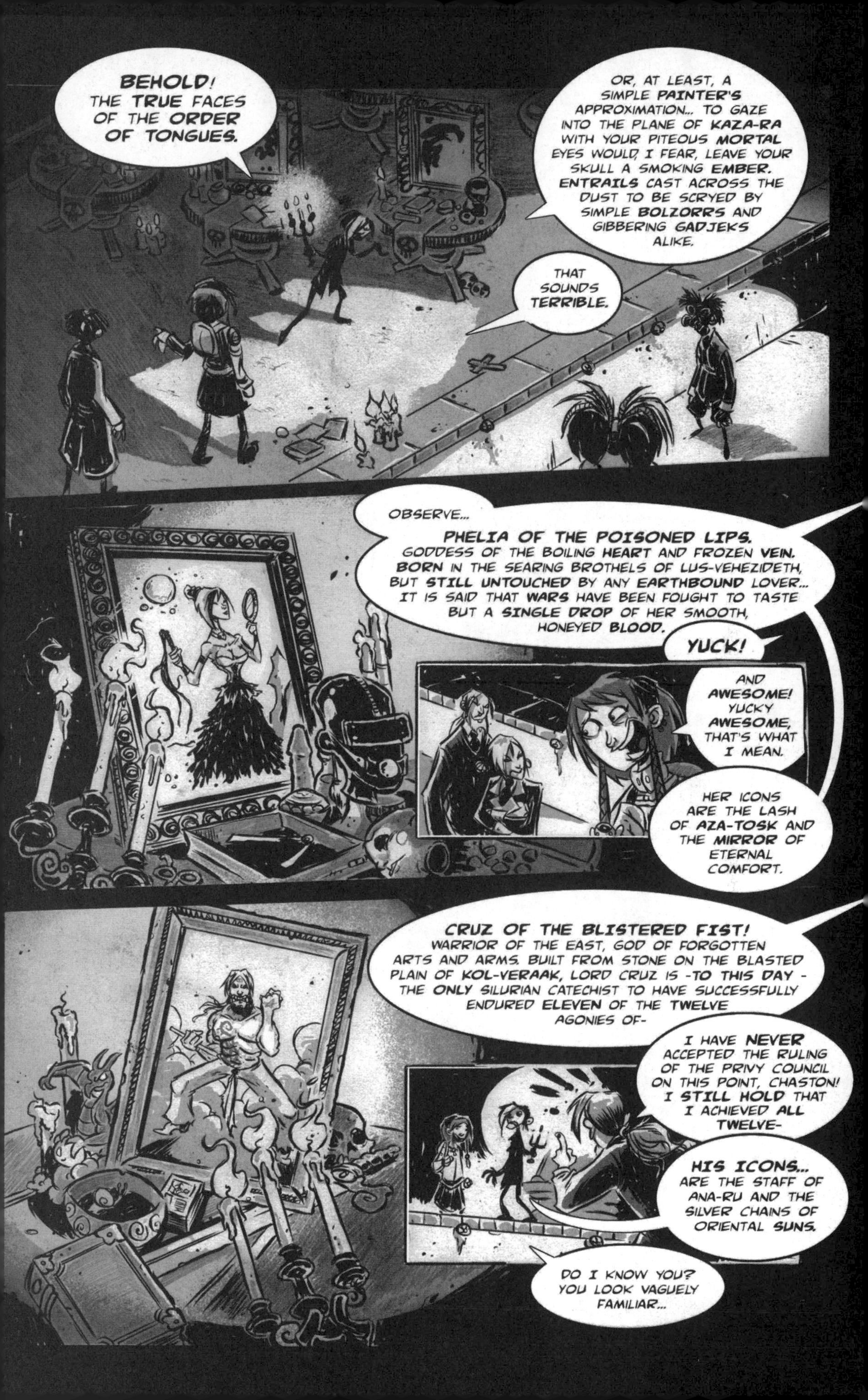
BEHOLD! THE TRUE FACES OF THE ORDER OF TONGUES.
OR, AT LEAST, A SIMPLE PAINTER'S APPROXIMATION... TO GAZE INTO THE PLANE OF KAZA-RA WITH YOUR PITEOUS MORTAL EYES WOULD, I FEAR, LEAVE YOUR SKULL A SMOKING EMBER. ENTRAILS CAST ACROSS THE DUST TO BE SCRYED BY SIMPLE BOLZORRS AND GIBBERING GADJEKS ALIKE.
THAT SOUNDS TERRIBLE.
OBSERVE...
PHELIA OF THE POISONED LIPS. GODDESS OF THE BOILING HEART AND FROZEN VEIN. BORN IN THE SEARING BROTHELS OF LUS-VEHEZIDETH, BUT STILL UNTOUCHED BY ANY EARTHBOUND LOVER... IT IS SAID THAT WARS HAVE BEEN FOUGHT TO TASTE BUT A SINGLE DROP OF HER SMOOTH, HONEYED BLOOD.
YUCK!
AND AWESOME! YUCKY AWESOME, THAT'S WHAT I MEAN.
HER ICONS ARE THE LASH OF AZA-TOSK AND THE MIRROR OF ETERNAL COMFORT.
CRUZ OF THE BLISTERED FIST! WARRIOR OF THE EAST, GOD OF FORGOTTEN ARTS AND ARMS. BUILT FROM STONE ON THE BLASTED PLAIN OF KOL-VERAAK, LORD CRUZ IS -TO THIS DAY- THE ONLY SILURIAN CATECHIST TO HAVE SUCCESSFULLY ENDURED ELEVEN OF THE TWELVE AGONIES OF-
I HAVE NEVER ACCEPTED THE RULING OF THE PRIVY COUNCIL ON THIS POINT, CHASTON! I STILL HOLD THAT I ACHIEVED ALL TWELVE-
HIS ICONS... ARE THE STAFF OF ANA-RU AND THE SILVER CHAINS OF ORIENTAL SUNS.
DO I KNOW YOU? YOU LOOK VAGUELY FAMILIAR...

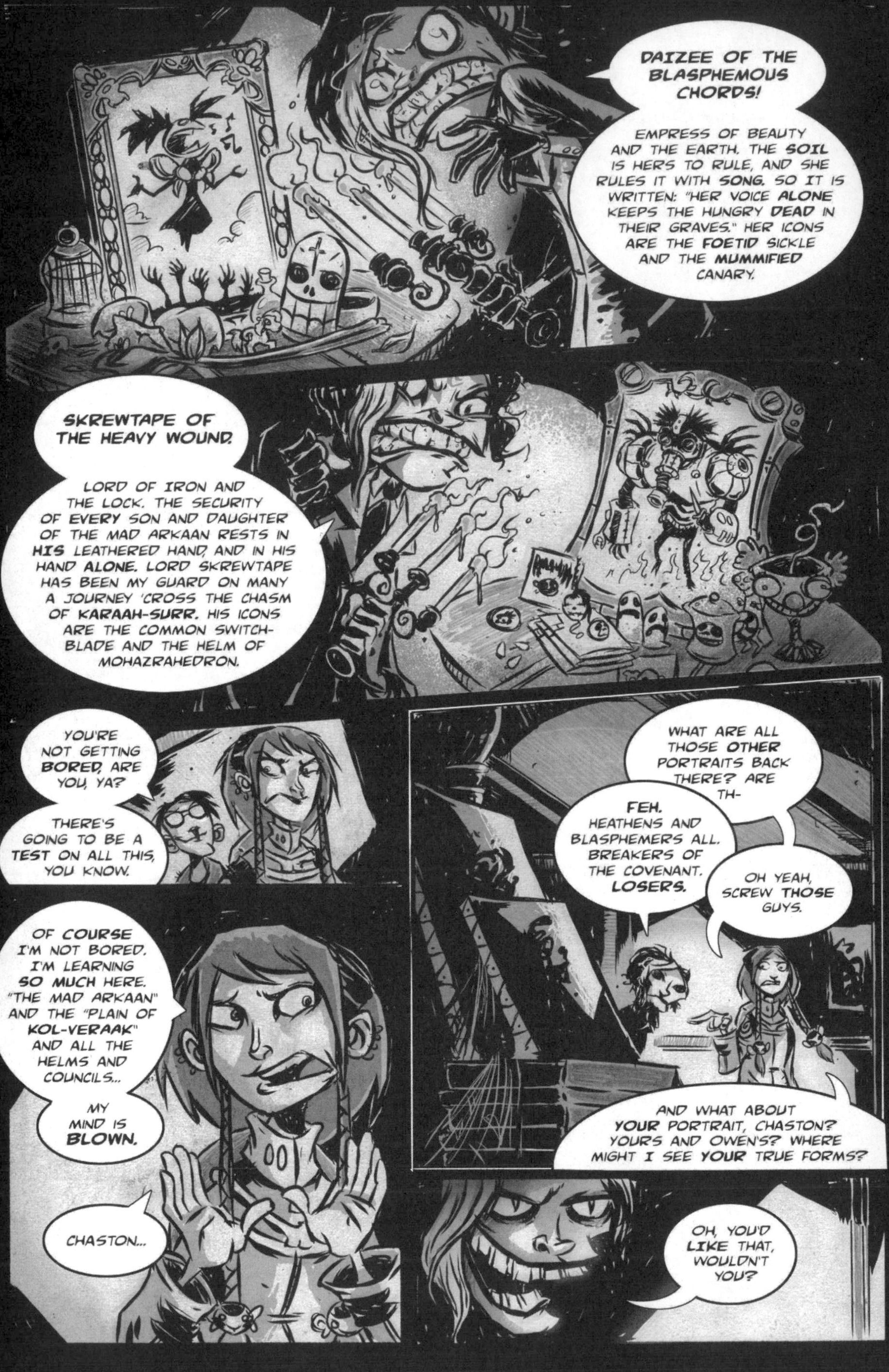
DAIZEE OF THE BLASPHEMOUS CHORDS!
EMPRESS OF BEAUTY AND THE EARTH. THE SOIL IS HERS TO RULE, AND SHE RULES IT WITH SONG. SO IT IS WRITTEN: "HER VOICE ALONE KEEPS THE HUNGRY DEAD IN THEIR GRAVES." HER ICONS ARE THE FOETID SICKLE AND THE MUMMIFIED CANARY.
SKREWTAPE OF THE HEAVY WOUND.
LORD OF IRON AND THE LOCK. THE SECURITY OF EVERY SON AND DAUGHTER OF THE MAD ARKAAN RESTS IN HIS LEATHERED HAND, AND IN HIS HAND ALONE. LORD SKREWTAPE HAS BEEN MY GUARD ON MANY A JOURNEY 'CROSS THE CHASM OF KARAAH-SURR. HIS ICONS ARE THE COMMON SWITCH-BLADE AND THE HELM OF MOHAZRAHEDRON.
YOU'RE NOT GETTING BORED, ARE YOU, YA?
THERE'S GOING TO BE A TEST ON ALL THIS, YOU KNOW.
OF COURSE I'M NOT BORED. I'M LEARNING SO MUCH HERE. "THE MAD ARKAAN" AND THE "PLAIN OF KOL-VERAAK" AND ALL THE HELMS AND COUNCILS...
MY MIND IS BLOWN.
CHASTON...
WHAT ARE ALL THOSE OTHER PORTRAITS BACK THERE? ARE TH-
FEH. HEATHENS AND BLASPHEMERS ALL. BREAKERS OF THE COVENANT. LOSERS.
OH YEAH, SCREW THOSE GUYS.
AND WHAT ABOUT YOUR PORTRAIT, CHASTON? YOURS AND OWEN'S? WHERE MIGHT I SEE YOUR TRUE FORMS?
OH, YOU'D LIKE THAT, WOULDN'T YOU?

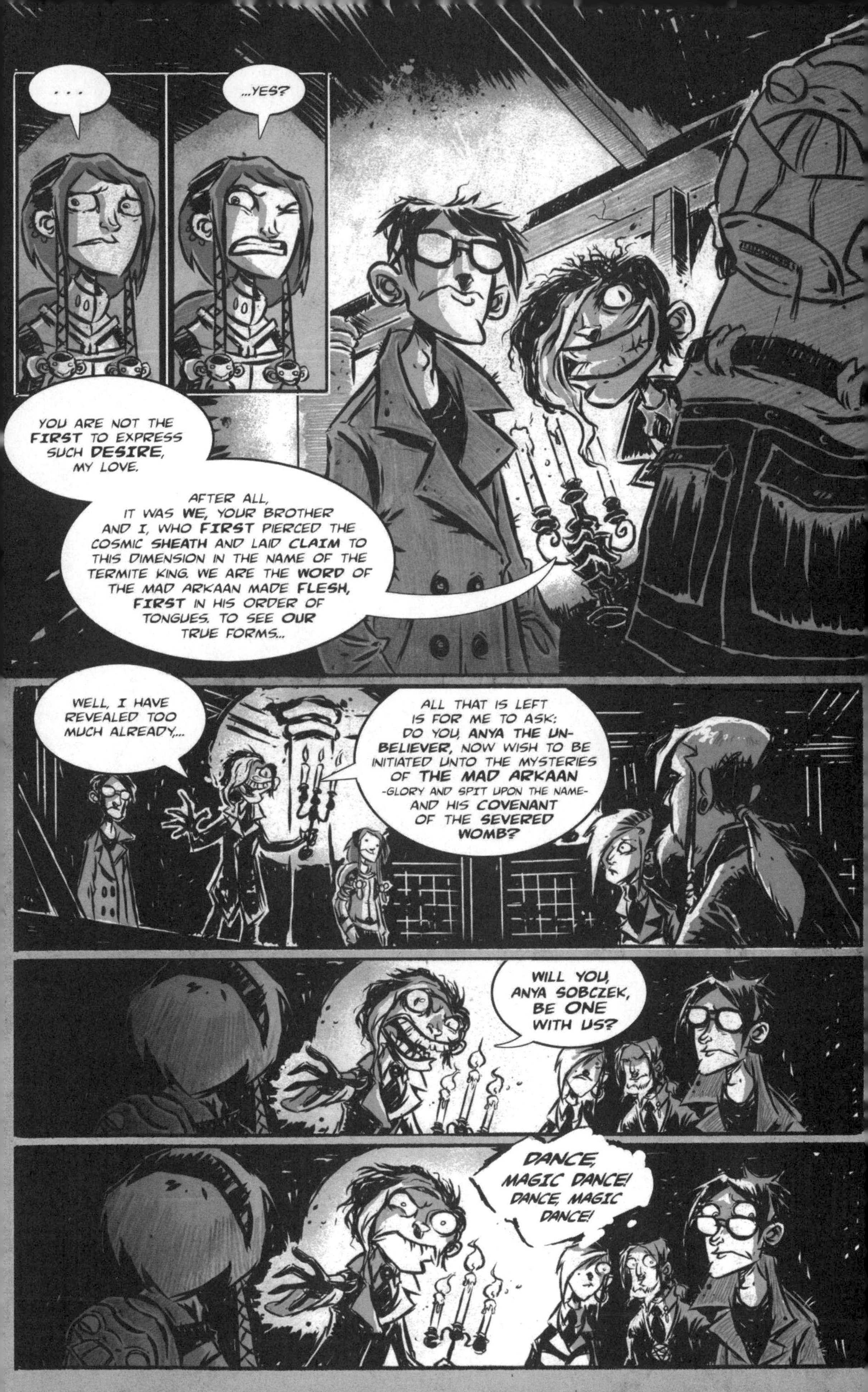
...
...YES?
YOU ARE NOT THE FIRST TO EXPRESS SUCH DESIRE, MY LOVE.
AFTER ALL, IT WAS WE, YOUR BROTHER AND I, WHO FIRST PIERCED THE COSMIC SHEATH AND LAID CLAIM TO THIS DIMENSION IN THE NAME OF THE TERMITE KING. WE ARE THE WORD OF THE MAD ARKAAN MADE FLESH, FIRST IN HIS ORDER OF TONGUES. TO SEE OUR TRUE FORMS...
WELL, I HAVE REVEALED TOO MUCH ALREADY,...
ALL THAT IS LEFT IS FOR ME TO ASK: DO YOU, ANYA THE UNBELIEVER, NOW WISH TO BE INITIATED UNTO THE MYSTERIES OF THE MAD ARKAAN -GLORY AND SPIT UPON THE NAME- AND HIS COVENANT OF THE SEVERED WOMB?
WILL YOU, ANYA SOBCZEK, BE ONE WITH US?
DANCE, MAGIC DANCE! DANCE, MAGIC DANCE!

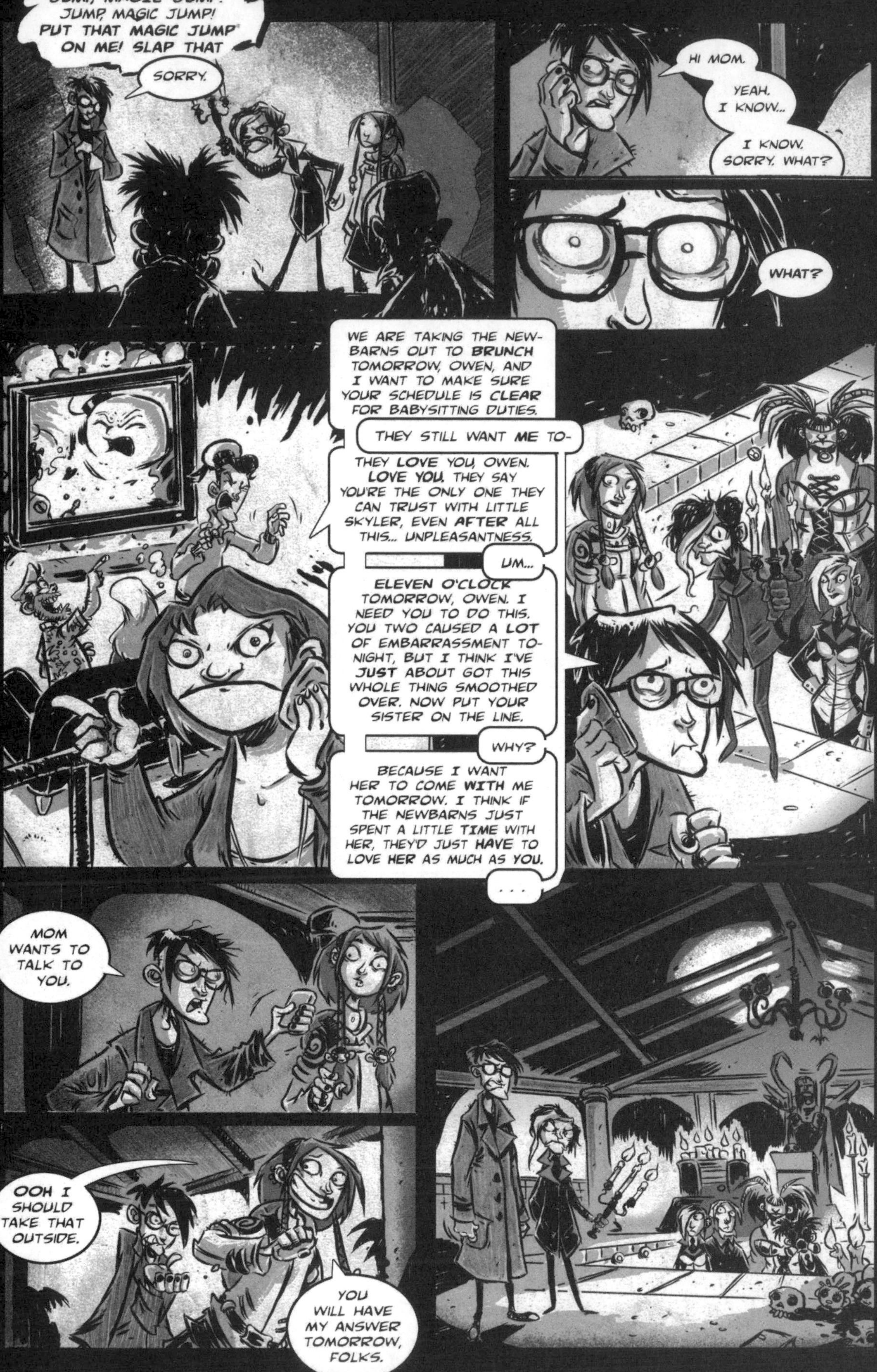
JUMP, MAGIC JUMP! JUMP, MAGIC JUMP! PUT THAT MAGIC JUMP ON ME! SLAP THAT
SORRY.
HI MOM.
YEAH. I KNOW...
I KNOW. SORRY. WHAT?
WHAT?
WE ARE TAKING THE NEW-BARNS OUT TO BRUNCH TOMORROW, OWEN, AND I WANT TO MAKE SURE YOUR SCHEDULE IS CLEAR FOR BABYSITTING DUTIES.
THEY STILL WANT ME TO-
THEY LOVE YOU, OWEN. LOVE YOU. THEY SAY YOU'RE THE ONLY ONE THEY CAN TRUST WITH LITTLE SKYLER, EVEN AFTER ALL THIS... UNPLEASANTNESS.
UM...
ELEVEN O'CLOCK TOMORROW, OWEN. I NEED YOU TO DO THIS. YOU TWO CAUSED A LOT OF EMBARRASSMENT TO-NIGHT, BUT I THINK I'VE JUST ABOUT GOT THIS WHOLE THING SMOOTHED OVER. NOW PUT YOUR SISTER ON THE LINE.
WHY?
BECAUSE I WANT HER TO COME WITH ME TOMORROW. I THINK IF THE NEWBARNS JUST SPENT A LITTLE TIME WITH HER, THEY'D JUST HAVE TO LOVE HER AS MUCH AS YOU.
. . .
MOM WANTS TO TALK TO YOU.
OOH I SHOULD TAKE THAT OUTSIDE.
YOU WILL HAVE MY ANSWER TOMORROW, FOLKS.

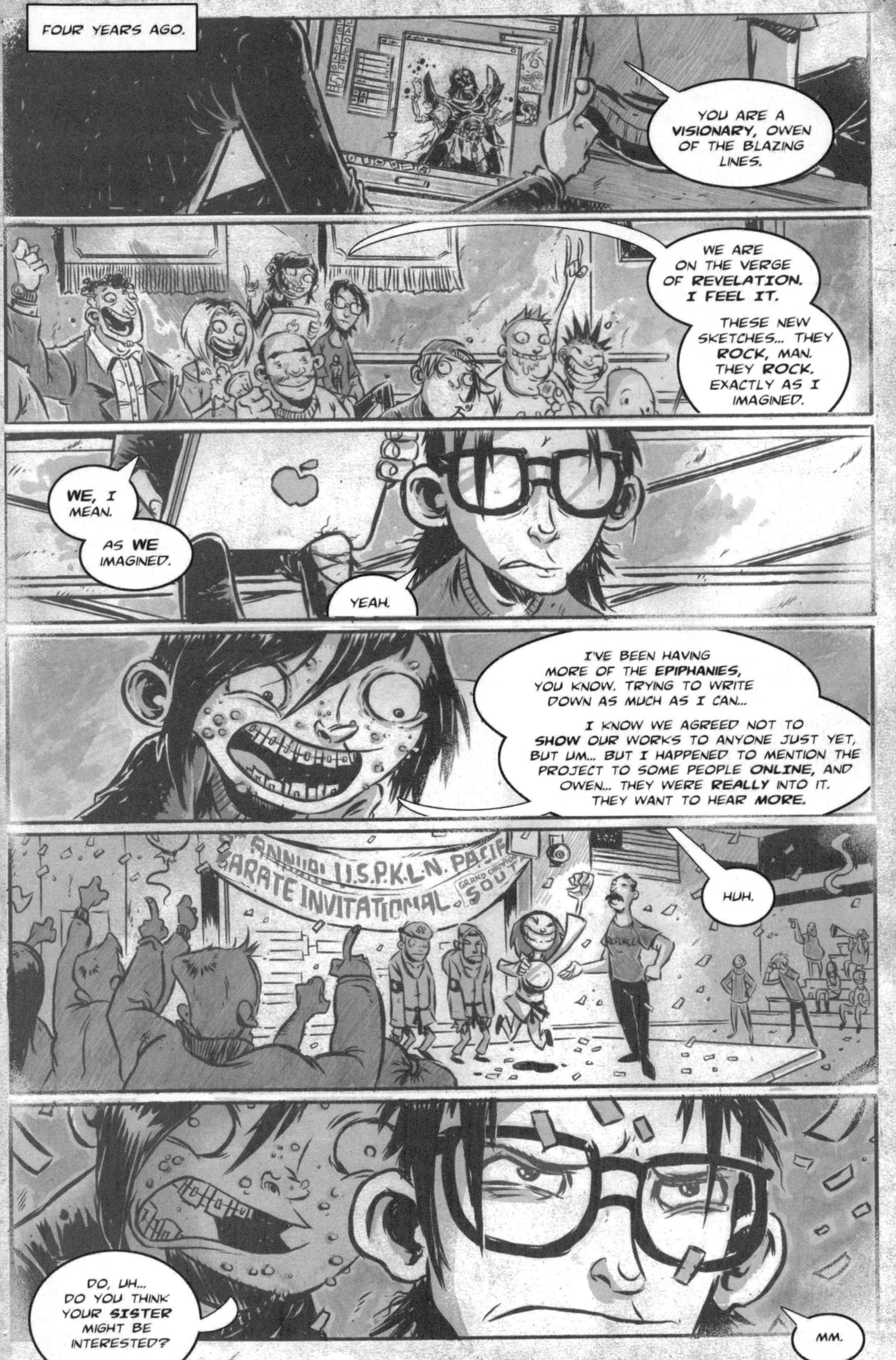
FOUR YEARS AGO.
YOU ARE A VISIONARY, OWEN OF THE BLAZING LINES.
WE ARE ON THE VERGE OF REVELATION. I FEEL IT.
THESE NEW SKETCHES... THEY ROCK, MAN. THEY ROCK. EXACTLY AS I IMAGINED.
WE, I MEAN.
AS WE IMAGINED.
YEAH.
I'VE BEEN HAVING MORE OF THE EPIPHANIES, YOU KNOW. TRYING TO WRITE DOWN AS MUCH AS I CAN...
I KNOW WE AGREED NOT TO SHOW OUR WORKS TO ANYONE JUST YET, BUT UM... BUT I HAPPENED TO MENTION THE PROJECT TO SOME PEOPLE ONLINE, AND OWEN... THEY WERE REALLY INTO IT. THEY WANT TO HEAR MORE.
ANNUAL U.S.P.K.L.N. PACIF
KARATE INVITATIONAL
GRAND CHAMPION SOUT
HUH.
DO, UH... DO YOU THINK YOUR SISTER MIGHT BE INTERESTED?
MM.

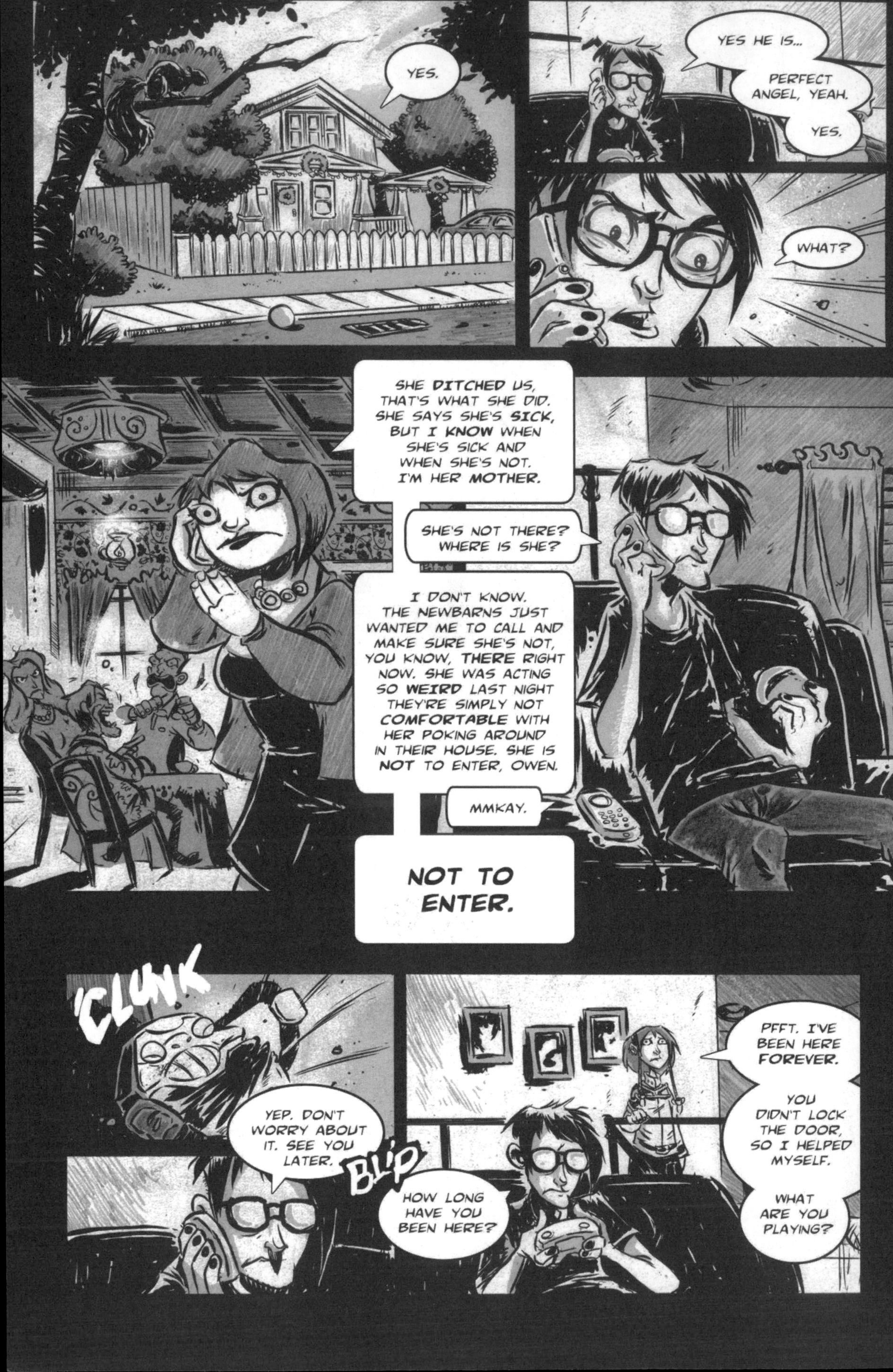
YES.
YES HE IS...
PERFECT ANGEL, YEAH.
YES.
WHAT?
SHE DITCHED US, THAT'S WHAT SHE DID. SHE SAYS SHE'S SICK, BUT I KNOW WHEN SHE'S SICK AND WHEN SHE'S NOT. I'M HER MOTHER.
SHE'S NOT THERE? WHERE IS SHE?
I DON'T KNOW. THE NEWBARNS JUST WANTED ME TO CALL AND MAKE SURE SHE'S NOT, YOU KNOW, THERE RIGHT NOW. SHE WAS ACTING SO WEIRD LAST NIGHT THEY'RE SIMPLY NOT COMFORTABLE WITH HER POKING AROUND IN THEIR HOUSE. SHE IS NOT TO ENTER, OWEN.
MMKAY.
NOT TO ENTER.
'CLUNK
YEP. DON'T WORRY ABOUT IT. SEE YOU LATER.
BLIP
HOW LONG HAVE YOU BEEN HERE?
PFFT. I'VE BEEN HERE FOREVER.
YOU DIDN'T LOCK THE DOOR, SO I HELPED MYSELF.
WHAT ARE YOU PLAYING?

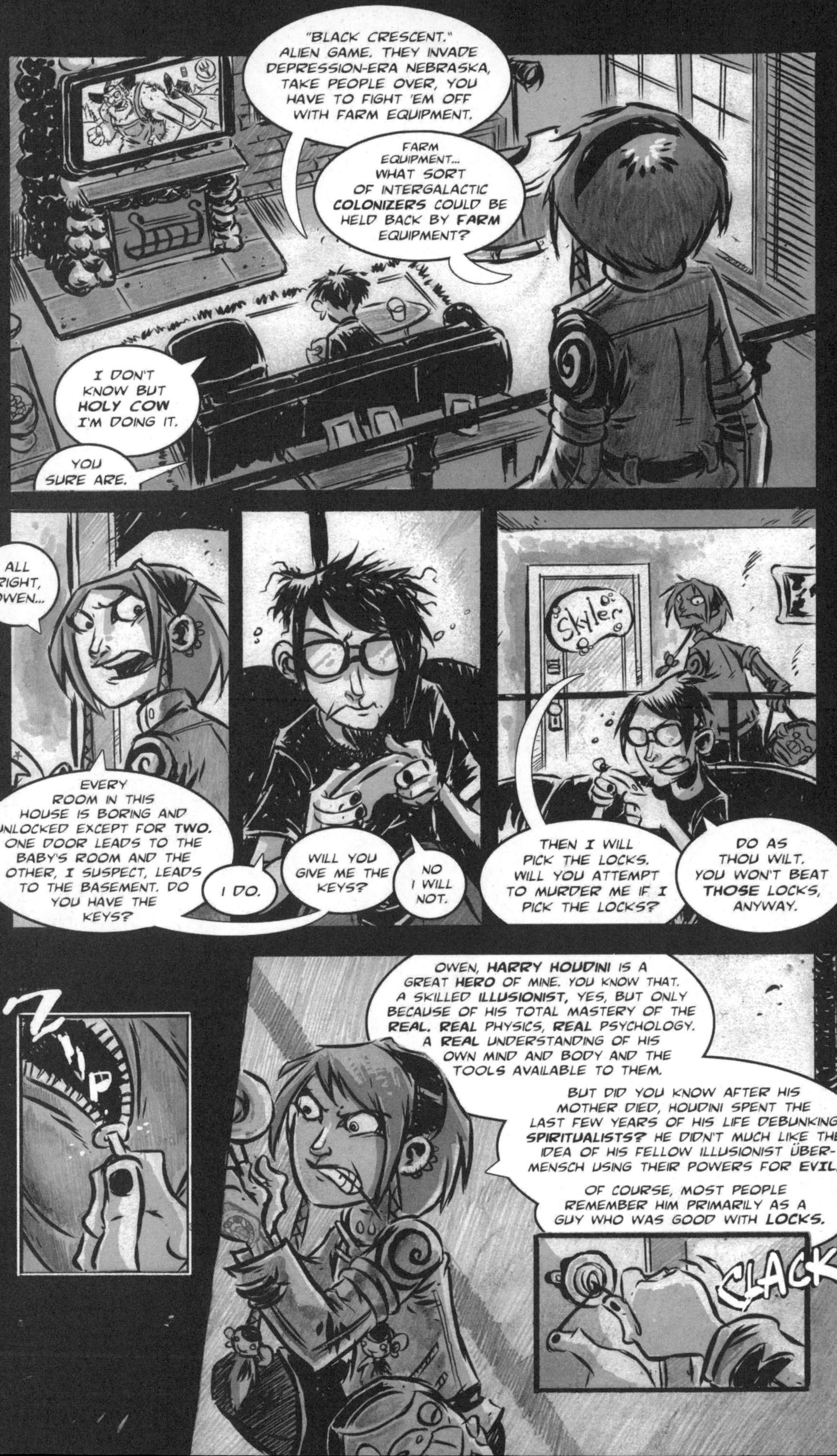

"BLACK CRESCENT." ALIEN GAME. THEY INVADE DEPRESSION-ERA NEBRASKA, TAKE PEOPLE OVER, YOU HAVE TO FIGHT 'EM OFF WITH FARM EQUIPMENT.
FARM EQUIPMENT... WHAT SORT OF INTERGALACTIC COLONIZERS COULD BE HELD BACK BY FARM EQUIPMENT?
I DON'T KNOW BUT HOLY COW I'M DOING IT.
YOU SURE ARE.
ALL RIGHT, OWEN...
EVERY ROOM IN THIS HOUSE IS BORING AND UNLOCKED EXCEPT FOR TWO. ONE DOOR LEADS TO THE BABY'S ROOM AND THE OTHER, I SUSPECT, LEADS TO THE BASEMENT. DO YOU HAVE THE KEYS?
I DO.
WILL YOU GIVE ME THE KEYS?
NO I WILL NOT.
Skyler
THEN I WILL PICK THE LOCKS. WILL YOU ATTEMPT TO MURDER ME IF I PICK THE LOCKS?
DO AS THOU WILT. YOU WON'T BEAT THOSE LOCKS, ANYWAY.
ZIIP
OWEN, HARRY HOUDINI IS A GREAT HERO OF MINE. YOU KNOW THAT. A SKILLED ILLUSIONIST, YES, BUT ONLY BECAUSE OF HIS TOTAL MASTERY OF THE REAL. REAL PHYSICS, REAL PSYCHOLOGY. A REAL UNDERSTANDING OF HIS OWN MIND AND BODY AND THE TOOLS AVAILABLE TO THEM.
BUT DID YOU KNOW AFTER HIS MOTHER DIED, HOUDINI SPENT THE LAST FEW YEARS OF HIS LIFE DEBUNKING SPIRITUALISTS? HE DIDN'T MUCH LIKE THE IDEA OF HIS FELLOW ILLUSIONIST ÜBER-MENSCH USING THEIR POWERS FOR EVIL.
OF COURSE, MOST PEOPLE REMEMBER HIM PRIMARILY AS A GUY WHO WAS GOOD WITH LOCKS.
CLACK

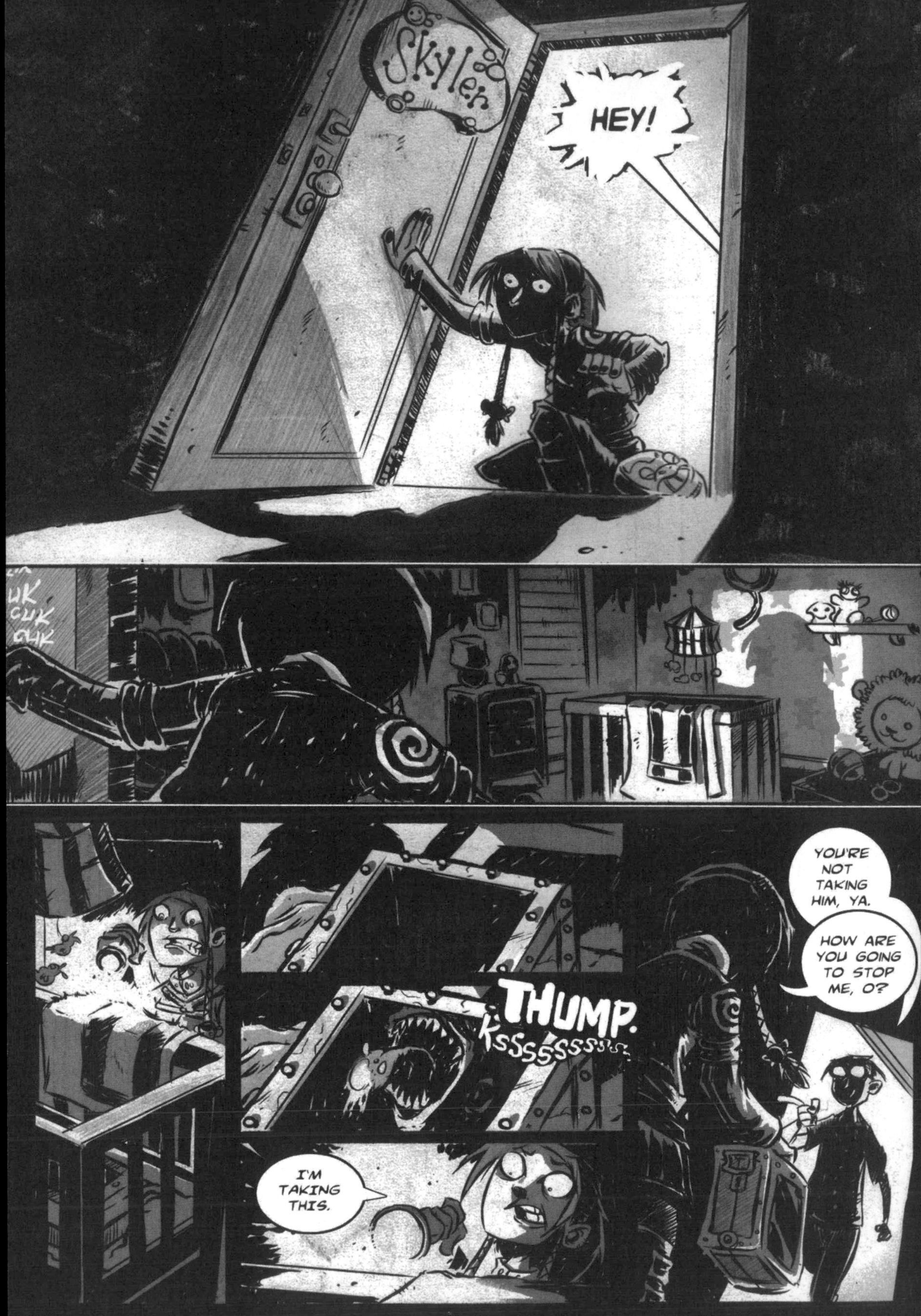
Skyler
HEY!
UK
CUK
CUK
YOU'RE NOT TAKING HIM, YA.
HOW ARE YOU GOING TO STOP ME, O?
THUMP.
KSSSSSSSS
I'M TAKING THIS.

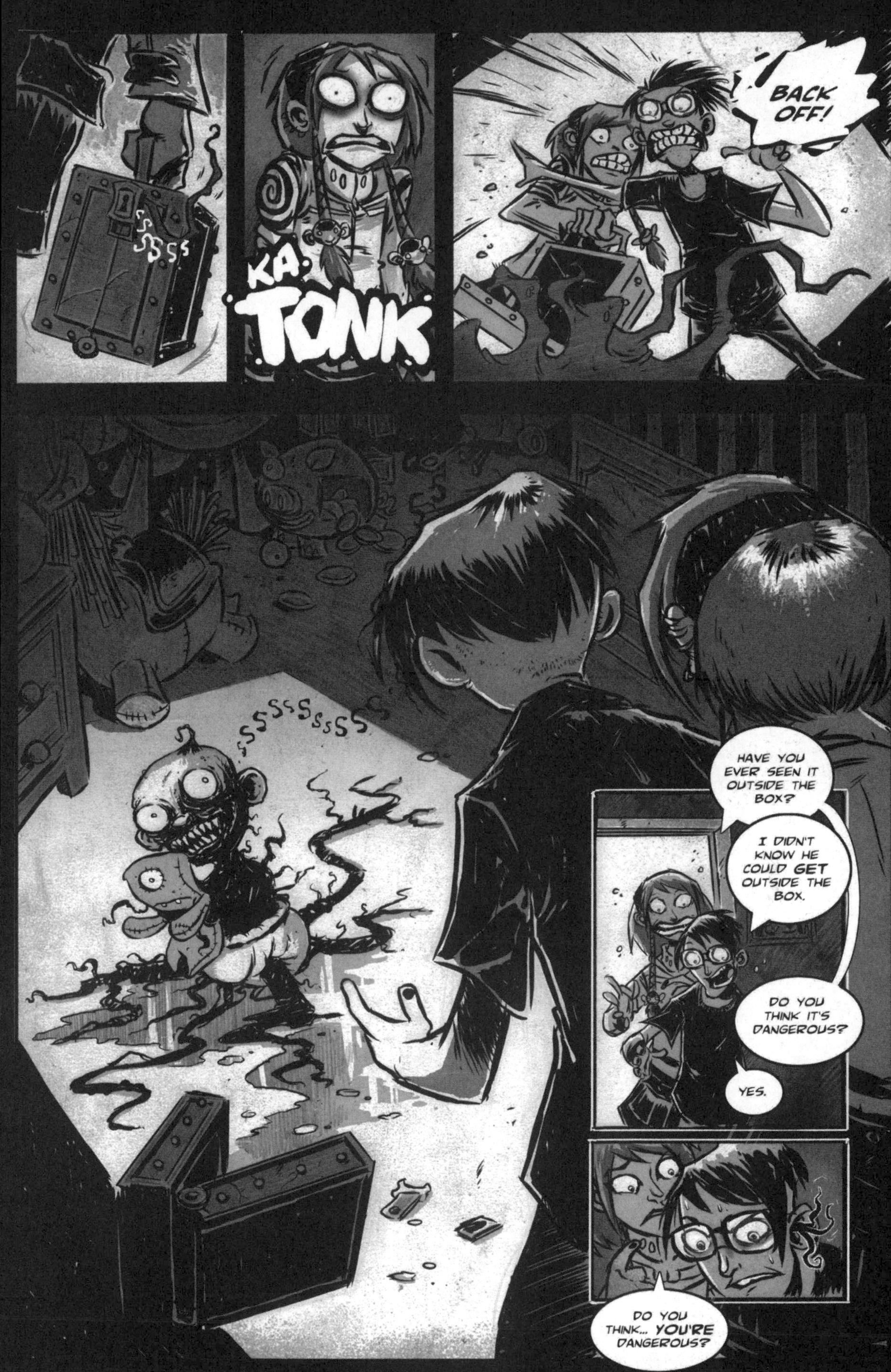

SSSSS
KA-TONK
BACK OFF!
SSSSSSSSS
HAVE YOU EVER SEEN IT OUTSIDE THE BOX?
I DIDN'T KNOW HE COULD GET OUTSIDE THE BOX.
DO YOU THINK IT'S DANGEROUS?
YES.
DO YOU THINK... YOU'RE DANGEROUS?

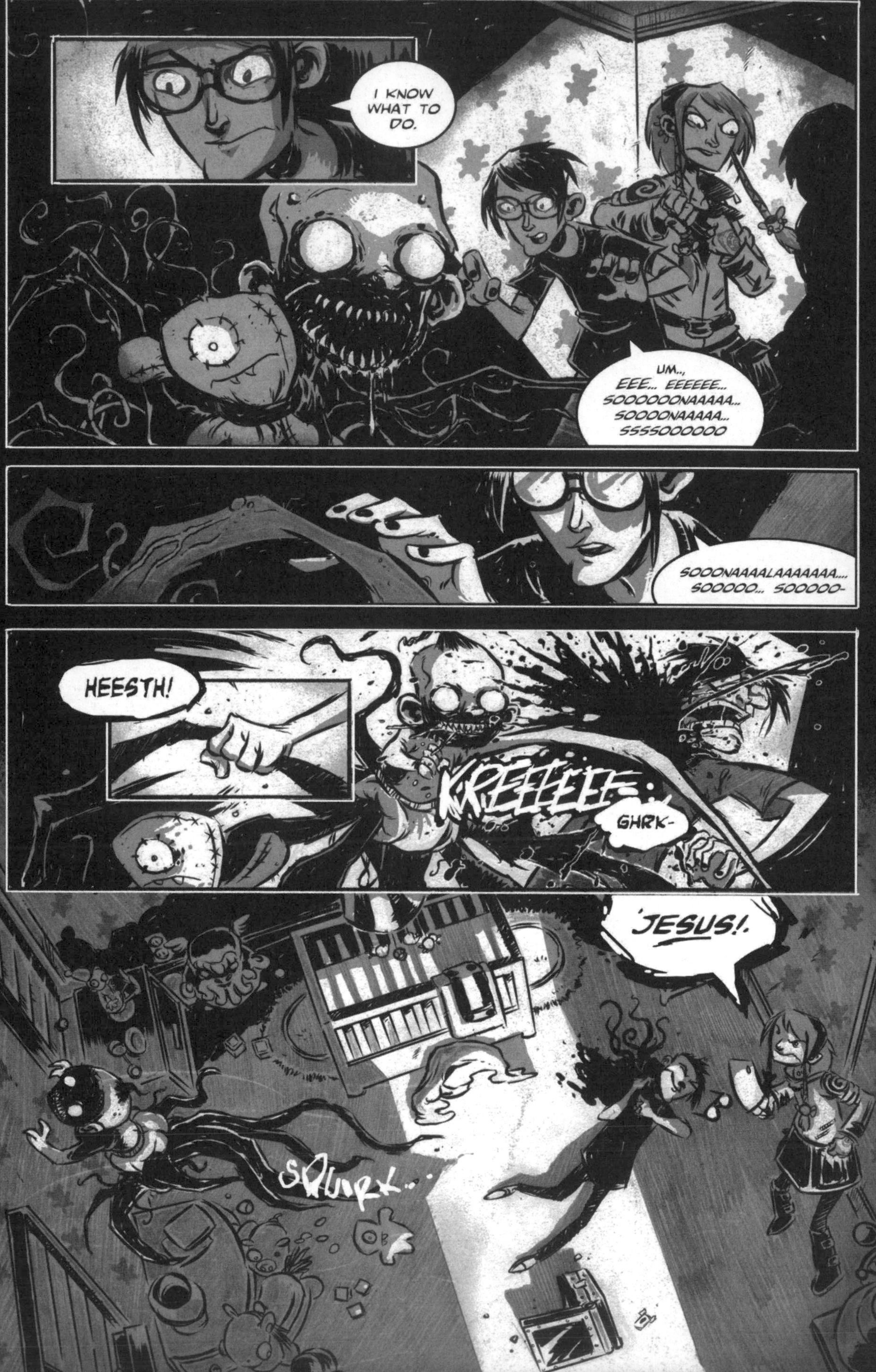
I KNOW WHAT TO DO.
UM.,, EEE... EEEEEE... SOOOOOONAAAAA... SOOOONAAAAA... SSSSOOOOOO
SOOONAAAALAAAAAAA.... SOOOOO... SOOOOO-
HEESTH!
KREEEEEE
GHRK-
JESUS!.
SQUIRK...

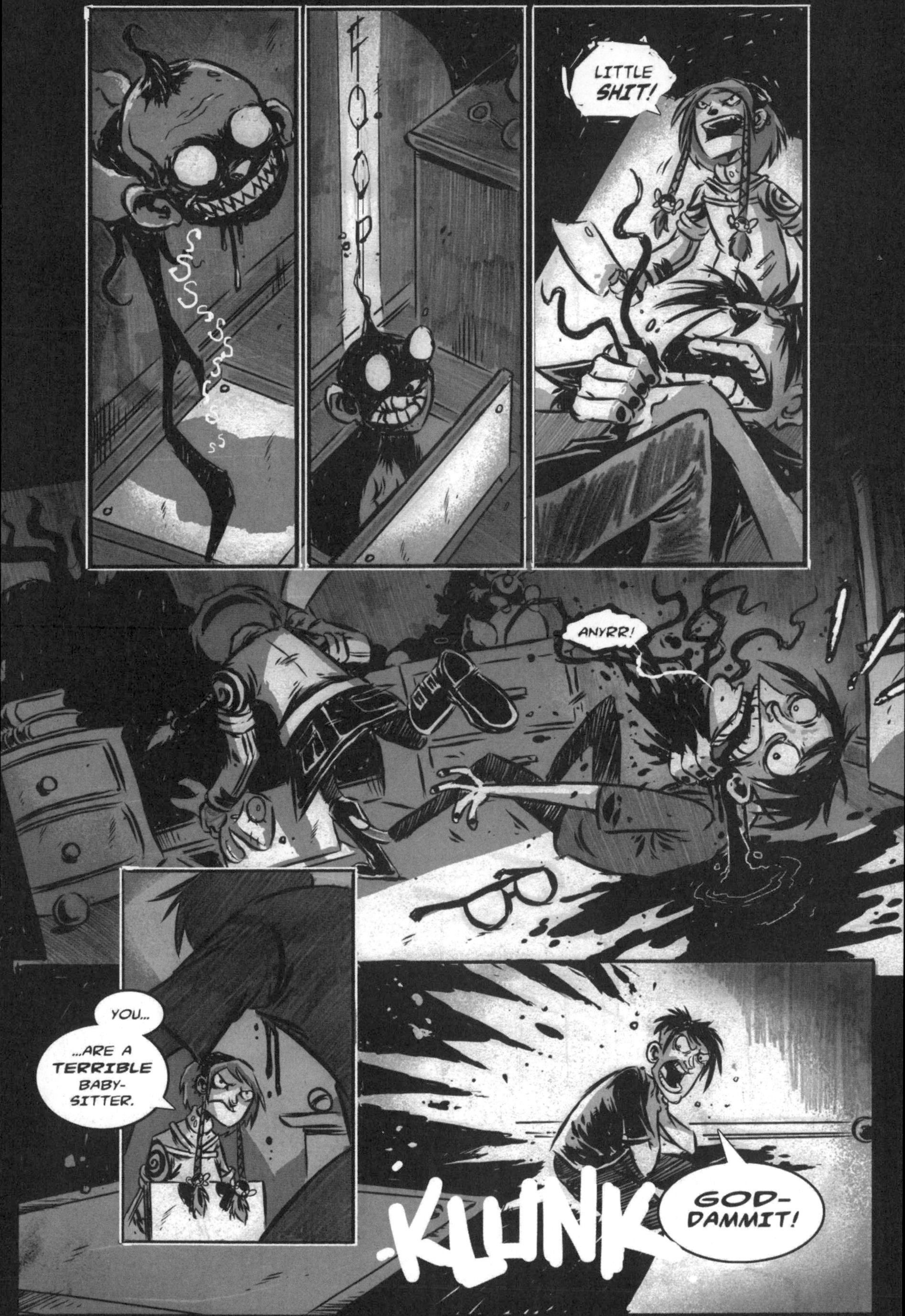

SSSSSSSSSSS
FOOP
LITTLE SHIT!
ANYRR!
YOU...
...ARE A TERRIBLE BABY-SITTER.
KLUNK
GOD-DAMMIT!

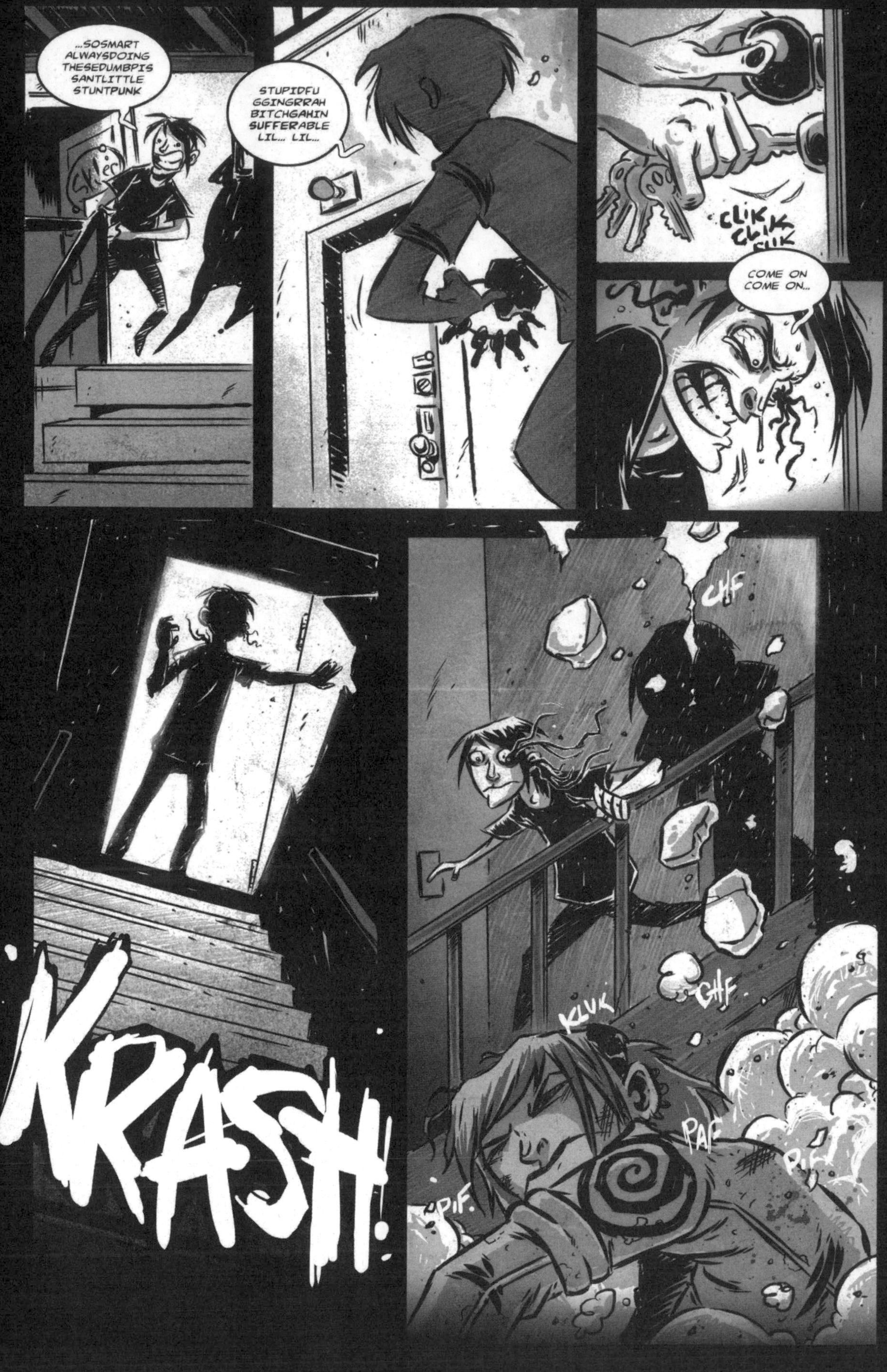
...SOSMART ALWAYSDOING THESEDUMBPIS SANTLITTLE STUNTPUNK
STUPIDFU GGINGRRAH BITCHGAHIN SUFFERABLE LIL... LIL...
CLIK CLIK CLIK
COME ON COME ON...
KRASH!
CHF
CHF
KLUK
PAF
PIF.
PIF.

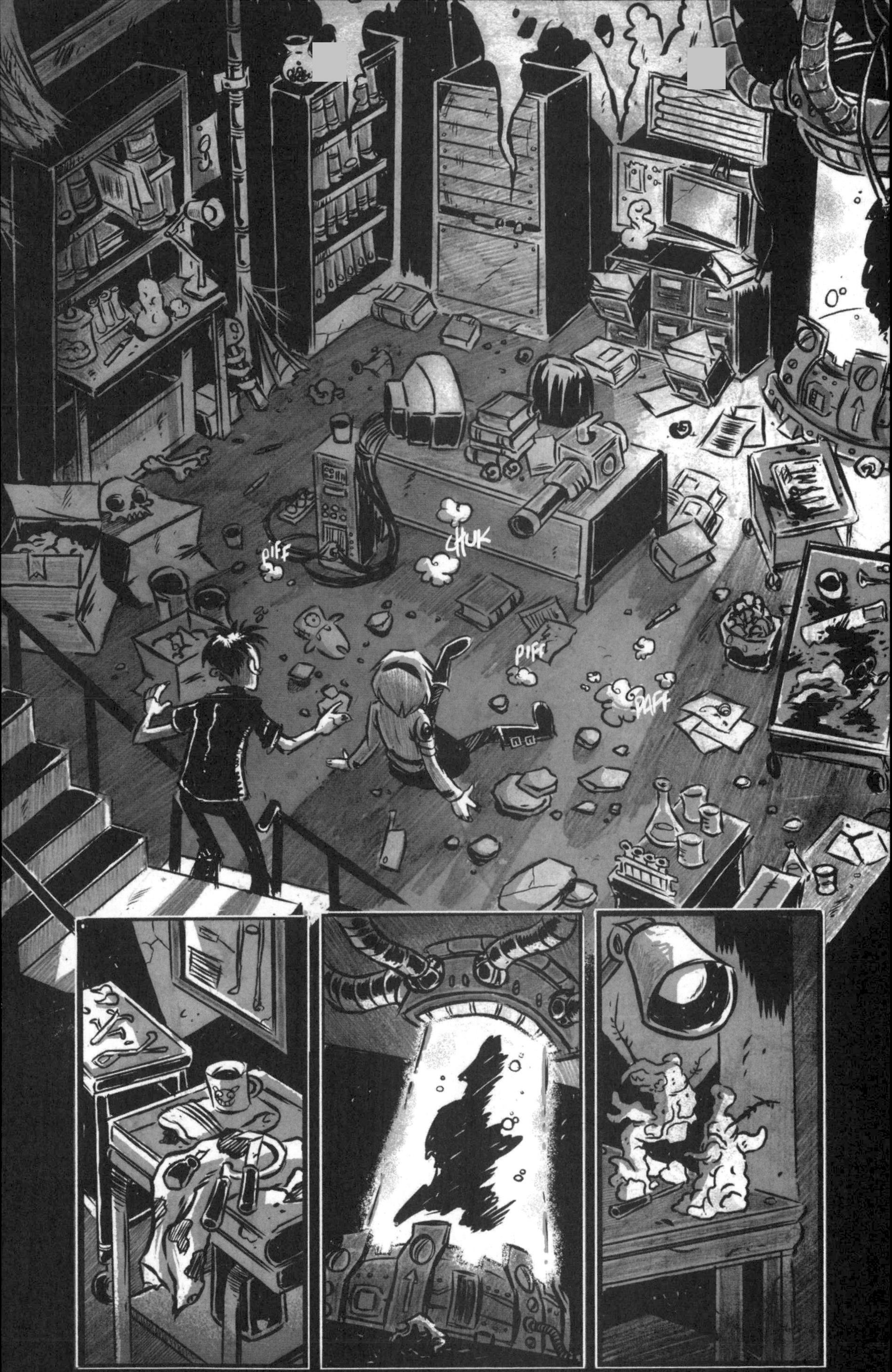
PIFF
CHUK
PIFF
PAFF

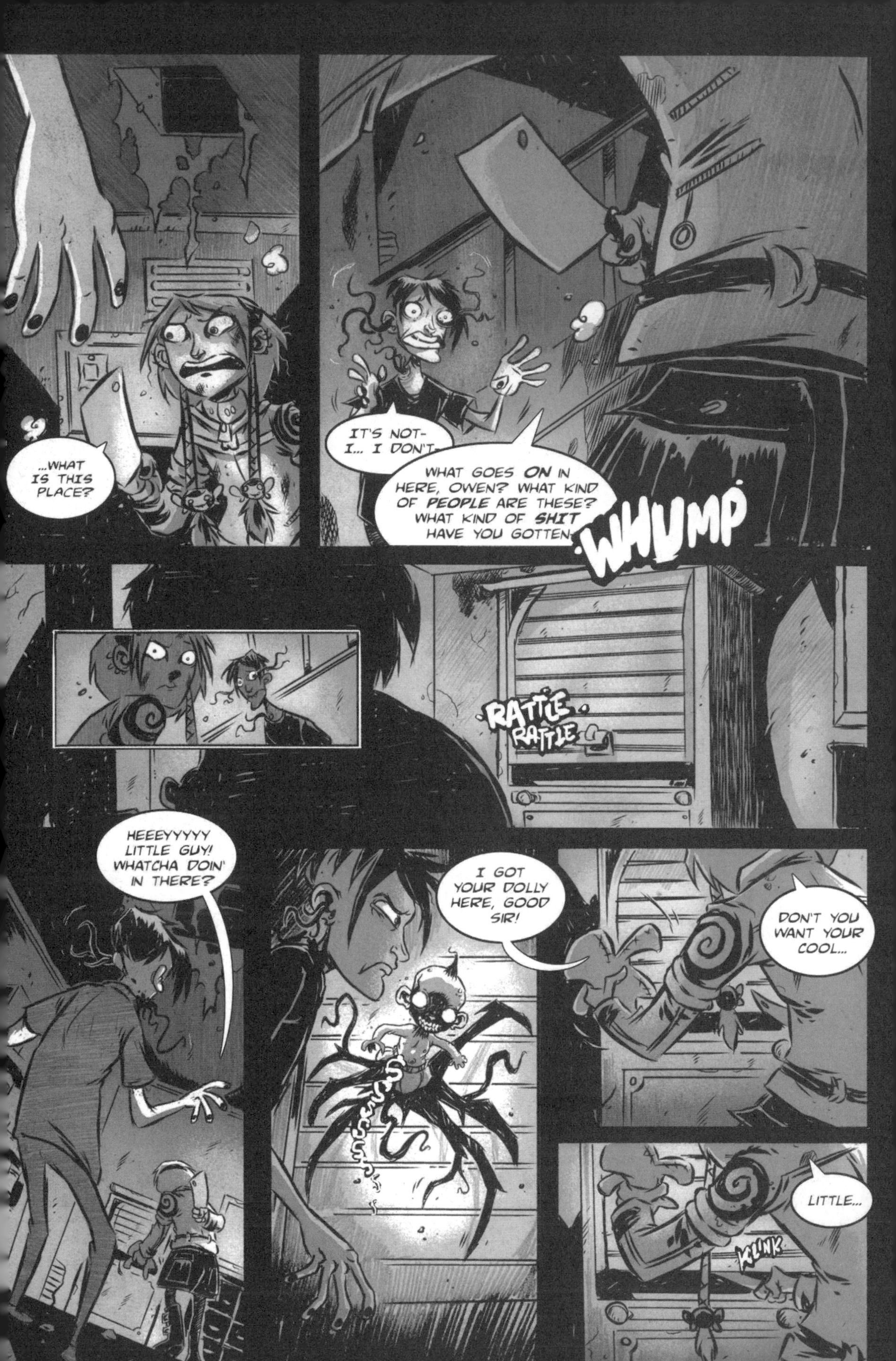
...WHAT IS THIS PLACE?
IT'S NOT- I... I DON'T-
WHAT GOES ON IN HERE, OWEN? WHAT KIND OF PEOPLE ARE THESE? WHAT KIND OF SHIT HAVE YOU GOTTEN-
WHUMP
RATTLE RATTLE
HEEEYYYYY LITTLE GUY! WHATCHA DOIN' IN THERE?
I GOT YOUR DOLLY HERE, GOOD SIR!
DON'T YOU WANT YOUR COOL...
LITTLE...
KLUNK

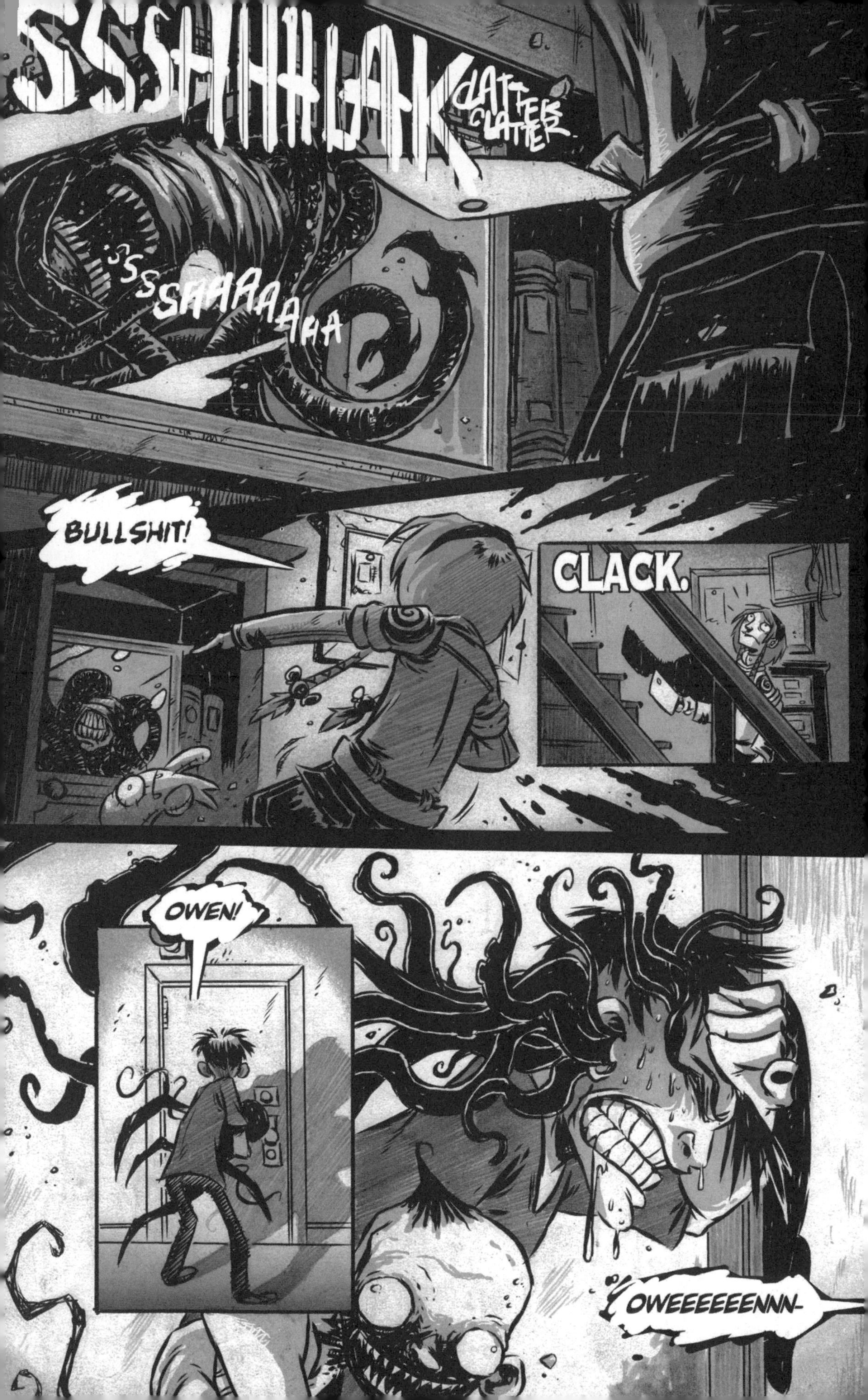
SSSHHHLAK
CLATTER CLATTER
SSSSHAAAAAHA
BULLSHIT!
CLACK.
OWEN!
OWEEEEEEENNN-

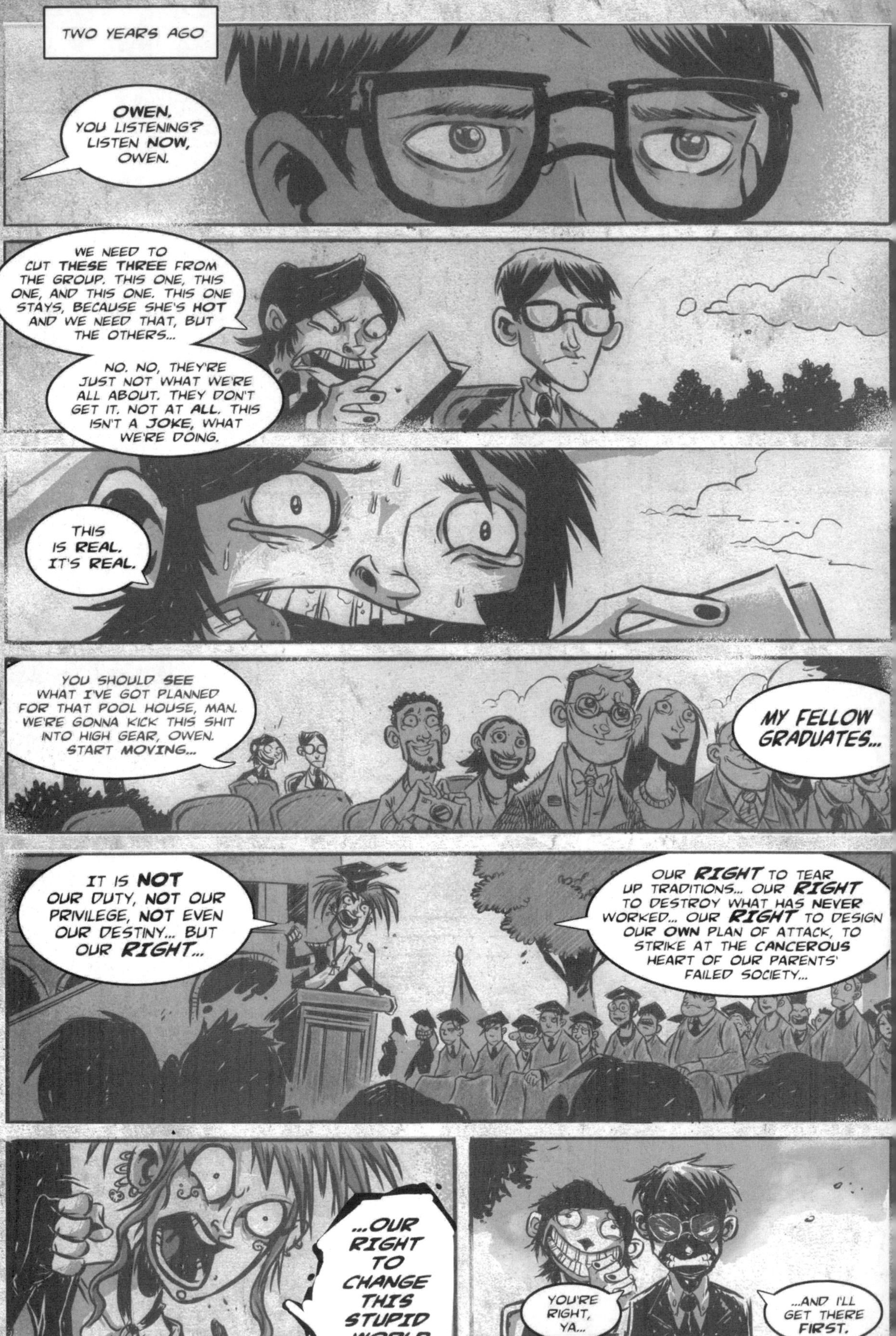
TWO YEARS AGO
OWEN. YOU LISTENING? LISTEN NOW, OWEN.
WE NEED TO CUT THESE THREE FROM THE GROUP. THIS ONE, THIS ONE, AND THIS ONE. THIS ONE STAYS, BECAUSE SHE'S HOT AND WE NEED THAT, BUT THE OTHERS...
NO. NO, THEY'RE JUST NOT WHAT WE'RE ALL ABOUT. THEY DON'T GET IT. NOT AT ALL. THIS ISN'T A JOKE, WHAT WE'RE DOING.
THIS IS REAL. IT'S REAL.
YOU SHOULD SEE WHAT I'VE GOT PLANNED FOR THAT POOL HOUSE, MAN. WE'RE GONNA KICK THIS SHIT INTO HIGH GEAR, OWEN. START MOVING...
MY FELLOW GRADUATES...
IT IS NOT OUR DUTY, NOT OUR PRIVILEGE, NOT EVEN OUR DESTINY... BUT OUR RIGHT...
OUR RIGHT TO TEAR UP TRADITIONS... OUR RIGHT TO DESTROY WHAT HAS NEVER WORKED... OUR RIGHT TO DESIGN OUR OWN PLAN OF ATTACK, TO STRIKE AT THE CANCEROUS HEART OF OUR PARENTS' FAILED SOCIETY...
...OUR RIGHT TO CHANGE THIS STUPID WORLD.
YOU'RE RIGHT, YA...
...AND I'LL GET THERE FIRST.

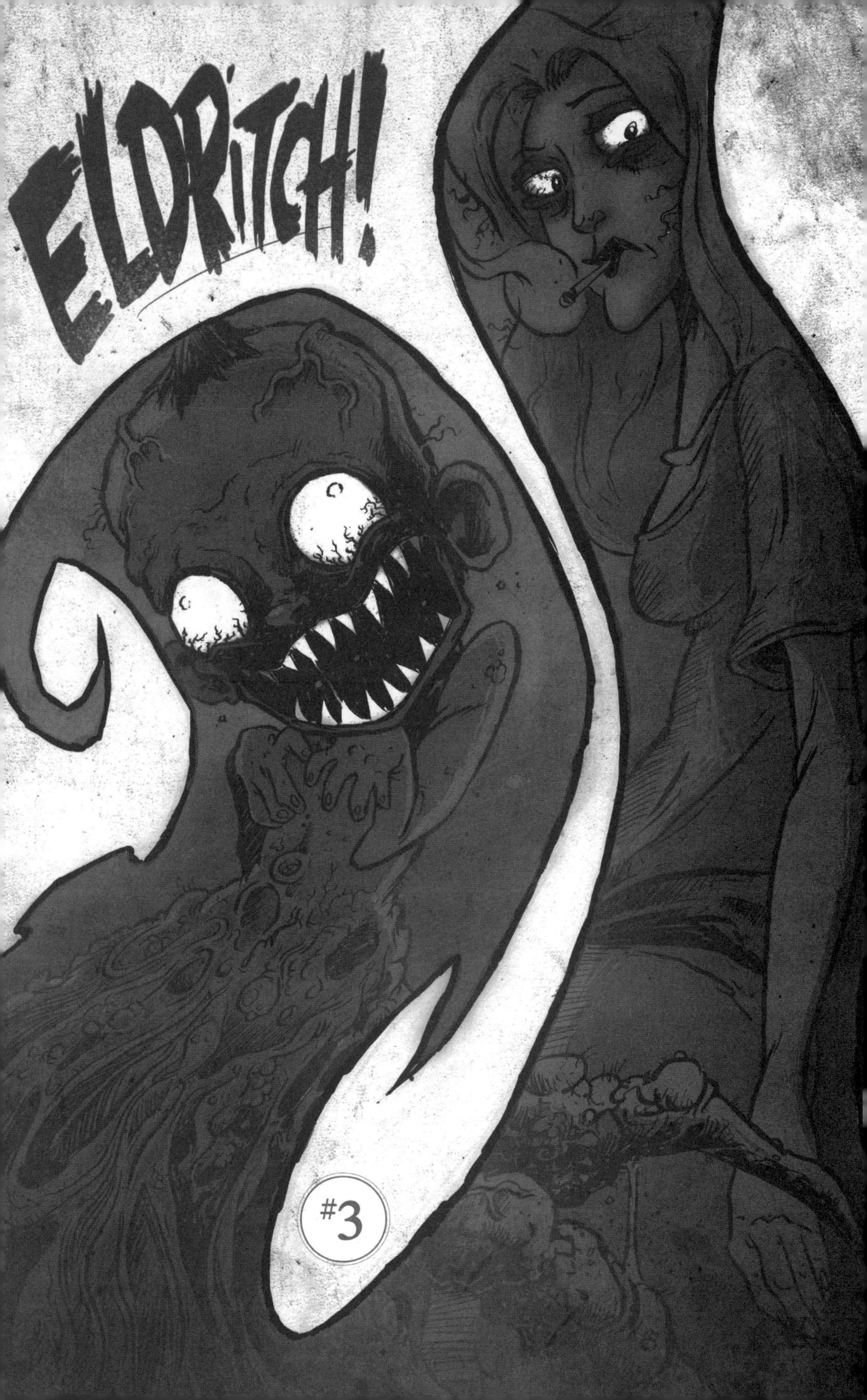
ELDRITCH!
#3

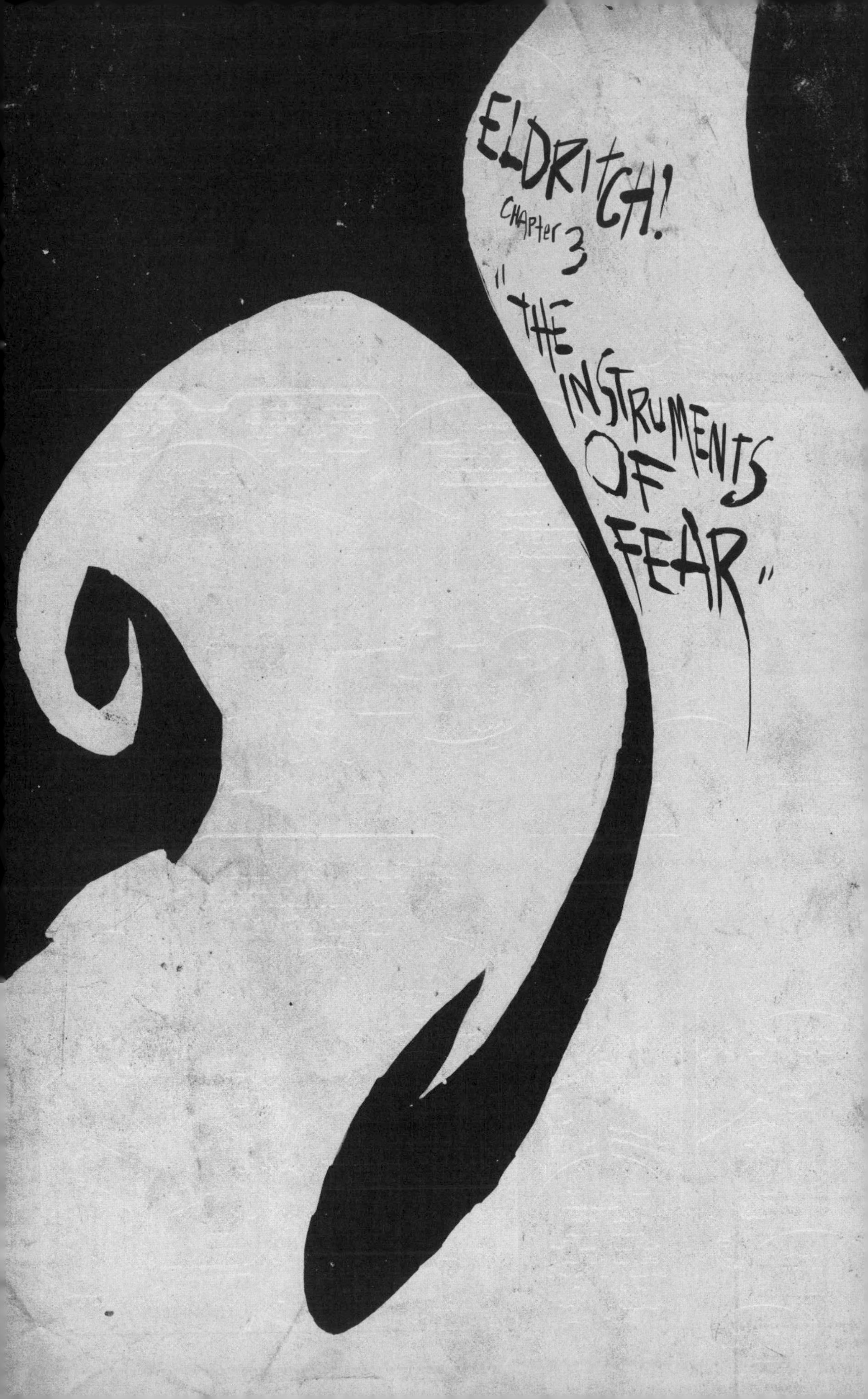
ELDRITCH!
Chapter 3
"THE INSTRUMENTS OF FEAR"

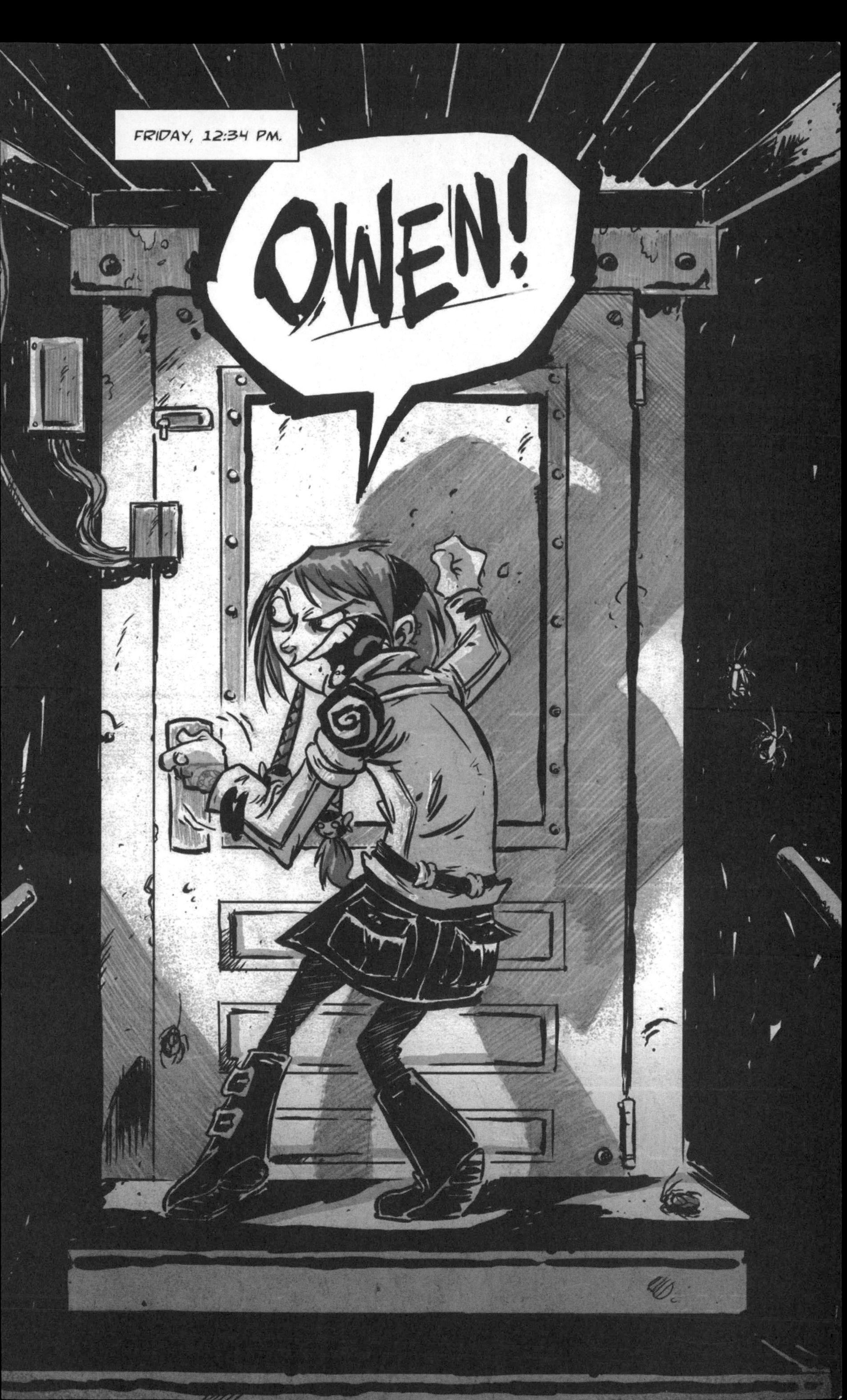
FRIDAY, 12:34 PM.
OWEN!

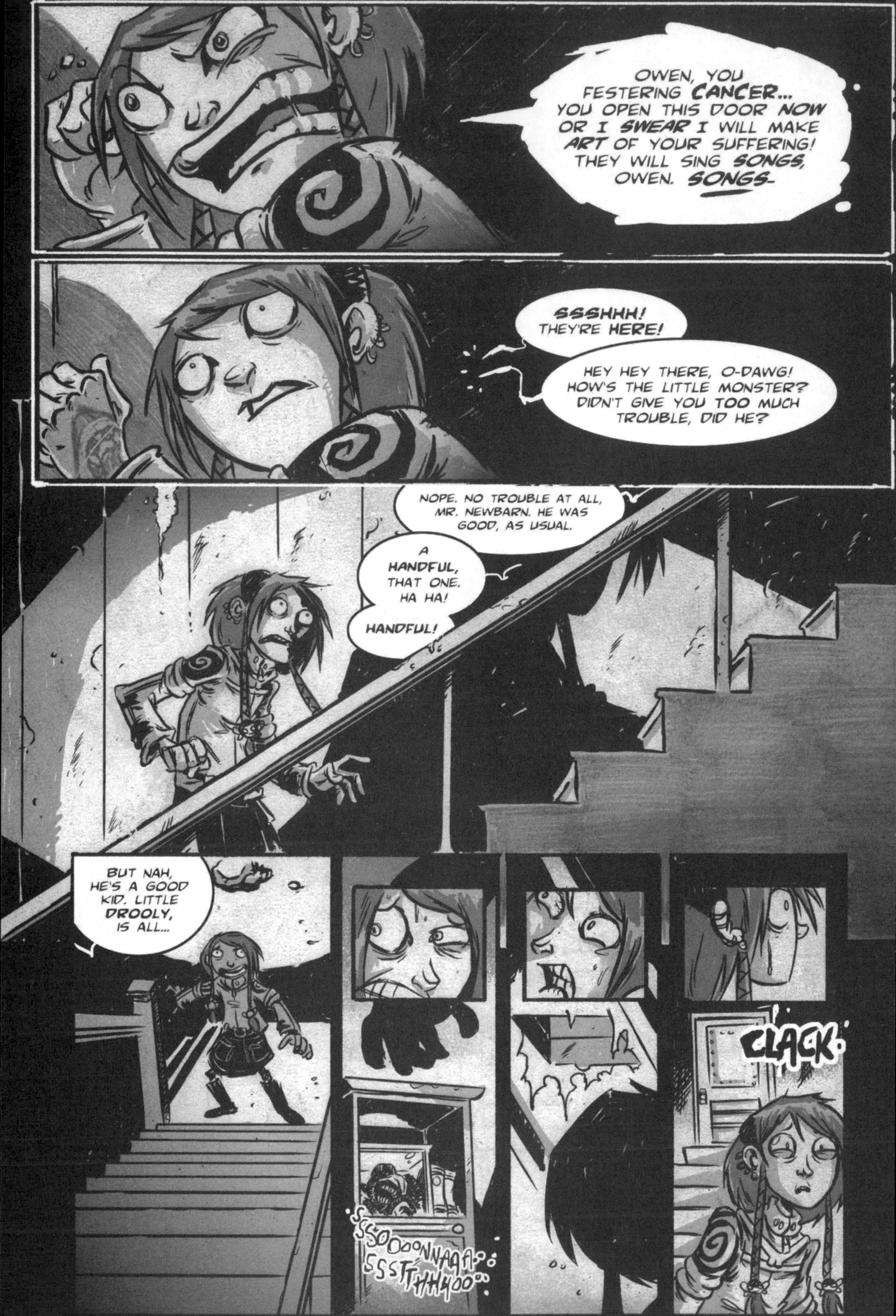

OWEN, YOU FESTERING CANCER... YOU OPEN THIS DOOR NOW OR I SWEAR I WILL MAKE ART OF YOUR SUFFERING! THEY WILL SING SONGS, OWEN. SONGS-
SSSHHH! THEY'RE HERE!
HEY HEY THERE, O-DAWG! HOW'S THE LITTLE MONSTER? DIDN'T GIVE YOU TOO MUCH TROUBLE, DID HE?
NOPE. NO TROUBLE AT ALL, MR. NEWBARN. HE WAS GOOD, AS USUAL.
A HANDFUL, THAT ONE. HA HA!
HANDFUL!
BUT NAH, HE'S A GOOD KID. LITTLE DROOLY, IS ALL...
SSSOOOONNAAA-SSSTTHHHOO
CLACK

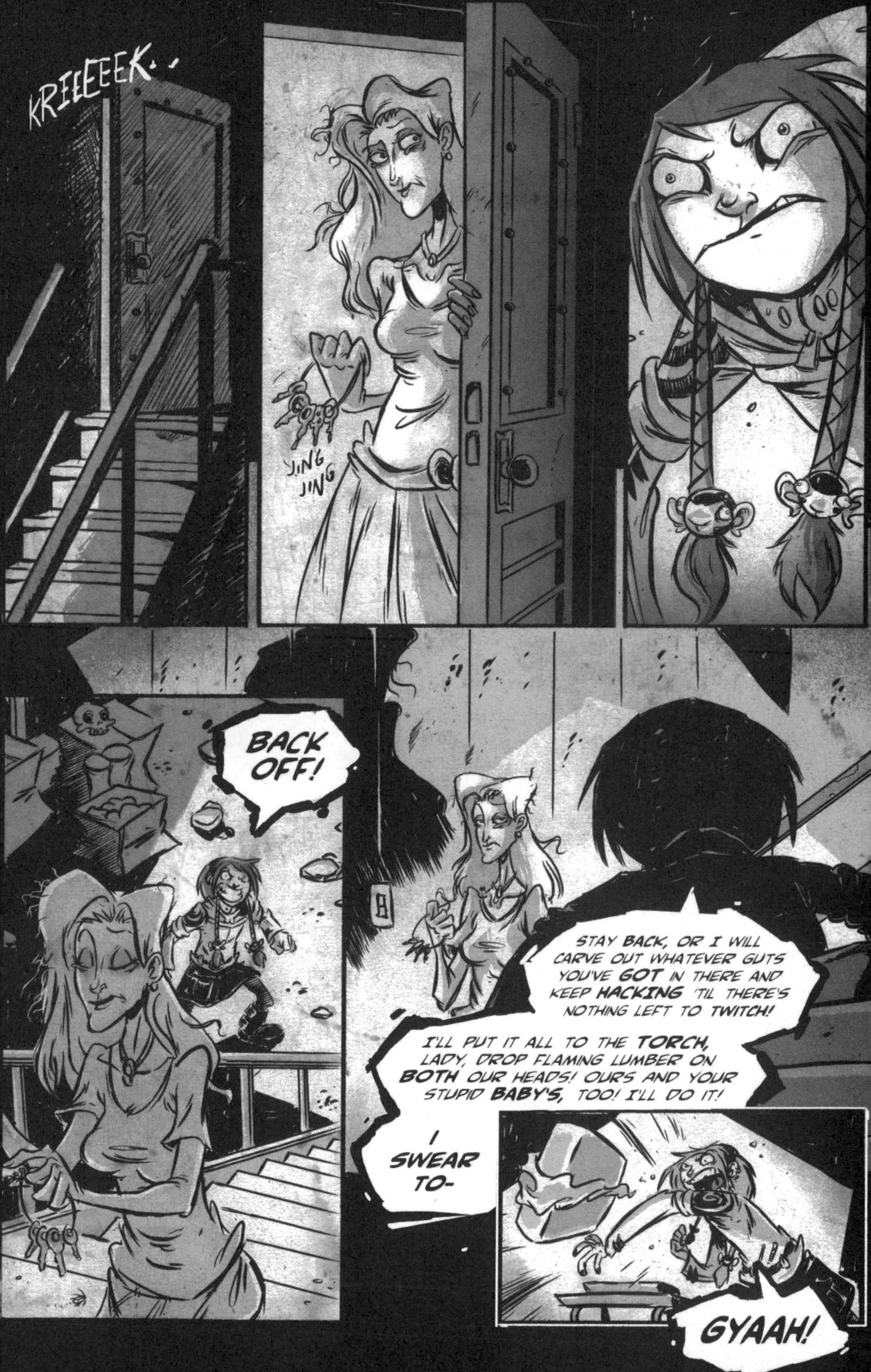
KREEEEEK...
JING JING
BACK OFF!
STAY BACK, OR I WILL CARVE OUT WHATEVER GUTS YOU'VE GOT IN THERE AND KEEP HACKING 'TIL THERE'S NOTHING LEFT TO TWITCH!
I'LL PUT IT ALL TO THE TORCH, LADY, DROP FLAMING LUMBER ON BOTH OUR HEADS! OURS AND YOUR STUPID BABY'S, TOO! I'LL DO IT!
I SWEAR TO-
GYAAH!

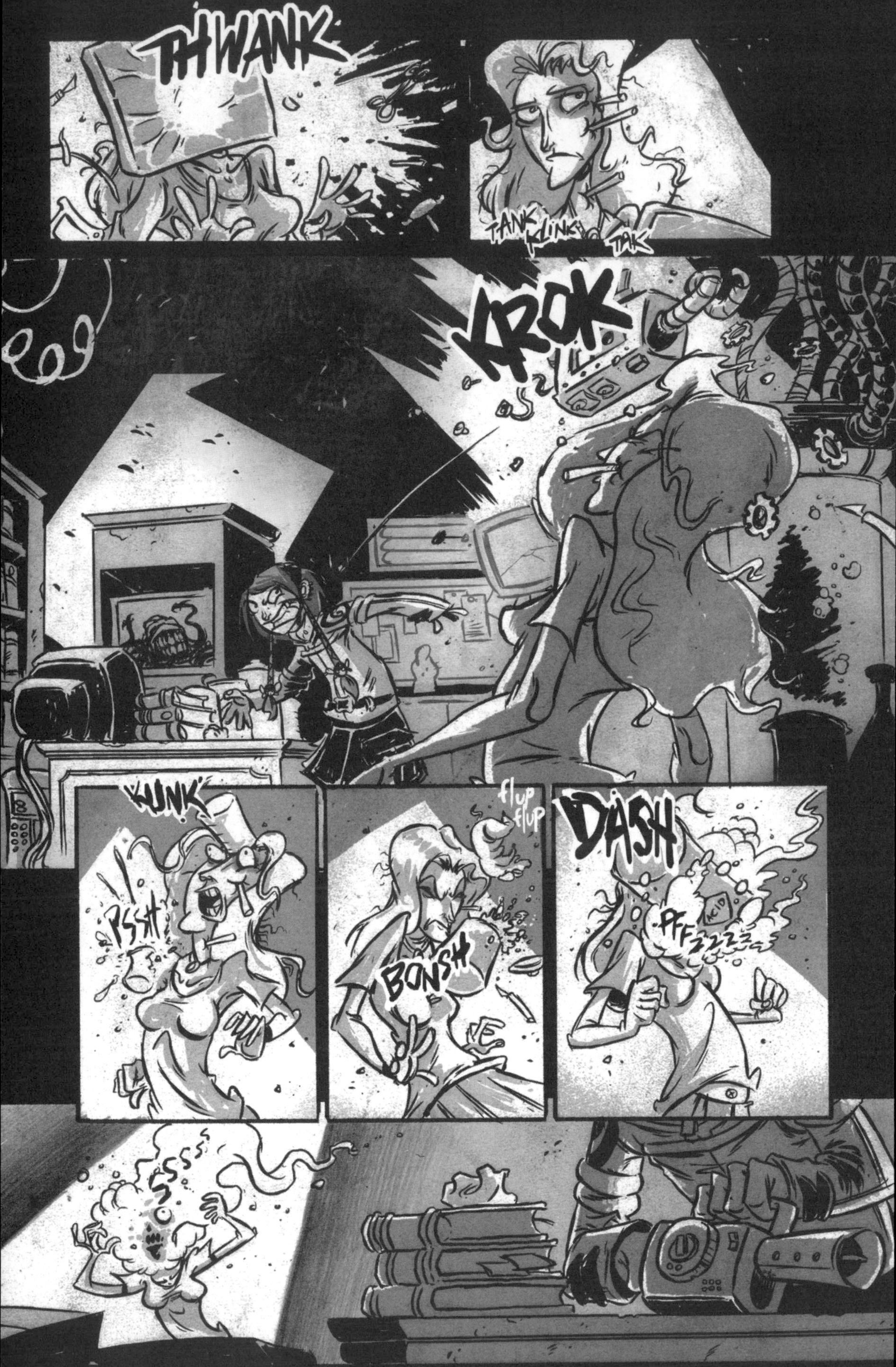
THWANK
TANK
KLINK
TAK
KROK
WUNK
PSSH
flup flup
BONSH
DASH
ACID
PFFZZZZ
SSSSS

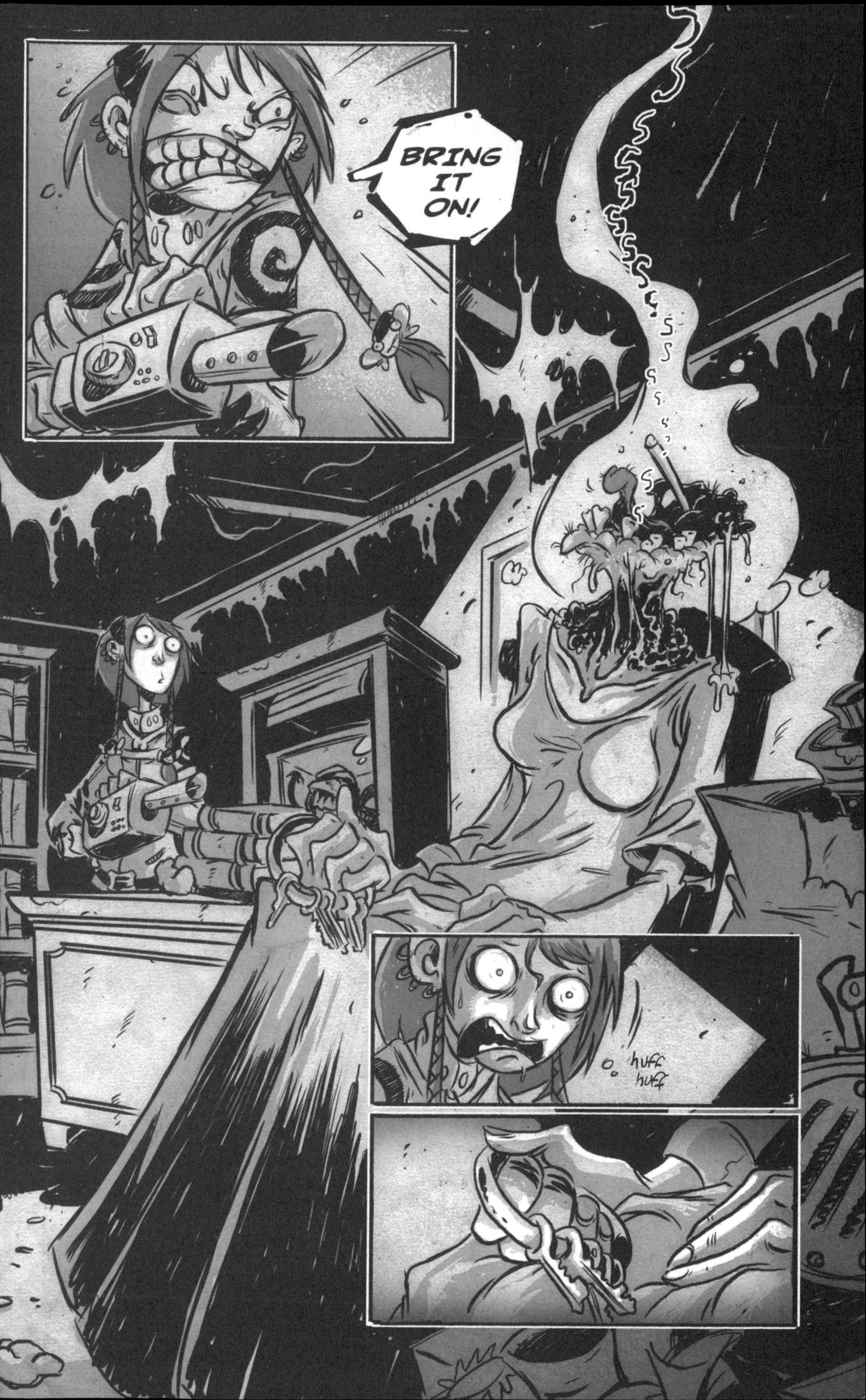

BRING IT ON!
SSSSSSSSSSSSS
huff huff

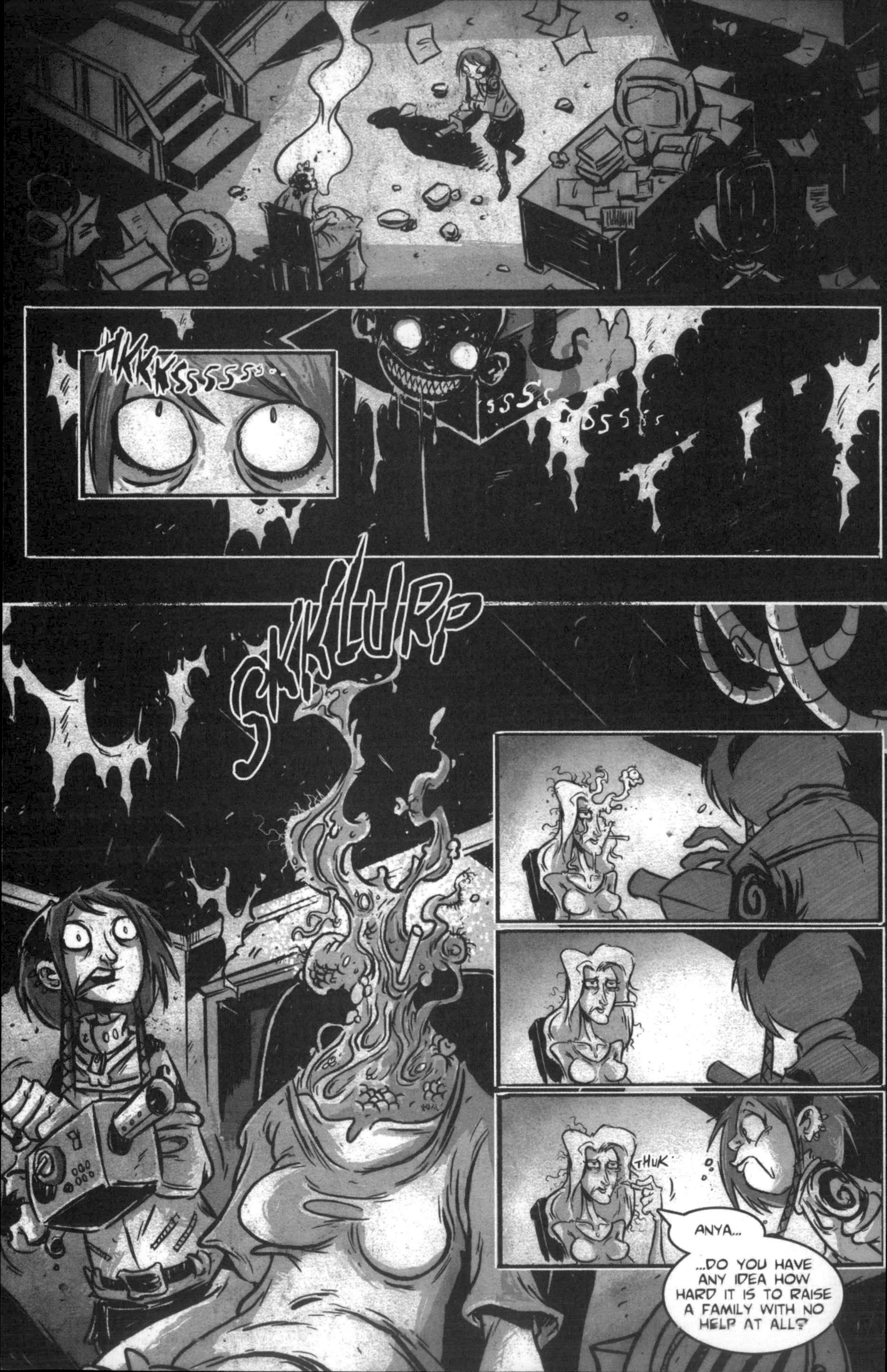
HKKKSSSSSS..
SSSS
SSSSS
SKKLURP
THUK
ANYA...
...DO YOU HAVE ANY IDEA HOW HARD IT IS TO RAISE A FAMILY WITH NO HELP AT ALL?

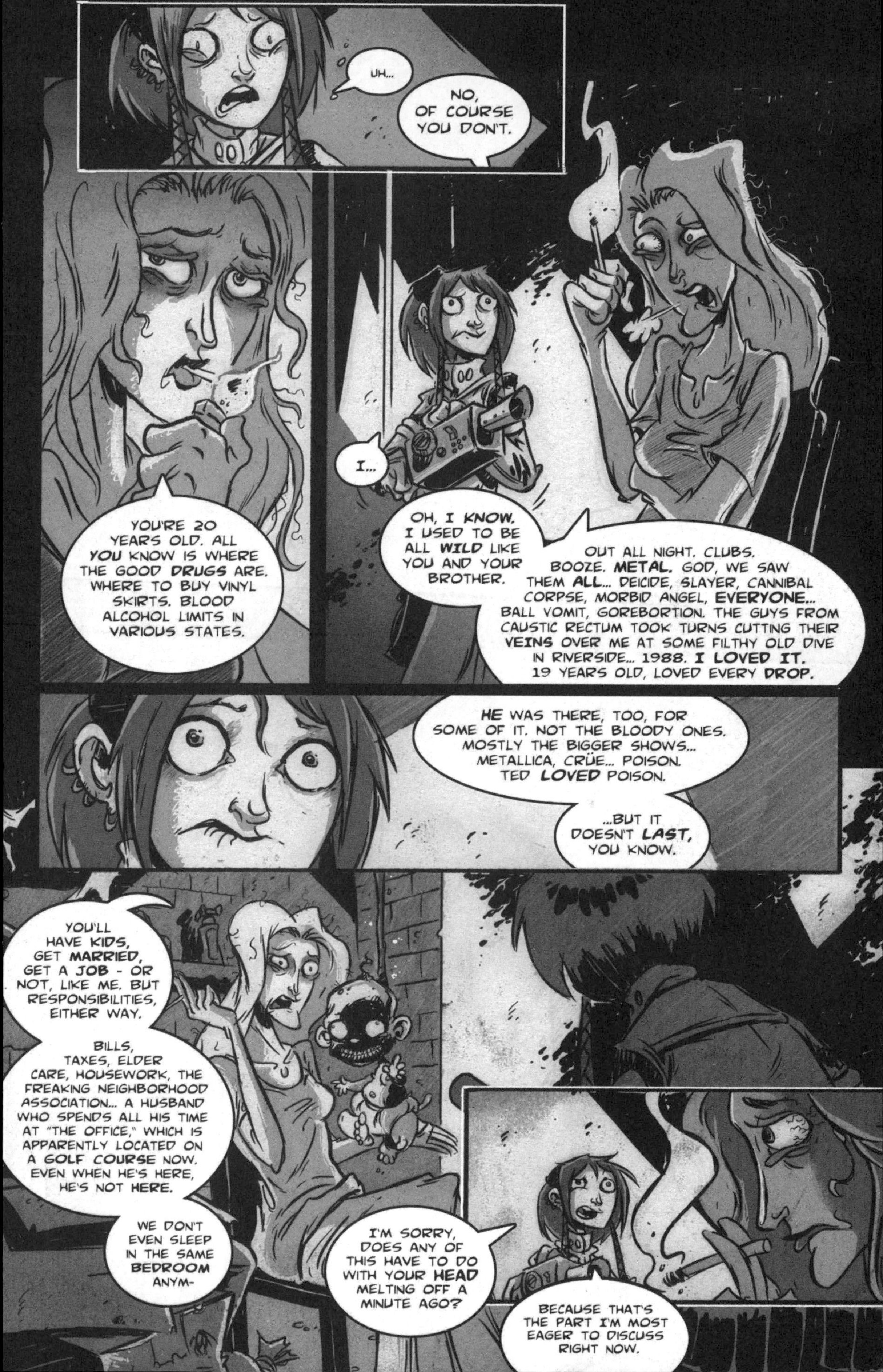
UH...
NO, OF COURSE YOU DON'T.
YOU'RE 20 YEARS OLD. ALL YOU KNOW IS WHERE THE GOOD DRUGS ARE. WHERE TO BUY VINYL SKIRTS. BLOOD ALCOHOL LIMITS IN VARIOUS STATES.
I...
OH, I KNOW. I USED TO BE ALL WILD LIKE YOU AND YOUR BROTHER.
OUT ALL NIGHT. CLUBS. BOOZE. METAL. GOD, WE SAW THEM ALL... DEICIDE, SLAYER, CANNIBAL CORPSE, MORBID ANGEL, EVERYONE... BALL VOMIT, GOREBORTION. THE GUYS FROM CAUSTIC RECTUM TOOK TURNS CUTTING THEIR VEINS OVER ME AT SOME FILTHY OLD DIVE IN RIVERSIDE... 1988. I LOVED IT. 19 YEARS OLD, LOVED EVERY DROP.
HE WAS THERE, TOO, FOR SOME OF IT. NOT THE BLOODY ONES. MOSTLY THE BIGGER SHOWS... METALLICA, CRÜE... POISON. TED LOVED POISON.
...BUT IT DOESN'T LAST, YOU KNOW.
YOU'LL HAVE KIDS, GET MARRIED, GET A JOB - OR NOT, LIKE ME. BUT RESPONSIBILITIES, EITHER WAY.
BILLS, TAXES, ELDER CARE, HOUSEWORK, THE FREAKING NEIGHBORHOOD ASSOCIATION... A HUSBAND WHO SPENDS ALL HIS TIME AT "THE OFFICE," WHICH IS APPARENTLY LOCATED ON A GOLF COURSE NOW. EVEN WHEN HE'S HERE, HE'S NOT HERE.
WE DON'T EVEN SLEEP IN THE SAME BEDROOM ANYM-
I'M SORRY, DOES ANY OF THIS HAVE TO DO WITH YOUR HEAD MELTING OFF A MINUTE AGO?
BECAUSE THAT'S THE PART I'M MOST EAGER TO DISCUSS RIGHT NOW.

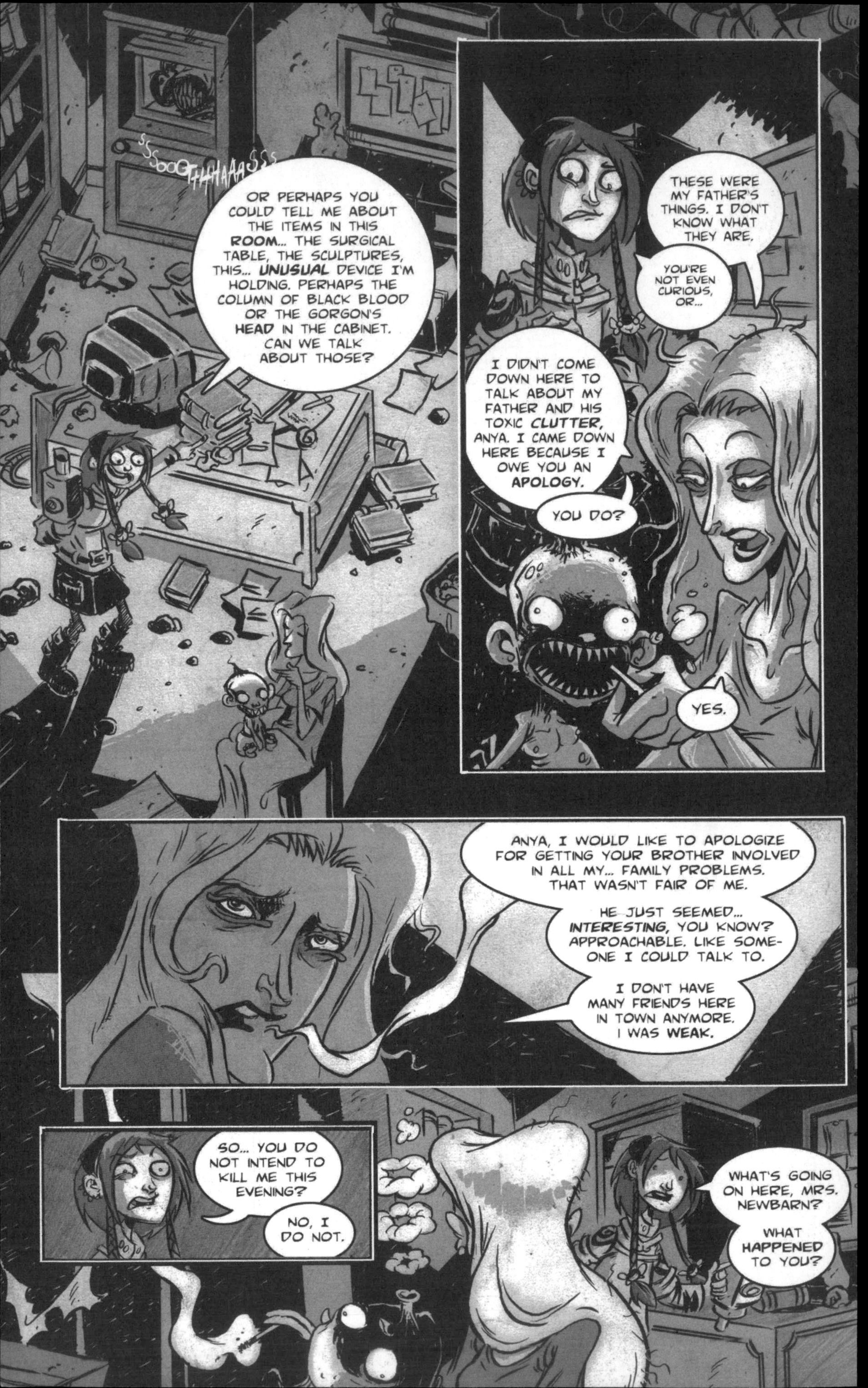
SSSOOOTHHHAAASSS
OR PERHAPS YOU COULD TELL ME ABOUT THE ITEMS IN THIS ROOM... THE SURGICAL TABLE, THE SCULPTURES, THIS... UNUSUAL DEVICE I'M HOLDING. PERHAPS THE COLUMN OF BLACK BLOOD OR THE GORGON'S HEAD IN THE CABINET. CAN WE TALK ABOUT THOSE?
THESE WERE MY FATHER'S THINGS. I DON'T KNOW WHAT THEY ARE.
YOU'RE NOT EVEN CURIOUS, OR...
I DIDN'T COME DOWN HERE TO TALK ABOUT MY FATHER AND HIS TOXIC CLUTTER, ANYA. I CAME DOWN HERE BECAUSE I OWE YOU AN APOLOGY.
YOU DO?
YES.
ANYA, I WOULD LIKE TO APOLOGIZE FOR GETTING YOUR BROTHER INVOLVED IN ALL MY... FAMILY PROBLEMS. THAT WASN'T FAIR OF ME.
HE JUST SEEMED... INTERESTING, YOU KNOW? APPROACHABLE. LIKE SOME-ONE I COULD TALK TO.
I DON'T HAVE MANY FRIENDS HERE IN TOWN ANYMORE. I WAS WEAK.
SO... YOU DO NOT INTEND TO KILL ME THIS EVENING?
NO, I DO NOT.
WHAT'S GOING ON HERE, MRS. NEWBARN?
WHAT HAPPENED TO YOU?

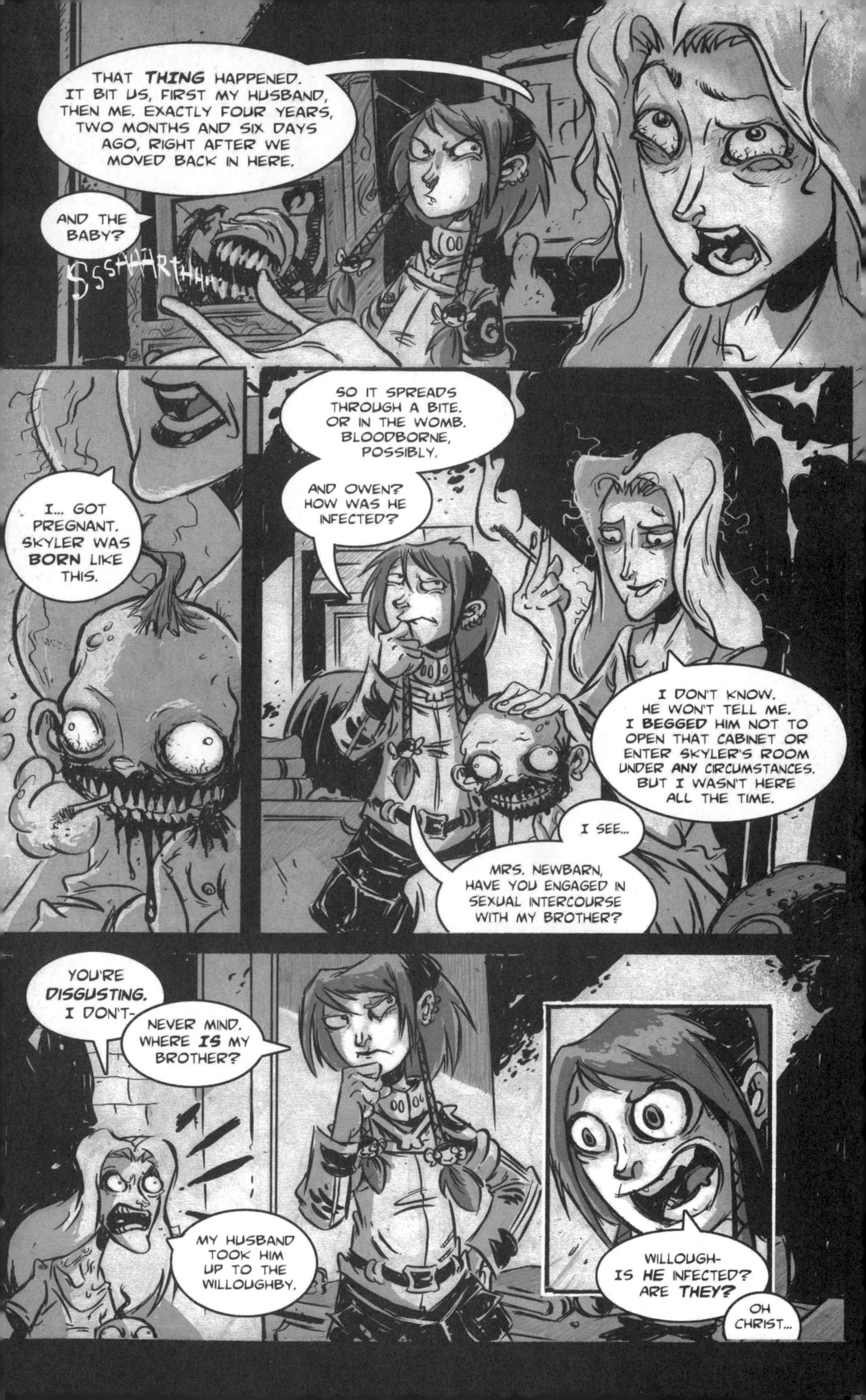

THAT THING HAPPENED. IT BIT US, FIRST MY HUSBAND, THEN ME. EXACTLY FOUR YEARS, TWO MONTHS AND SIX DAYS AGO, RIGHT AFTER WE MOVED BACK IN HERE.
AND THE BABY?
SSSHAARTHHH...
I... GOT PREGNANT. SKYLER WAS BORN LIKE THIS.
SO IT SPREADS THROUGH A BITE. OR IN THE WOMB. BLOODBORNE, POSSIBLY.
AND OWEN? HOW WAS HE INFECTED?
I DON'T KNOW. HE WON'T TELL ME. I BEGGED HIM NOT TO OPEN THAT CABINET OR ENTER SKYLER'S ROOM UNDER ANY CIRCUMSTANCES. BUT I WASN'T HERE ALL THE TIME.
I SEE...
MRS. NEWBARN, HAVE YOU ENGAGED IN SEXUAL INTERCOURSE WITH MY BROTHER?
YOU'RE DISGUSTING. I DON'T-
NEVER MIND. WHERE IS MY BROTHER?
MY HUSBAND TOOK HIM UP TO THE WILLOUGHBY.
WILLOUGH- IS HE INFECTED? ARE THEY?
OH CHRIST...

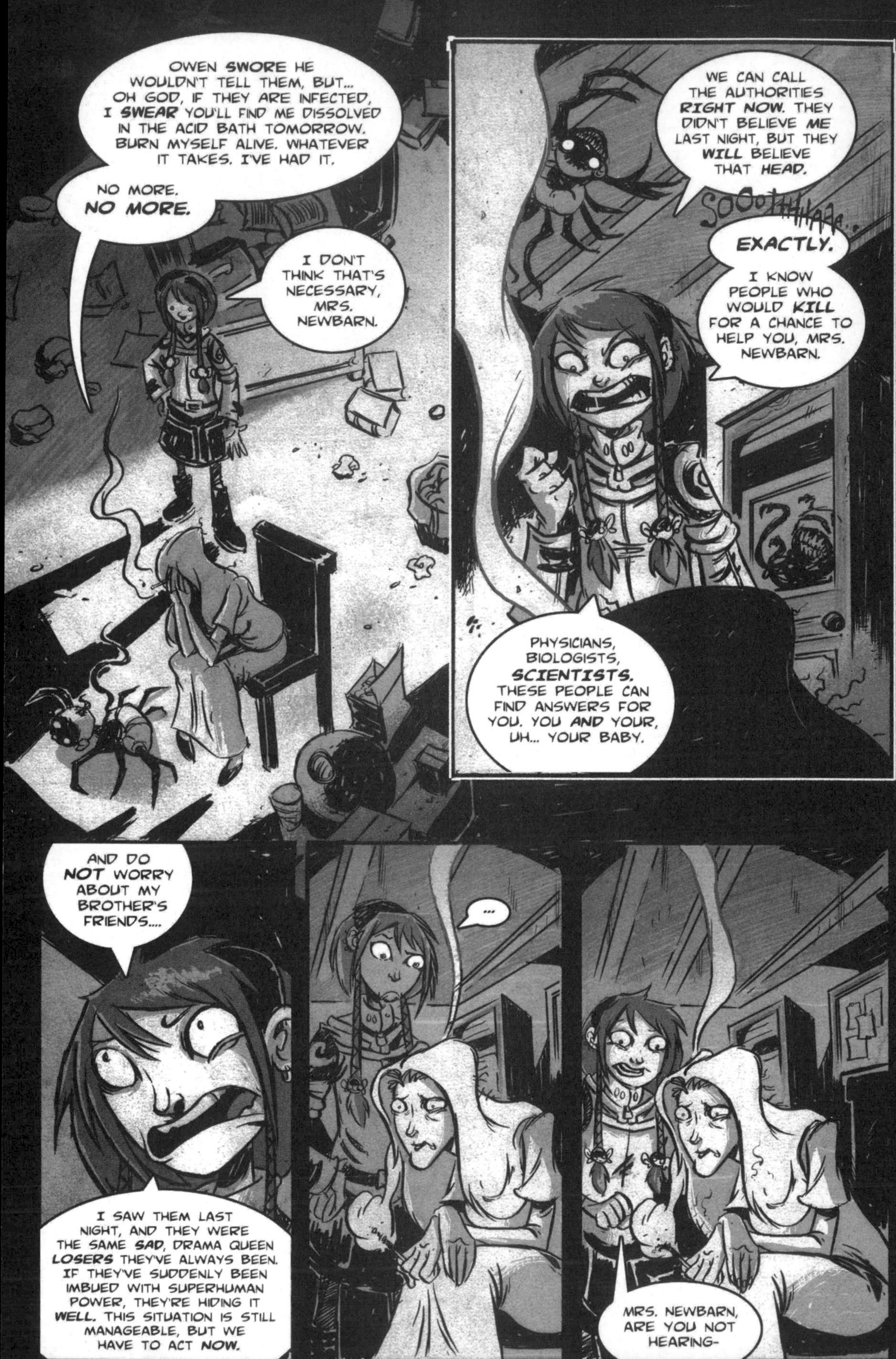
OWEN **SWORE** HE WOULDN'T TELL THEM, BUT... OH GOD, IF THEY ARE INFECTED, **I SWEAR** YOU'LL FIND ME DISSOLVED IN THE ACID BATH TOMORROW. BURN MYSELF ALIVE. WHATEVER IT TAKES. I'VE HAD IT.
NO MORE. **NO MORE.**
I DON'T THINK THAT'S NECESSARY, MRS. NEWBARN.
WE CAN CALL THE AUTHORITIES **RIGHT NOW.** THEY DIDN'T BELIEVE **ME** LAST NIGHT, BUT THEY **WILL** BELIEVE THAT **HEAD.**
SOOOTHHAAA...
EXACTLY.
I KNOW PEOPLE WHO WOULD **KILL** FOR A CHANCE TO HELP YOU, MRS. NEWBARN.
PHYSICIANS, BIOLOGISTS, **SCIENTISTS.** THESE PEOPLE CAN FIND ANSWERS FOR YOU. YOU **AND** YOUR, UH... YOUR BABY.
AND DO **NOT** WORRY ABOUT MY BROTHER'S FRIENDS....
I SAW THEM LAST NIGHT, AND THEY WERE THE SAME **SAD**, DRAMA QUEEN **LOSERS** THEY'VE ALWAYS BEEN. IF THEY'VE SUDDENLY BEEN IMBUED WITH SUPERHUMAN POWER, THEY'RE HIDING IT **WELL.** THIS SITUATION IS STILL MANAGEABLE, BUT WE HAVE TO ACT **NOW.**
...
MRS. NEWBARN, ARE YOU NOT HEARING-

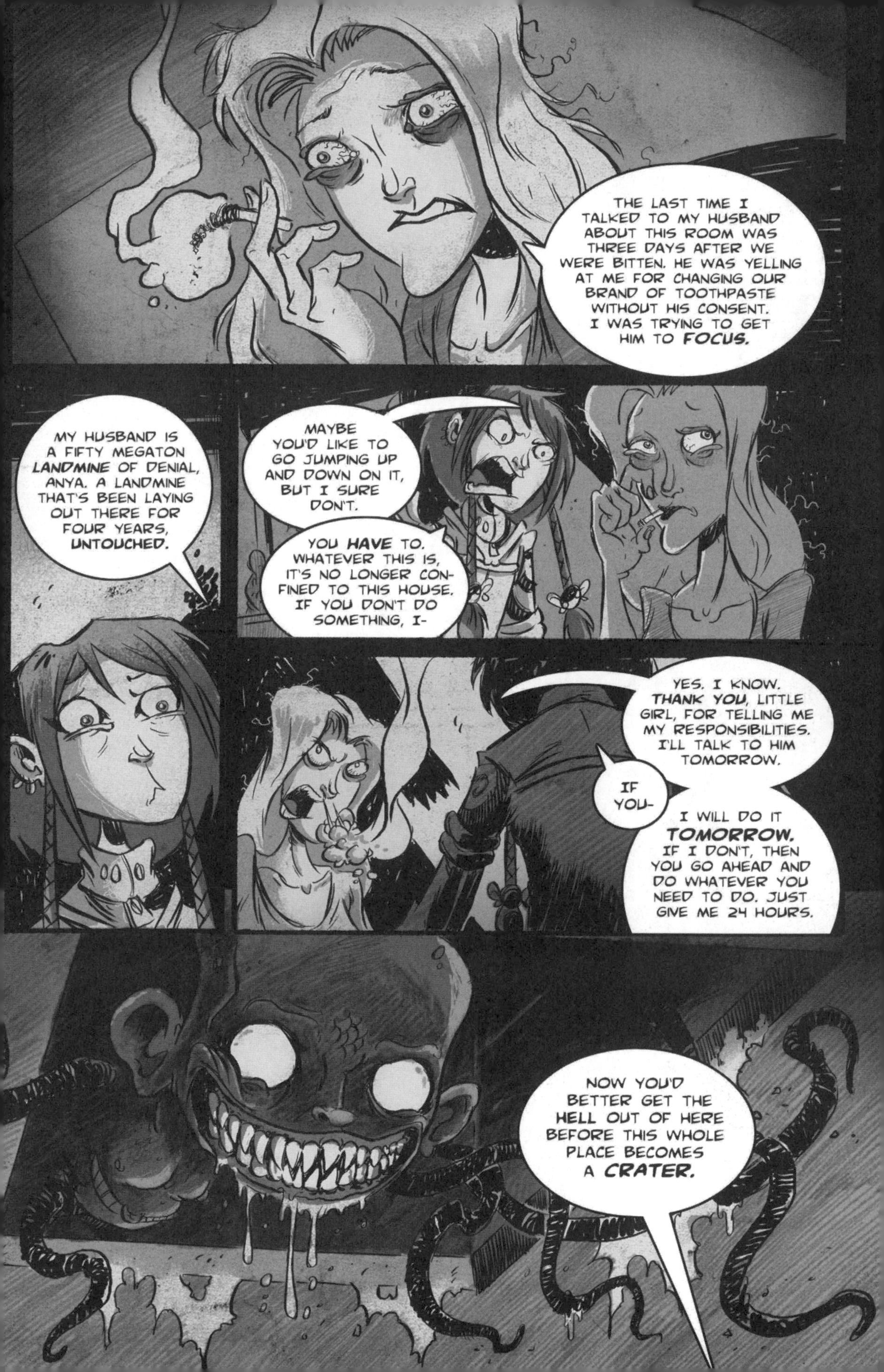
THE LAST TIME I TALKED TO MY HUSBAND ABOUT THIS ROOM WAS THREE DAYS AFTER WE WERE BITTEN. HE WAS YELLING AT ME FOR CHANGING OUR BRAND OF TOOTHPASTE WITHOUT HIS CONSENT. I WAS TRYING TO GET HIM TO FOCUS.
MY HUSBAND IS A FIFTY MEGATON LANDMINE OF DENIAL, ANYA. A LANDMINE THAT'S BEEN LAYING OUT THERE FOR FOUR YEARS, UNTOUCHED.
MAYBE YOU'D LIKE TO GO JUMPING UP AND DOWN ON IT, BUT I SURE DON'T.
YOU HAVE TO. WHATEVER THIS IS, IT'S NO LONGER CONFINED TO THIS HOUSE. IF YOU DON'T DO SOMETHING, I-
YES. I KNOW. THANK YOU, LITTLE GIRL, FOR TELLING ME MY RESPONSIBILITIES. I'LL TALK TO HIM TOMORROW.
IF YOU-
I WILL DO IT TOMORROW. IF I DON'T, THEN YOU GO AHEAD AND DO WHATEVER YOU NEED TO DO. JUST GIVE ME 24 HOURS.
NOW YOU'D BETTER GET THE HELL OUT OF HERE BEFORE THIS WHOLE PLACE BECOMES A CRATER.

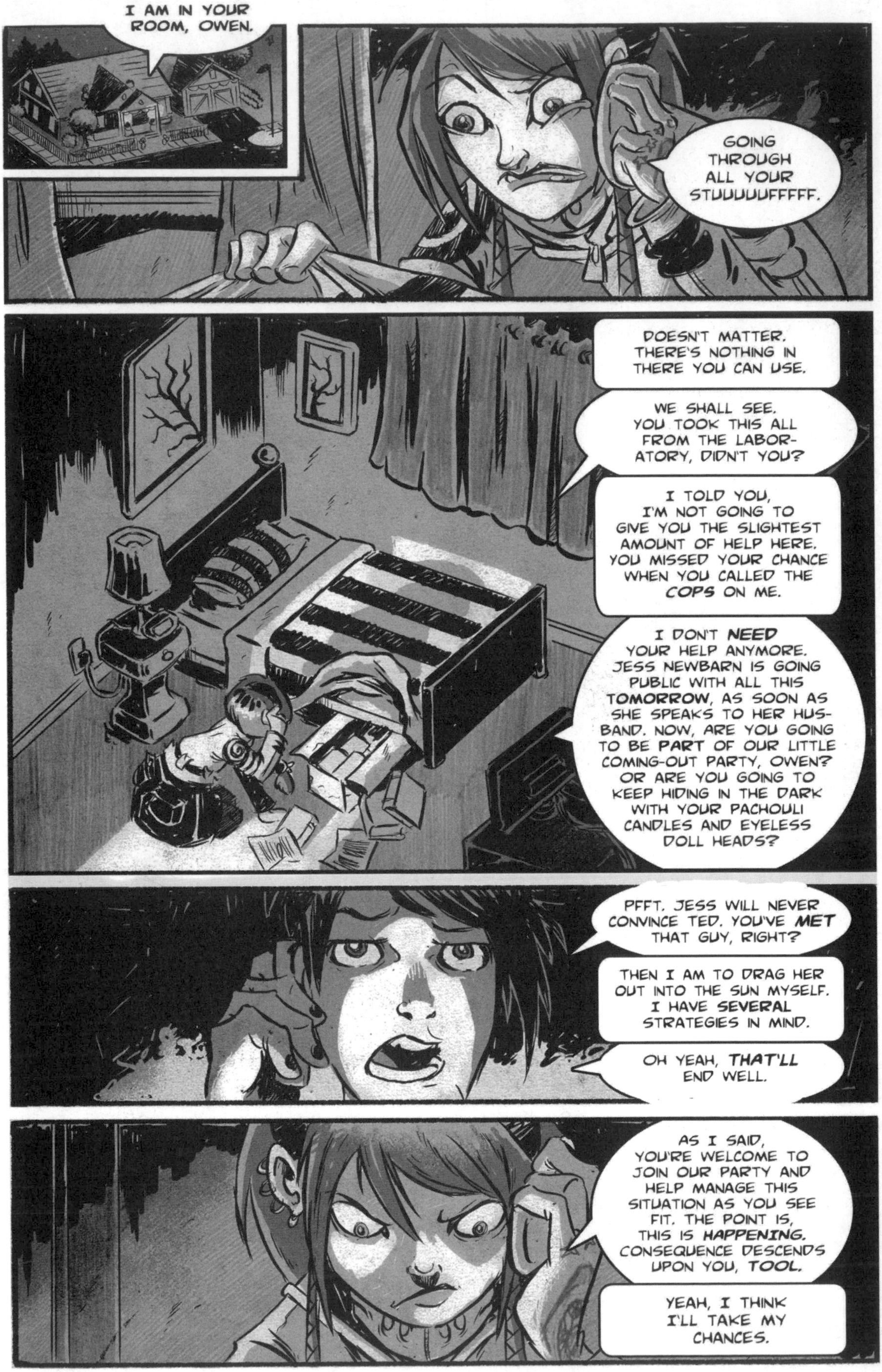
I AM IN YOUR ROOM, OWEN.
GOING THROUGH ALL YOUR STUUUUUFFFFF.
DOESN'T MATTER. THERE'S NOTHING IN THERE YOU CAN USE.
WE SHALL SEE. YOU TOOK THIS ALL FROM THE LABORATORY, DIDN'T YOU?
I TOLD YOU, I'M NOT GOING TO GIVE YOU THE SLIGHTEST AMOUNT OF HELP HERE. YOU MISSED YOUR CHANCE WHEN YOU CALLED THE *COPS* ON ME.
I DON'T **NEED** YOUR HELP ANYMORE. JESS NEWBARN IS GOING PUBLIC WITH ALL THIS **TOMORROW**, AS SOON AS SHE SPEAKS TO HER HUSBAND. NOW, ARE YOU GOING TO BE **PART** OF OUR LITTLE COMING-OUT PARTY, OWEN? OR ARE YOU GOING TO KEEP HIDING IN THE DARK WITH YOUR PACHOULI CANDLES AND EYELESS DOLL HEADS?
PFFT. JESS WILL NEVER CONVINCE TED. YOU'VE ***MET*** THAT GUY, RIGHT?
THEN I AM TO DRAG HER OUT INTO THE SUN MYSELF. I HAVE **SEVERAL** STRATEGIES IN MIND.
OH YEAH, ***THAT'LL*** END WELL.
AS I SAID, YOU'RE WELCOME TO JOIN OUR PARTY AND HELP MANAGE THIS SITUATION AS YOU SEE FIT. THE POINT IS, THIS IS ***HAPPENING.*** CONSEQUENCE DESCENDS UPON YOU, ***TOOL.***
YEAH, I THINK I'LL TAKE MY CHANCES.

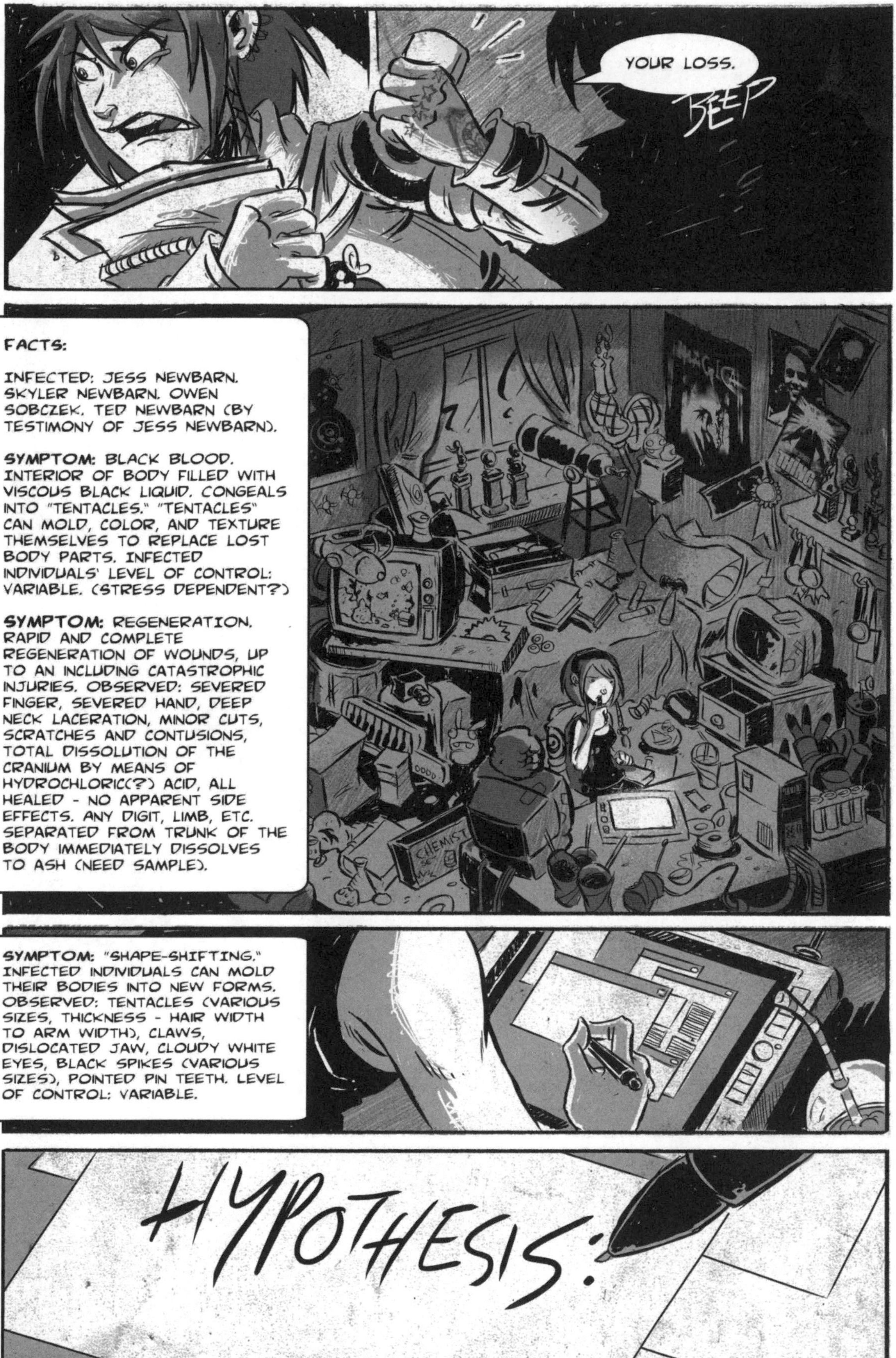
YOUR LOSS.
BEEP
FACTS:
INFECTED: JESS NEWBARN. SKYLER NEWBARN. OWEN SOBCZEK. TED NEWBARN (BY TESTIMONY OF JESS NEWBARN).
SYMPTOM: BLACK BLOOD. INTERIOR OF BODY FILLED WITH VISCOUS BLACK LIQUID. CONGEALS INTO "TENTACLES." "TENTACLES" CAN MOLD, COLOR, AND TEXTURE THEMSELVES TO REPLACE LOST BODY PARTS. INFECTED INDIVIDUALS' LEVEL OF CONTROL: VARIABLE. (STRESS DEPENDENT?)
SYMPTOM: REGENERATION. RAPID AND COMPLETE REGENERATION OF WOUNDS, UP TO AN INCLUDING CATASTROPHIC INJURIES. OBSERVED: SEVERED FINGER, SEVERED HAND, DEEP NECK LACERATION, MINOR CUTS, SCRATCHES AND CONTUSIONS, TOTAL DISSOLUTION OF THE CRANIUM BY MEANS OF HYDROCHLORIC(?) ACID, ALL HEALED - NO APPARENT SIDE EFFECTS. ANY DIGIT, LIMB, ETC. SEPARATED FROM TRUNK OF THE BODY IMMEDIATELY DISSOLVES TO ASH (NEED SAMPLE).
CHEMIST
SYMPTOM: "SHAPE-SHIFTING." INFECTED INDIVIDUALS CAN MOLD THEIR BODIES INTO NEW FORMS. OBSERVED: TENTACLES (VARIOUS SIZES, THICKNESS - HAIR WIDTH TO ARM WIDTH), CLAWS, DISLOCATED JAW, CLOUDY WHITE EYES, BLACK SPIKES (VARIOUS SIZES), POINTED PIN TEETH. LEVEL OF CONTROL: VARIABLE.
HYPOTHESIS:

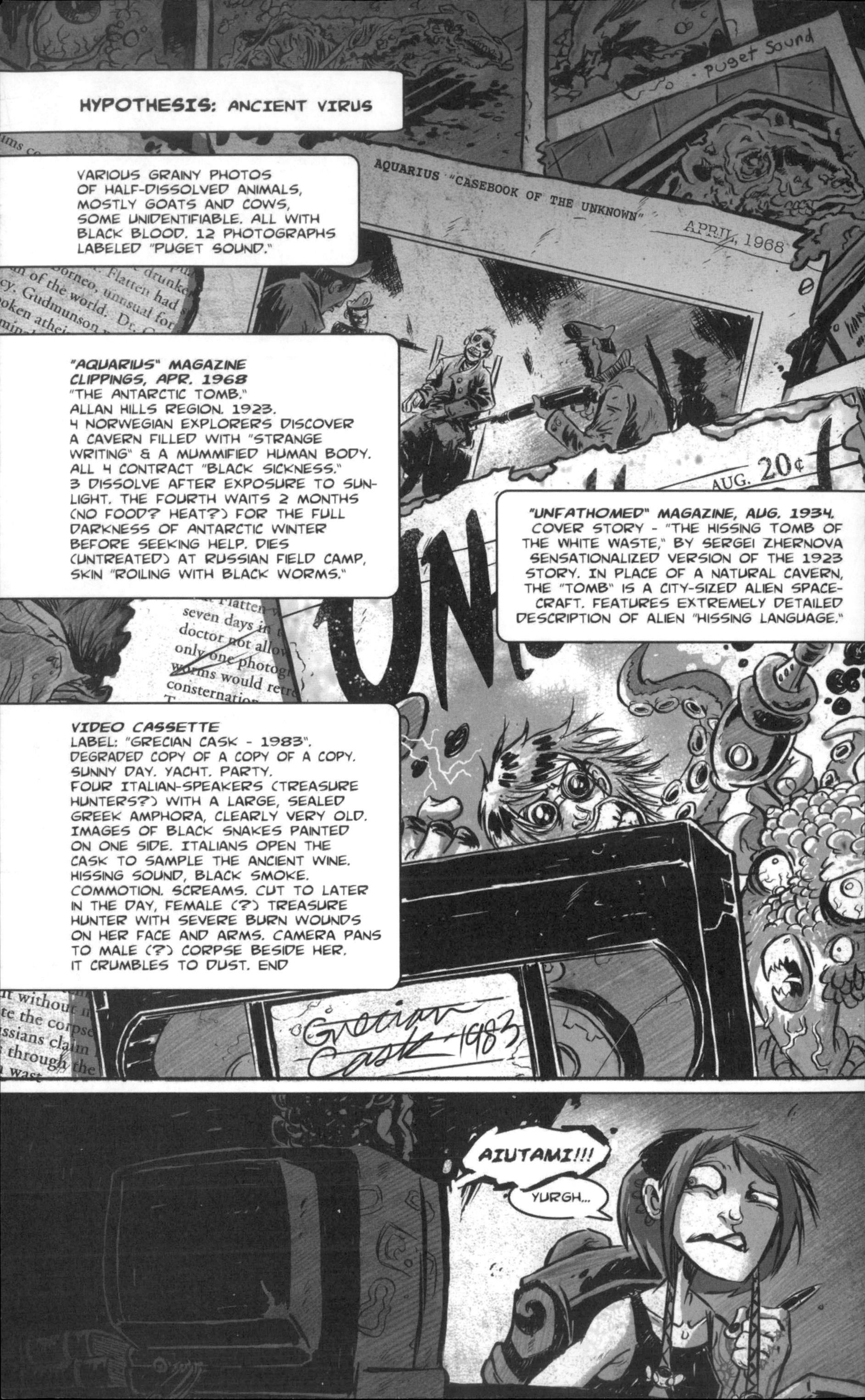
HYPOTHESIS: ANCIENT VIRUS
VARIOUS GRAINY PHOTOS OF HALF-DISSOLVED ANIMALS, MOSTLY GOATS AND COWS, SOME UNIDENTIFIABLE. ALL WITH BLACK BLOOD. 12 PHOTOGRAPHS LABELED "PUGET SOUND."
Puget Sound
AQUARIUS "CASEBOOK OF THE UNKNOWN"
APRIL, 1968
"AQUARIUS" MAGAZINE CLIPPINGS, APR. 1968
"THE ANTARCTIC TOMB."
ALLAN HILLS REGION. 1923.
4 NORWEGIAN EXPLORERS DISCOVER A CAVERN FILLED WITH "STRANGE WRITING" & A MUMMIFIED HUMAN BODY. ALL 4 CONTRACT "BLACK SICKNESS." 3 DISSOLVE AFTER EXPOSURE TO SUNLIGHT. THE FOURTH WAITS 2 MONTHS (NO FOOD? HEAT?) FOR THE FULL DARKNESS OF ANTARCTIC WINTER BEFORE SEEKING HELP. DIES (UNTREATED) AT RUSSIAN FIELD CAMP, SKIN "ROILING WITH BLACK WORMS."
AUG. 20¢
"UNFATHOMED" MAGAZINE, AUG. 1934.
COVER STORY - "THE HISSING TOMB OF THE WHITE WASTE," BY SERGEI ZHERNOVA SENSATIONALIZED VERSION OF THE 1923 STORY. IN PLACE OF A NATURAL CAVERN, THE "TOMB" IS A CITY-SIZED ALIEN SPACECRAFT. FEATURES EXTREMELY DETAILED DESCRIPTION OF ALIEN "HISSING LANGUAGE."
VIDEO CASSETTE
LABEL: "GRECIAN CASK - 1983".
DEGRADED COPY OF A COPY OF A COPY. SUNNY DAY. YACHT. PARTY.
FOUR ITALIAN-SPEAKERS (TREASURE HUNTERS?) WITH A LARGE, SEALED GREEK AMPHORA, CLEARLY VERY OLD. IMAGES OF BLACK SNAKES PAINTED ON ONE SIDE. ITALIANS OPEN THE CASK TO SAMPLE THE ANCIENT WINE. HISSING SOUND, BLACK SMOKE. COMMOTION. SCREAMS. CUT TO LATER IN THE DAY, FEMALE (?) TREASURE HUNTER WITH SEVERE BURN WOUNDS ON HER FACE AND ARMS. CAMERA PANS TO MALE (?) CORPSE BESIDE HER. IT CRUMBLES TO DUST. END
Grecian Cask 1983
AIUTAMI!!!
YURGH...

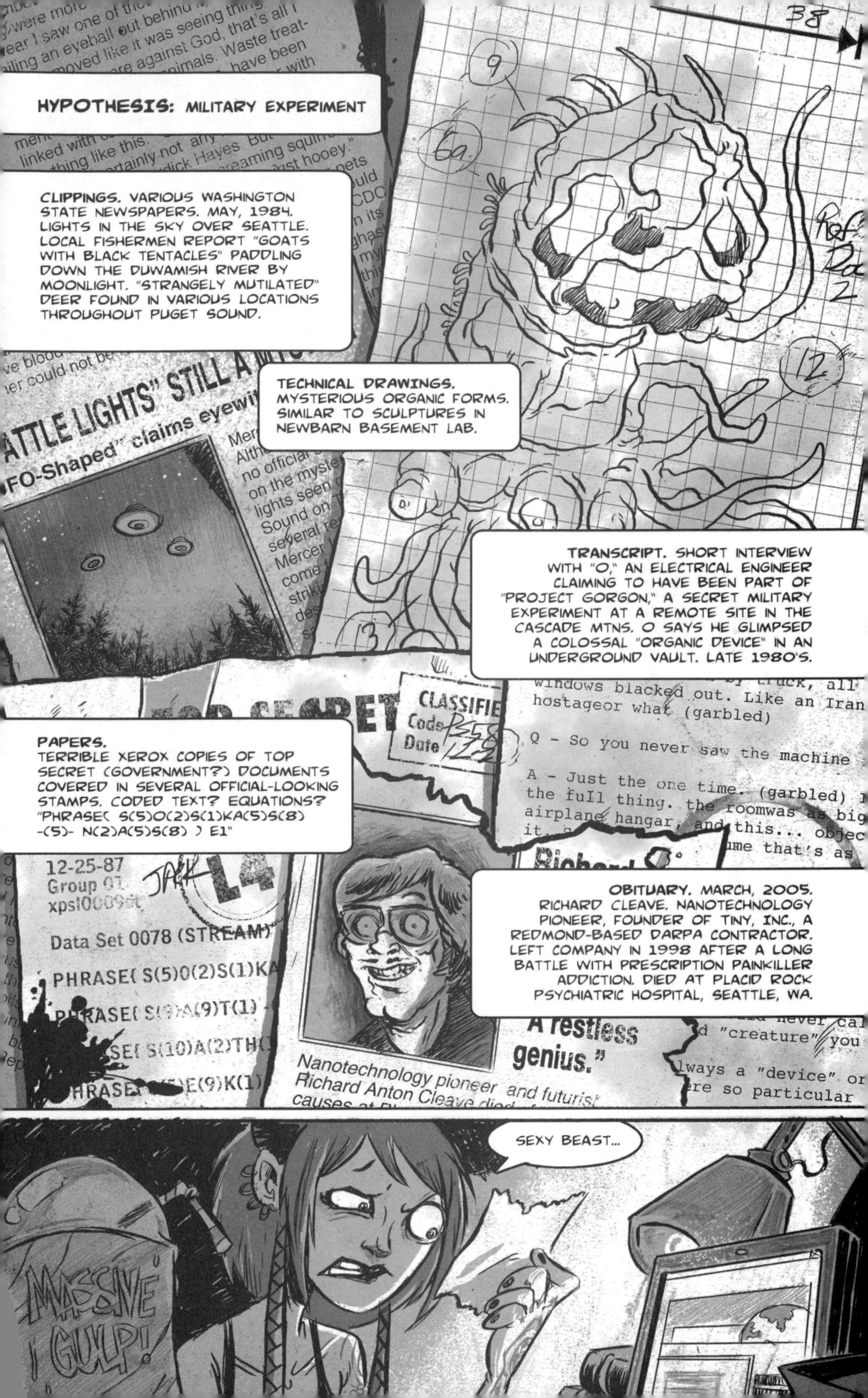
HYPOTHESIS: MILITARY EXPERIMENT
CLIPPINGS. VARIOUS WASHINGTON STATE NEWSPAPERS. MAY, 1984. LIGHTS IN THE SKY OVER SEATTLE. LOCAL FISHERMEN REPORT "GOATS WITH BLACK TENTACLES" PADDLING DOWN THE DUWAMISH RIVER BY MOONLIGHT. "STRANGELY MUTILATED" DEER FOUND IN VARIOUS LOCATIONS THROUGHOUT PUGET SOUND.
TECHNICAL DRAWINGS. MYSTERIOUS ORGANIC FORMS. SIMILAR TO SCULPTURES IN NEWBARN BASEMENT LAB.
TRANSCRIPT. SHORT INTERVIEW WITH "O," AN ELECTRICAL ENGINEER CLAIMING TO HAVE BEEN PART OF "PROJECT GORGON," A SECRET MILITARY EXPERIMENT AT A REMOTE SITE IN THE CASCADE MTNS. O SAYS HE GLIMPSED A COLOSSAL "ORGANIC DEVICE" IN AN UNDERGROUND VAULT. LATE 1980'S.
PAPERS. TERRIBLE XEROX COPIES OF TOP SECRET (GOVERNMENT?) DOCUMENTS COVERED IN SEVERAL OFFICIAL-LOOKING STAMPS. CODED TEXT? EQUATIONS? "PHRASE(S(5)O(2)S(1)KA(5)S(8) -(5)- N(2)A(5)S(8)) E1"
OBITUARY. MARCH, 2005. RICHARD CLEAVE. NANOTECHNOLOGY PIONEER, FOUNDER OF TINY, INC., A REDMOND-BASED DARPA CONTRACTOR. LEFT COMPANY IN 1998 AFTER A LONG BATTLE WITH PRESCRIPTION PAINKILLER ADDICTION. DIED AT PLACID ROCK PSYCHIATRIC HOSPITAL, SEATTLE, WA.
SEXY BEAST...
MASSIVE GULP!

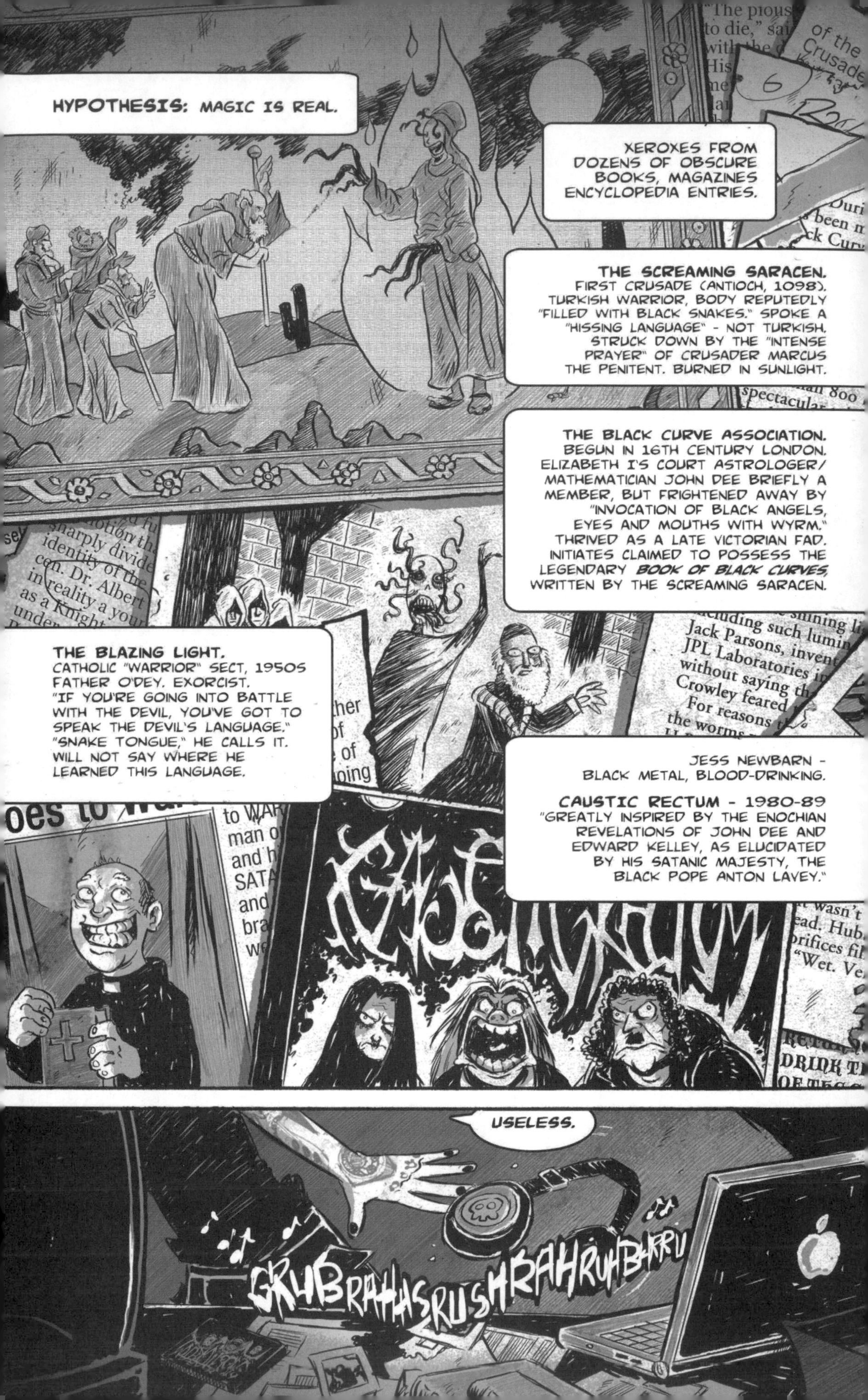
HYPOTHESIS: MAGIC IS REAL.
XEROXES FROM DOZENS OF OBSCURE BOOKS, MAGAZINES ENCYCLOPEDIA ENTRIES.
THE SCREAMING SARACEN. FIRST CRUSADE (ANTIOCH, 1098). TURKISH WARRIOR, BODY REPUTEDLY "FILLED WITH BLACK SNAKES." SPOKE A "HISSING LANGUAGE" - NOT TURKISH. STRUCK DOWN BY THE "INTENSE PRAYER" OF CRUSADER MARCUS THE PENITENT. BURNED IN SUNLIGHT.
THE BLACK CURVE ASSOCIATION. BEGUN IN 16TH CENTURY LONDON. ELIZABETH I'S COURT ASTROLOGER/ MATHEMATICIAN JOHN DEE BRIEFLY A MEMBER, BUT FRIGHTENED AWAY BY "INVOCATION OF BLACK ANGELS, EYES AND MOUTHS WITH WYRM." THRIVED AS A LATE VICTORIAN FAD. INITIATES CLAIMED TO POSSESS THE LEGENDARY *BOOK OF BLACK CURVES*, WRITTEN BY THE SCREAMING SARACEN.
THE BLAZING LIGHT. CATHOLIC "WARRIOR" SECT, 1950S FATHER O'DEY. EXORCIST. "IF YOU'RE GOING INTO BATTLE WITH THE DEVIL, YOU'VE GOT TO SPEAK THE DEVIL'S LANGUAGE." "SNAKE TONGUE," HE CALLS IT. WILL NOT SAY WHERE HE LEARNED THIS LANGUAGE.
JESS NEWBARN - BLACK METAL, BLOOD-DRINKING.
CAUSTIC RECTUM - 1980-89 "GREATLY INSPIRED BY THE ENOCHIAN REVELATIONS OF JOHN DEE AND EDWARD KELLEY, AS ELUCIDATED BY HIS SATANIC MAJESTY, THE BLACK POPE ANTON LAVEY."
USELESS.
GRUBRAHASRUSHRAHRUHBARRU

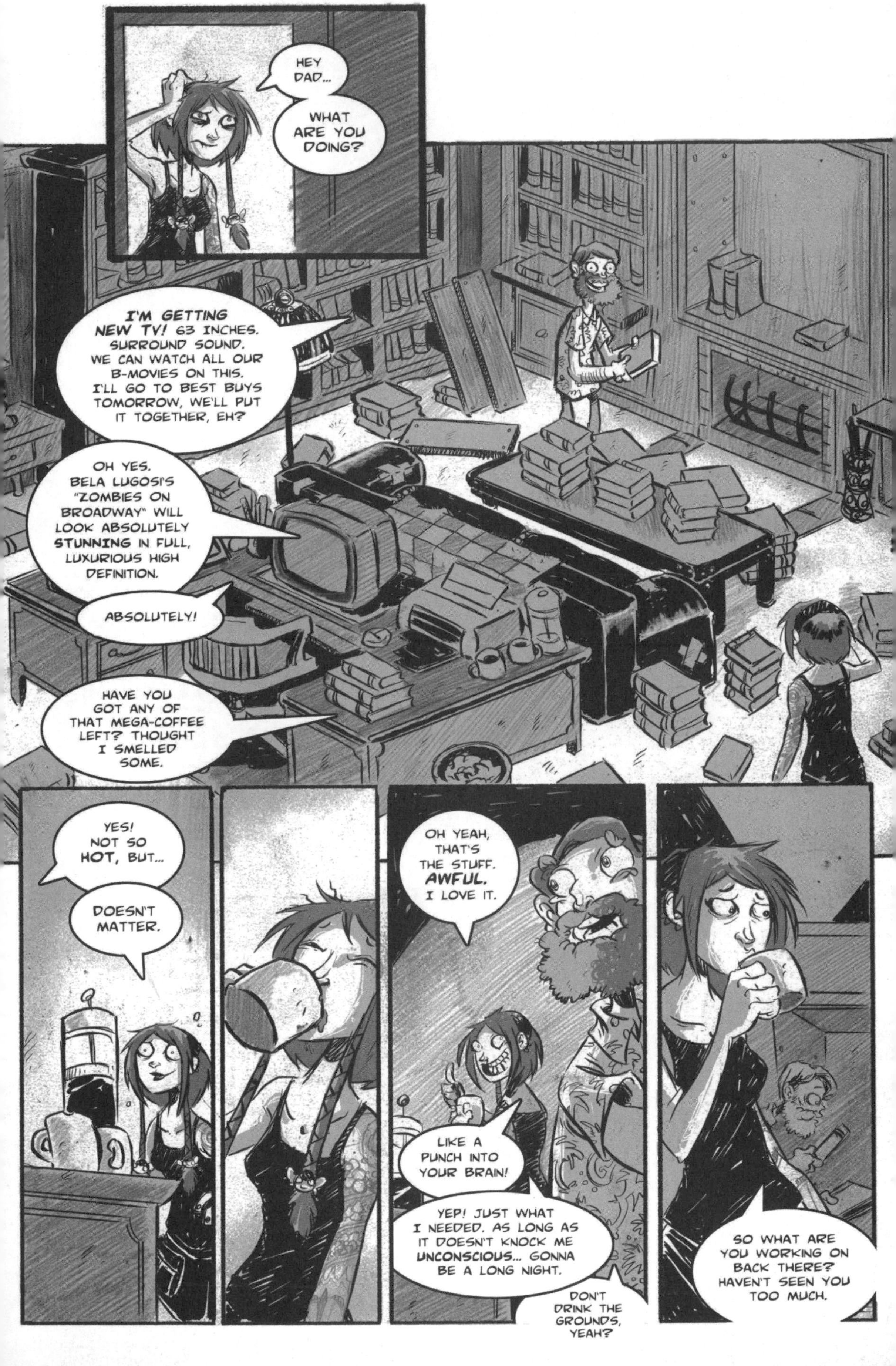
HEY DAD...
WHAT ARE YOU DOING?
I'M GETTING NEW TV! 63 INCHES. SURROUND SOUND. WE CAN WATCH ALL OUR B-MOVIES ON THIS. I'LL GO TO BEST BUYS TOMORROW, WE'LL PUT IT TOGETHER, EH?
OH YES. BELA LUGOSI'S "ZOMBIES ON BROADWAY" WILL LOOK ABSOLUTELY STUNNING IN FULL, LUXURIOUS HIGH DEFINITION.
ABSOLUTELY!
HAVE YOU GOT ANY OF THAT MEGA-COFFEE LEFT? THOUGHT I SMELLED SOME.
YES! NOT SO HOT, BUT...
DOESN'T MATTER.
OH YEAH, THAT'S THE STUFF. AWFUL. I LOVE IT.
LIKE A PUNCH INTO YOUR BRAIN!
YEP! JUST WHAT I NEEDED. AS LONG AS IT DOESN'T KNOCK ME UNCONSCIOUS... GONNA BE A LONG NIGHT.
DON'T DRINK THE GROUNDS, YEAH?
SO WHAT ARE YOU WORKING ON BACK THERE? HAVEN'T SEEN YOU TOO MUCH.

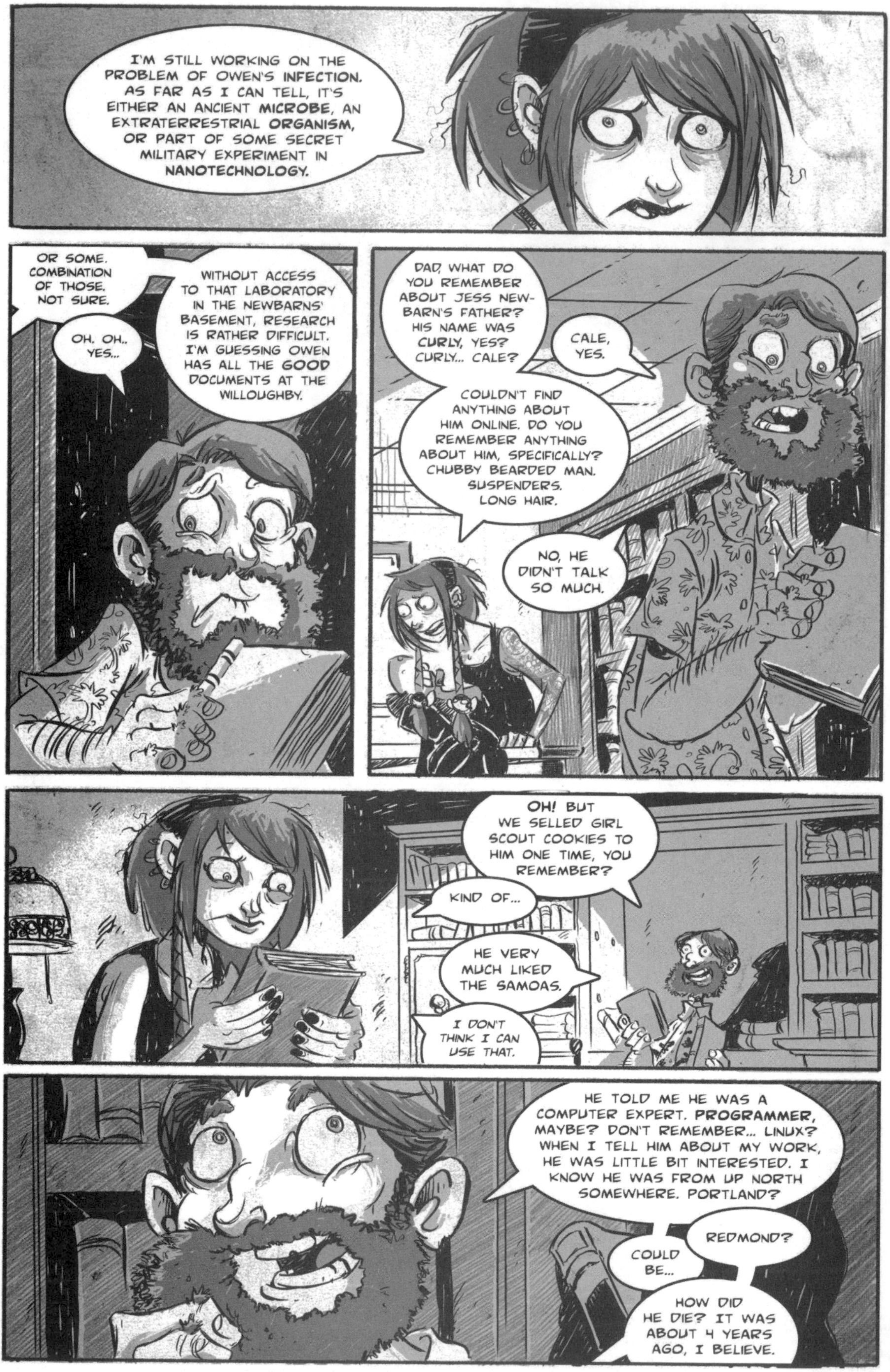
I'M STILL WORKING ON THE PROBLEM OF OWEN'S INFECTION. AS FAR AS I CAN TELL, IT'S EITHER AN ANCIENT MICROBE, AN EXTRATERRESTRIAL ORGANISM, OR PART OF SOME SECRET MILITARY EXPERIMENT IN NANOTECHNOLOGY.
OR SOME. COMBINATION OF THOSE. NOT SURE.
OH. OH.. YES...
WITHOUT ACCESS TO THAT LABORATORY IN THE NEWBARNS' BASEMENT, RESEARCH IS RATHER DIFFICULT. I'M GUESSING OWEN HAS ALL THE GOOD DOCUMENTS AT THE WILLOUGHBY.
DAD, WHAT DO YOU REMEMBER ABOUT JESS NEW-BARN'S FATHER? HIS NAME WAS CURLY, YES? CURLY... CALE?
CALE, YES.
COULDN'T FIND ANYTHING ABOUT HIM ONLINE. DO YOU REMEMBER ANYTHING ABOUT HIM, SPECIFICALLY? CHUBBY BEARDED MAN. SUSPENDERS. LONG HAIR.
NO, HE DIDN'T TALK SO MUCH.
OH! BUT WE SELLED GIRL SCOUT COOKIES TO HIM ONE TIME, YOU REMEMBER?
KIND OF...
HE VERY MUCH LIKED THE SAMOAS.
I DON'T THINK I CAN USE THAT.
HE TOLD ME HE WAS A COMPUTER EXPERT. PROGRAMMER, MAYBE? DON'T REMEMBER... LINUX? WHEN I TELL HIM ABOUT MY WORK, HE WAS LITTLE BIT INTERESTED. I KNOW HE WAS FROM UP NORTH SOMEWHERE. PORTLAND?
REDMOND?
COULD BE...
HOW DID HE DIE? IT WAS ABOUT 4 YEARS AGO, I BELIEVE.

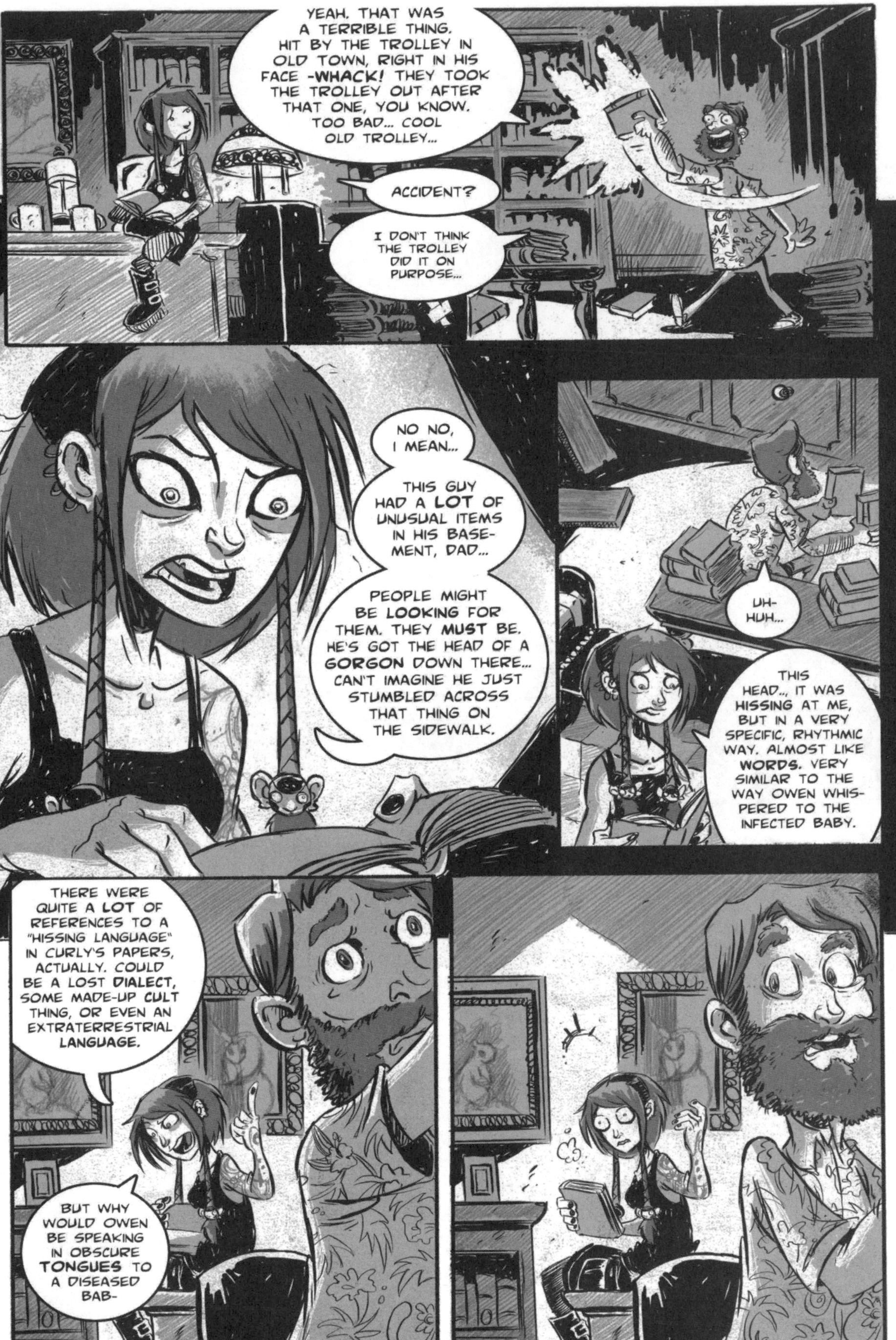

YEAH. THAT WAS A TERRIBLE THING. HIT BY THE TROLLEY IN OLD TOWN, RIGHT IN HIS FACE -WHACK! THEY TOOK THE TROLLEY OUT AFTER THAT ONE, YOU KNOW. TOO BAD... COOL OLD TROLLEY...
ACCIDENT?
I DON'T THINK THE TROLLEY DID IT ON PURPOSE...
NO NO, I MEAN...
THIS GUY HAD A LOT OF UNUSUAL ITEMS IN HIS BASE-MENT, DAD...
PEOPLE MIGHT BE LOOKING FOR THEM. THEY MUST BE. HE'S GOT THE HEAD OF A GORGON DOWN THERE... CAN'T IMAGINE HE JUST STUMBLED ACROSS THAT THING ON THE SIDEWALK.
UH-HUH...
THIS HEAD.., IT WAS HISSING AT ME, BUT IN A VERY SPECIFIC, RHYTHMIC WAY. ALMOST LIKE WORDS. VERY SIMILAR TO THE WAY OWEN WHIS-PERED TO THE INFECTED BABY.
THERE WERE QUITE A LOT OF REFERENCES TO A "HISSING LANGUAGE" IN CURLY'S PAPERS, ACTUALLY. COULD BE A LOST DIALECT, SOME MADE-UP CULT THING, OR EVEN AN EXTRATERRESTRIAL LANGUAGE.
BUT WHY WOULD OWEN BE SPEAKING IN OBSCURE TONGUES TO A DISEASED BAB-

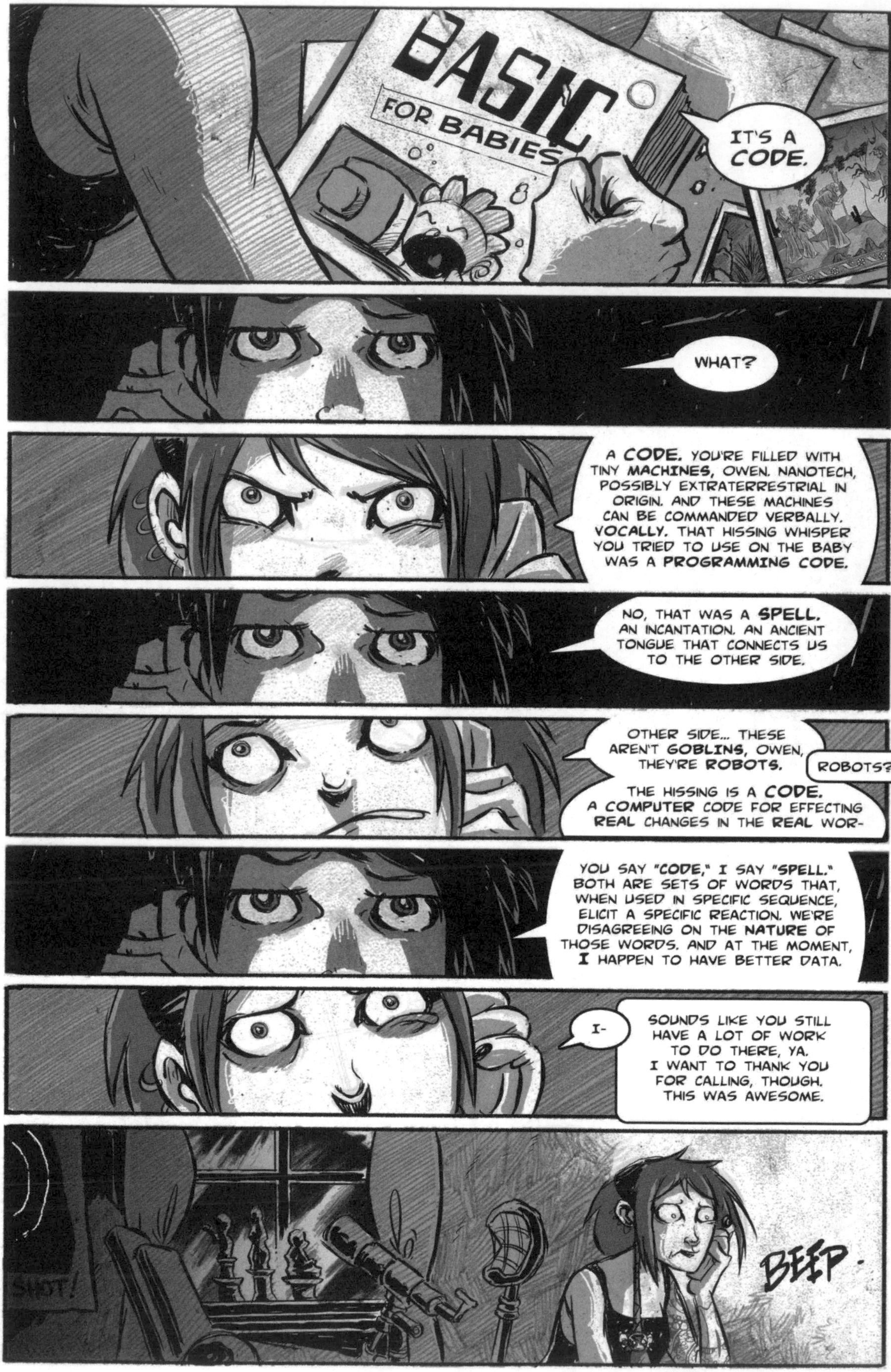
BASIC FOR BABIES
IT'S A CODE.
WHAT?
A CODE. YOU'RE FILLED WITH TINY MACHINES, OWEN. NANOTECH, POSSIBLY EXTRATERRESTRIAL IN ORIGIN. AND THESE MACHINES CAN BE COMMANDED VERBALLY. VOCALLY. THAT HISSING WHISPER YOU TRIED TO USE ON THE BABY WAS A PROGRAMMING CODE.
NO, THAT WAS A SPELL. AN INCANTATION. AN ANCIENT TONGUE THAT CONNECTS US TO THE OTHER SIDE.
OTHER SIDE... THESE AREN'T GOBLINS, OWEN, THEY'RE ROBOTS.
ROBOTS?
THE HISSING IS A CODE. A COMPUTER CODE FOR EFFECTING REAL CHANGES IN THE REAL WOR-
YOU SAY "CODE," I SAY "SPELL." BOTH ARE SETS OF WORDS THAT, WHEN USED IN SPECIFIC SEQUENCE, ELICIT A SPECIFIC REACTION. WE'RE DISAGREEING ON THE NATURE OF THOSE WORDS. AND AT THE MOMENT, I HAPPEN TO HAVE BETTER DATA.
I-
SOUNDS LIKE YOU STILL HAVE A LOT OF WORK TO DO THERE, YA. I WANT TO THANK YOU FOR CALLING, THOUGH. THIS WAS AWESOME.
SHOT!
BEEP.

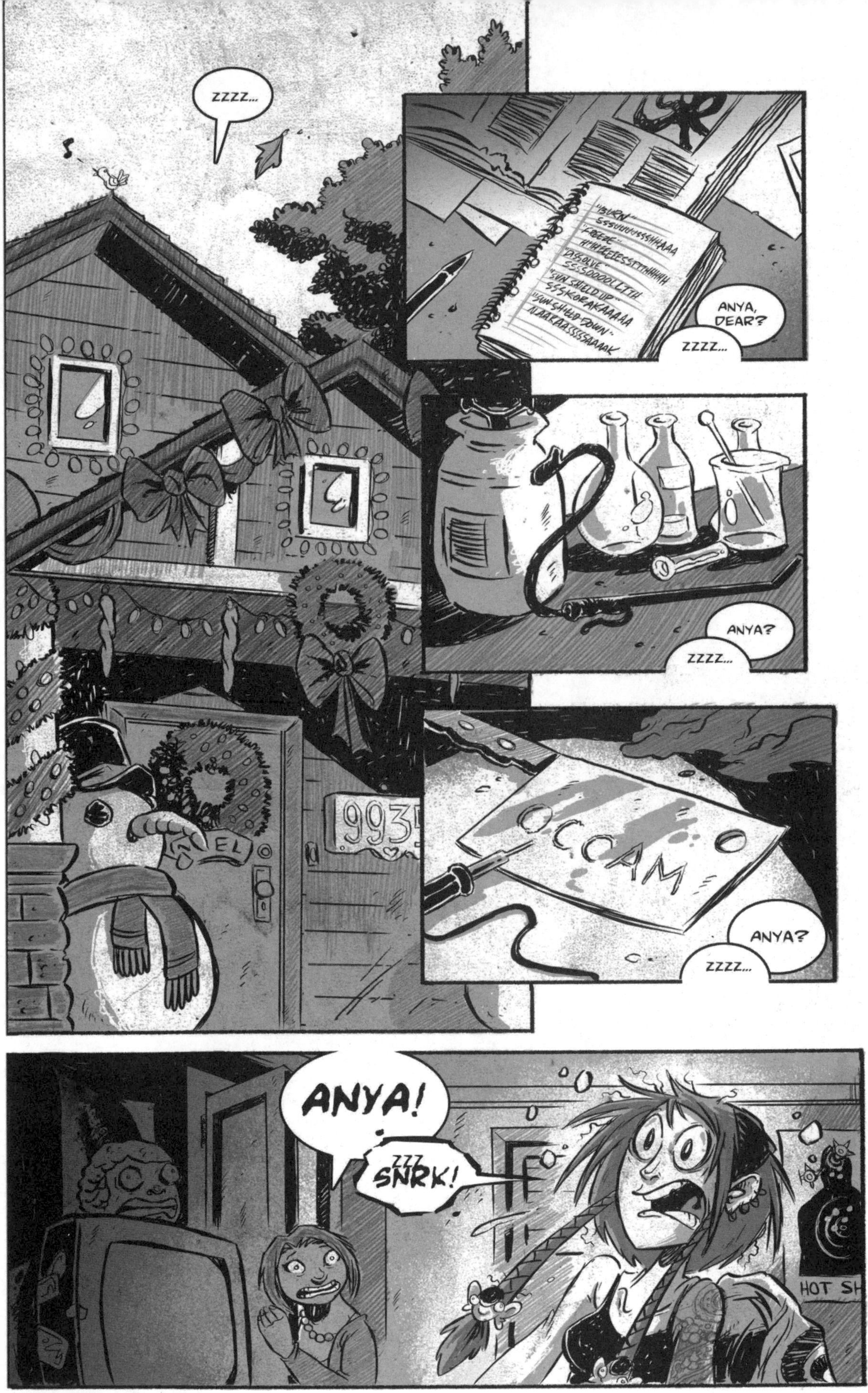
ZZZZ...
"BURN"
SSSUUUUUSSSHHAAA
"FREEZE"
HHHEEEEESSSTTHHHHH
"DISSOLVE"
SSSSOOOOOLLLTTH
"SUN SHIELD UP"
SSSKORAKAAAAAA
"SUN SHIELD DOWN"
NAARAASSSSSAAAAK
ANYA, DEAR?
ZZZZ...
ANYA?
ZZZZ...
OCCAM
ANYA?
ZZZZ...
9935
EL
ANYA!
ZZZ SNRK!
HOT SH

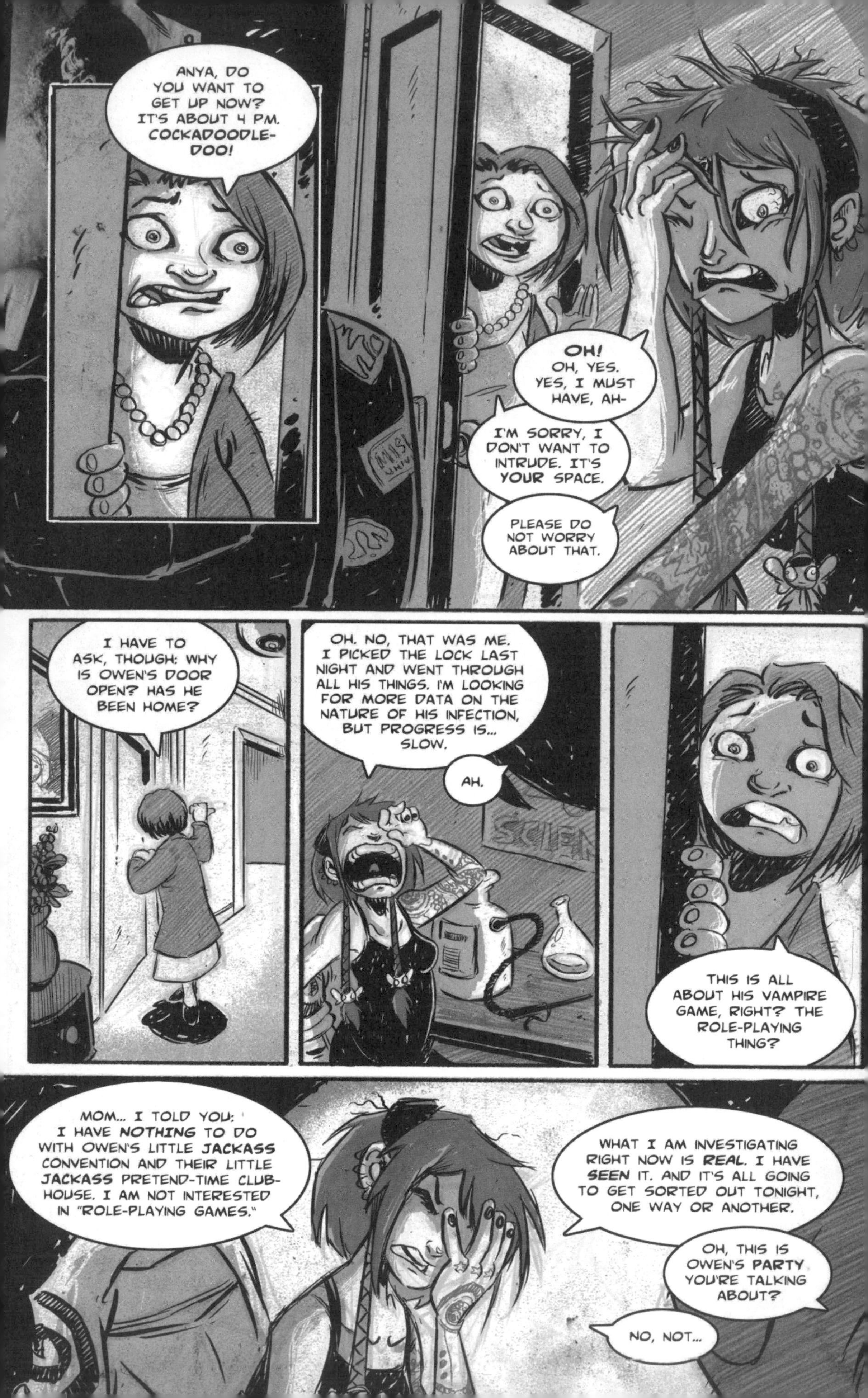
ANYA, DO YOU WANT TO GET UP NOW? IT'S ABOUT 4 PM. COCKADOODLE-DOO!
OH! OH, YES. YES, I MUST HAVE, AH-
I'M SORRY, I DON'T WANT TO INTRUDE. IT'S YOUR SPACE.
PLEASE DO NOT WORRY ABOUT THAT.
I HAVE TO ASK, THOUGH: WHY IS OWEN'S DOOR OPEN? HAS HE BEEN HOME?
OH. NO, THAT WAS ME. I PICKED THE LOCK LAST NIGHT AND WENT THROUGH ALL HIS THINGS. I'M LOOKING FOR MORE DATA ON THE NATURE OF HIS INFECTION, BUT PROGRESS IS... SLOW.
AH.
THIS IS ALL ABOUT HIS VAMPIRE GAME, RIGHT? THE ROLE-PLAYING THING?
MOM... I TOLD YOU: I HAVE NOTHING TO DO WITH OWEN'S LITTLE JACKASS CONVENTION AND THEIR LITTLE JACKASS PRETEND-TIME CLUB-HOUSE. I AM NOT INTERESTED IN "ROLE-PLAYING GAMES."
WHAT I AM INVESTIGATING RIGHT NOW IS REAL. I HAVE SEEN IT. AND IT'S ALL GOING TO GET SORTED OUT TONIGHT, ONE WAY OR ANOTHER.
OH, THIS IS OWEN'S PARTY YOU'RE TALKING ABOUT?
NO, NOT...

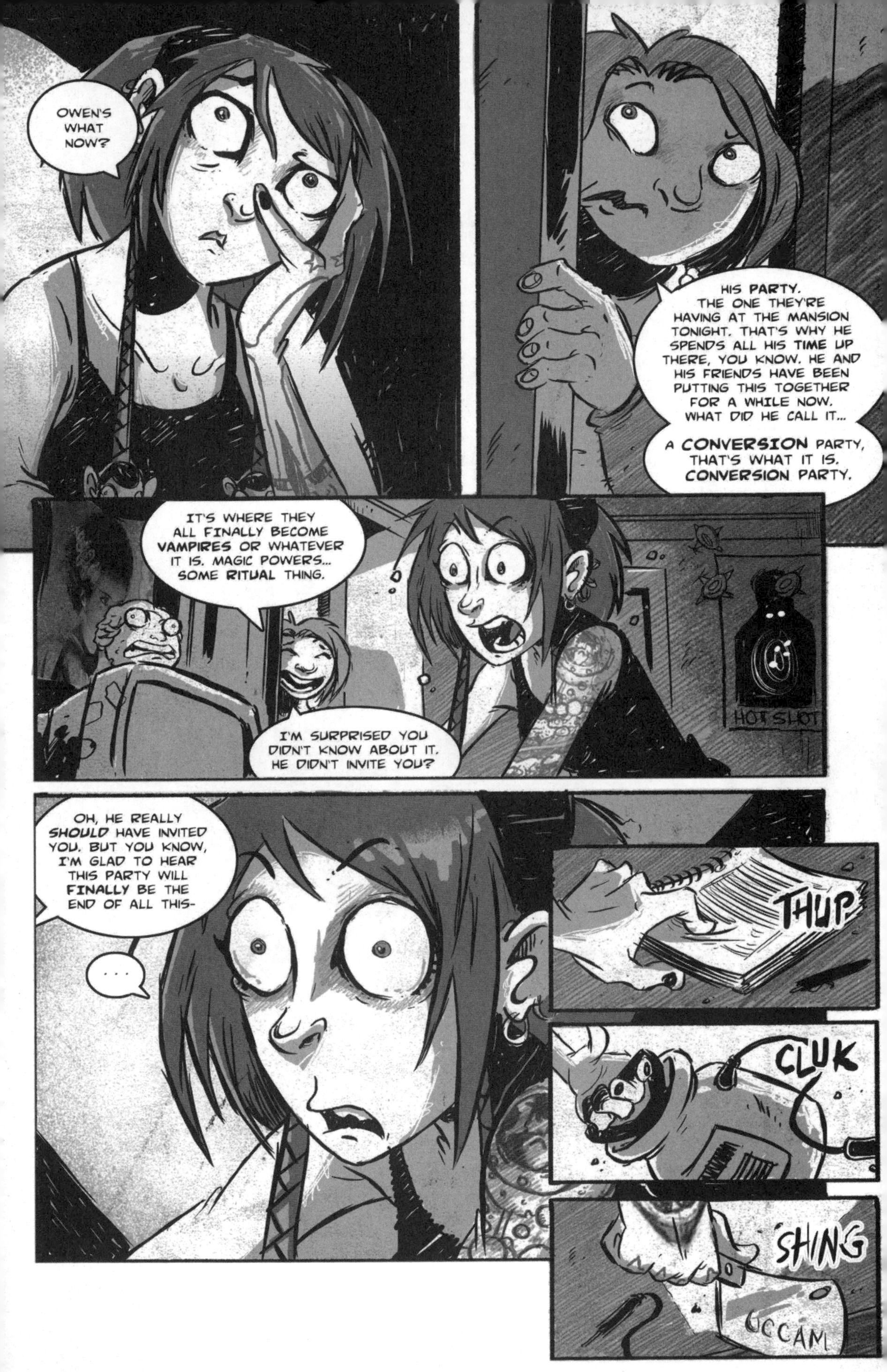
OWEN'S WHAT NOW?
HIS PARTY. THE ONE THEY'RE HAVING AT THE MANSION TONIGHT. THAT'S WHY HE SPENDS ALL HIS TIME UP THERE, YOU KNOW. HE AND HIS FRIENDS HAVE BEEN PUTTING THIS TOGETHER FOR A WHILE NOW. WHAT DID HE CALL IT...
A CONVERSION PARTY, THAT'S WHAT IT IS. CONVERSION PARTY.
IT'S WHERE THEY ALL FINALLY BECOME VAMPIRES OR WHATEVER IT IS. MAGIC POWERS... SOME RITUAL THING.
HOT SHOT
I'M SURPRISED YOU DIDN'T KNOW ABOUT IT. HE DIDN'T INVITE YOU?
OH, HE REALLY SHOULD HAVE INVITED YOU. BUT YOU KNOW, I'M GLAD TO HEAR THIS PARTY WILL FINALLY BE THE END OF ALL THIS-
...
THUP
CLUK
SHING
OCCAM

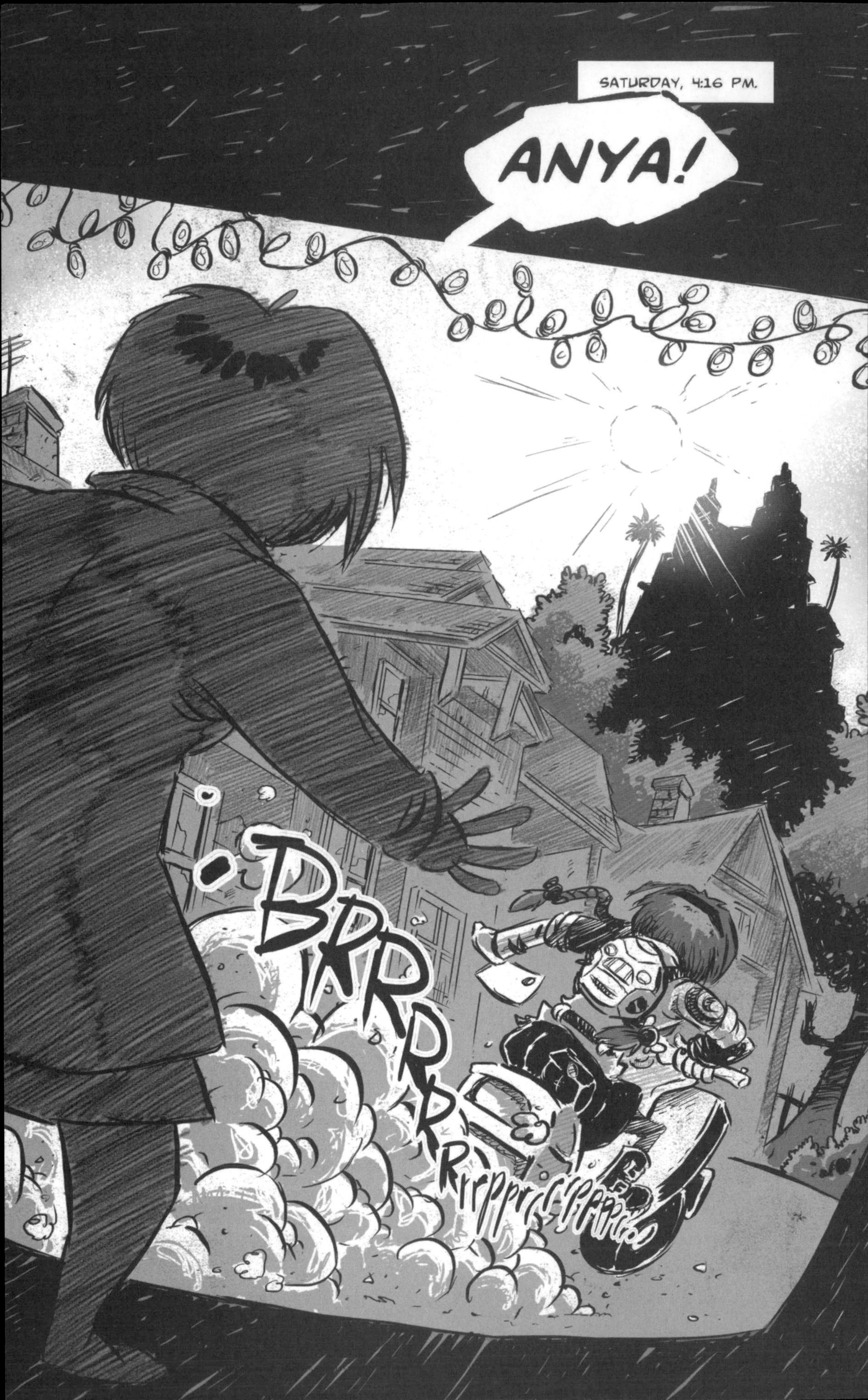
SATURDAY, 4:16 PM.
ANYA!
BRRRRRrrrpprr

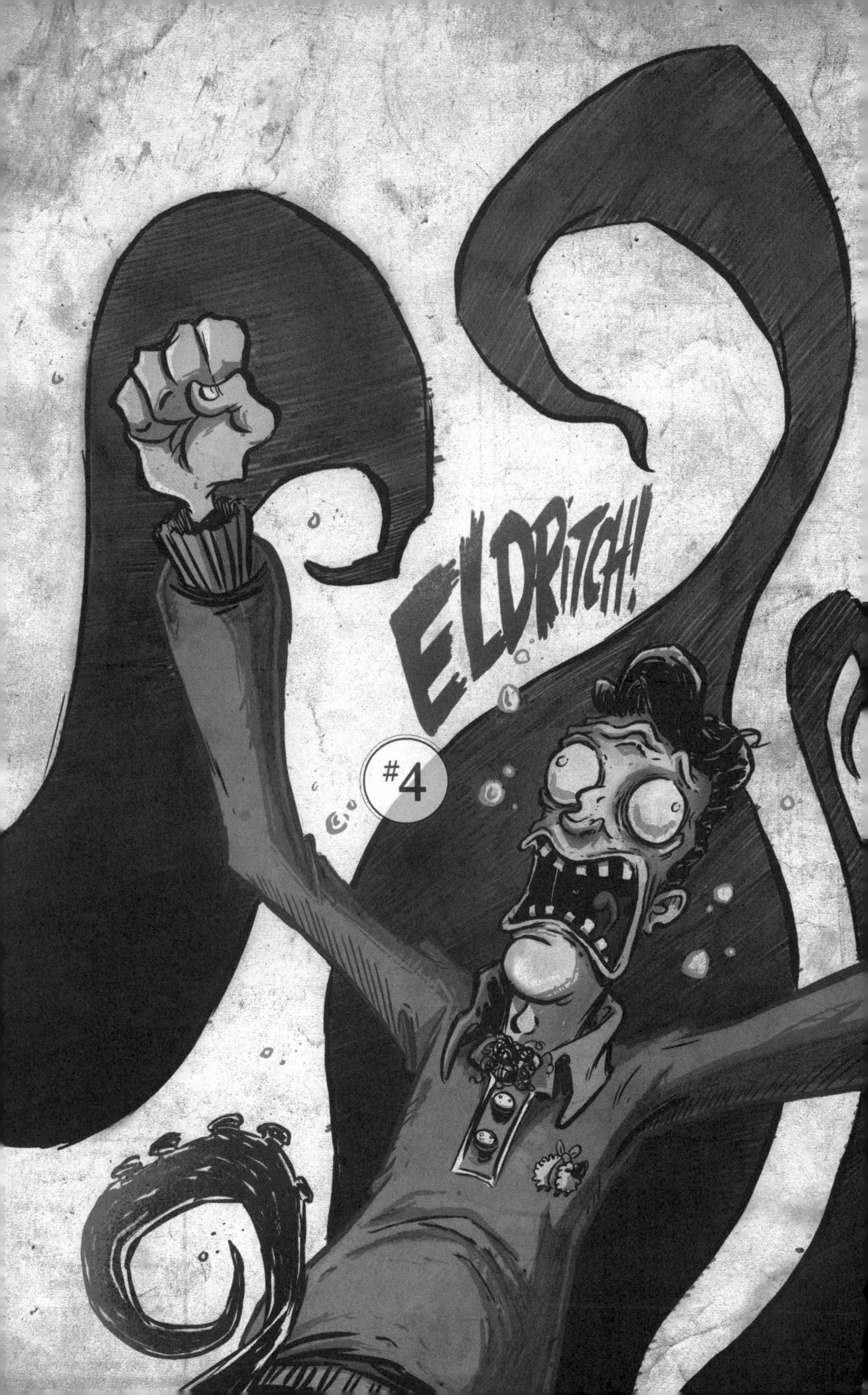
ELDRITCH!
#4

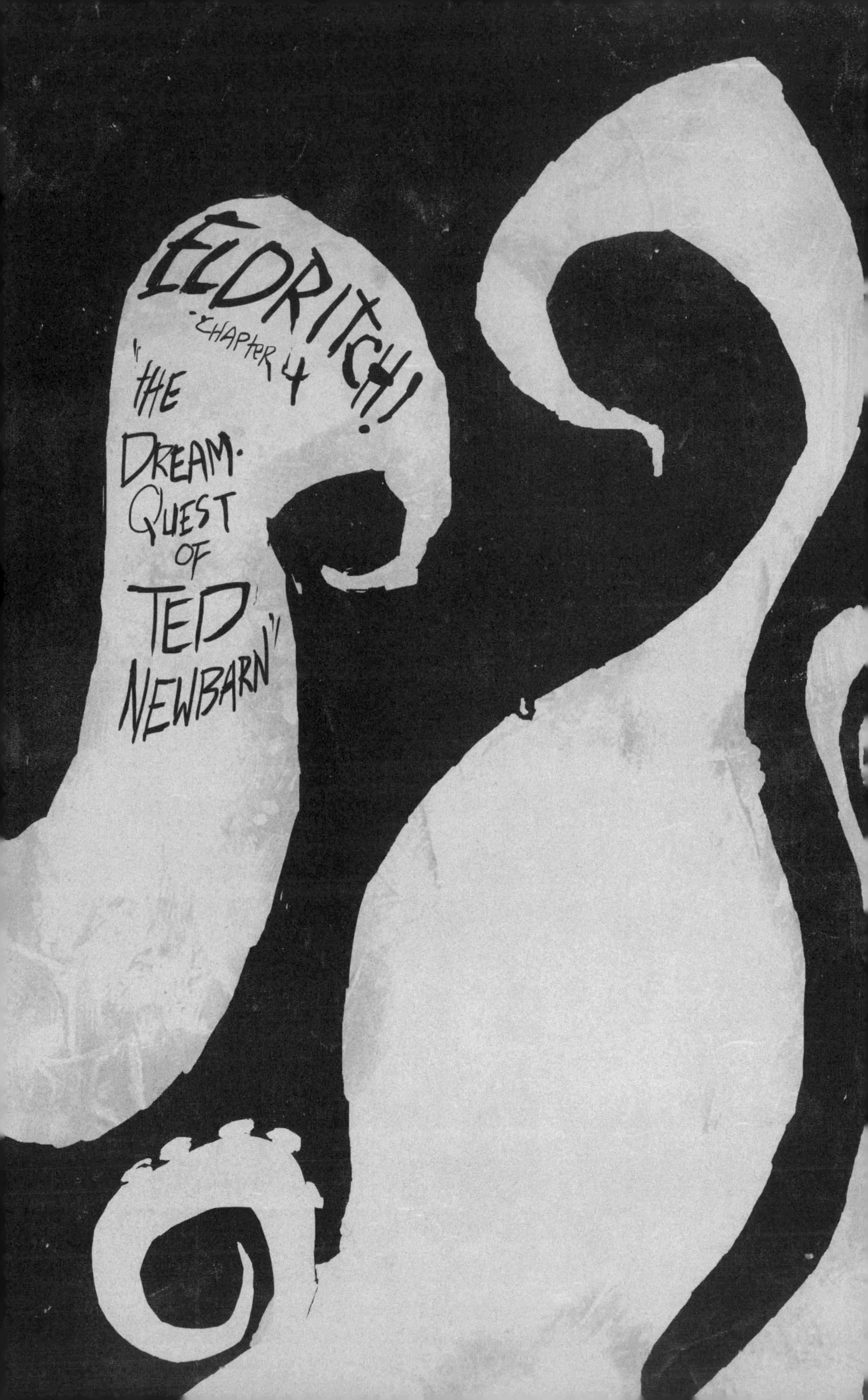
ELDRITCH!
CHAPTER 4
"THE
DREAM-
QUEST
OF
TED
NEWBARN"

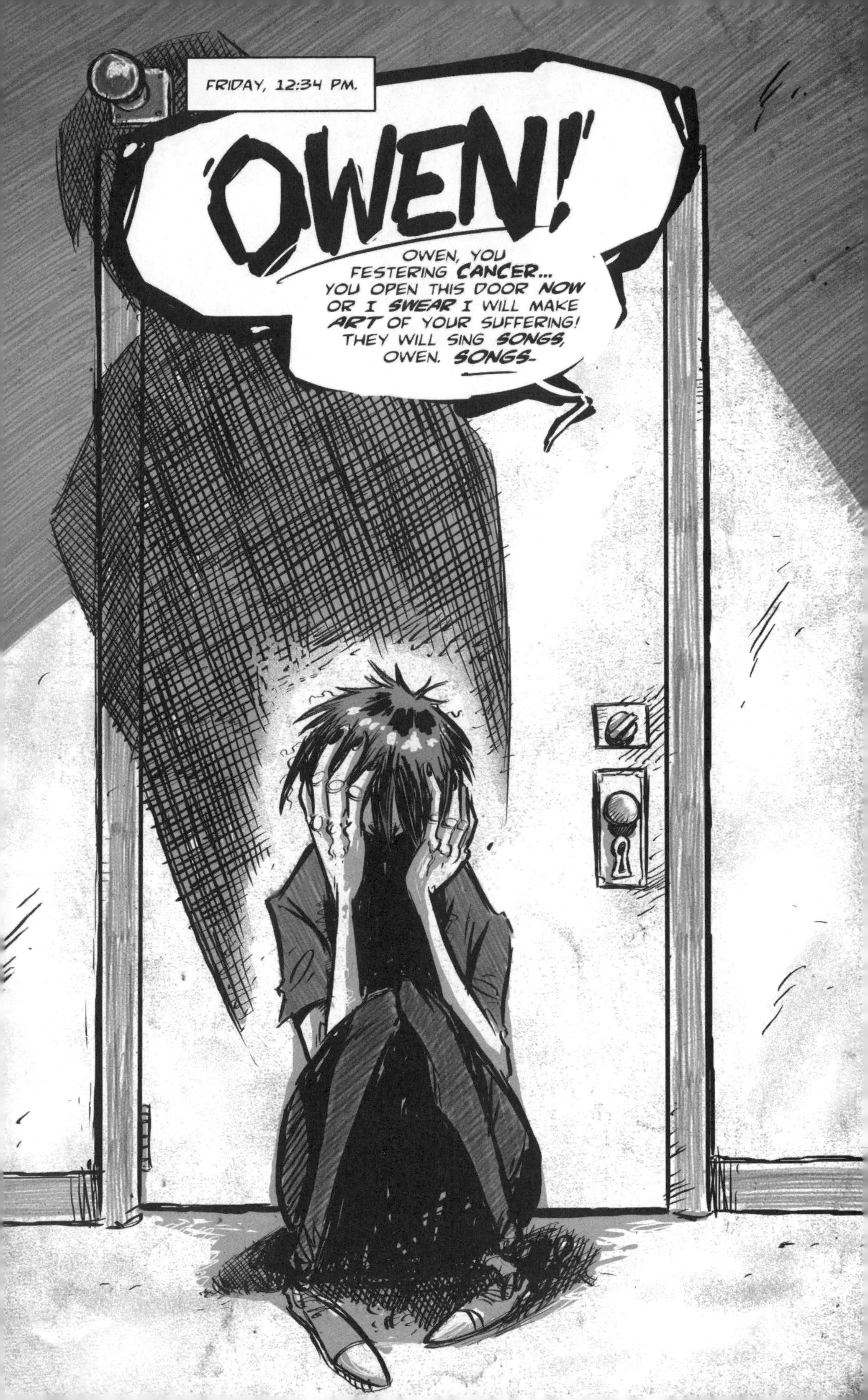
FRIDAY, 12:34 PM.
OWEN!
OWEN, YOU FESTERING CANCER... YOU OPEN THIS DOOR NOW OR I SWEAR I WILL MAKE ART OF YOUR SUFFERING! THEY WILL SING SONGS, OWEN. SONGS-

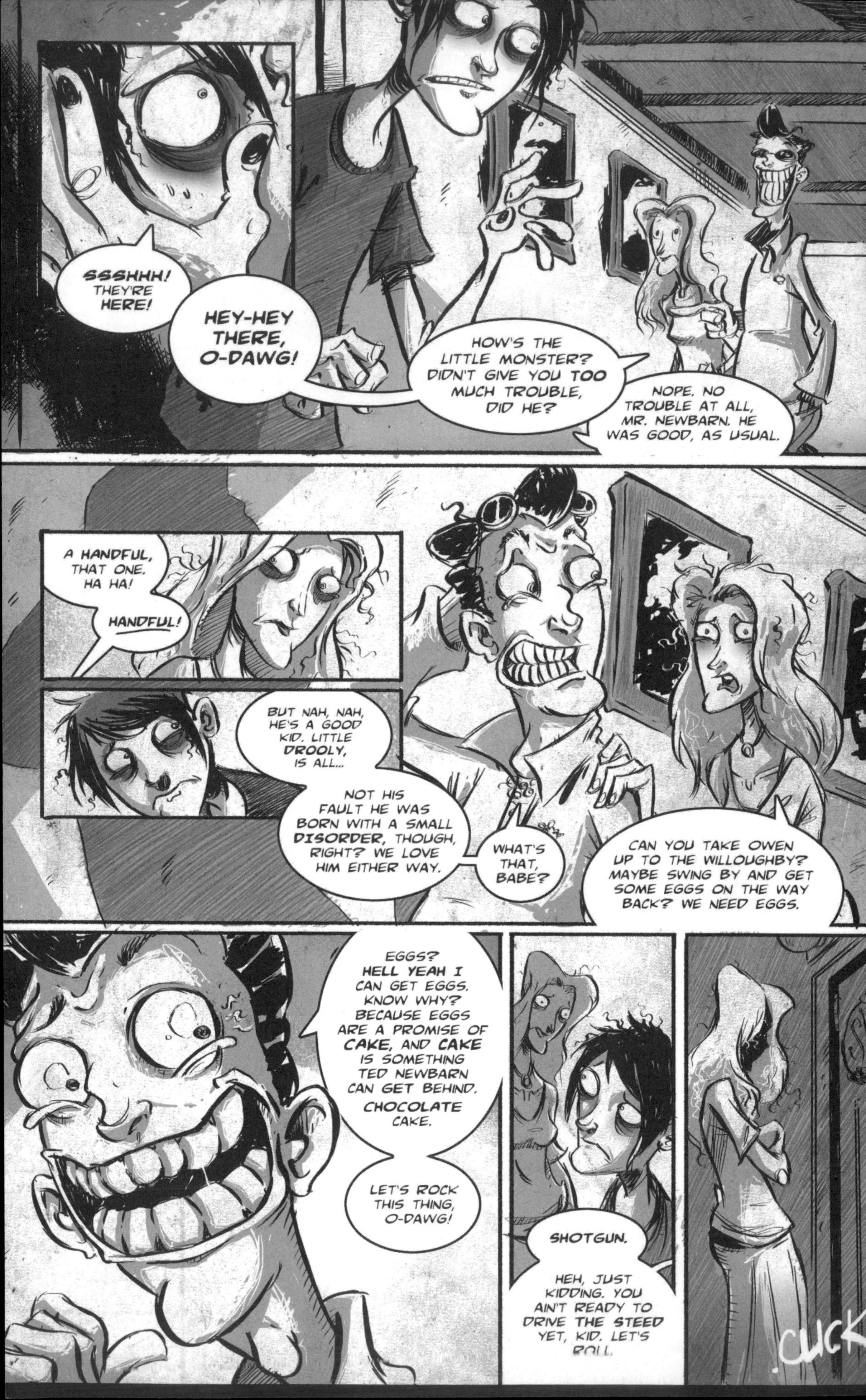
SSSHHH! THEY'RE HERE!
HEY-HEY THERE, O-DAWG!
HOW'S THE LITTLE MONSTER? DIDN'T GIVE YOU TOO MUCH TROUBLE, DID HE?
NOPE. NO TROUBLE AT ALL, MR. NEWBARN. HE WAS GOOD, AS USUAL.
A HANDFUL, THAT ONE. HA HA!
HANDFUL!
BUT NAH, NAH, HE'S A GOOD KID. LITTLE DROOLY, IS ALL...
NOT HIS FAULT HE WAS BORN WITH A SMALL DISORDER, THOUGH, RIGHT? WE LOVE HIM EITHER WAY.
WHAT'S THAT, BABE?
CAN YOU TAKE OWEN UP TO THE WILLOUGHBY? MAYBE SWING BY AND GET SOME EGGS ON THE WAY BACK? WE NEED EGGS.
EGGS? HELL YEAH I CAN GET EGGS. KNOW WHY? BECAUSE EGGS ARE A PROMISE OF CAKE, AND CAKE IS SOMETHING TED NEWBARN CAN GET BEHIND. CHOCOLATE CAKE.
LET'S ROCK THIS THING, O-DAWG!
SHOTGUN.
HEH, JUST KIDDING. YOU AIN'T READY TO DRIVE THE STEED YET, KID. LET'S ROLL.
CLICK

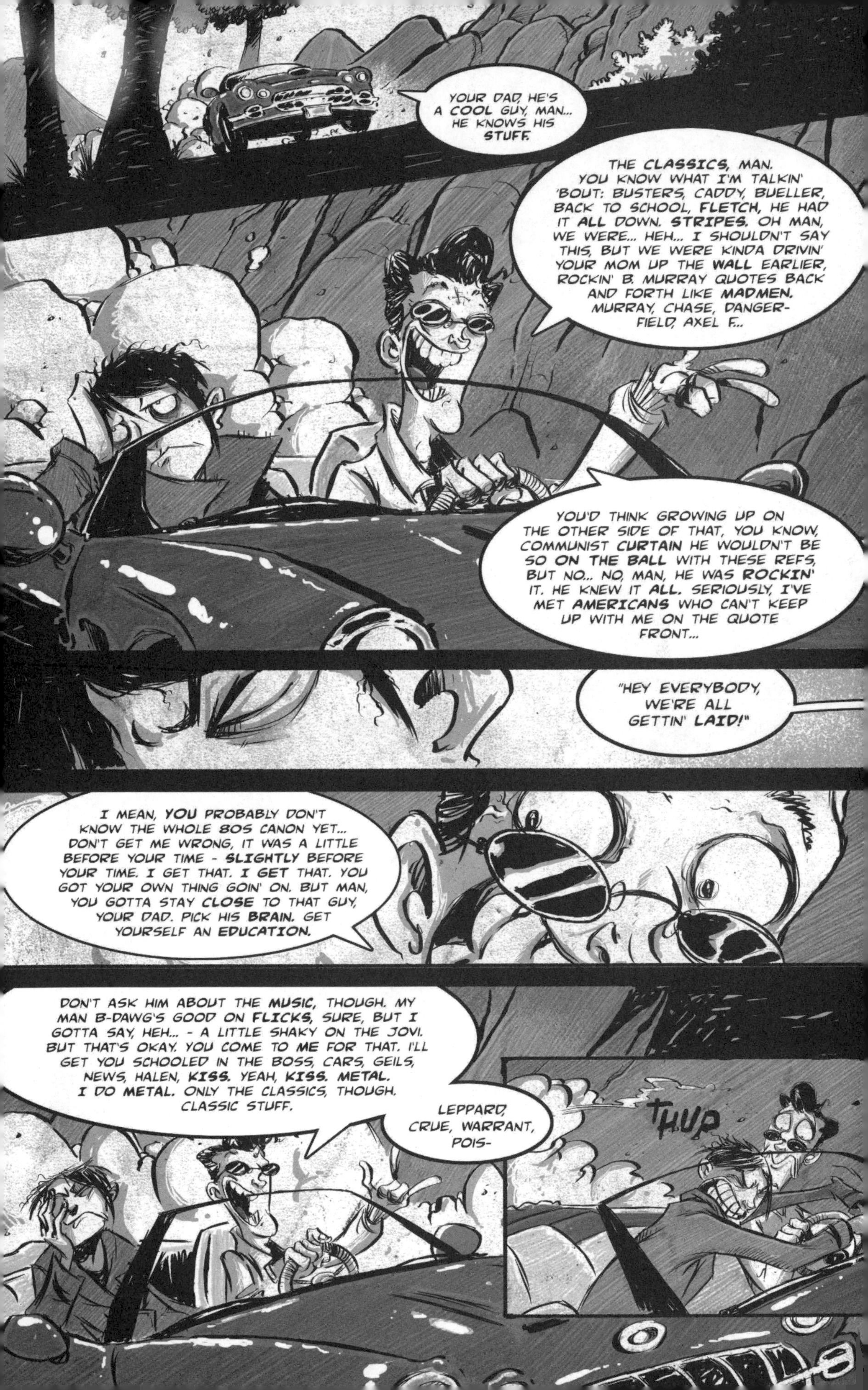
YOUR DAD, HE'S A COOL GUY, MAN... HE KNOWS HIS STUFF.
THE CLASSICS, MAN. YOU KNOW WHAT I'M TALKIN' 'BOUT: BUSTERS, CADDY, BUELLER, BACK TO SCHOOL, FLETCH, HE HAD IT ALL DOWN. STRIPES. OH MAN, WE WERE... HEH... I SHOULDN'T SAY THIS, BUT WE WERE KINDA DRIVIN' YOUR MOM UP THE WALL EARLIER, ROCKIN' B. MURRAY QUOTES BACK AND FORTH LIKE MADMEN. MURRAY, CHASE, DANGER-FIELD, AXEL F...
YOU'D THINK GROWING UP ON THE OTHER SIDE OF THAT, YOU KNOW, COMMUNIST CURTAIN HE WOULDN'T BE SO ON THE BALL WITH THESE REFS, BUT NO... NO, MAN, HE WAS ROCKIN' IT. HE KNEW IT ALL. SERIOUSLY, I'VE MET AMERICANS WHO CAN'T KEEP UP WITH ME ON THE QUOTE FRONT...
"HEY EVERYBODY, WE'RE ALL GETTIN' LAID!"
I MEAN, YOU PROBABLY DON'T KNOW THE WHOLE 80S CANON YET... DON'T GET ME WRONG, IT WAS A LITTLE BEFORE YOUR TIME - SLIGHTLY BEFORE YOUR TIME. I GET THAT. I GET THAT. YOU GOT YOUR OWN THING GOIN' ON. BUT MAN, YOU GOTTA STAY CLOSE TO THAT GUY, YOUR DAD. PICK HIS BRAIN. GET YOURSELF AN EDUCATION.
DON'T ASK HIM ABOUT THE MUSIC, THOUGH. MY MAN B-DAWG'S GOOD ON FLICKS, SURE, BUT I GOTTA SAY, HEH... - A LITTLE SHAKY ON THE JOVI. BUT THAT'S OKAY. YOU COME TO ME FOR THAT. I'LL GET YOU SCHOOLED IN THE BOSS, CARS, GEILS, NEWS, HALEN, KISS. YEAH, KISS. METAL. I DO METAL. ONLY THE CLASSICS, THOUGH. CLASSIC STUFF.
LEPPARD, CRUE, WARRANT, POIS-
THUP

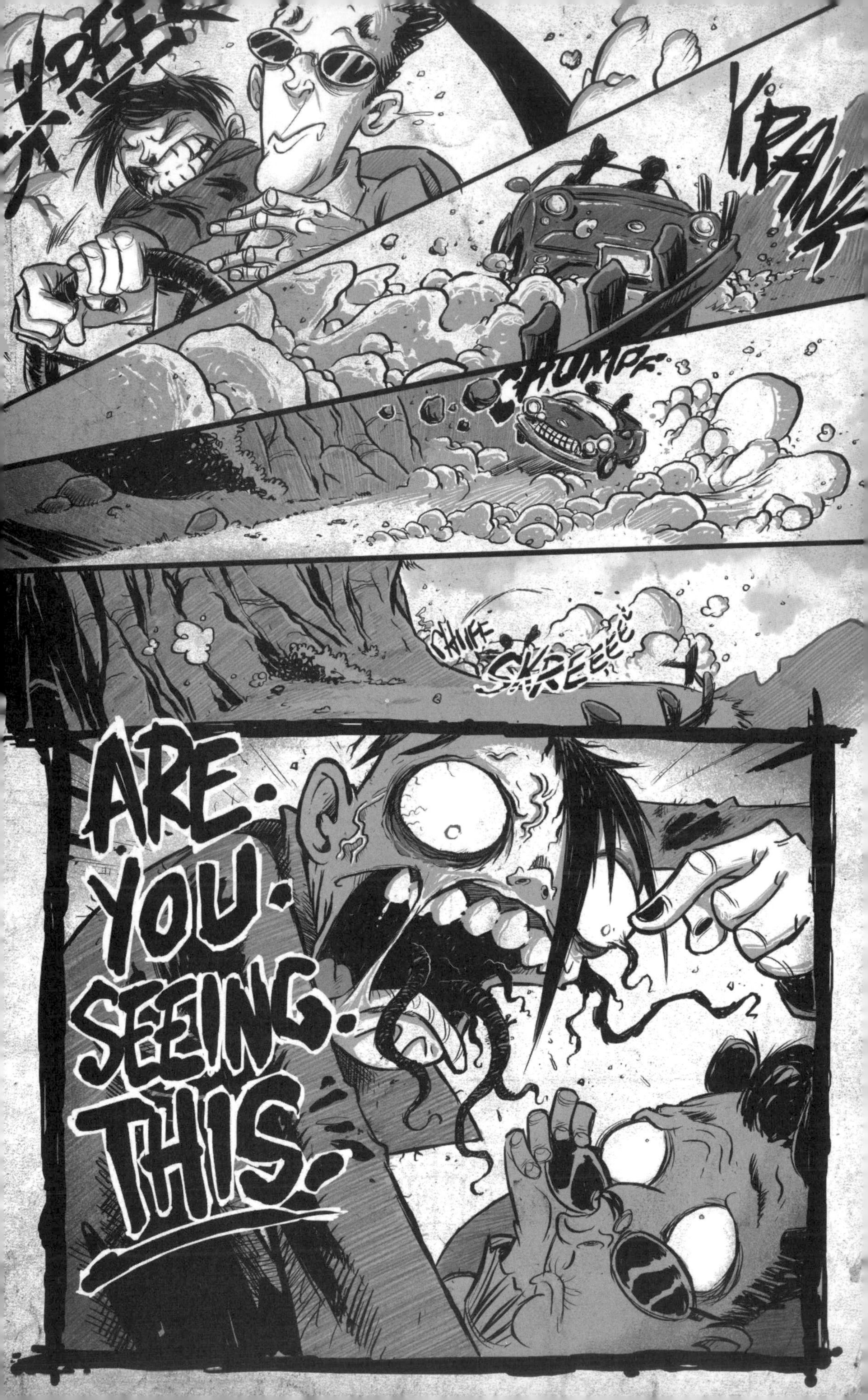
KRANK
CHUMPF
CHUFF
SKREEEEEE
ARE. YOU. SEEING. THIS.

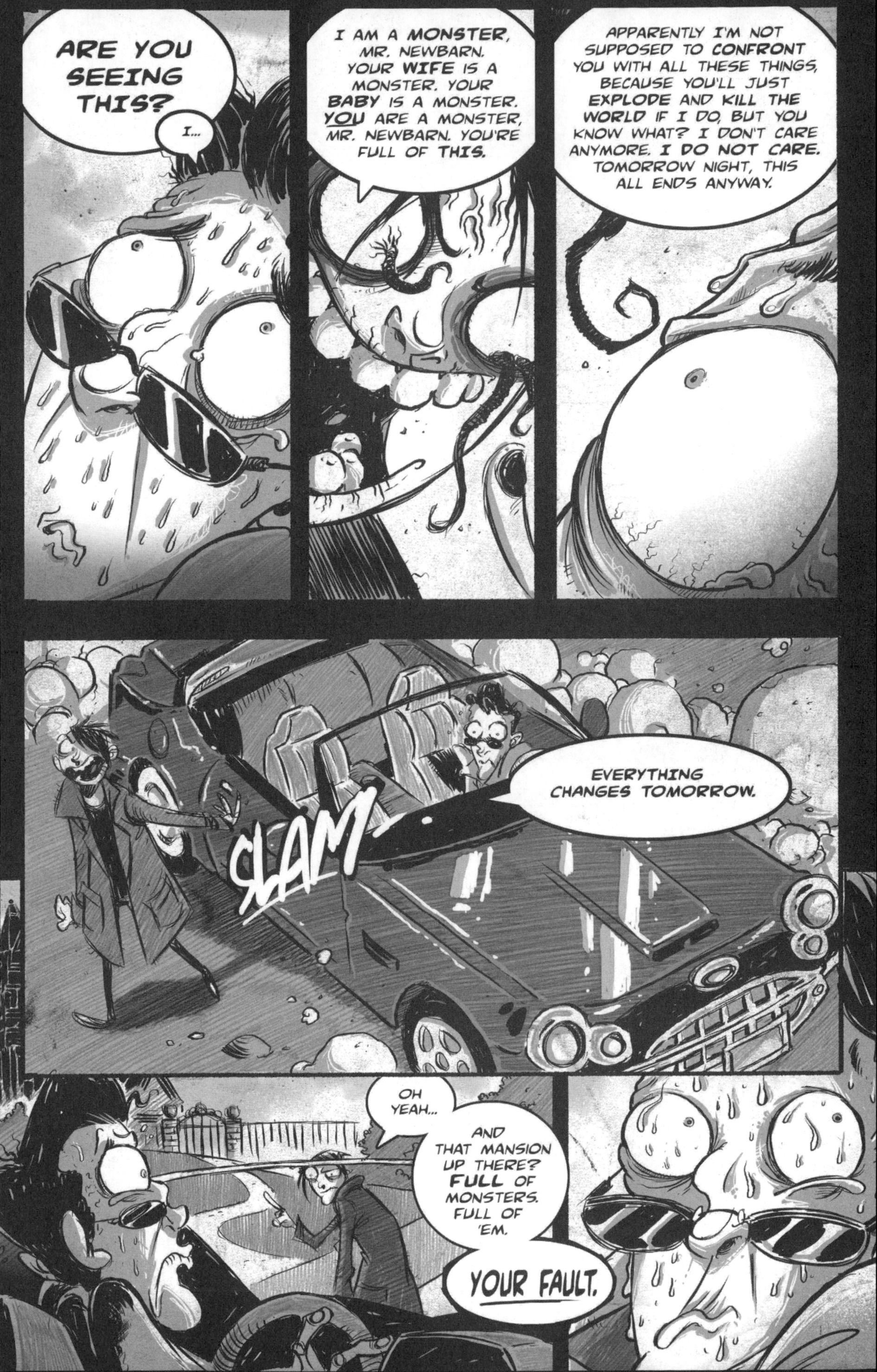
ARE YOU SEEING THIS?
I...
I AM A MONSTER, MR. NEWBARN. YOUR WIFE IS A MONSTER. YOUR BABY IS A MONSTER. YOU ARE A MONSTER, MR. NEWBARN. YOU'RE FULL OF THIS.
APPARENTLY I'M NOT SUPPOSED TO CONFRONT YOU WITH ALL THESE THINGS, BECAUSE YOU'LL JUST EXPLODE AND KILL THE WORLD IF I DO, BUT YOU KNOW WHAT? I DON'T CARE ANYMORE. I DO NOT CARE. TOMORROW NIGHT, THIS ALL ENDS ANYWAY.
EVERYTHING CHANGES TOMORROW.
SLAM
OH YEAH...
AND THAT MANSION UP THERE? FULL OF MONSTERS. FULL OF 'EM.
YOUR FAULT.

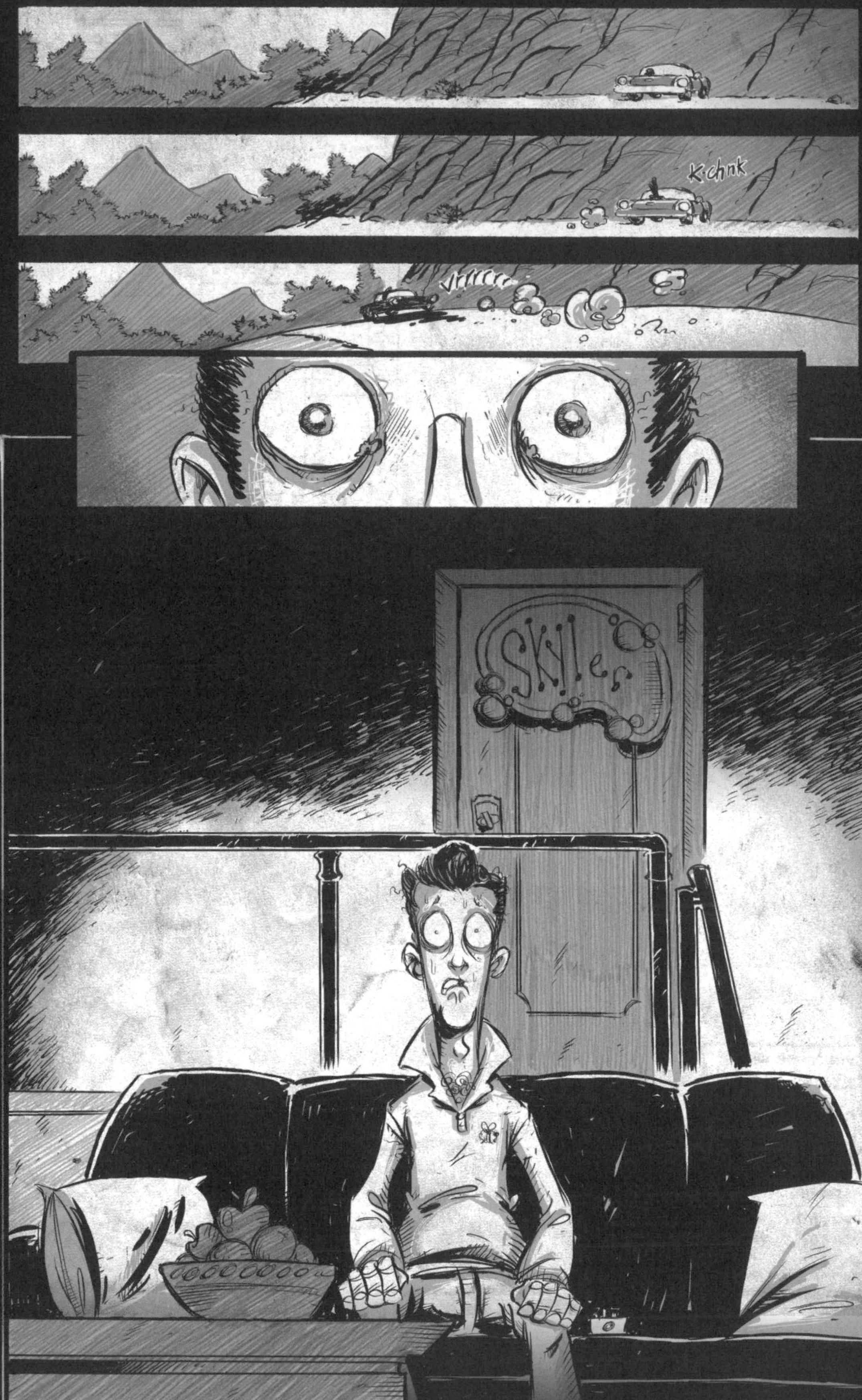
K·chnk
Vrrrrrr

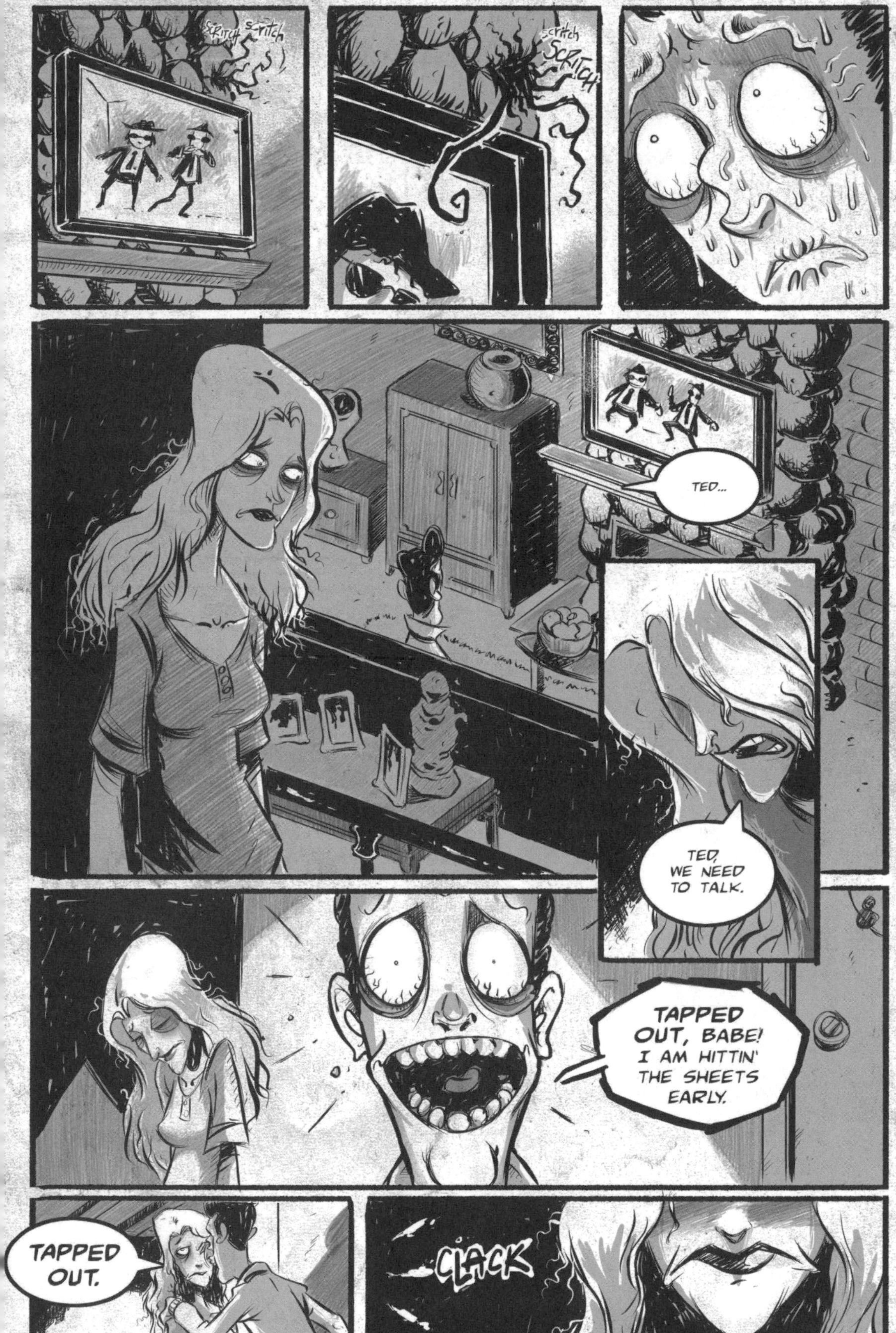

SCRITCH SCRITCH
SCRITCH SCRITCH
TED...
TED, WE NEED TO TALK.
TAPPED OUT, BABE! I AM HITTIN' THE SHEETS EARLY.
TAPPED OUT.
CLACK

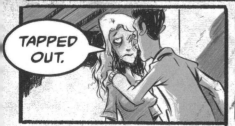

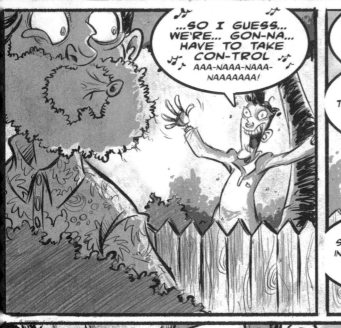

...SO I GUESS... WE'RE... GON-NA... HAVE TO TAKE CON-TROL ♪♪ AAA-NAAA-NAAA-NAAAAAAA!

BOBBY BROWN. 'BUSTERS 2 SOUND-TRACK. CLASSIC. HOW'S IT HANGIN', HOSER?

OH! HI, TED! YES, I WATCH THE MOVIE AGAIN LAST NIGHT. VERY GOOD.

AN UNDERRATED GEM. SIGOURNEY IS SMOKIN' IN THAT. SMOKIN'. EVEN AFTER HAVING THAT KID. UNBELIEVABLE.

YEAH! OKAY!

HEY-HEY, LISTEN... I JUST WANTED TO, UH, STOP ON BY AND MAKE SURE, Y'KNOW... WELL, THE WIFE WAS A LITTLE WORRIED ABOUT YOUR, UH... YOUR DAUGHTER LAST NIGHT...

EVERYTHING ALL, UH... RIGHT... THERE?

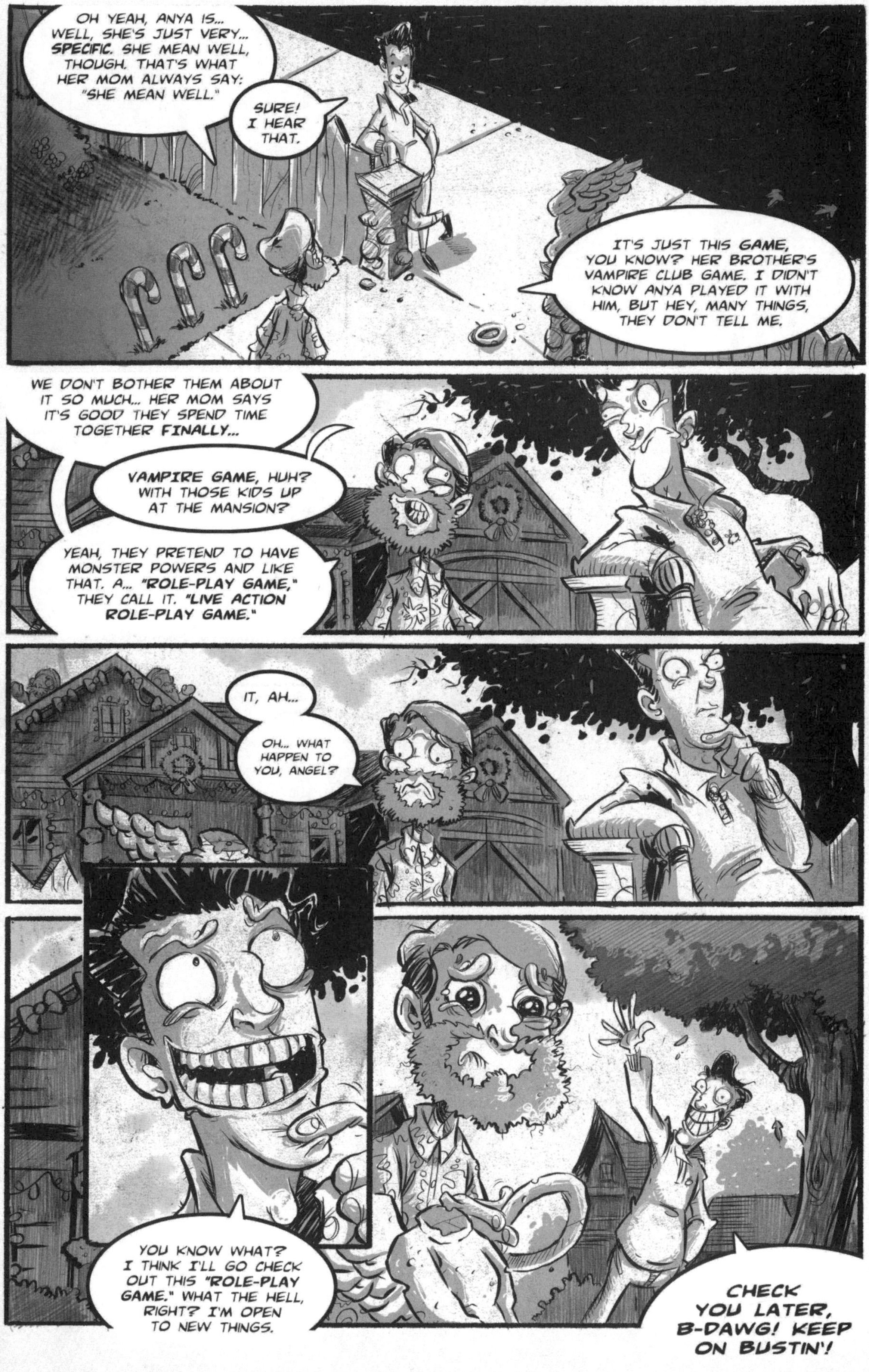
OH YEAH, ANYA IS... WELL, SHE'S JUST VERY... SPECIFIC. SHE MEAN WELL, THOUGH. THAT'S WHAT HER MOM ALWAYS SAY: "SHE MEAN WELL."
SURE! I HEAR THAT.
IT'S JUST THIS GAME, YOU KNOW? HER BROTHER'S VAMPIRE CLUB GAME. I DIDN'T KNOW ANYA PLAYED IT WITH HIM, BUT HEY, MANY THINGS, THEY DON'T TELL ME.
WE DON'T BOTHER THEM ABOUT IT SO MUCH... HER MOM SAYS IT'S GOOD THEY SPEND TIME TOGETHER FINALLY...
VAMPIRE GAME, HUH? WITH THOSE KIDS UP AT THE MANSION?
YEAH, THEY PRETEND TO HAVE MONSTER POWERS AND LIKE THAT. A... "ROLE-PLAY GAME," THEY CALL IT. "LIVE ACTION ROLE-PLAY GAME."
IT, AH...
OH... WHAT HAPPEN TO YOU, ANGEL?
YOU KNOW WHAT? I THINK I'LL GO CHECK OUT THIS "ROLE-PLAY GAME." WHAT THE HELL, RIGHT? I'M OPEN TO NEW THINGS.
CHECK YOU LATER, B-DAWG! KEEP ON BUSTIN'!

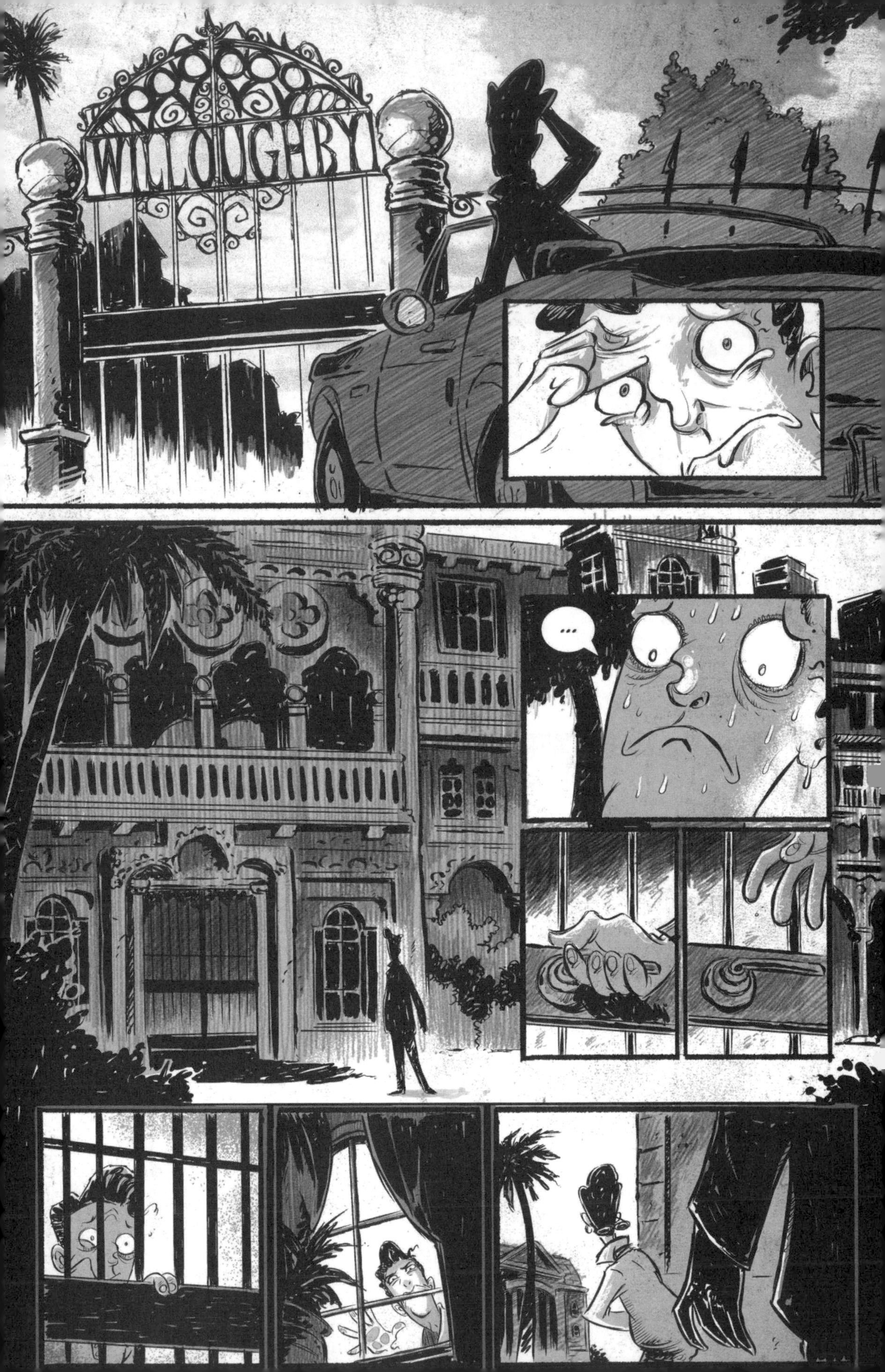
WILLOUGHBY
...

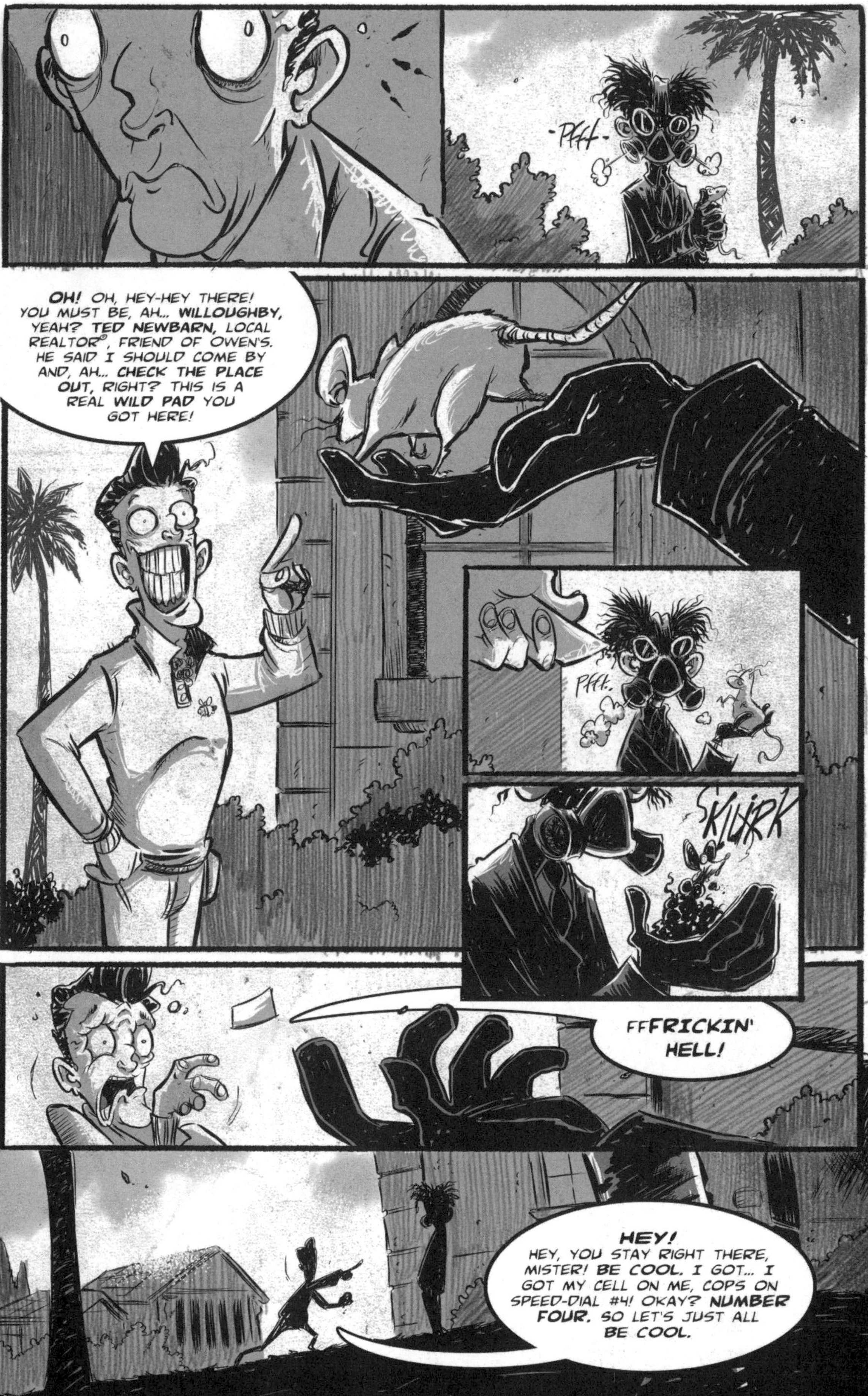
-PFFT-
OH! OH, HEY-HEY THERE! YOU MUST BE, AH... WILLOUGHBY, YEAH? TED NEWBARN, LOCAL REALTOR®, FRIEND OF OWEN'S. HE SAID I SHOULD COME BY AND, AH... CHECK THE PLACE OUT, RIGHT? THIS IS A REAL WILD PAD YOU GOT HERE!
PFFT.
KLURK
FFFRICKIN' HELL!
HEY! HEY, YOU STAY RIGHT THERE, MISTER! BE COOL. I GOT... I GOT MY CELL ON ME, COPS ON SPEED-DIAL #4! OKAY? NUMBER FOUR. SO LET'S JUST ALL BE COOL.

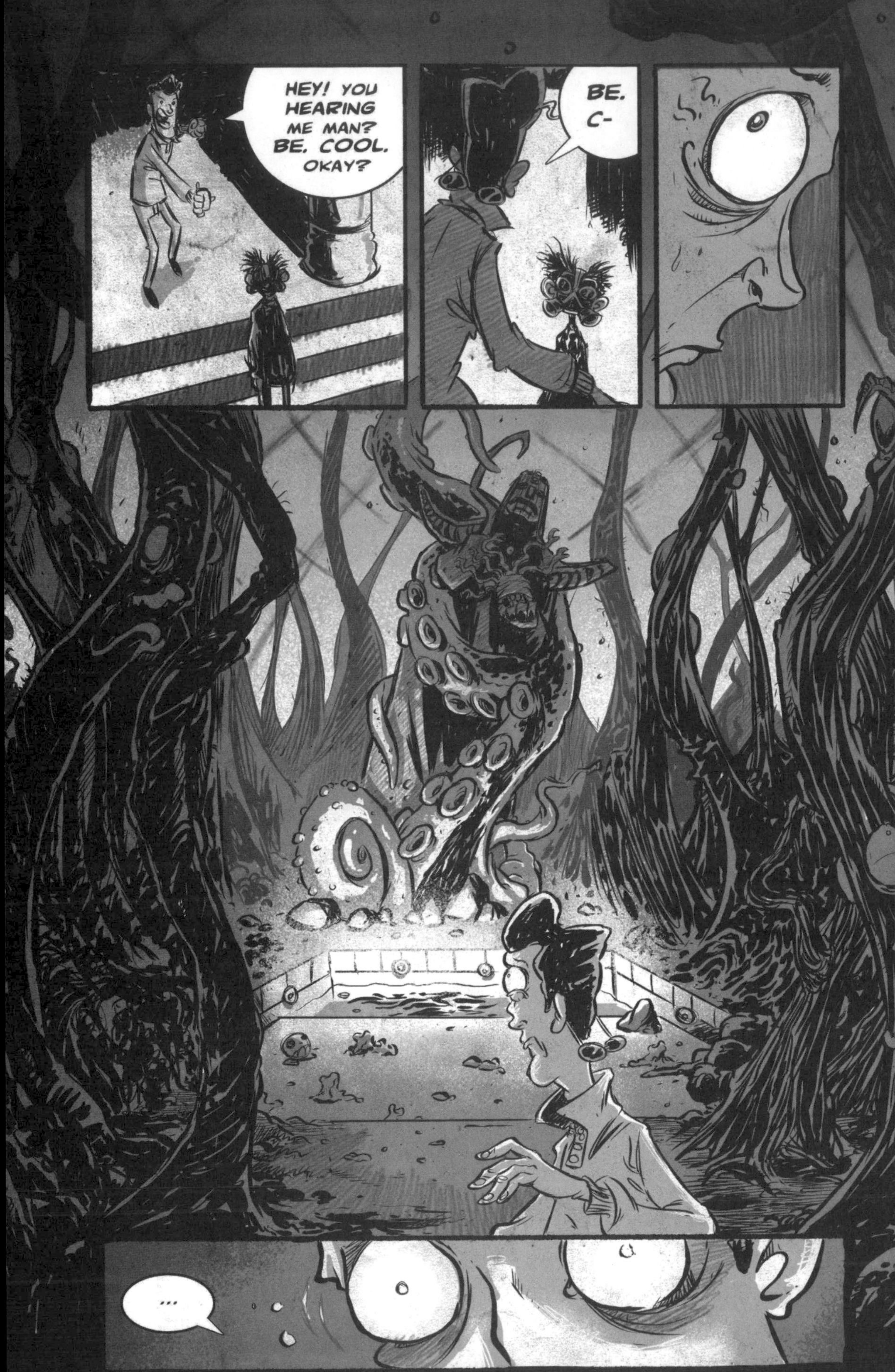
HEY! YOU HEARING ME MAN? BE. COOL. OKAY?
BE. C-
...

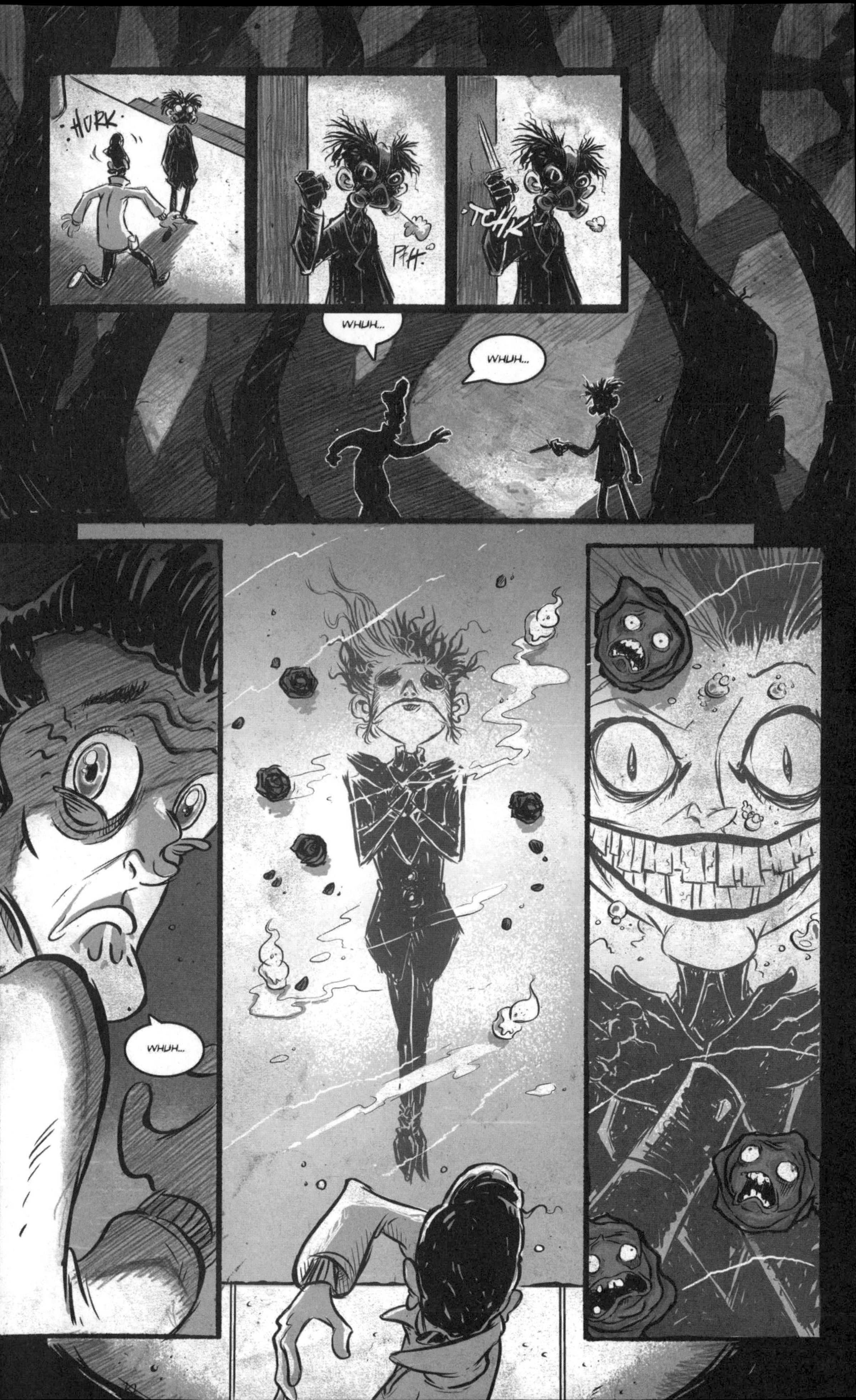
HORK
PFH.
TCHK
WHUH...
WHUH...
WHUH...

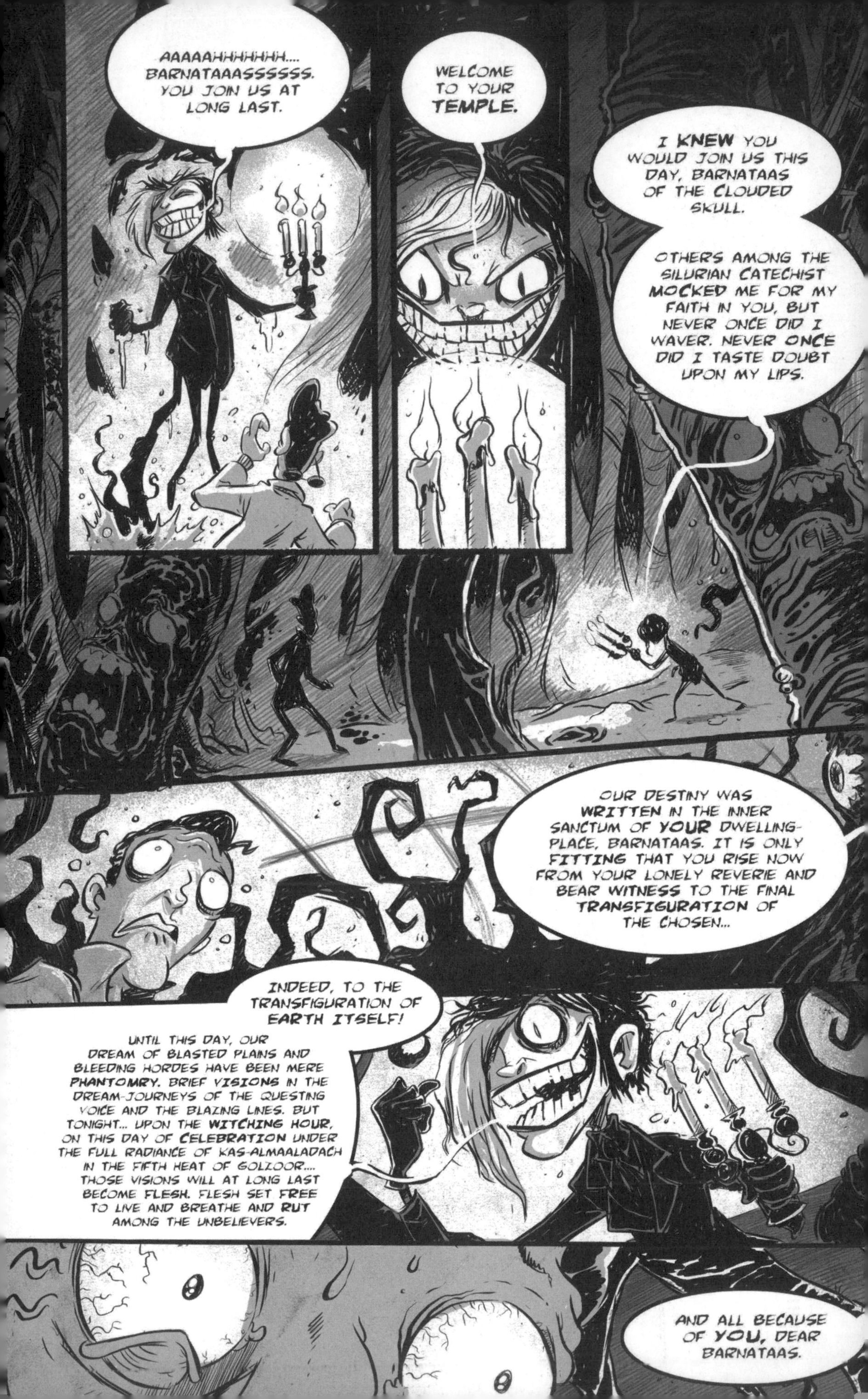
AAAAAHHHHHHH.... BARNATAAASSSSSS. YOU JOIN US AT LONG LAST.
WELCOME TO YOUR TEMPLE.
I KNEW YOU WOULD JOIN US THIS DAY, BARNATAAS OF THE CLOUDED SKULL.
OTHERS AMONG THE SILURIAN CATECHIST MOCKED ME FOR MY FAITH IN YOU, BUT NEVER ONCE DID I WAVER. NEVER ONCE DID I TASTE DOUBT UPON MY LIPS.
OUR DESTINY WAS WRITTEN IN THE INNER SANCTUM OF YOUR DWELLING-PLACE, BARNATAAS. IT IS ONLY FITTING THAT YOU RISE NOW FROM YOUR LONELY REVERIE AND BEAR WITNESS TO THE FINAL TRANSFIGURATION OF THE CHOSEN...
INDEED, TO THE TRANSFIGURATION OF EARTH ITSELF!
UNTIL THIS DAY, OUR DREAM OF BLASTED PLAINS AND BLEEDING HORDES HAVE BEEN MERE PHANTOMRY. BRIEF VISIONS IN THE DREAM-JOURNEYS OF THE QUESTING VOICE AND THE BLAZING LINES. BUT TONIGHT... UPON THE WITCHING HOUR, ON THIS DAY OF CELEBRATION UNDER THE FULL RADIANCE OF KAS-ALMAALADACH IN THE FIFTH HEAT OF GOLZOOR.... THOSE VISIONS WILL AT LONG LAST BECOME FLESH. FLESH SET FREE TO LIVE AND BREATHE AND RUT AMONG THE UNBELIEVERS.
AND ALL BECAUSE OF YOU, DEAR BARNATAAS.

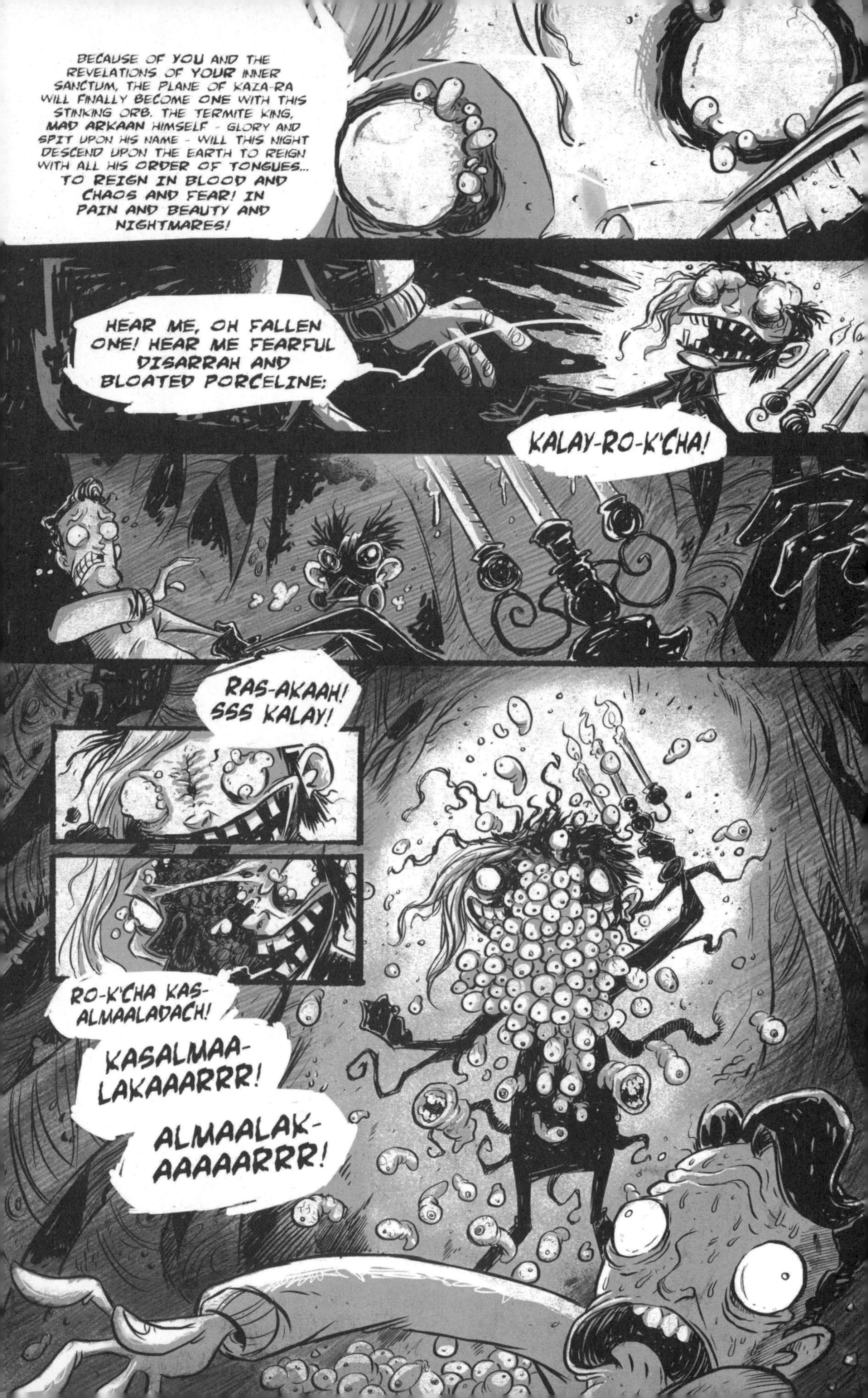
BECAUSE OF YOU AND THE REVELATIONS OF YOUR INNER SANCTUM, THE PLANE OF KAZA-RA WILL FINALLY BECOME ONE WITH THIS STINKING ORB. THE TERMITE KING, MAD ARKAAN HIMSELF - GLORY AND SPIT UPON HIS NAME - WILL THIS NIGHT DESCEND UPON THE EARTH TO REIGN WITH ALL HIS ORDER OF TONGUES... TO REIGN IN BLOOD AND CHAOS AND FEAR! IN PAIN AND BEAUTY AND NIGHTMARES!
HEAR ME, OH FALLEN ONE! HEAR ME FEARFUL DISARRAH AND BLOATED PORCELINE:
KALAY-RO-K'CHA!
RAS-AKAAH! SSS KALAY!
RO-K'CHA KAS-ALMAALADACH!
KASALMAA-LAKAAARRR!
ALMAALAK-AAAAARRR!

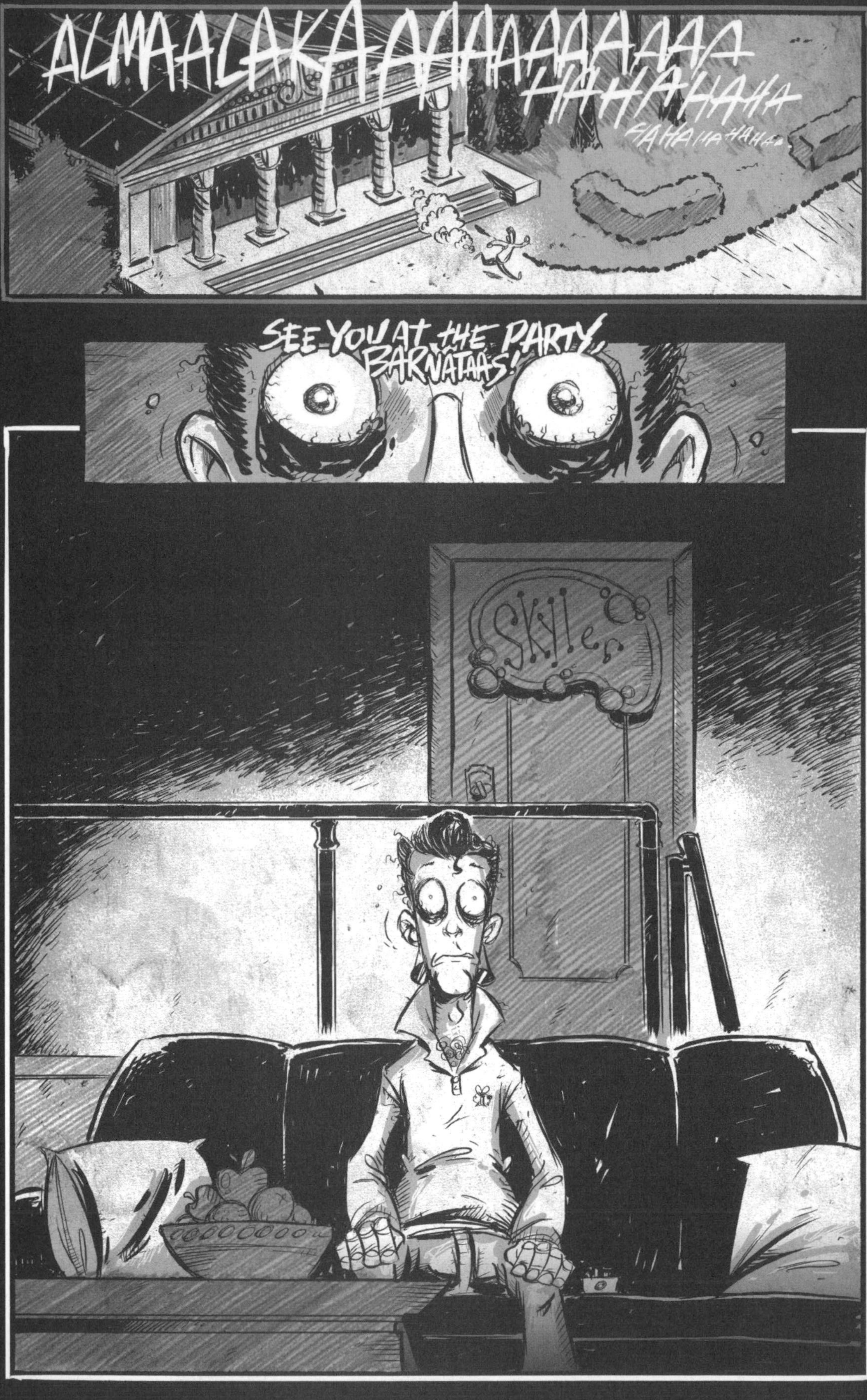
ALMAALAKAAAAAAAAAAA HAHAHAHAHA HAHAHAHAHA
SEE YOU AT THE PARTY, BARNATAAS!
SKYLER

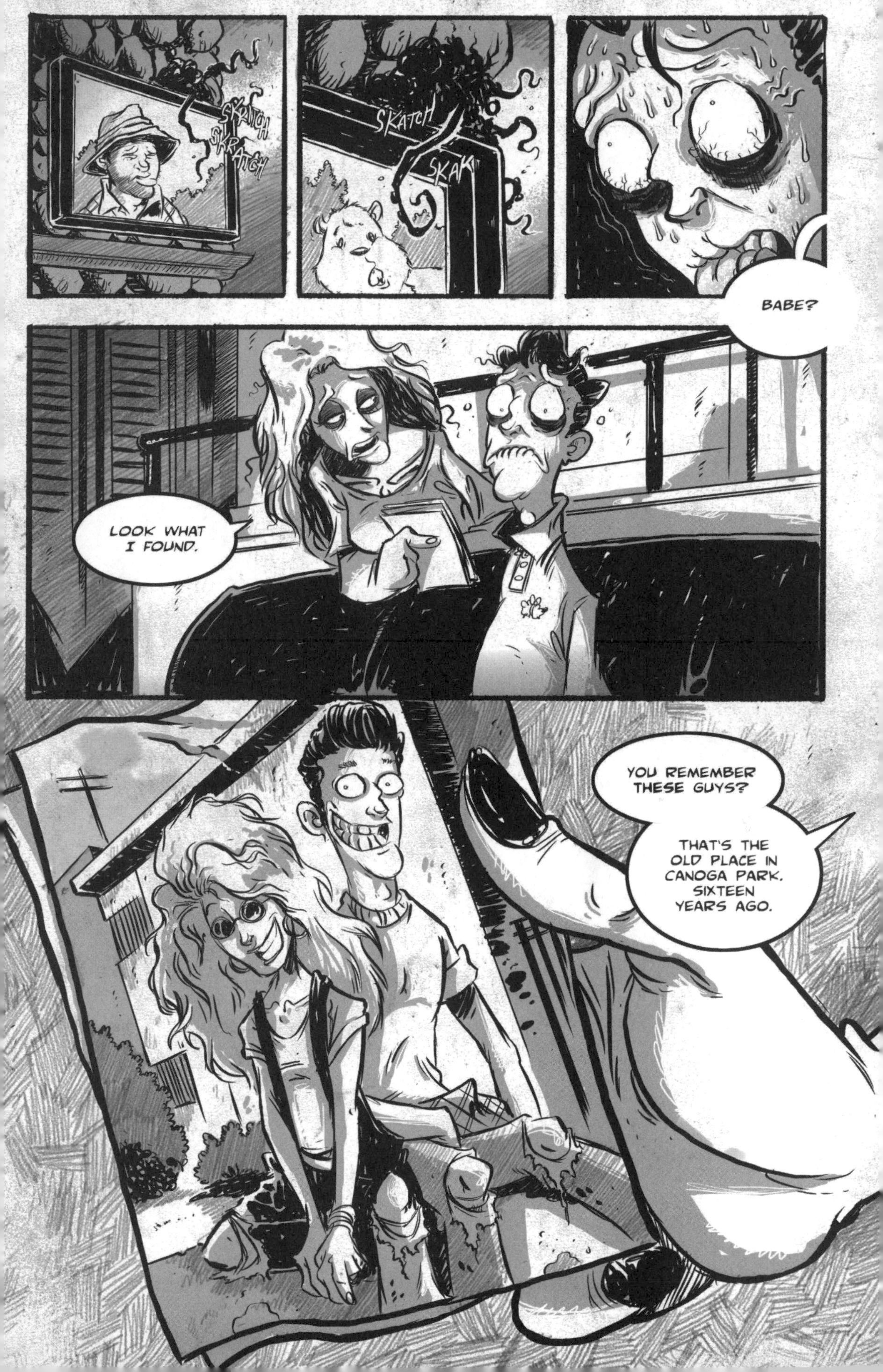
SKRATCH SKRATCH
SKATCH SKAK
BABE?
LOOK WHAT I FOUND.
YOU REMEMBER THESE GUYS?
THAT'S THE OLD PLACE IN CANOGA PARK. SIXTEEN YEARS AGO.

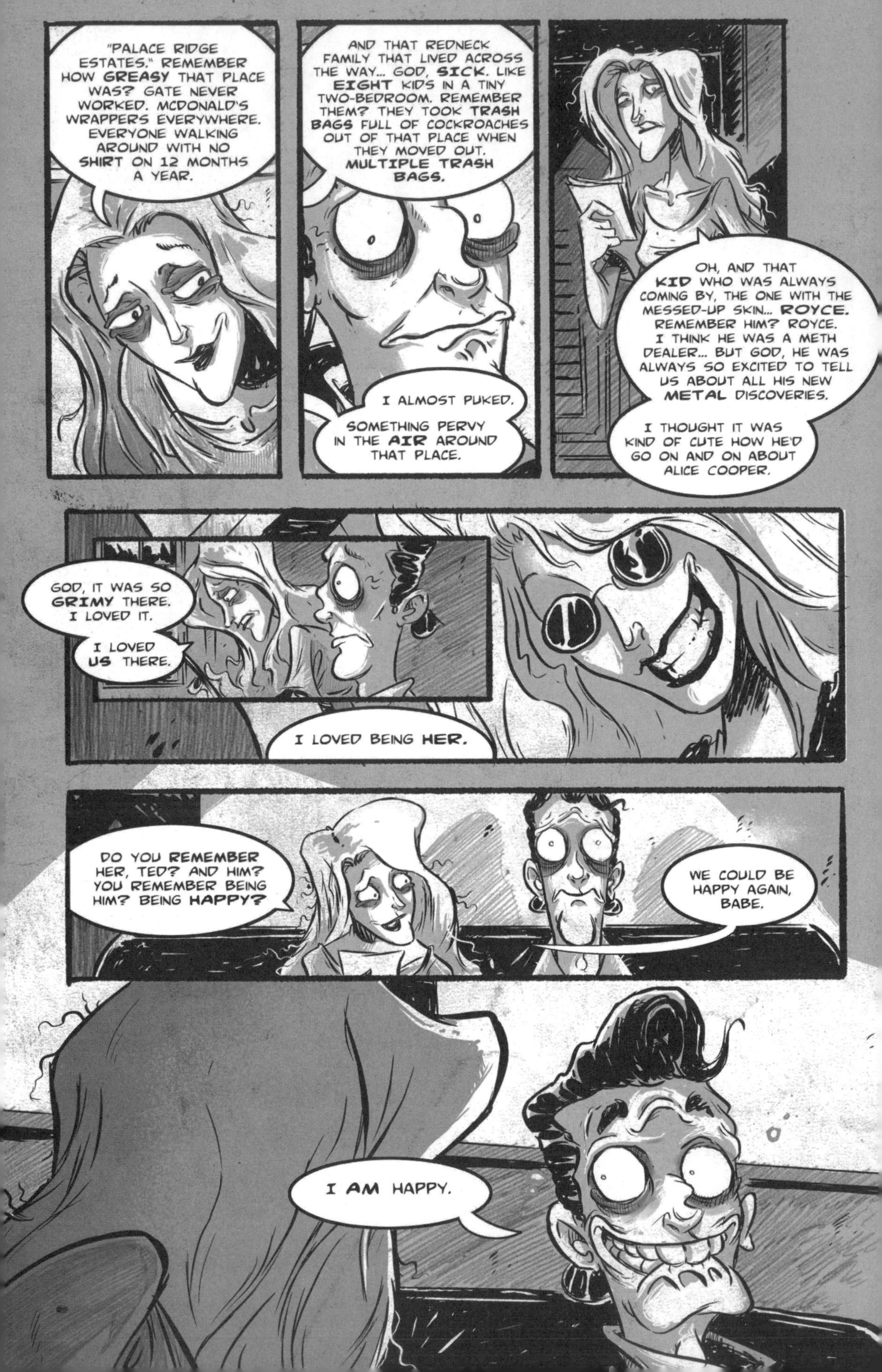
"PALACE RIDGE ESTATES." REMEMBER HOW GREASY THAT PLACE WAS? GATE NEVER WORKED. MCDONALD'S WRAPPERS EVERYWHERE. EVERYONE WALKING AROUND WITH NO SHIRT ON 12 MONTHS A YEAR.
AND THAT REDNECK FAMILY THAT LIVED ACROSS THE WAY... GOD, SICK. LIKE EIGHT KIDS IN A TINY TWO-BEDROOM. REMEMBER THEM? THEY TOOK TRASH BAGS FULL OF COCKROACHES OUT OF THAT PLACE WHEN THEY MOVED OUT. MULTIPLE TRASH BAGS.
I ALMOST PUKED.
SOMETHING PERVY IN THE AIR AROUND THAT PLACE.
OH, AND THAT KID WHO WAS ALWAYS COMING BY, THE ONE WITH THE MESSED-UP SKIN... ROYCE. REMEMBER HIM? ROYCE. I THINK HE WAS A METH DEALER... BUT GOD, HE WAS ALWAYS SO EXCITED TO TELL US ABOUT ALL HIS NEW METAL DISCOVERIES.
I THOUGHT IT WAS KIND OF CUTE HOW HE'D GO ON AND ON ABOUT ALICE COOPER.
GOD, IT WAS SO GRIMY THERE. I LOVED IT.
I LOVED US THERE.
I LOVED BEING HER.
DO YOU REMEMBER HER, TED? AND HIM? YOU REMEMBER BEING HIM? BEING HAPPY?
WE COULD BE HAPPY AGAIN, BABE.
I AM HAPPY.

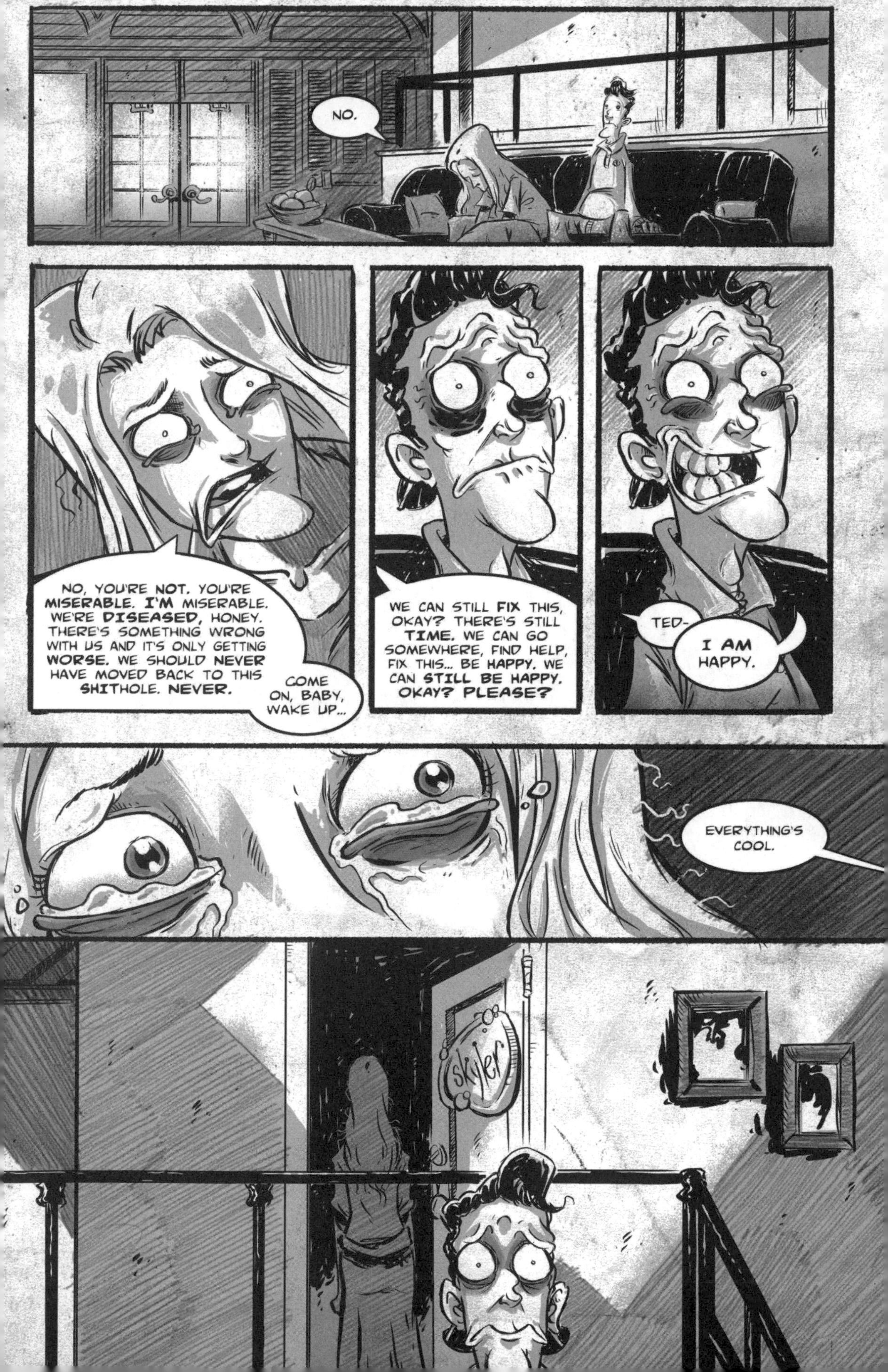
NO.
NO, YOU'RE NOT. YOU'RE MISERABLE. I'M MISERABLE. WE'RE DISEASED, HONEY. THERE'S SOMETHING WRONG WITH US AND IT'S ONLY GETTING WORSE. WE SHOULD NEVER HAVE MOVED BACK TO THIS SHITHOLE. NEVER.
COME ON, BABY, WAKE UP...
WE CAN STILL FIX THIS, OKAY? THERE'S STILL TIME. WE CAN GO SOMEWHERE, FIND HELP, FIX THIS... BE HAPPY. WE CAN STILL BE HAPPY. OKAY? PLEASE?
TED-
I AM HAPPY.
EVERYTHING'S COOL.
skyler

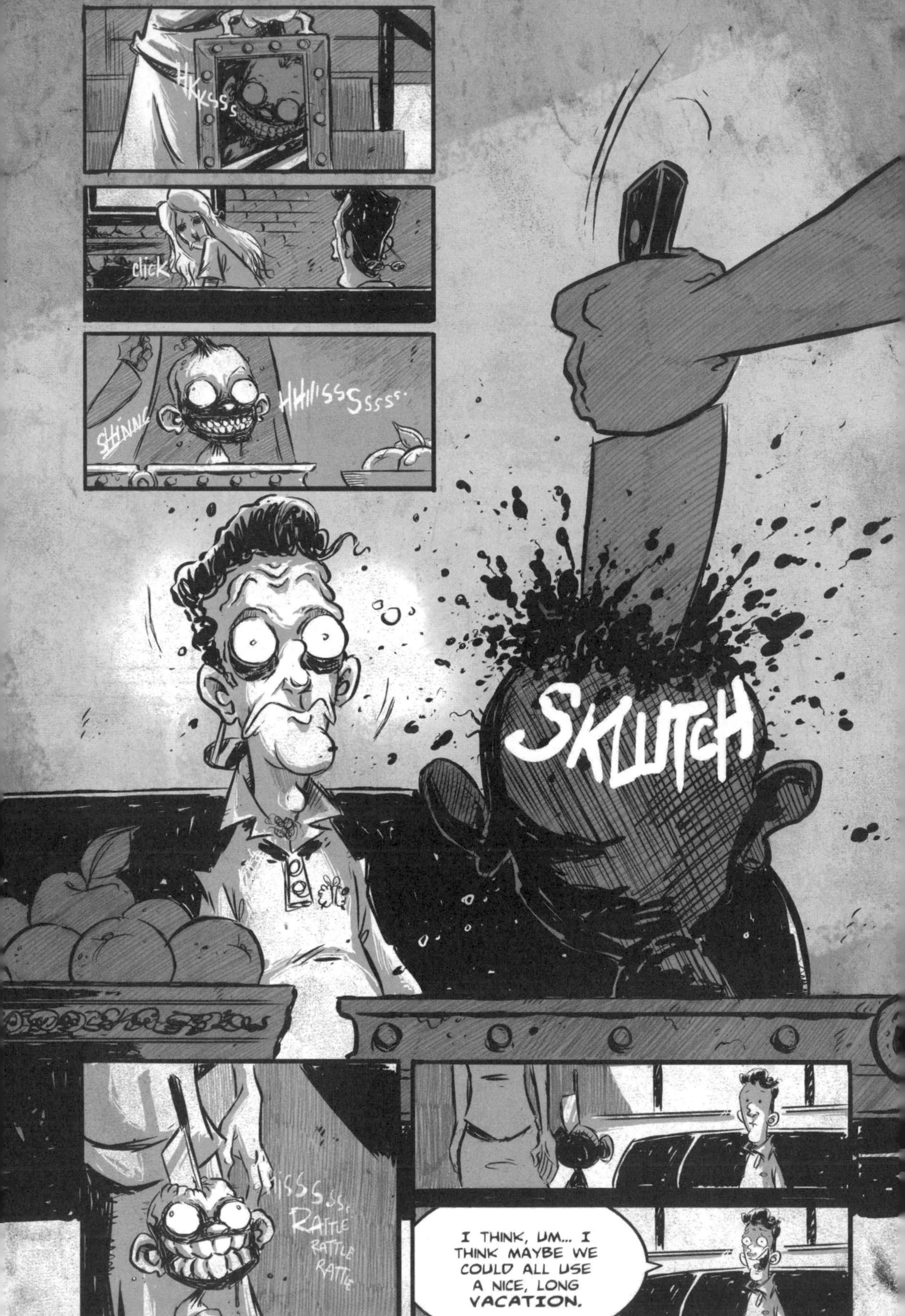

HKKSSS
click
SHING
HHISSSSSSS
SKLUTCH
HISSSSS
RATTLE
RATTLE
RATTLE
I THINK, UM... I THINK MAYBE WE COULD ALL USE A NICE, LONG VACATION.

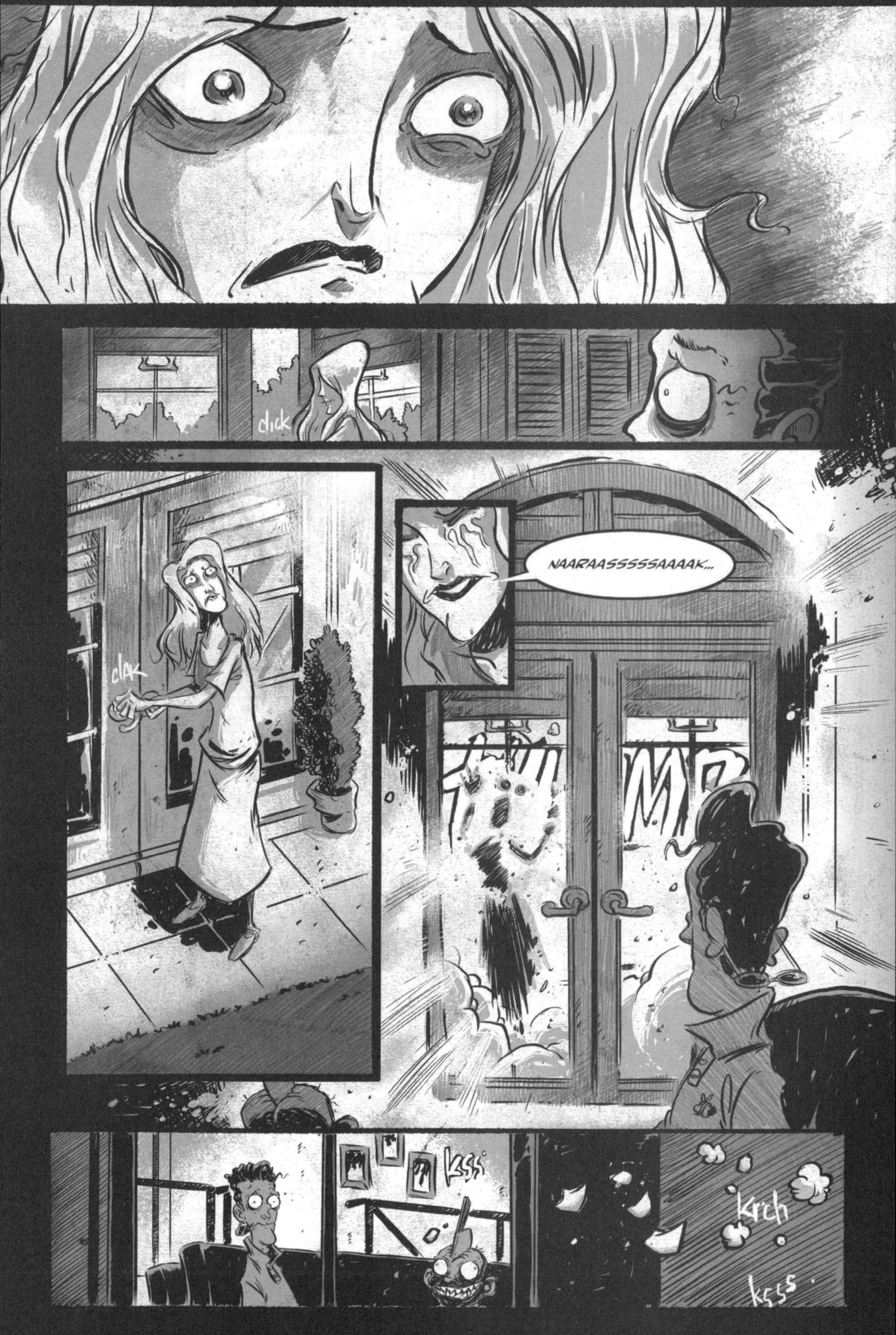
click
clak
NAARAASSSSSAAAAK...
ksss
krch
ksss

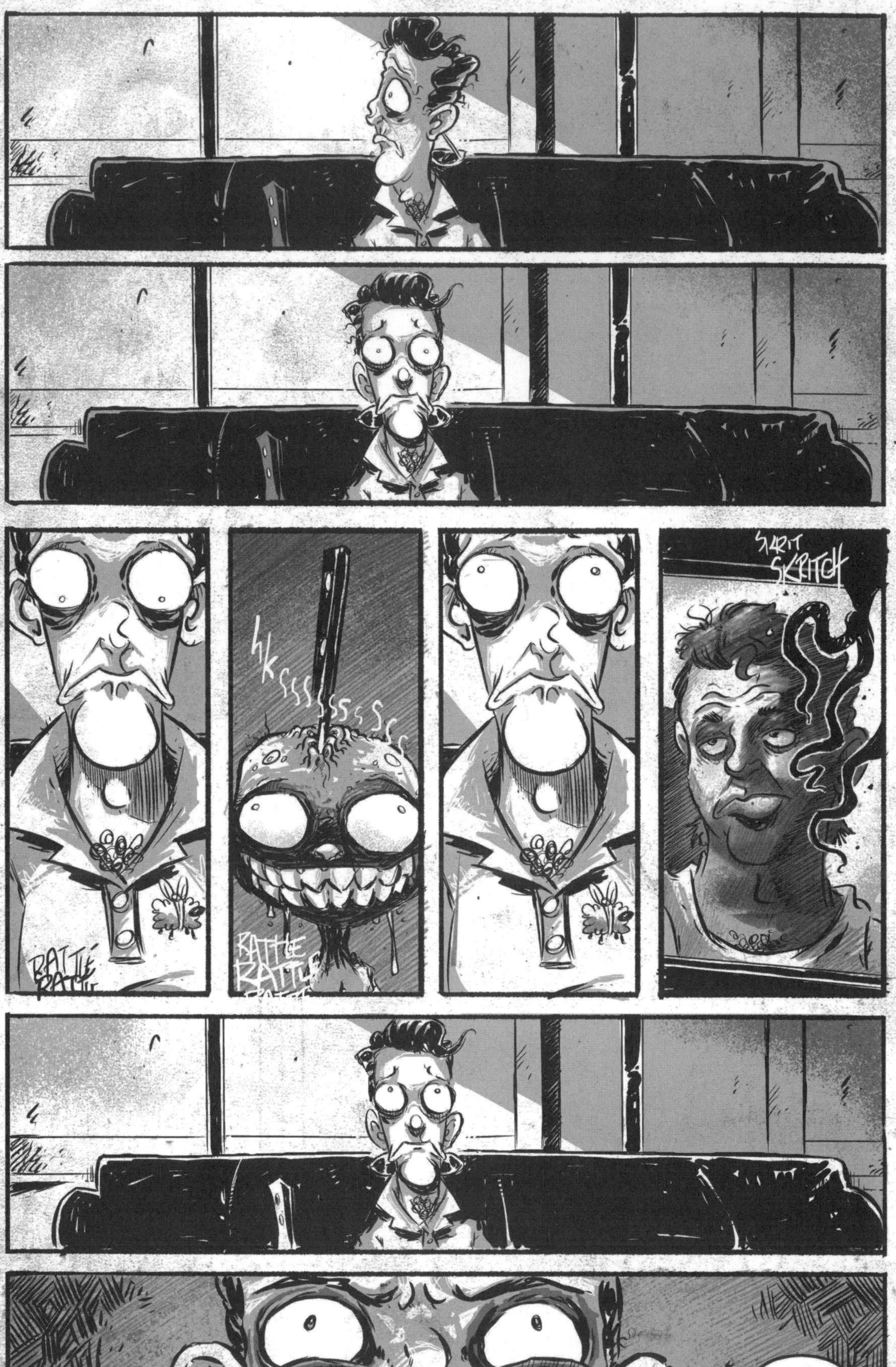
RATTLE
RATTLE
SKRIT
SKRITCH
OKAY.

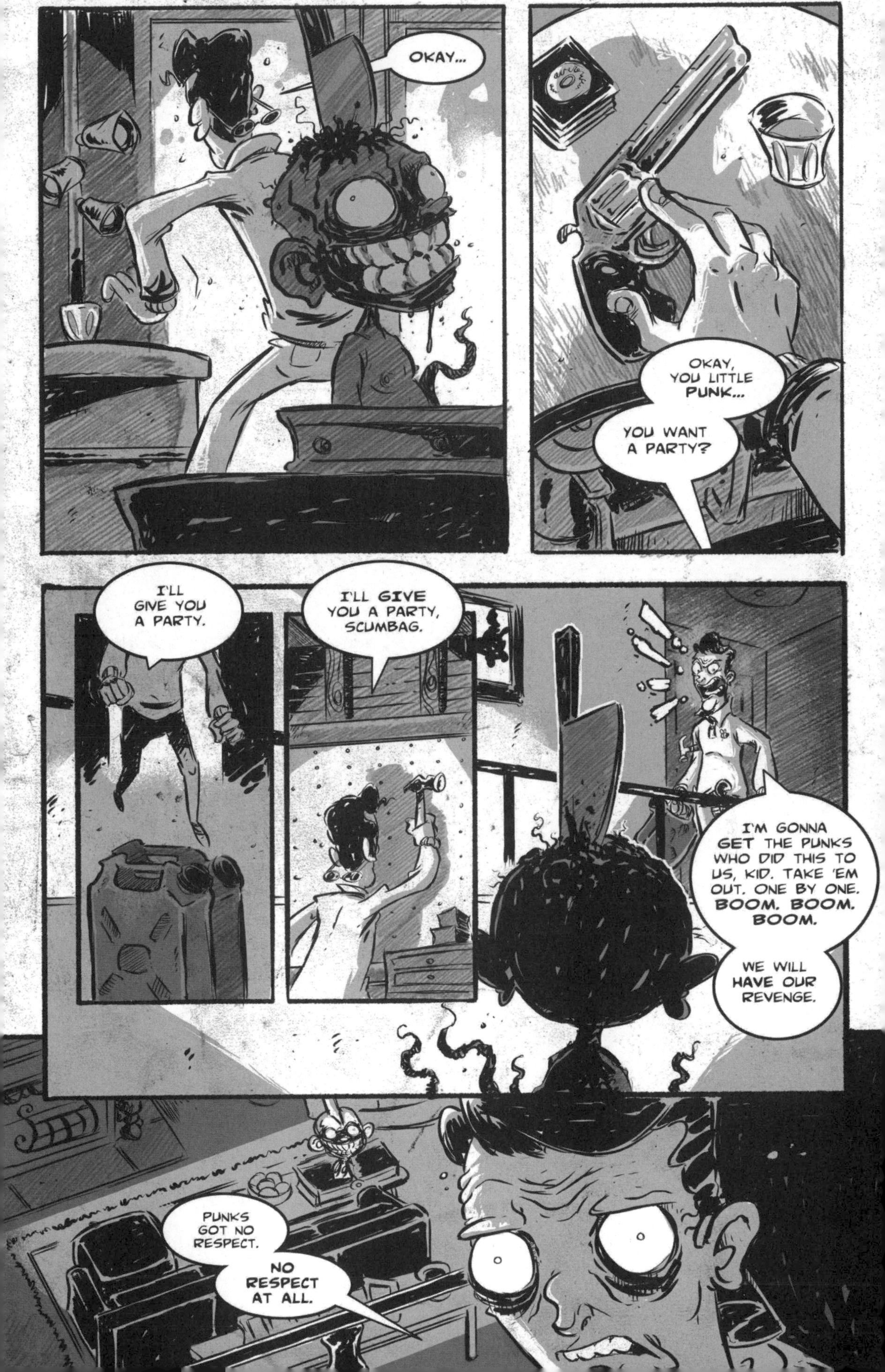
OKAY...
OKAY, YOU LITTLE PUNK...
YOU WANT A PARTY?
I'LL GIVE YOU A PARTY.
I'LL GIVE YOU A PARTY, SCUMBAG.
I'M GONNA GET THE PUNKS WHO DID THIS TO US, KID. TAKE 'EM OUT. ONE BY ONE. BOOM. BOOM. BOOM.
WE WILL HAVE OUR REVENGE.
PUNKS GOT NO RESPECT.
NO RESPECT AT ALL.

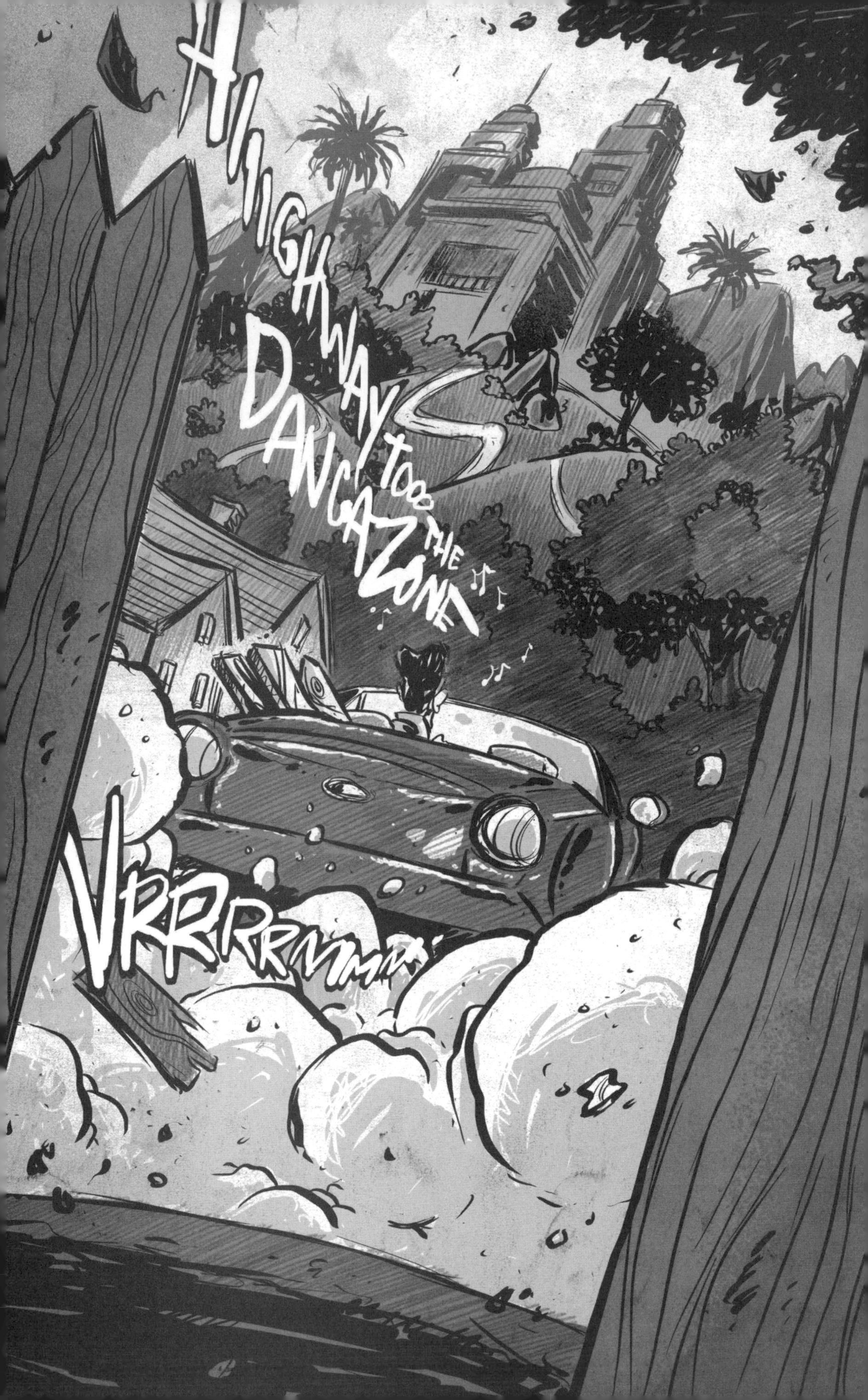
HIIIGHWAYS TOOO THE DANGAZONE
VRRRRMMMM

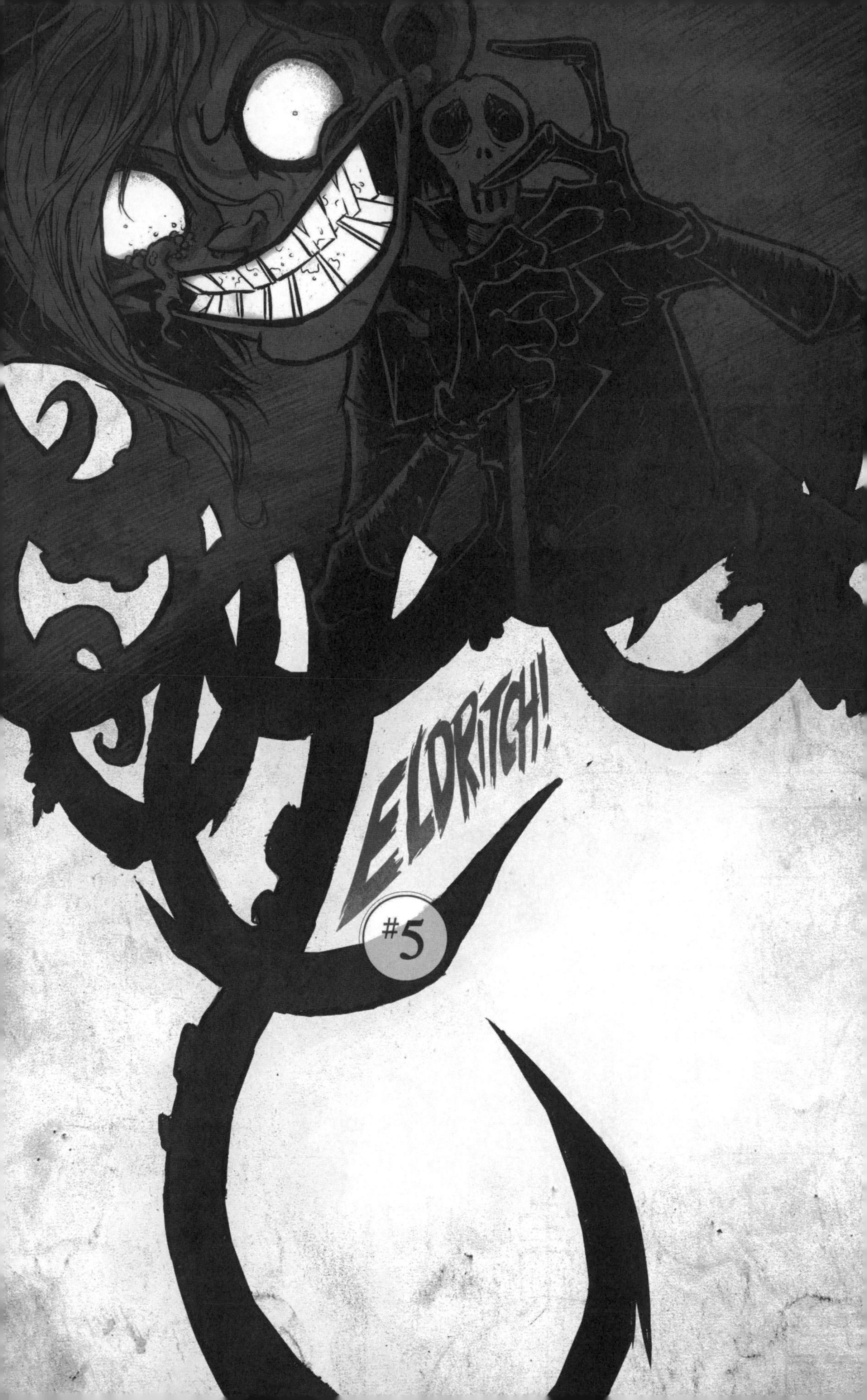
ELDRITCH!
#5

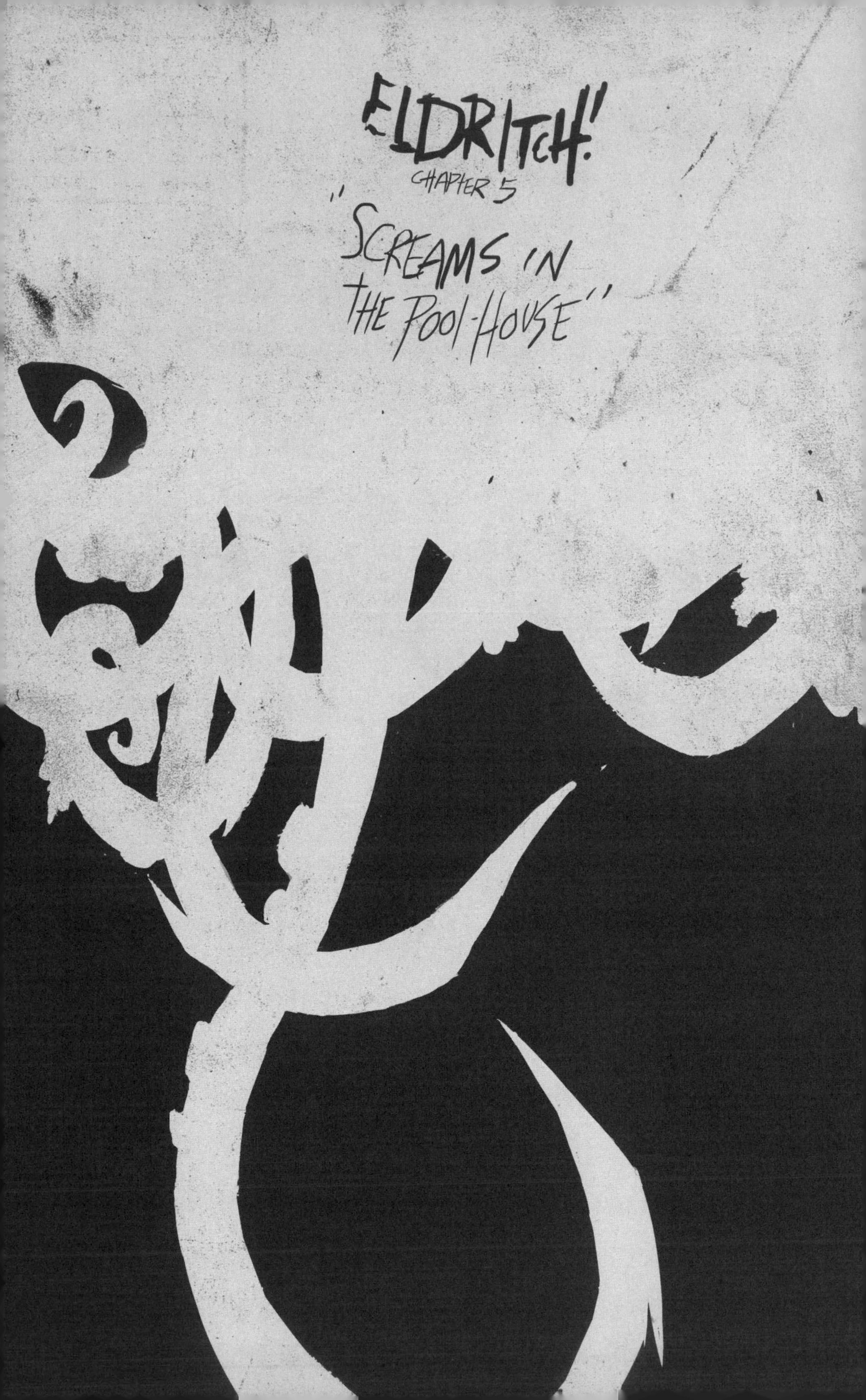
ELDRITCH!
CHAPTER 5
"SCREAMS IN THE POOL-HOUSE"

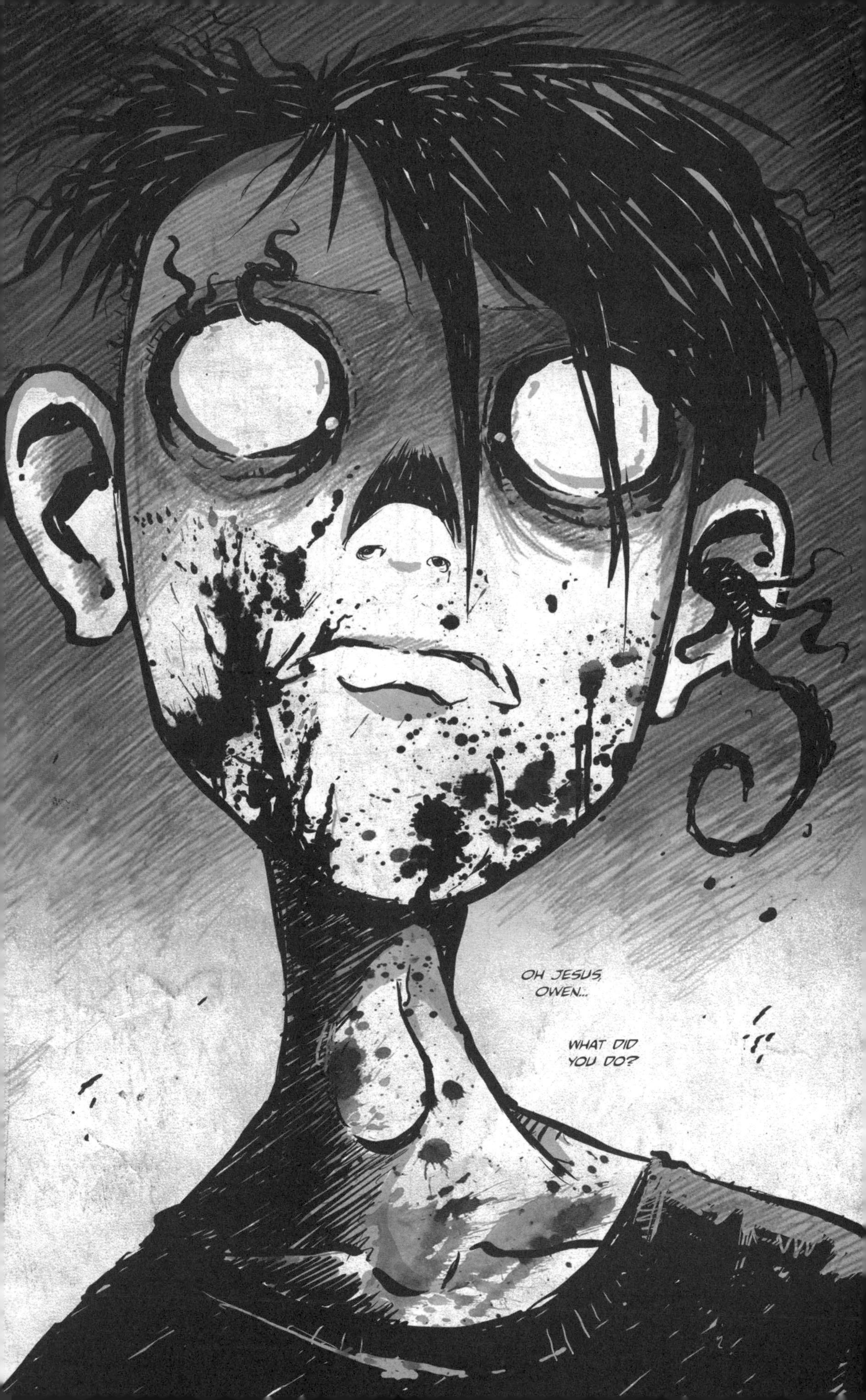
OH JESUS,
OWEN...
WHAT DID
YOU DO?

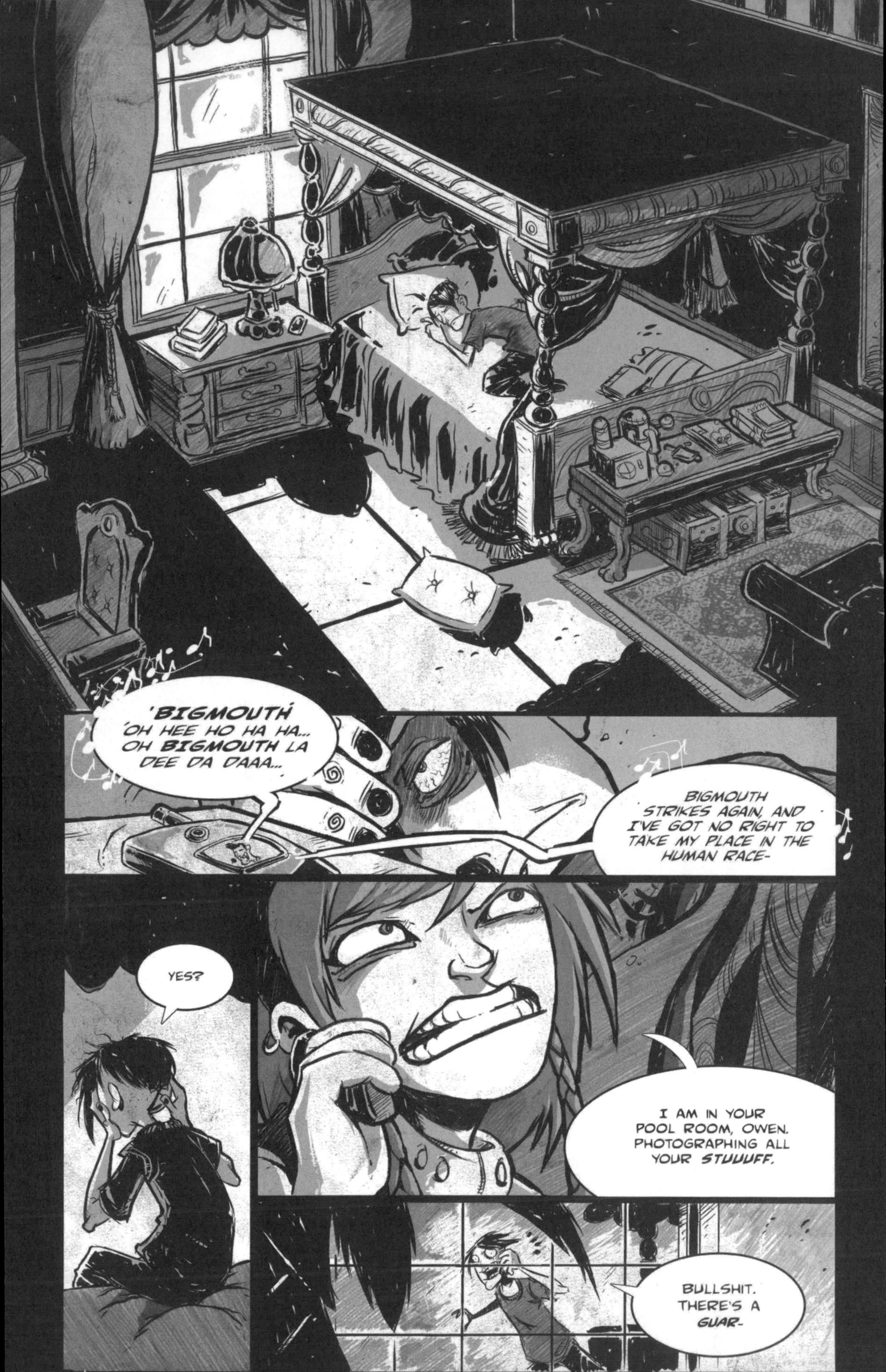
'BIGMOUTH
OH HEE HO HA HA... OH BIGMOUTH LA DEE DA DAAA...
BIGMOUTH STRIKES AGAIN, AND I'VE GOT NO RIGHT TO TAKE MY PLACE IN THE HUMAN RACE-
YES?
I AM IN YOUR POOL ROOM, OWEN. PHOTOGRAPHING ALL YOUR STUUUFF.
BULLSHIT. THERE'S A GUAR-

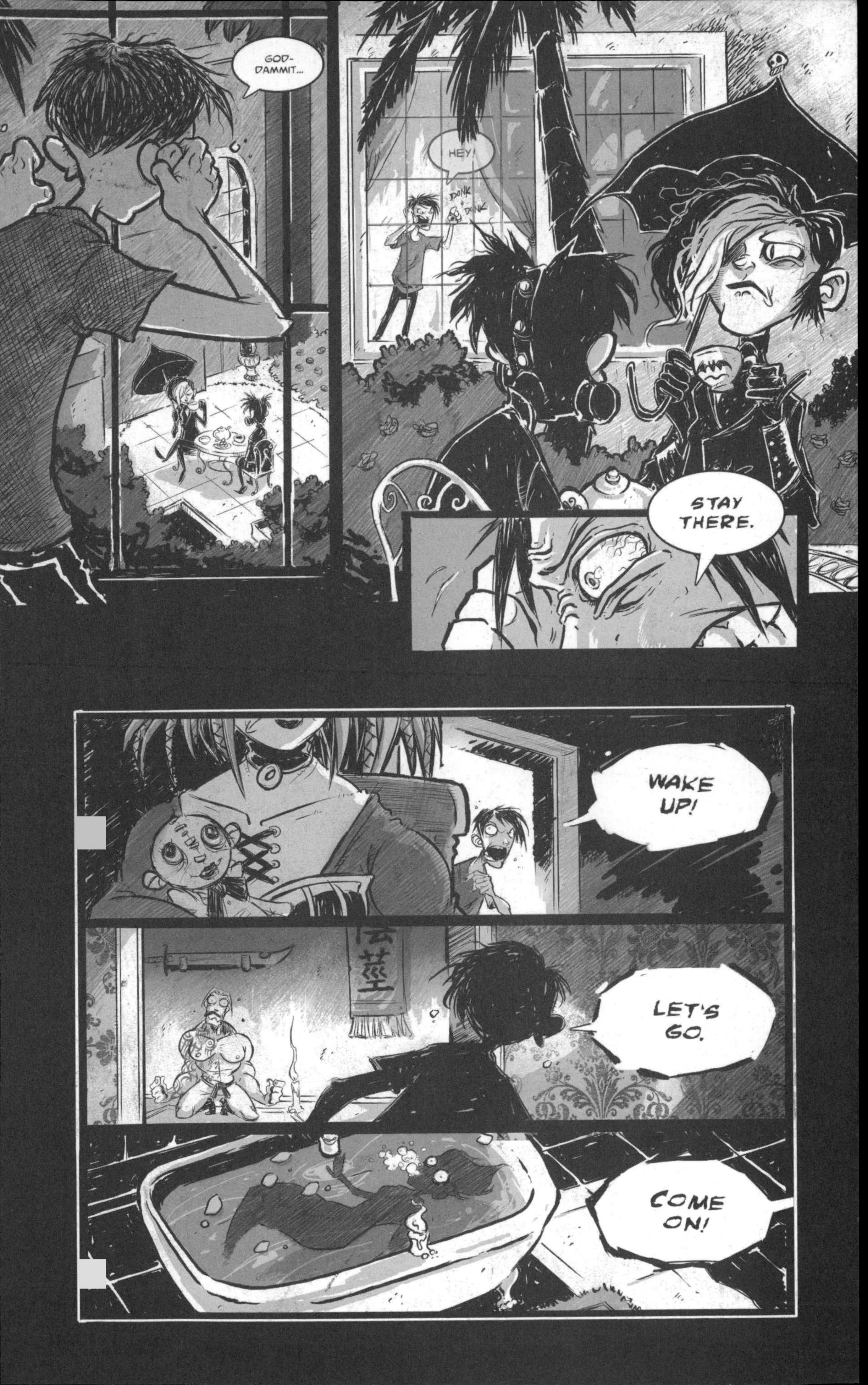
GOD-DAMMIT...
HEY!
DONK
DONK
STAY THERE.
WAKE UP!
LET'S GO.
COME ON!

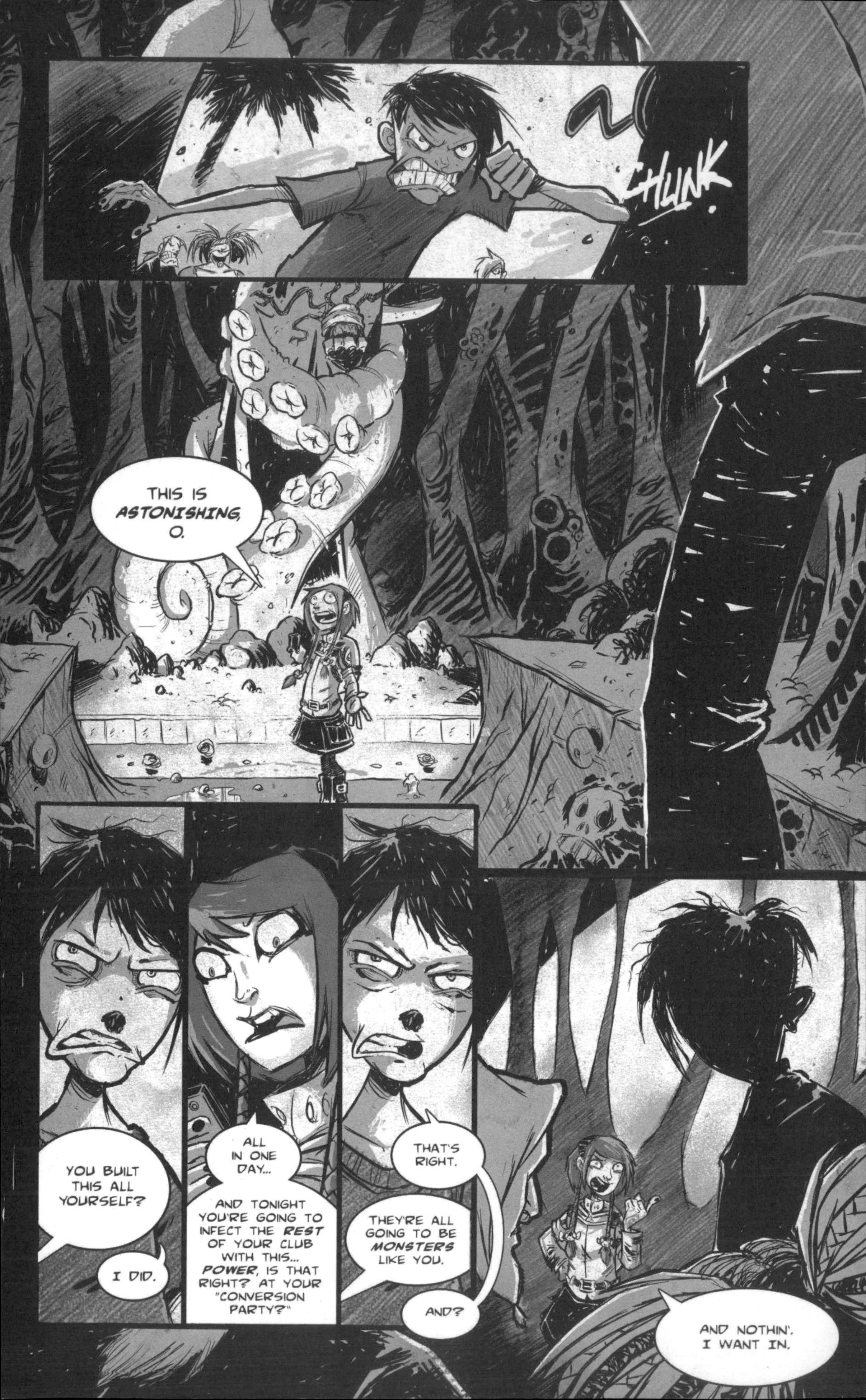
CHUNK
THIS IS ASTONISHING, O.
YOU BUILT THIS ALL YOURSELF?
I DID.
ALL IN ONE DAY...
AND TONIGHT YOU'RE GOING TO INFECT THE REST OF YOUR CLUB WITH THIS... POWER, IS THAT RIGHT? AT YOUR "CONVERSION PARTY?"
THAT'S RIGHT.
THEY'RE ALL GOING TO BE MONSTERS LIKE YOU.
AND?
AND NOTHIN'. I WANT IN.

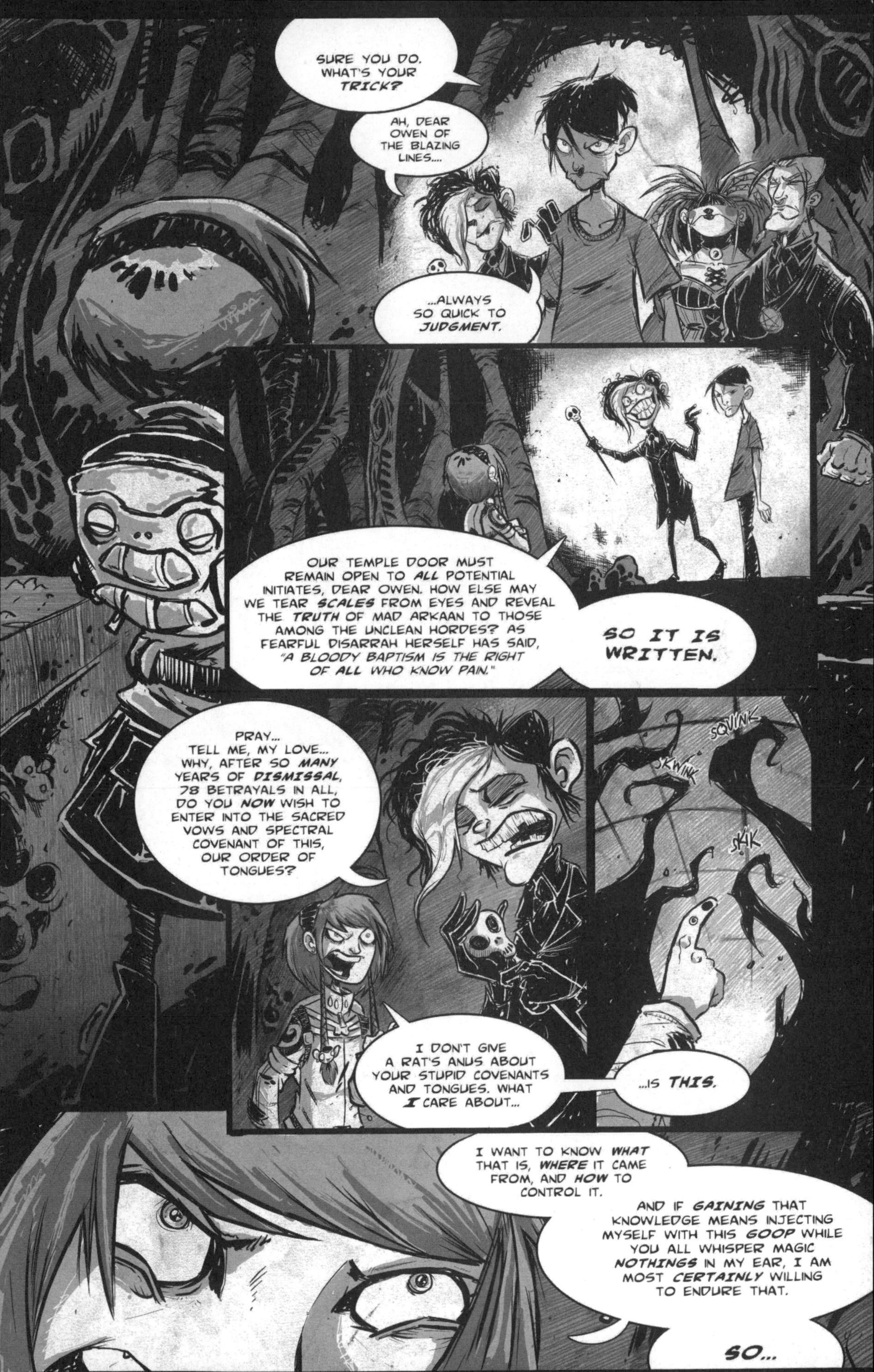

SURE YOU DO. WHAT'S YOUR TRICK?
AH, DEAR OWEN OF THE BLAZING LINES....
...ALWAYS SO QUICK TO JUDGMENT.
OUR TEMPLE DOOR MUST REMAIN OPEN TO ALL POTENTIAL INITIATES, DEAR OWEN. HOW ELSE MAY WE TEAR SCALES FROM EYES AND REVEAL THE TRUTH OF MAD ARKAAN TO THOSE AMONG THE UNCLEAN HORDES? AS FEARFUL DISARRAH HERSELF HAS SAID, "A BLOODY BAPTISM IS THE RIGHT OF ALL WHO KNOW PAIN."
SO IT IS WRITTEN.
PRAY... TELL ME, MY LOVE... WHY, AFTER SO MANY YEARS OF DISMISSAL, 78 BETRAYALS IN ALL, DO YOU NOW WISH TO ENTER INTO THE SACRED VOWS AND SPECTRAL COVENANT OF THIS, OUR ORDER OF TONGUES?
SQUINK
SKWINK
SKIK
I DON'T GIVE A RAT'S ANUS ABOUT YOUR STUPID COVENANTS AND TONGUES. WHAT I CARE ABOUT...
...IS THIS.
I WANT TO KNOW WHAT THAT IS, WHERE IT CAME FROM, AND HOW TO CONTROL IT.
AND IF GAINING THAT KNOWLEDGE MEANS INJECTING MYSELF WITH THIS GOOP WHILE YOU ALL WHISPER MAGIC NOTHINGS IN MY EAR, I AM MOST CERTAINLY WILLING TO ENDURE THAT.
SO...

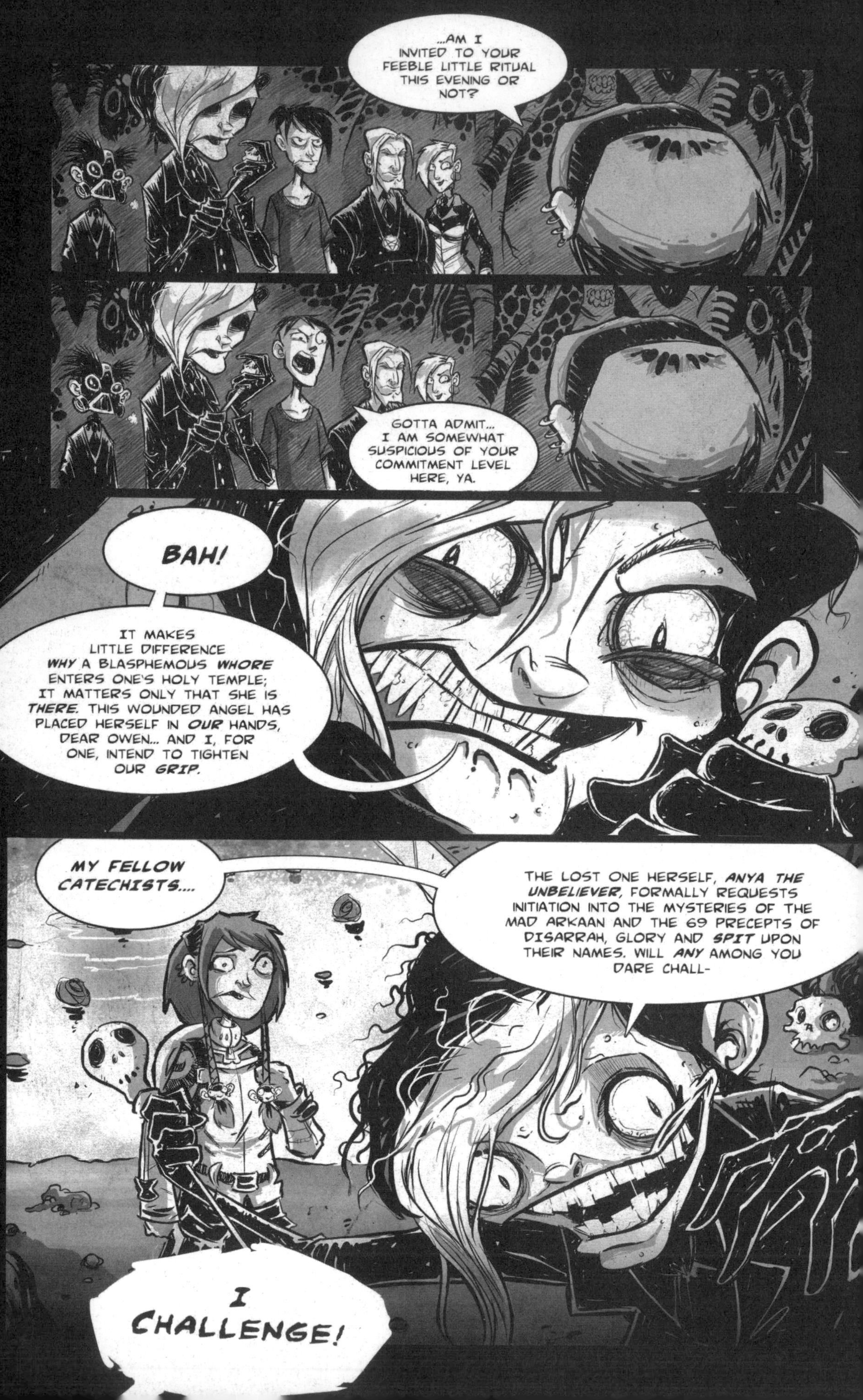
...AM I INVITED TO YOUR FEEBLE LITTLE RITUAL THIS EVENING OR NOT?
GOTTA ADMIT... I AM SOMEWHAT SUSPICIOUS OF YOUR COMMITMENT LEVEL HERE, YA.
BAH!
IT MAKES LITTLE DIFFERENCE WHY A BLASPHEMOUS WHORE ENTERS ONE'S HOLY TEMPLE; IT MATTERS ONLY THAT SHE IS THERE. THIS WOUNDED ANGEL HAS PLACED HERSELF IN OUR HANDS, DEAR OWEN... AND I, FOR ONE, INTEND TO TIGHTEN OUR GRIP.
MY FELLOW CATECHISTS....
THE LOST ONE HERSELF, ANYA THE UNBELIEVER, FORMALLY REQUESTS INITIATION INTO THE MYSTERIES OF THE MAD ARKAAN AND THE 69 PRECEPTS OF DISARRAH, GLORY AND SPIT UPON THEIR NAMES. WILL ANY AMONG YOU DARE CHALL-
I CHALLENGE!

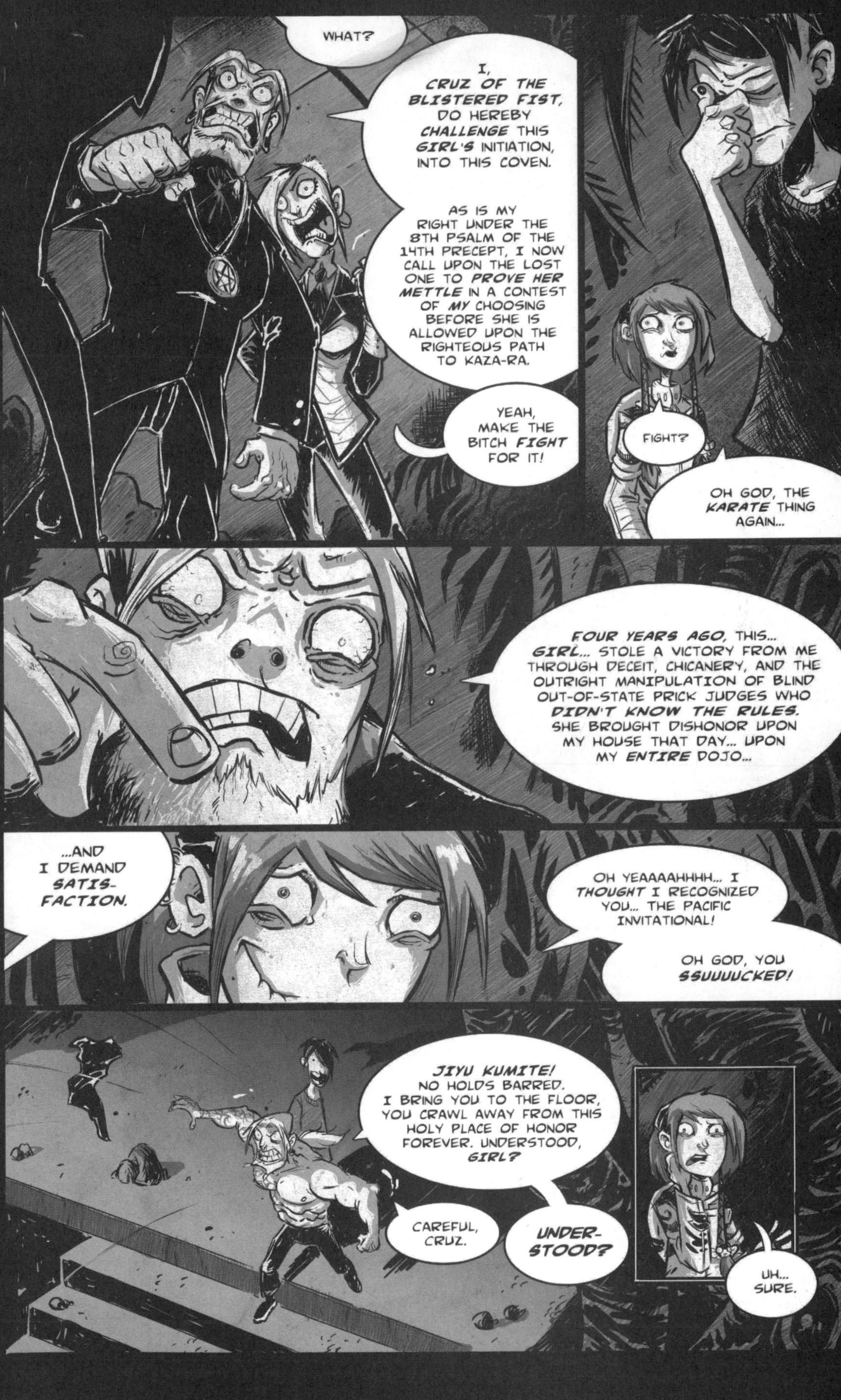
WHAT?
I, CRUZ OF THE BLISTERED FIST, DO HEREBY CHALLENGE THIS GIRL'S INITIATION, INTO THIS COVEN.
AS IS MY RIGHT UNDER THE 8TH PSALM OF THE 14TH PRECEPT, I NOW CALL UPON THE LOST ONE TO PROVE HER METTLE IN A CONTEST OF MY CHOOSING BEFORE SHE IS ALLOWED UPON THE RIGHTEOUS PATH TO KAZA-RA.
YEAH, MAKE THE BITCH FIGHT FOR IT!
FIGHT?
OH GOD, THE KARATE THING AGAIN...
FOUR YEARS AGO, THIS... GIRL... STOLE A VICTORY FROM ME THROUGH DECEIT, CHICANERY, AND THE OUTRIGHT MANIPULATION OF BLIND OUT-OF-STATE PRICK JUDGES WHO DIDN'T KNOW THE RULES. SHE BROUGHT DISHONOR UPON MY HOUSE THAT DAY... UPON MY ENTIRE DOJO...
...AND I DEMAND SATIS-FACTION.
OH YEAAAAHHHH... I THOUGHT I RECOGNIZED YOU... THE PACIFIC INVITATIONAL!
OH GOD, YOU SSUUUUCKED!
JIYU KUMITE! NO HOLDS BARRED. I BRING YOU TO THE FLOOR, YOU CRAWL AWAY FROM THIS HOLY PLACE OF HONOR FOREVER. UNDERSTOOD, GIRL?
CAREFUL, CRUZ.
UNDER-STOOD?
UH... SURE.

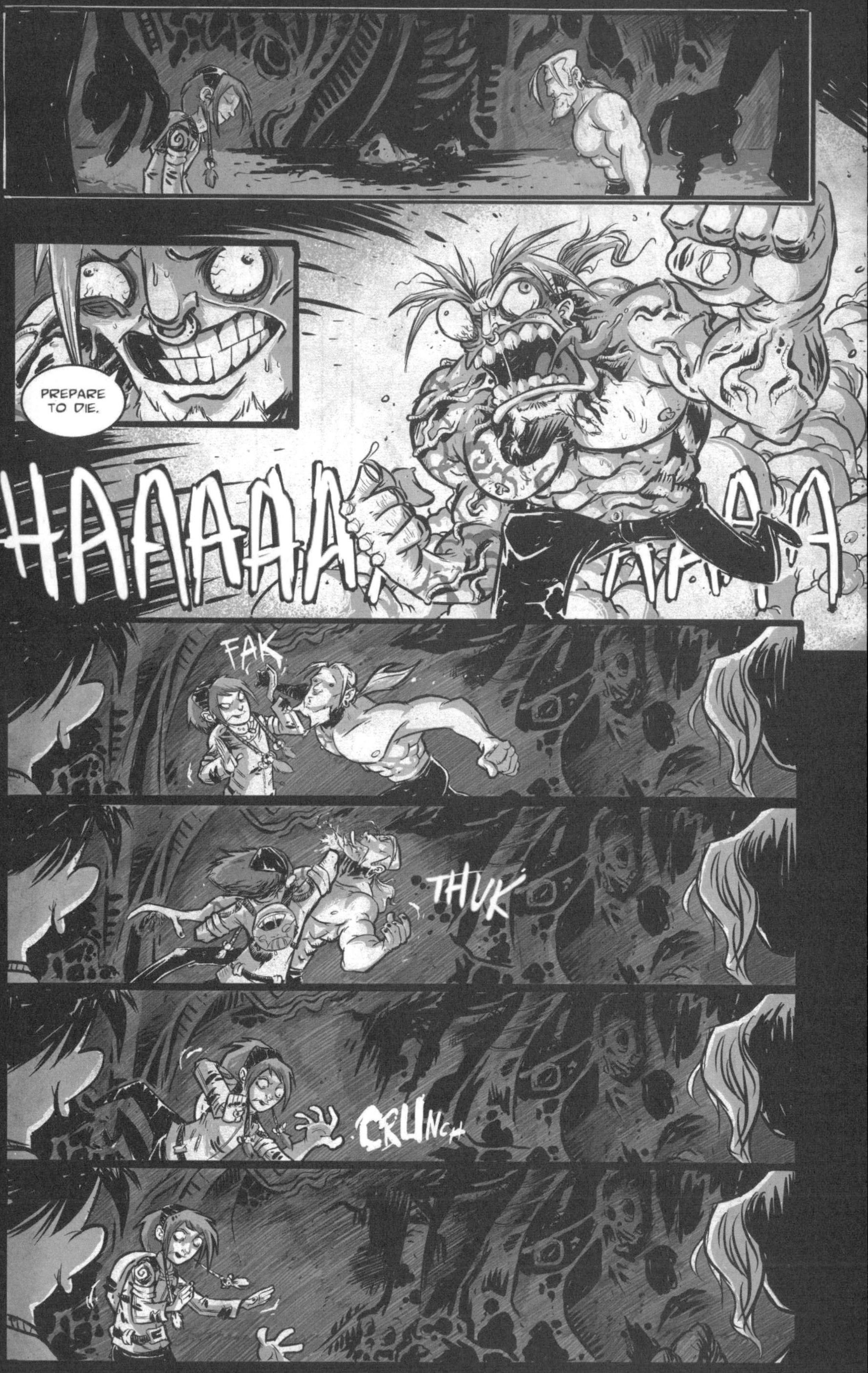
PREPARE TO DIE.
HAAAAAAAAAA
FAK
THUK
CRUNCH

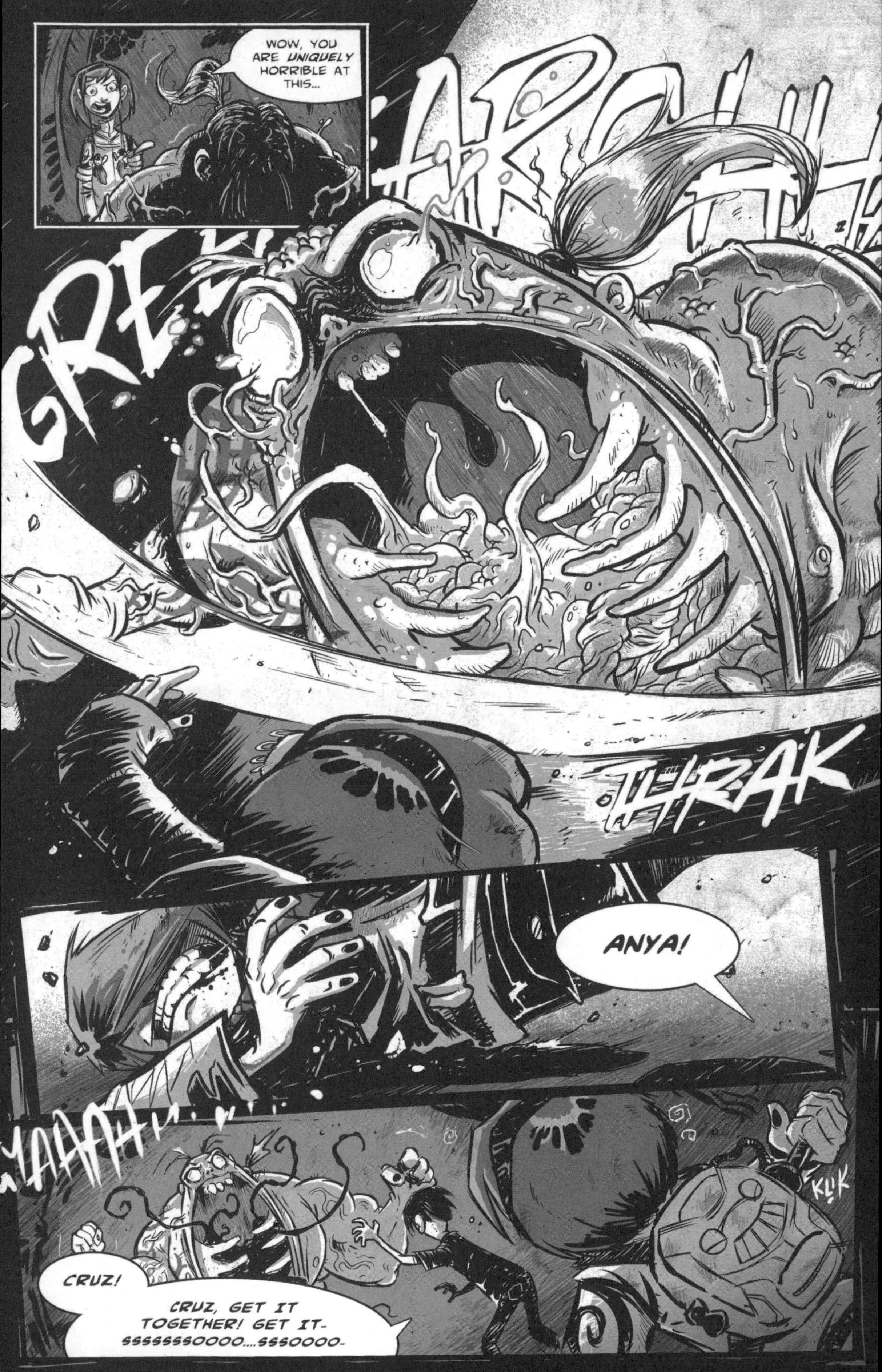
WOW, YOU ARE *UNIQUELY* HORRIBLE AT THIS...
THRAK
ANYA!
KLIK
CRUZ!
CRUZ, GET IT TOGETHER! GET IT-SSSSSSSOOOO....SSSOOOO-

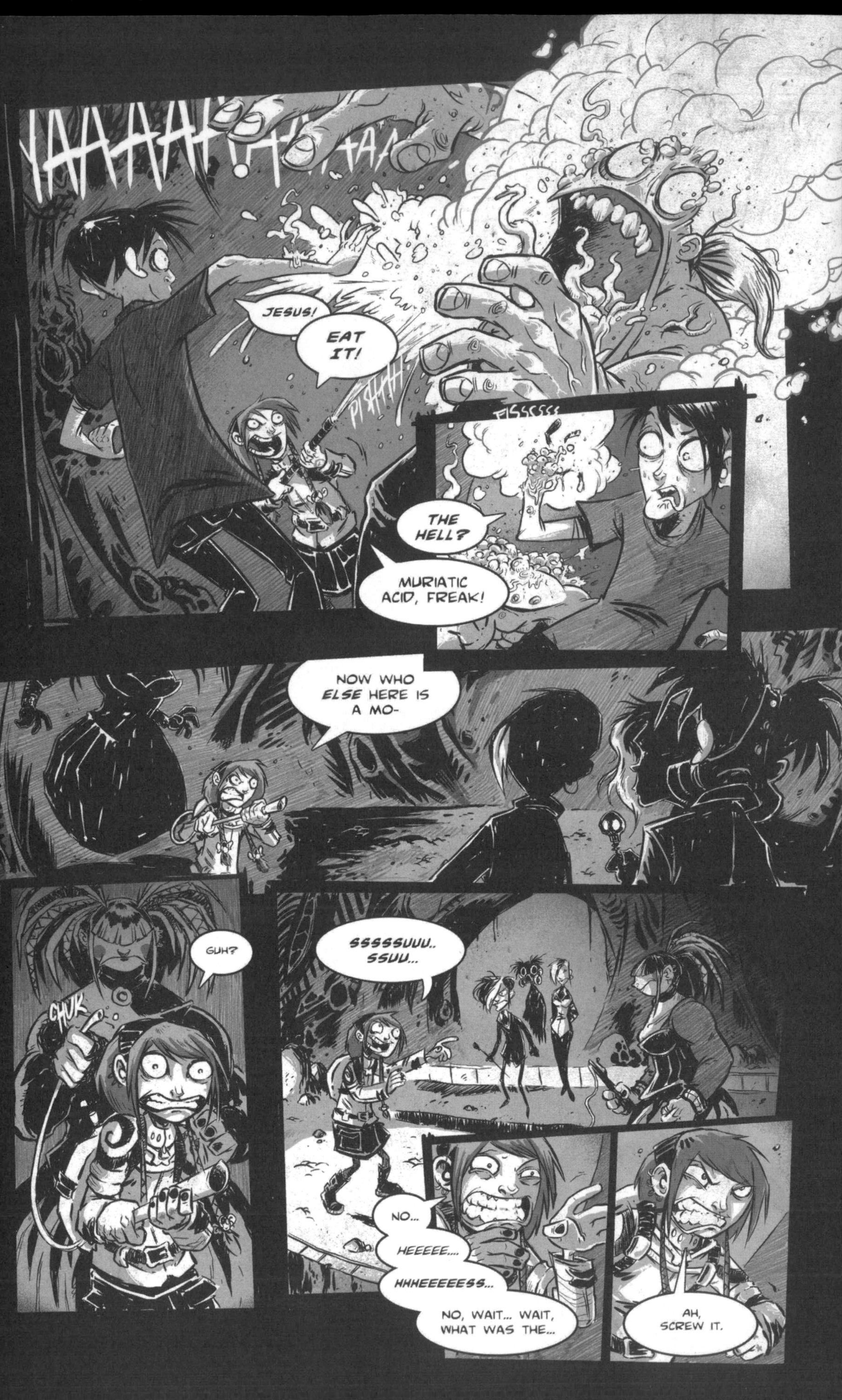
YAAAAH!
JESUS!
EAT IT!
PISHHH!
FISSSSS
THE HELL?
MURIATIC ACID, FREAK!
NOW WHO ELSE HERE IS A MO-
GUH?
CHUK
SSSSSUUU.. SSUU...
NO...
HEEEEE....
HHHEEEEESS...
NO, WAIT... WAIT, WHAT WAS THE...
AH, SCREW IT.

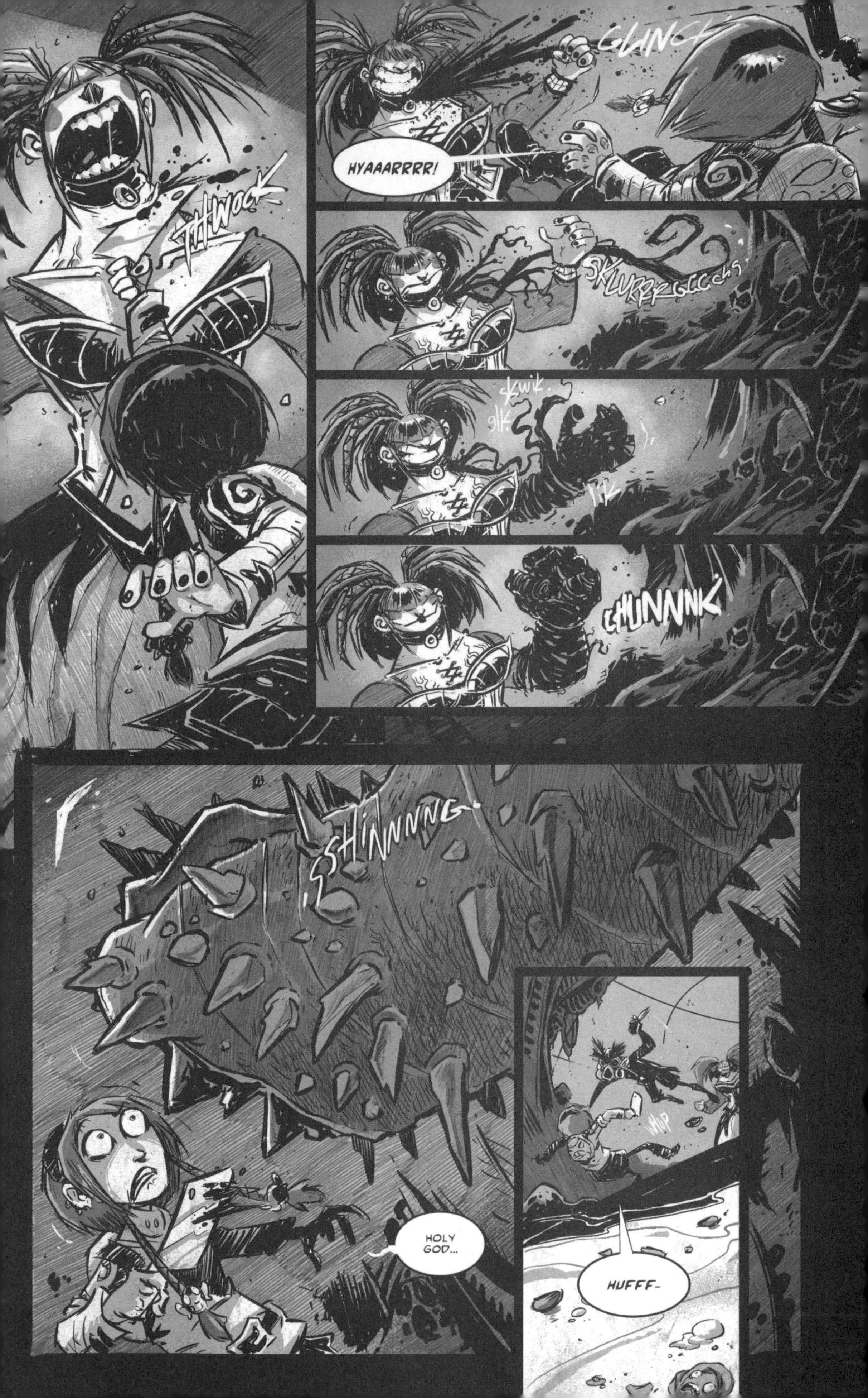
THWOCK
GLUNCK
HYAAARRRR!
SKLURRRGGCchs
CHUNNNK
SHINNNNG
HOLY GOD...
HUFFF-

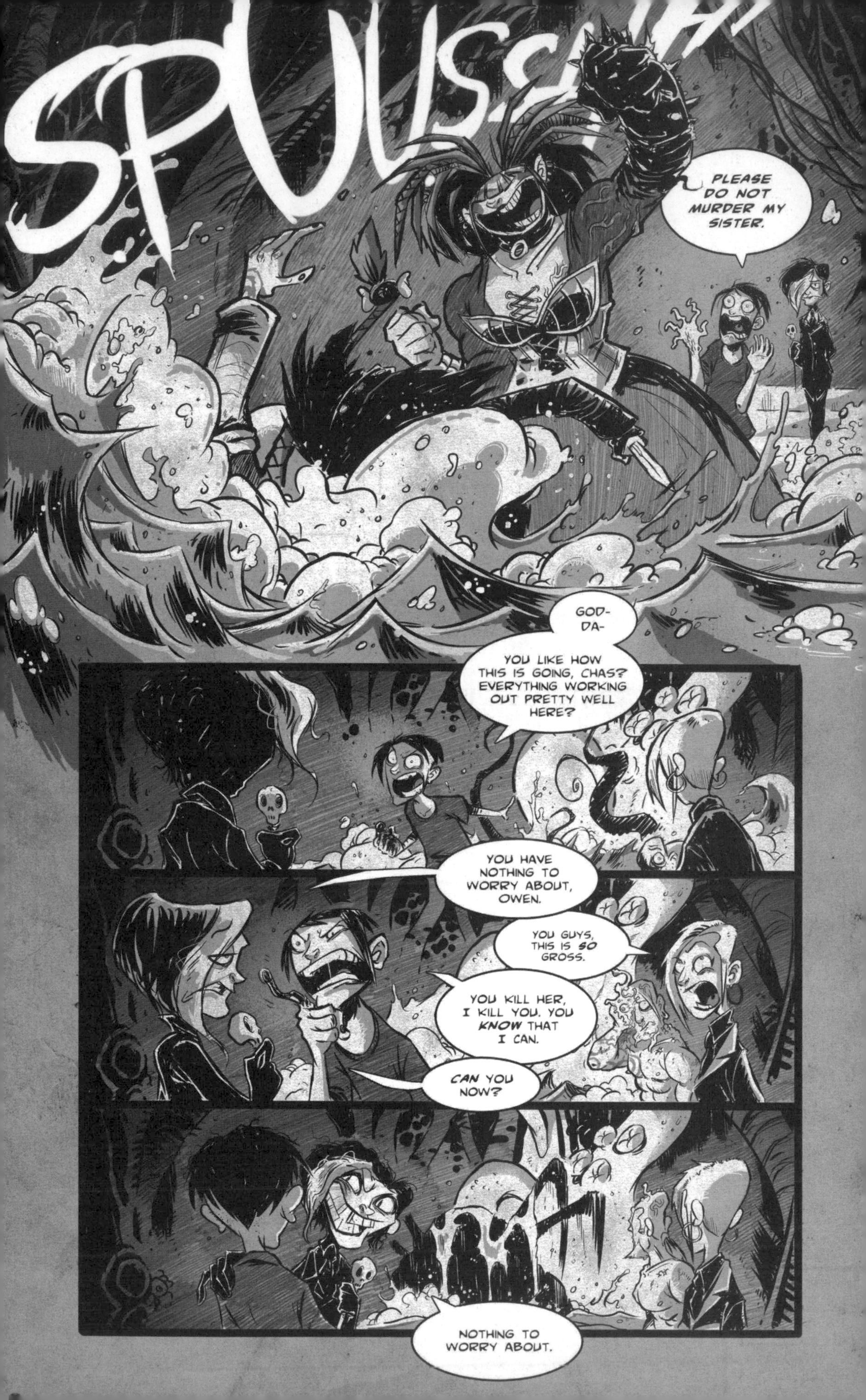
SPLUSSH!
PLEASE DO NOT MURDER MY SISTER.
GOD-DA-
YOU LIKE HOW THIS IS GOING, CHAS? EVERYTHING WORKING OUT PRETTY WELL HERE?
YOU HAVE NOTHING TO WORRY ABOUT, OWEN.
YOU GUYS, THIS IS SO GROSS.
YOU KILL HER, I KILL YOU. YOU KNOW THAT I CAN.
CAN YOU NOW?
NOTHING TO WORRY ABOUT.

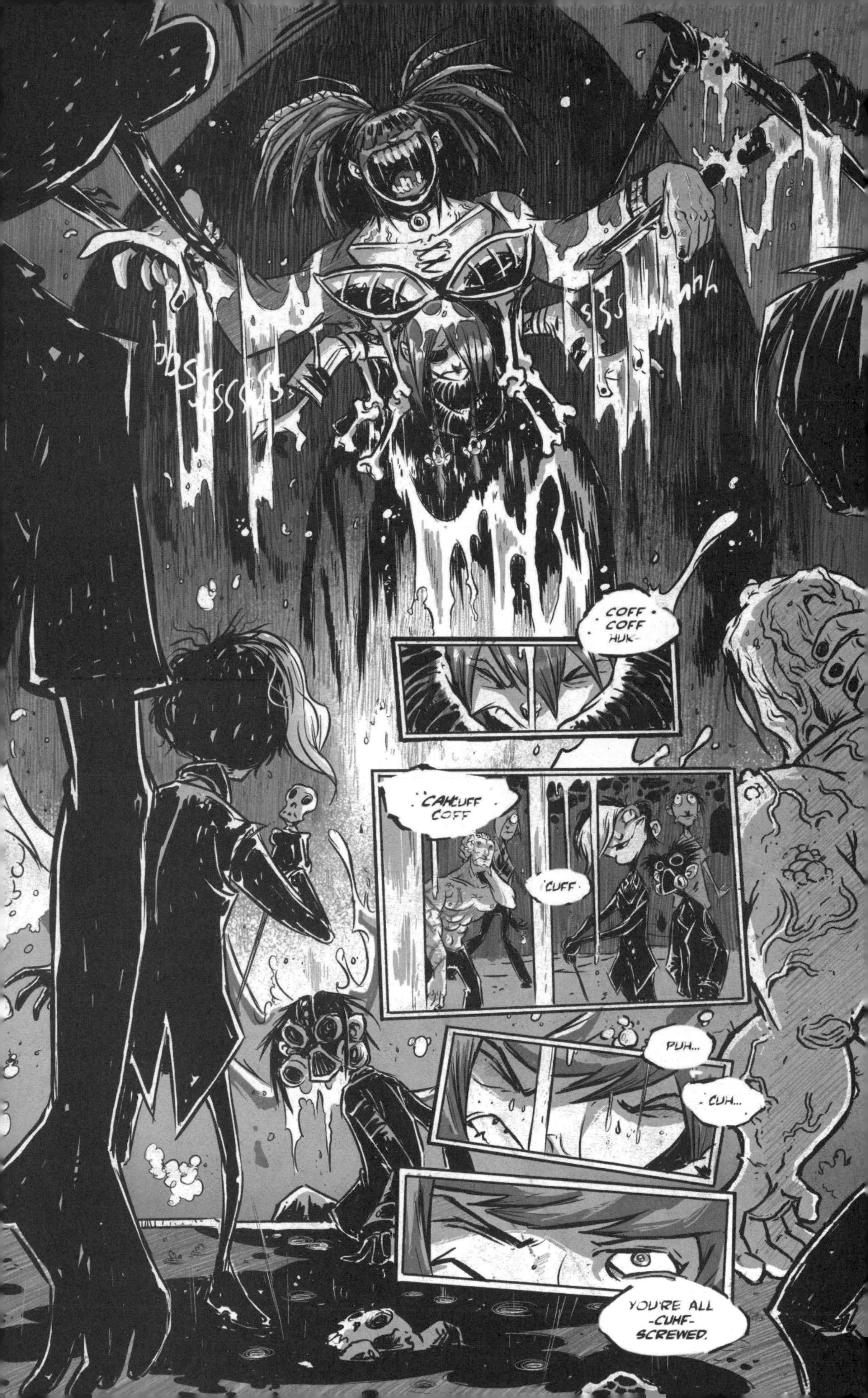
hssssssss
sssshhh
COFF COFF HUK-
CAHCUFF COFF
CUFF
PUH...
-CUH...
YOU'RE ALL -CUHF- SCREWED.

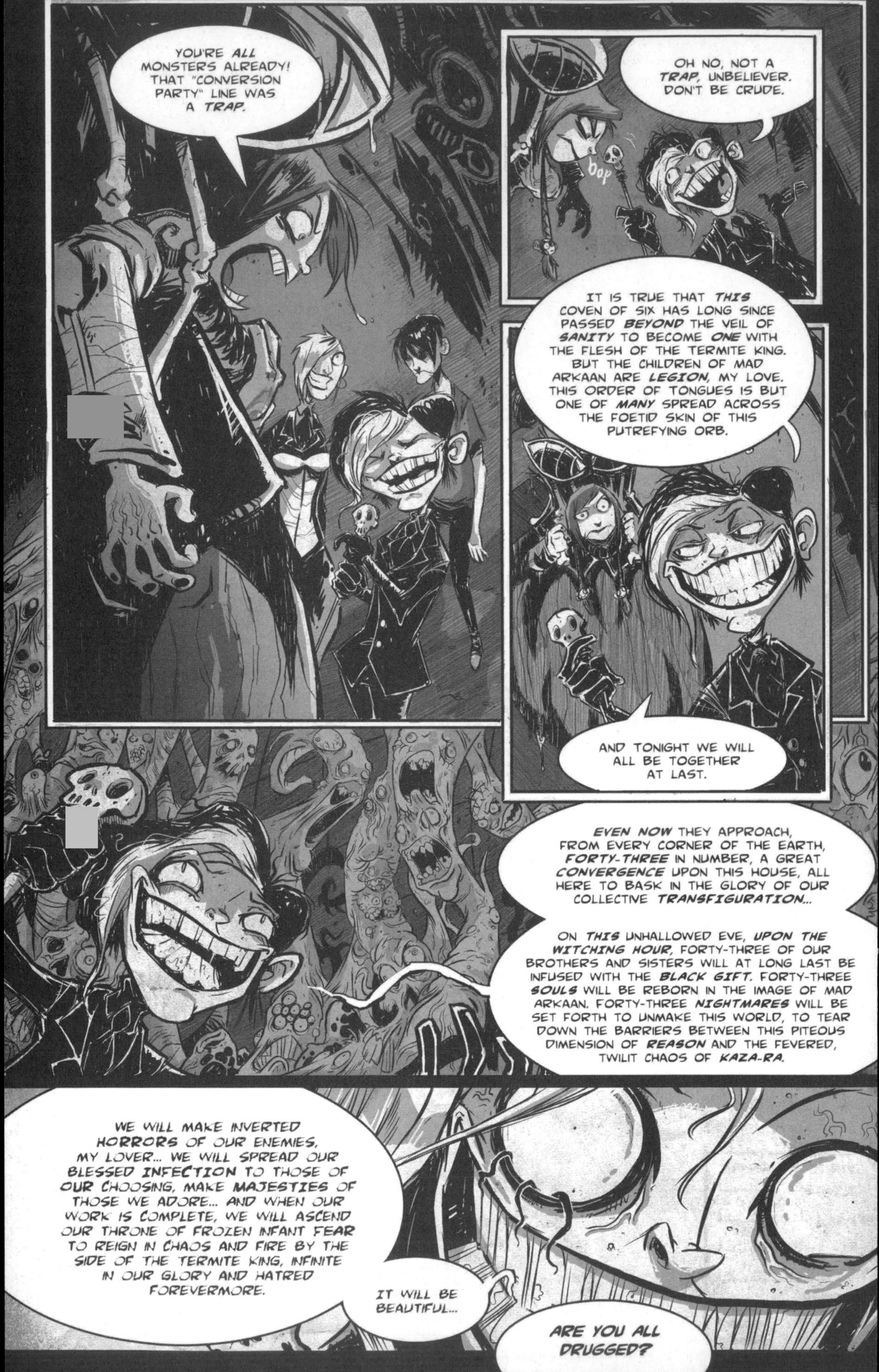
YOU'RE ALL MONSTERS ALREADY! THAT "CONVERSION PARTY" LINE WAS A TRAP.
OH NO, NOT A TRAP, UNBELIEVER. DON'T BE CRUDE.
bop
IT IS TRUE THAT THIS COVEN OF SIX HAS LONG SINCE PASSED BEYOND THE VEIL OF SANITY TO BECOME ONE WITH THE FLESH OF THE TERMITE KING. BUT THE CHILDREN OF MAD ARKAAN ARE LEGION, MY LOVE. THIS ORDER OF TONGUES IS BUT ONE OF MANY SPREAD ACROSS THE FOETID SKIN OF THIS PUTREFYING ORB.
AND TONIGHT WE WILL ALL BE TOGETHER AT LAST.
EVEN NOW THEY APPROACH, FROM EVERY CORNER OF THE EARTH, FORTY-THREE IN NUMBER, A GREAT CONVERGENCE UPON THIS HOUSE, ALL HERE TO BASK IN THE GLORY OF OUR COLLECTIVE TRANSFIGURATION...
ON THIS UNHALLOWED EVE, UPON THE WITCHING HOUR, FORTY-THREE OF OUR BROTHERS AND SISTERS WILL AT LONG LAST BE INFUSED WITH THE BLACK GIFT. FORTY-THREE SOULS WILL BE REBORN IN THE IMAGE OF MAD ARKAAN. FORTY-THREE NIGHTMARES WILL BE SET FORTH TO UNMAKE THIS WORLD, TO TEAR DOWN THE BARRIERS BETWEEN THIS PITEOUS DIMENSION OF REASON AND THE FEVERED, TWILIT CHAOS OF KAZA-RA.
WE WILL MAKE INVERTED HORRORS OF OUR ENEMIES, MY LOVER... WE WILL SPREAD OUR BLESSED INFECTION TO THOSE OF OUR CHOOSING, MAKE MAJESTIES OF THOSE WE ADORE... AND WHEN OUR WORK IS COMPLETE, WE WILL ASCEND OUR THRONE OF FROZEN INFANT FEAR TO REIGN IN CHAOS AND FIRE BY THE SIDE OF THE TERMITE KING, INFINITE IN OUR GLORY AND HATRED FOREVERMORE.
IT WILL BE BEAUTIFUL...
ARE YOU ALL DRUGGED?

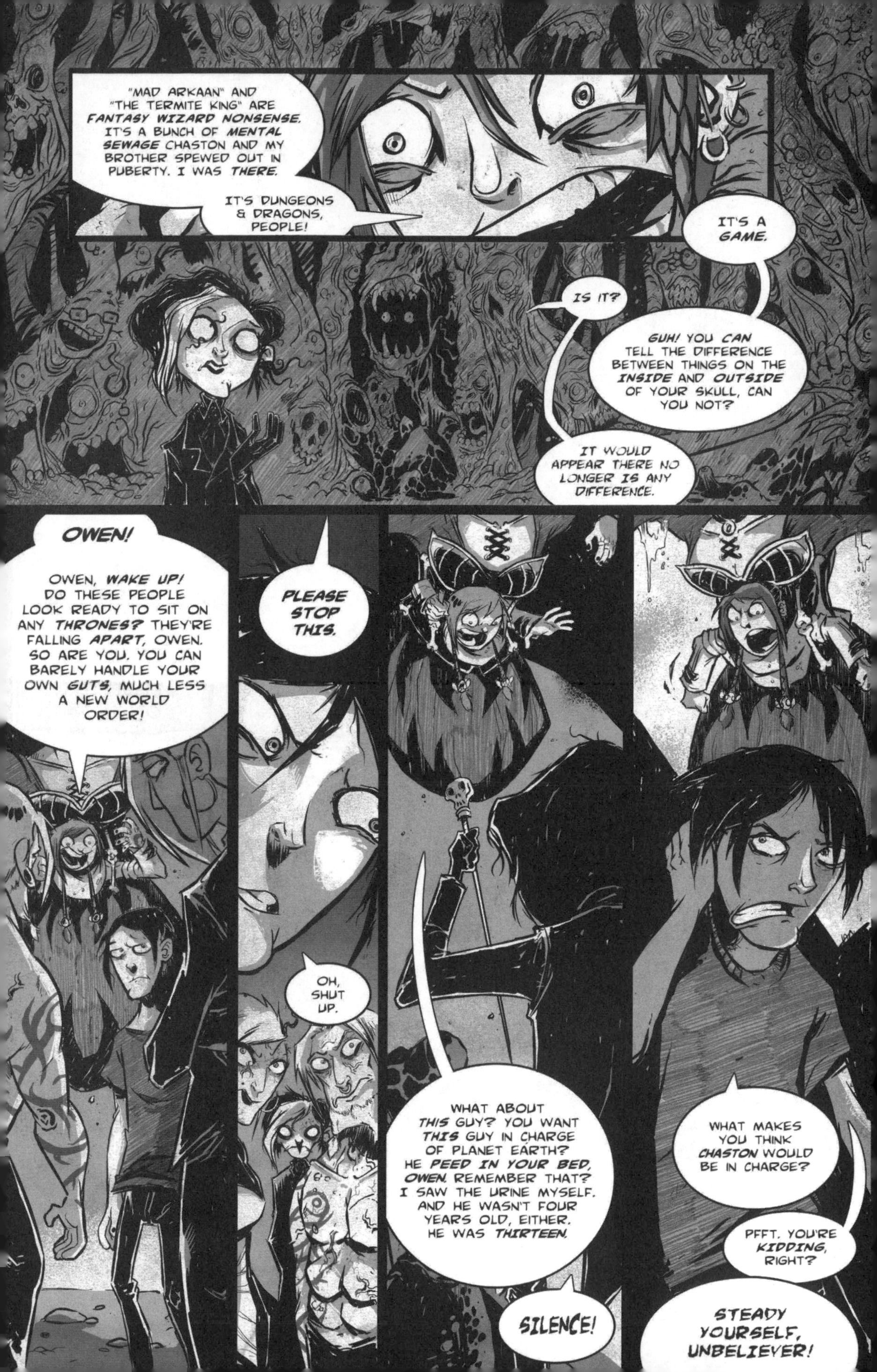
"MAD ARKAAN" AND "THE TERMITE KING" ARE *FANTASY WIZARD NONSENSE.* IT'S A BUNCH OF *MENTAL SEWAGE* CHASTON AND MY BROTHER SPEWED OUT IN PUBERTY. I WAS *THERE.*
IT'S DUNGEONS & DRAGONS, PEOPLE!
IT'S A *GAME.*
IS IT?
GUH! YOU *CAN* TELL THE DIFFERENCE BETWEEN THINGS ON THE *INSIDE* AND *OUTSIDE* OF YOUR SKULL, CAN YOU NOT?
IT WOULD APPEAR THERE NO LONGER *IS* ANY DIFFERENCE.
OWEN!
OWEN, *WAKE UP!* DO THESE PEOPLE LOOK READY TO SIT ON ANY *THRONES?* THEY'RE FALLING *APART,* OWEN. SO ARE YOU. YOU CAN BARELY HANDLE YOUR OWN *GUTS,* MUCH LESS A NEW WORLD ORDER!
PLEASE STOP THIS.
OH, SHUT UP.
WHAT ABOUT *THIS* GUY? YOU WANT *THIS* GUY IN CHARGE OF PLANET EARTH? HE *PEED IN YOUR BED, OWEN.* REMEMBER THAT? I SAW THE URINE MYSELF. AND HE WASN'T FOUR YEARS OLD, EITHER. HE WAS *THIRTEEN.*
SILENCE!
WHAT MAKES YOU THINK *CHASTON* WOULD BE IN CHARGE?
PFFT. YOU'RE *KIDDING,* RIGHT?
STEADY YOURSELF, UNBELIEVER!

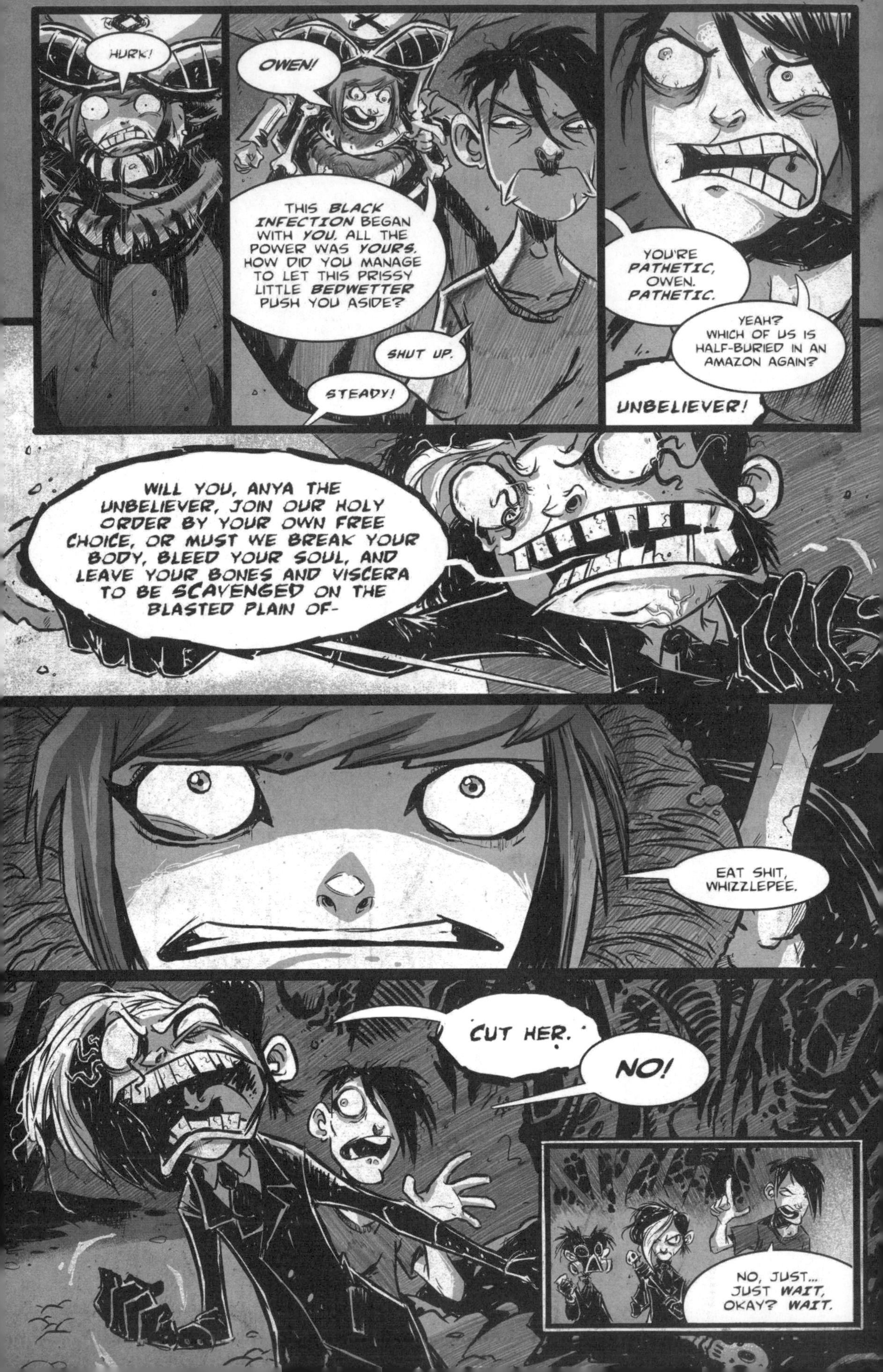
HURK!
OWEN!
THIS BLACK INFECTION BEGAN WITH YOU. ALL THE POWER WAS YOURS. HOW DID YOU MANAGE TO LET THIS PRISSY LITTLE BEDWETTER PUSH YOU ASIDE?
SHUT UP.
STEADY!
YOU'RE PATHETIC, OWEN. PATHETIC.
YEAH? WHICH OF US IS HALF-BURIED IN AN AMAZON AGAIN?
UNBELIEVER!
WILL YOU, ANYA THE UNBELIEVER, JOIN OUR HOLY ORDER BY YOUR OWN FREE CHOICE, OR MUST WE BREAK YOUR BODY, BLEED YOUR SOUL, AND LEAVE YOUR BONES AND VISCERA TO BE SCAVENGED ON THE BLASTED PLAIN OF-
EAT SHIT, WHIZZLEPEE.
CUT HER.
NO!
NO, JUST... JUST WAIT, OKAY? WAIT.

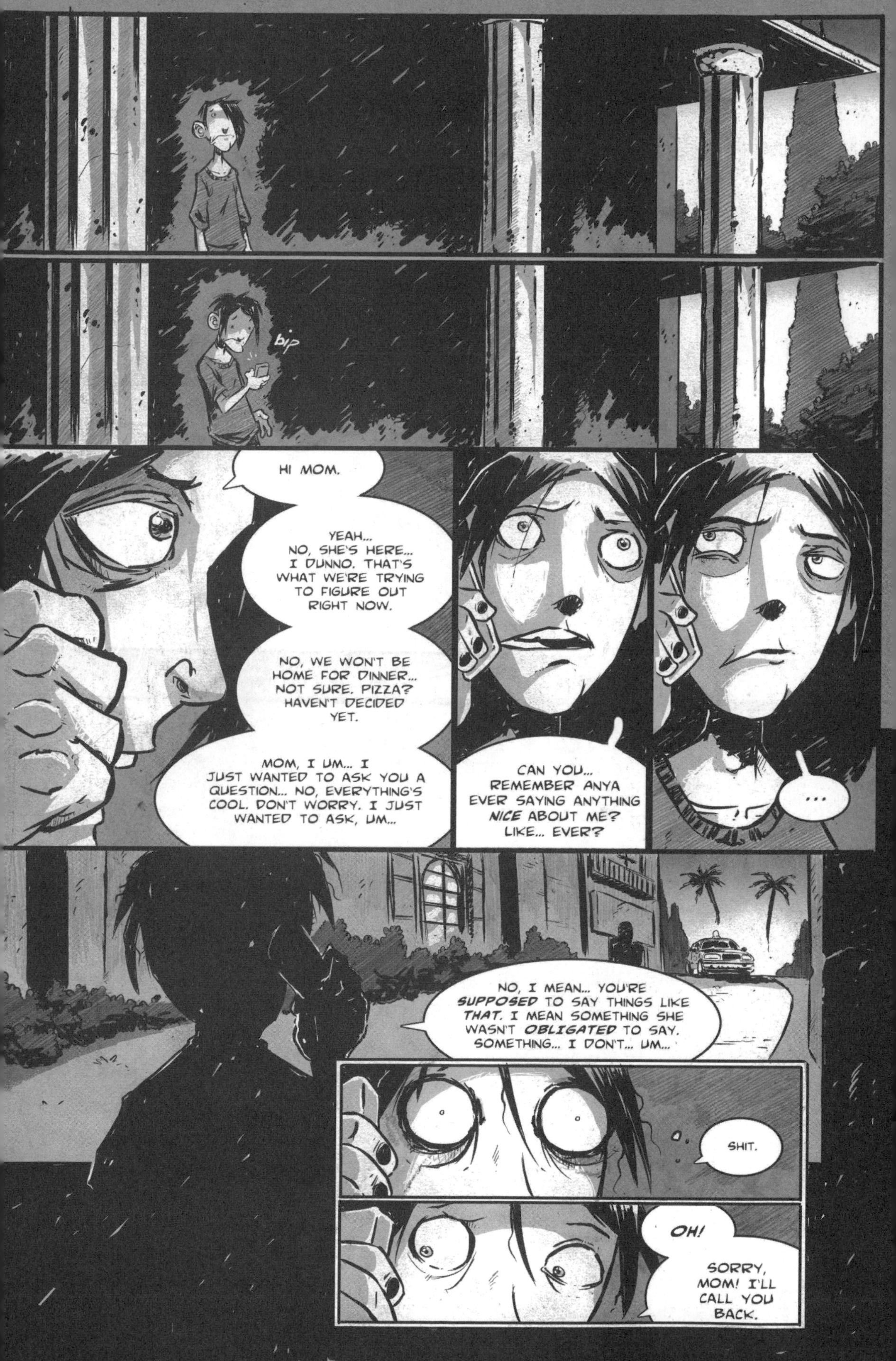
bip
HI MOM.
YEAH... NO, SHE'S HERE... I DUNNO. THAT'S WHAT WE'RE TRYING TO FIGURE OUT RIGHT NOW.
NO, WE WON'T BE HOME FOR DINNER... NOT SURE. PIZZA? HAVEN'T DECIDED YET.
MOM, I UM... I JUST WANTED TO ASK YOU A QUESTION... NO, EVERYTHING'S COOL. DON'T WORRY. I JUST WANTED TO ASK, UM...
CAN YOU... REMEMBER ANYA EVER SAYING ANYTHING NICE ABOUT ME? LIKE... EVER?
...
NO, I MEAN... YOU'RE SUPPOSED TO SAY THINGS LIKE THAT. I MEAN SOMETHING SHE WASN'T OBLIGATED TO SAY. SOMETHING... I DON'T... UM...
SHIT.
OH!
SORRY, MOM! I'LL CALL YOU BACK.

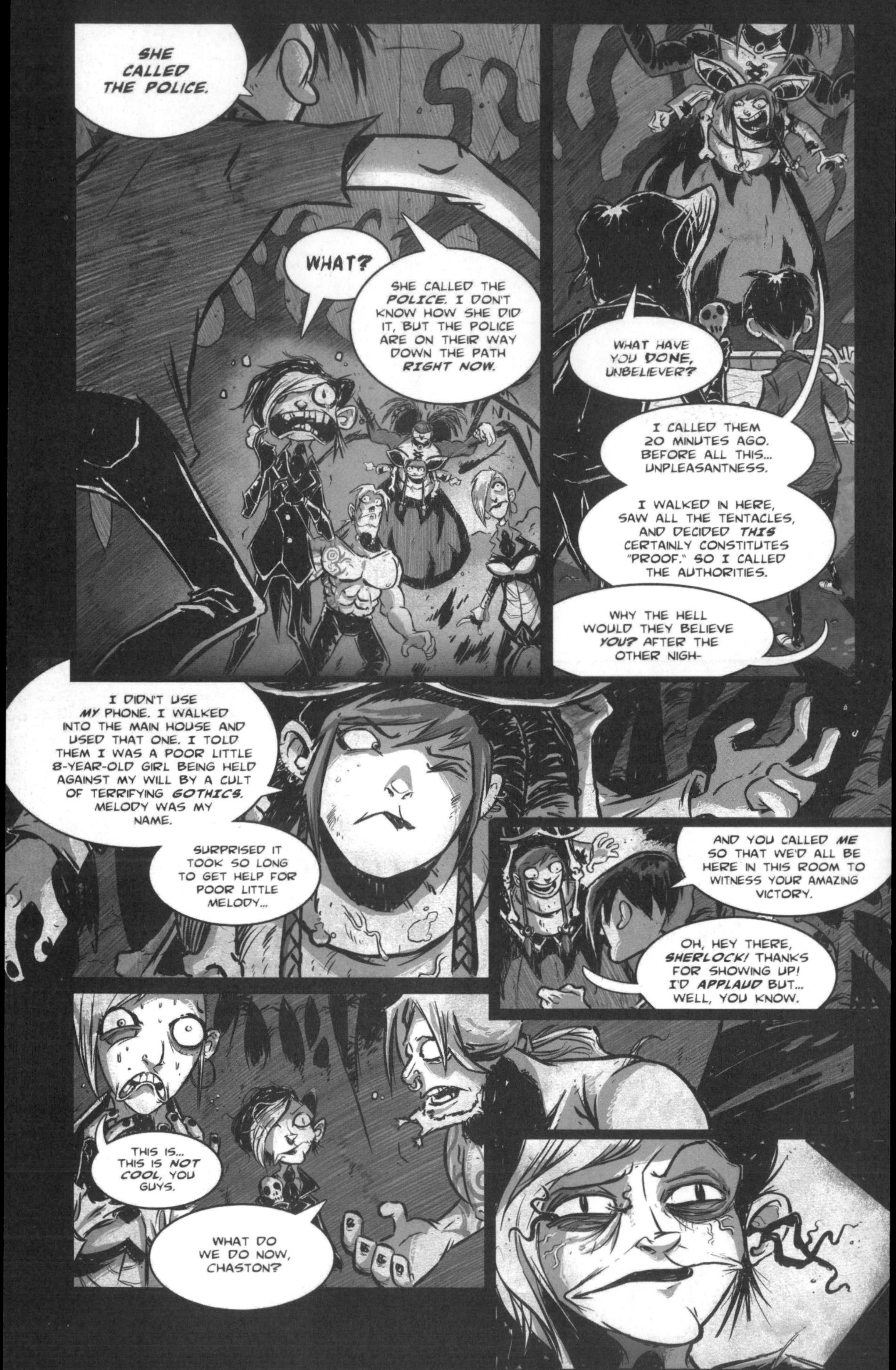
SHE CALLED THE POLICE.
WHAT?
SHE CALLED THE POLICE. I DON'T KNOW HOW SHE DID IT, BUT THE POLICE ARE ON THEIR WAY DOWN THE PATH RIGHT NOW.
WHAT HAVE YOU DONE, UNBELIEVER?
I CALLED THEM 20 MINUTES AGO. BEFORE ALL THIS... UNPLEASANTNESS.
I WALKED IN HERE, SAW ALL THE TENTACLES, AND DECIDED THIS CERTAINLY CONSTITUTES "PROOF." SO I CALLED THE AUTHORITIES.
WHY THE HELL WOULD THEY BELIEVE YOU? AFTER THE OTHER NIGH-
I DIDN'T USE MY PHONE. I WALKED INTO THE MAIN HOUSE AND USED THAT ONE. I TOLD THEM I WAS A POOR LITTLE 8-YEAR-OLD GIRL BEING HELD AGAINST MY WILL BY A CULT OF TERRIFYING GOTHICS. MELODY WAS MY NAME.
SURPRISED IT TOOK SO LONG TO GET HELP FOR POOR LITTLE MELODY...
AND YOU CALLED ME SO THAT WE'D ALL BE HERE IN THIS ROOM TO WITNESS YOUR AMAZING VICTORY.
OH, HEY THERE, SHERLOCK! THANKS FOR SHOWING UP! I'D APPLAUD BUT... WELL, YOU KNOW.
THIS IS... THIS IS NOT COOL, YOU GUYS.
WHAT DO WE DO NOW, CHASTON?

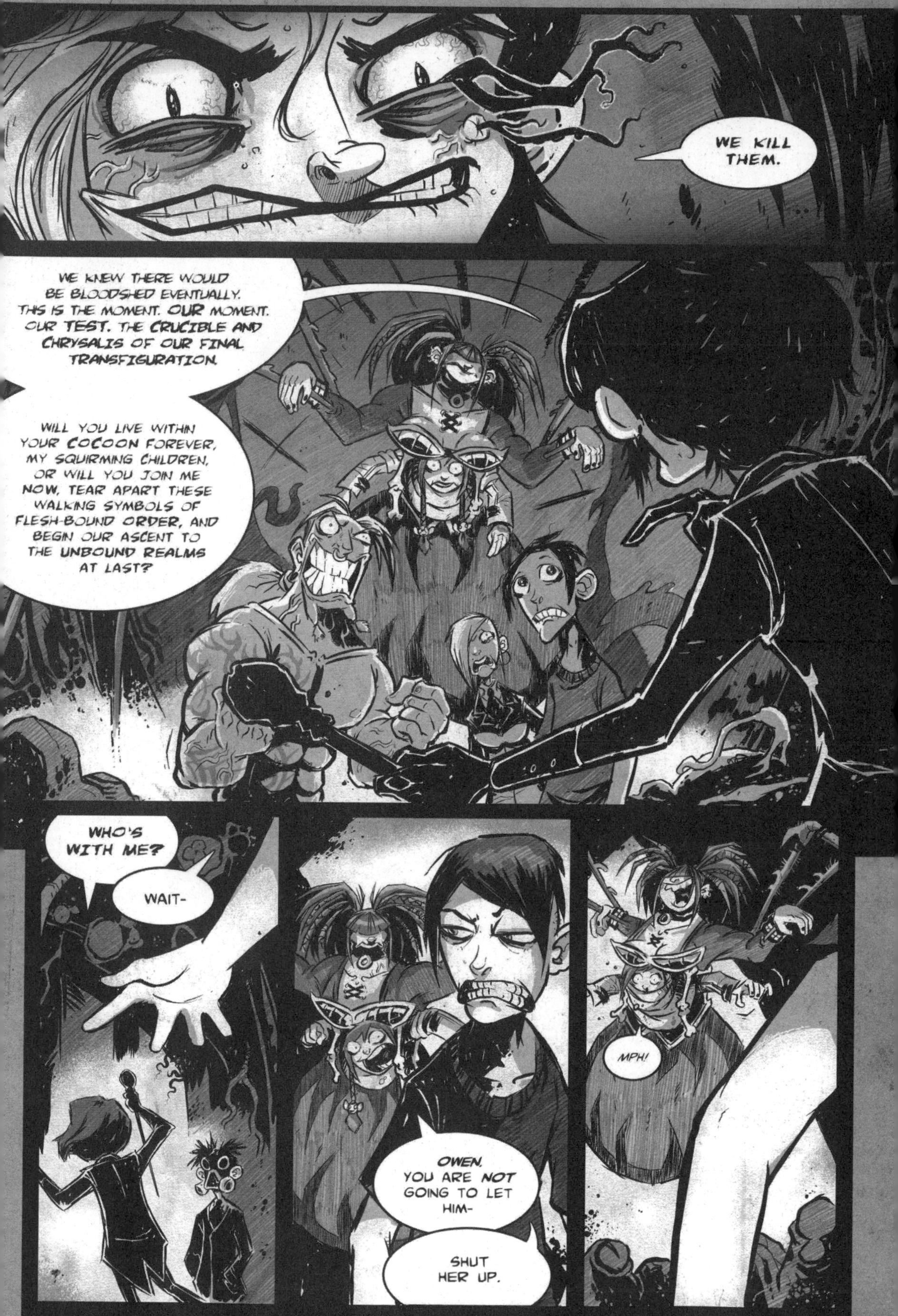
WE KILL THEM.
WE KNEW THERE WOULD BE BLOODSHED EVENTUALLY. THIS IS THE MOMENT. OUR MOMENT. OUR TEST. THE CRUCIBLE AND CHRYSALIS OF OUR FINAL TRANSFIGURATION.
WILL YOU LIVE WITHIN YOUR COCOON FOREVER, MY SQUIRMING CHILDREN, OR WILL YOU JOIN ME NOW, TEAR APART THESE WALKING SYMBOLS OF FLESH-BOUND ORDER, AND BEGIN OUR ASCENT TO THE UNBOUND REALMS AT LAST?
WHO'S WITH ME?
WAIT-
OWEN, YOU ARE NOT GOING TO LET HIM-
SHUT HER UP.
MPH!

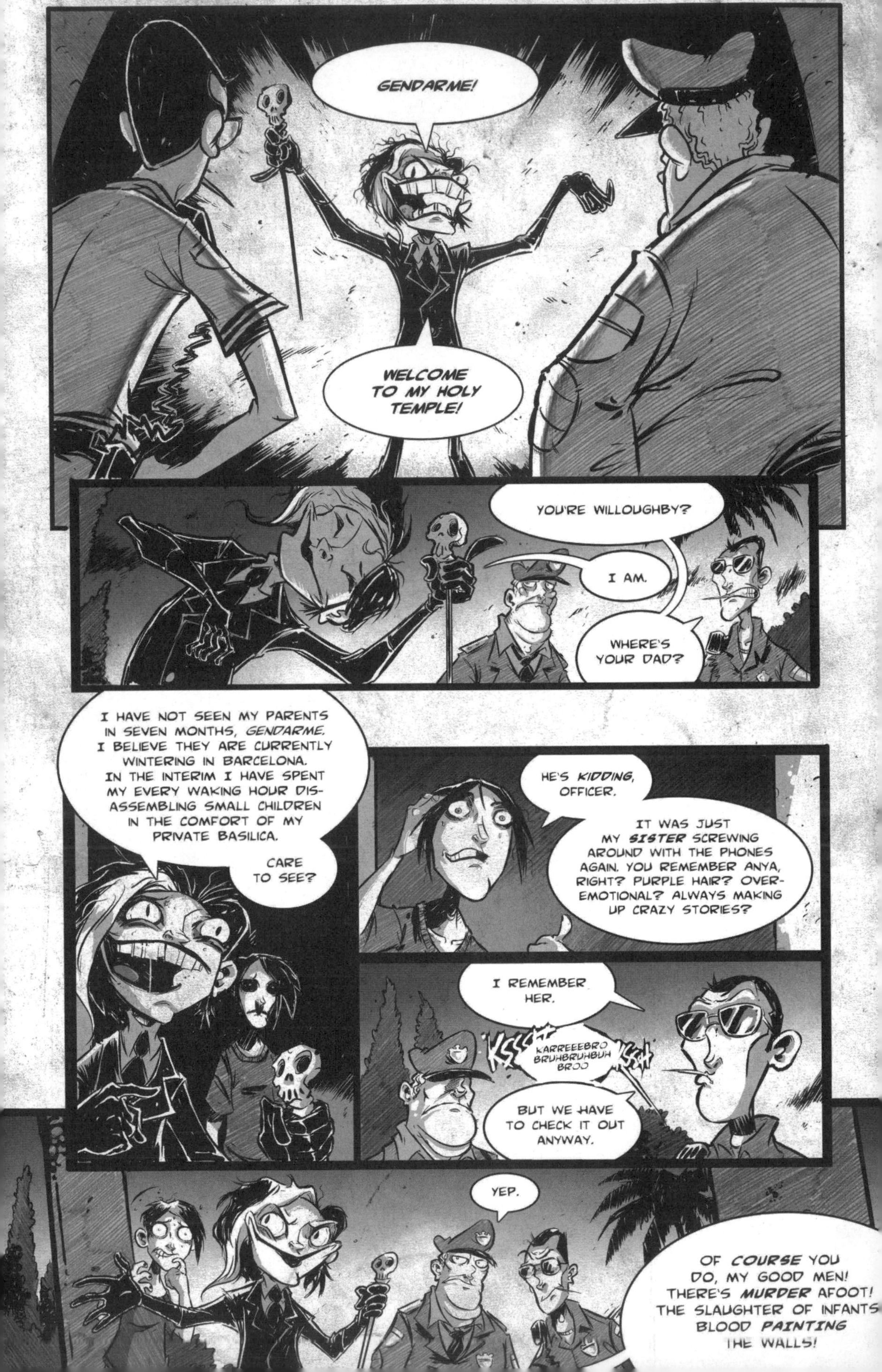
GENDARME!
WELCOME TO MY HOLY TEMPLE!
YOU'RE WILLOUGHBY?
I AM.
WHERE'S YOUR DAD?
I HAVE NOT SEEN MY PARENTS IN SEVEN MONTHS, GENDARME. I BELIEVE THEY ARE CURRENTLY WINTERING IN BARCELONA. IN THE INTERIM I HAVE SPENT MY EVERY WAKING HOUR DIS-ASSEMBLING SMALL CHILDREN IN THE COMFORT OF MY PRIVATE BASILICA.
CARE TO SEE?
HE'S KIDDING, OFFICER.
IT WAS JUST MY SISTER SCREWING AROUND WITH THE PHONES AGAIN. YOU REMEMBER ANYA, RIGHT? PURPLE HAIR? OVER-EMOTIONAL? ALWAYS MAKING UP CRAZY STORIES?
I REMEMBER HER.
KARREEEBRO BRUHBRUHBUH BROO
BUT WE HAVE TO CHECK IT OUT ANYWAY.
YEP.
OF COURSE YOU DO, MY GOOD MEN! THERE'S MURDER AFOOT! THE SLAUGHTER OF INFANTS BLOOD PAINTING THE WALLS!

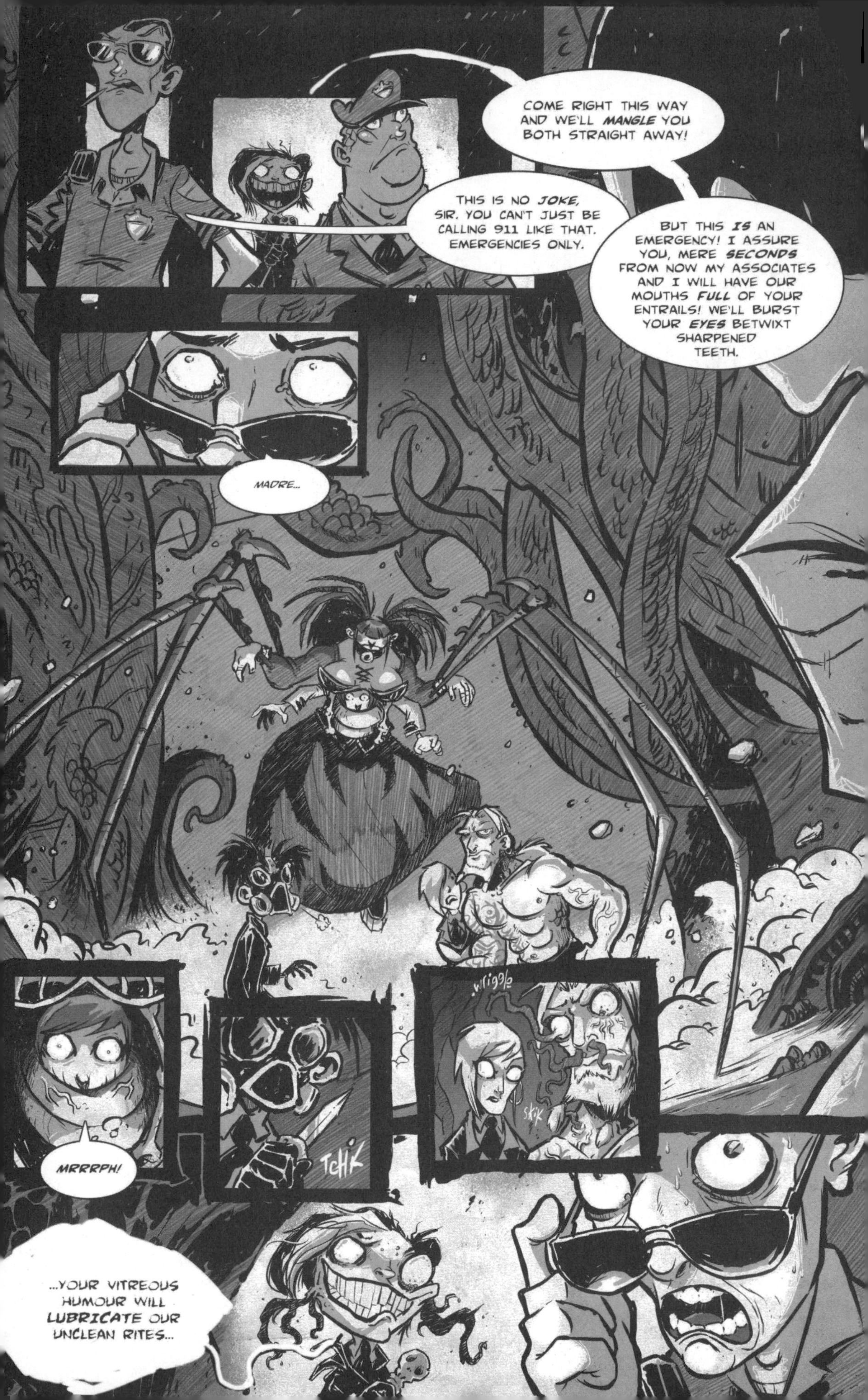
COME RIGHT THIS WAY AND WE'LL MANGLE YOU BOTH STRAIGHT AWAY!
THIS IS NO JOKE, SIR. YOU CAN'T JUST BE CALLING 911 LIKE THAT. EMERGENCIES ONLY.
BUT THIS IS AN EMERGENCY! I ASSURE YOU, MERE SECONDS FROM NOW MY ASSOCIATES AND I WILL HAVE OUR MOUTHS FULL OF YOUR ENTRAILS! WE'LL BURST YOUR EYES BETWIXT SHARPENED TEETH.
MADRE...
MRRRPH!
TCHIK
wriggle
SKIK
...YOUR VITREOUS HUMOUR WILL LUBRICATE OUR UNCLEAN RITES...

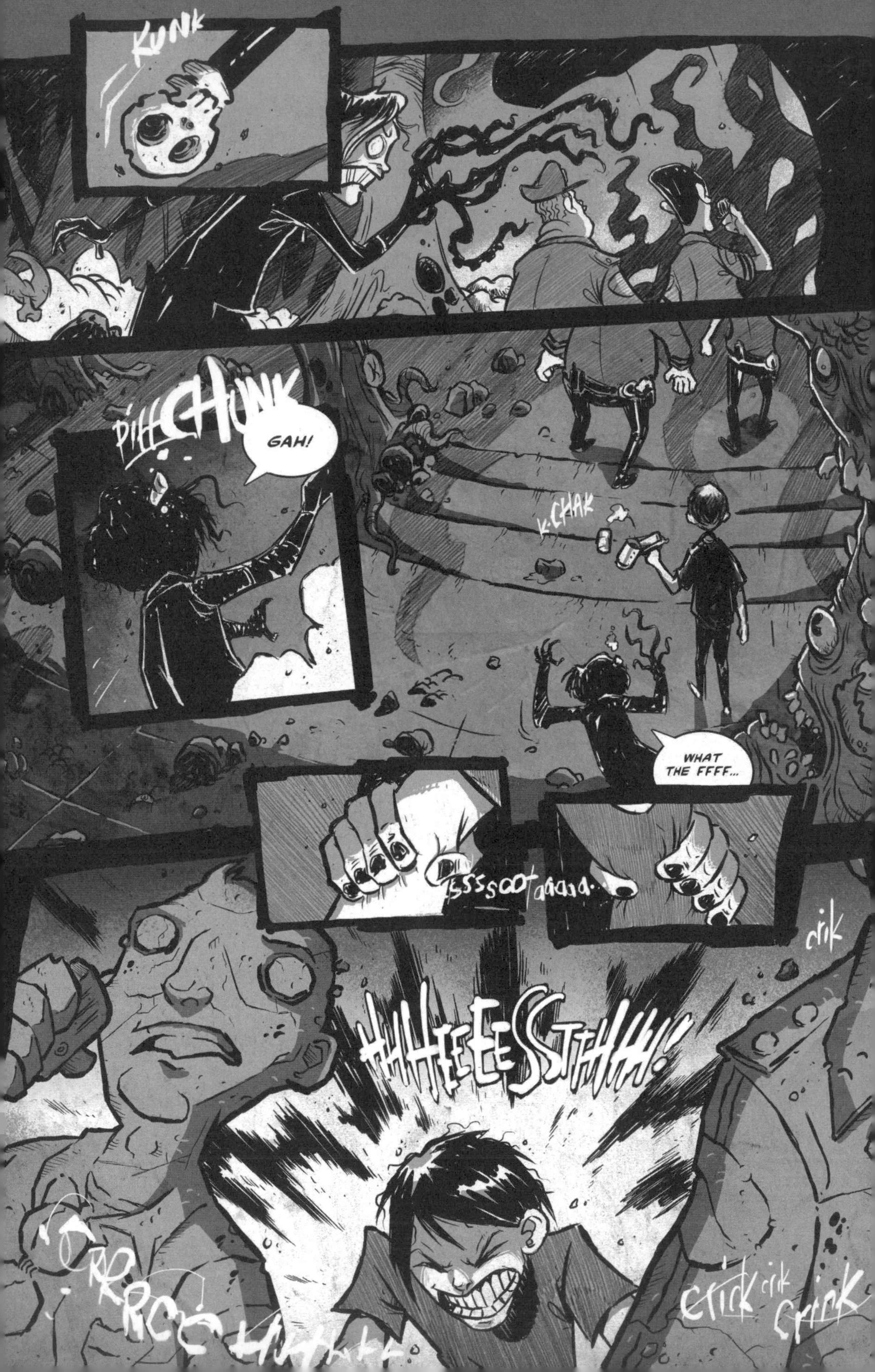
KUNK
PIH CHUNK
GAH!
K-CHAK
WHAT THE FFFF...
SSSSCOOTAAAAA..
crik
HHHEEEESSTHHH!
CRRRCCC
crick crik crick

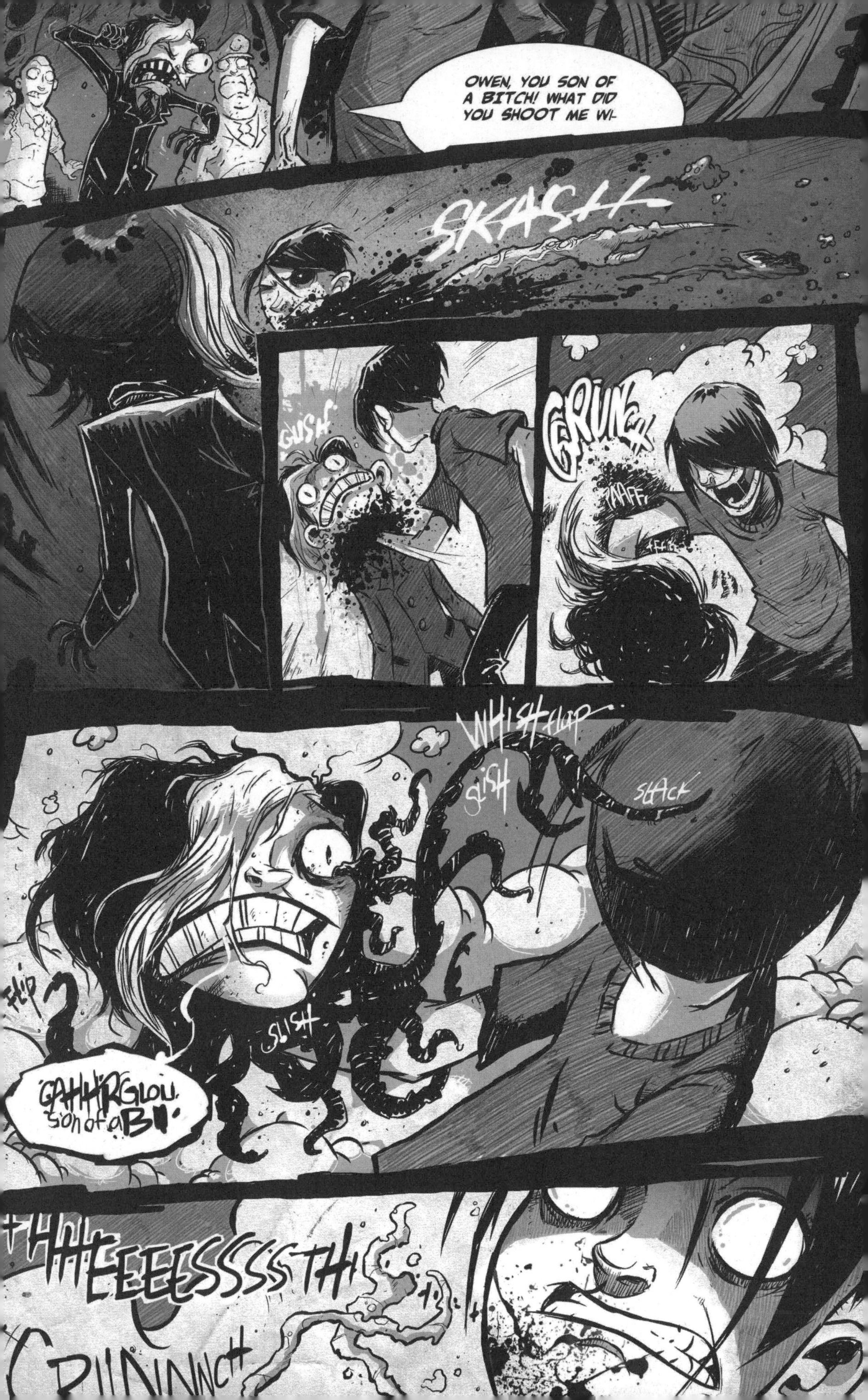
OWEN, YOU SON OF A BITCH! WHAT DID YOU SHOOT ME WI-
SKASH
GUSH
CRUNCH
PAAFF
WHISH flap
SLISH
SLACK
FLIP
SLISH
GAHHRGLOU. son of a BI
THHEEEESSSSTH
CRUNNNCH

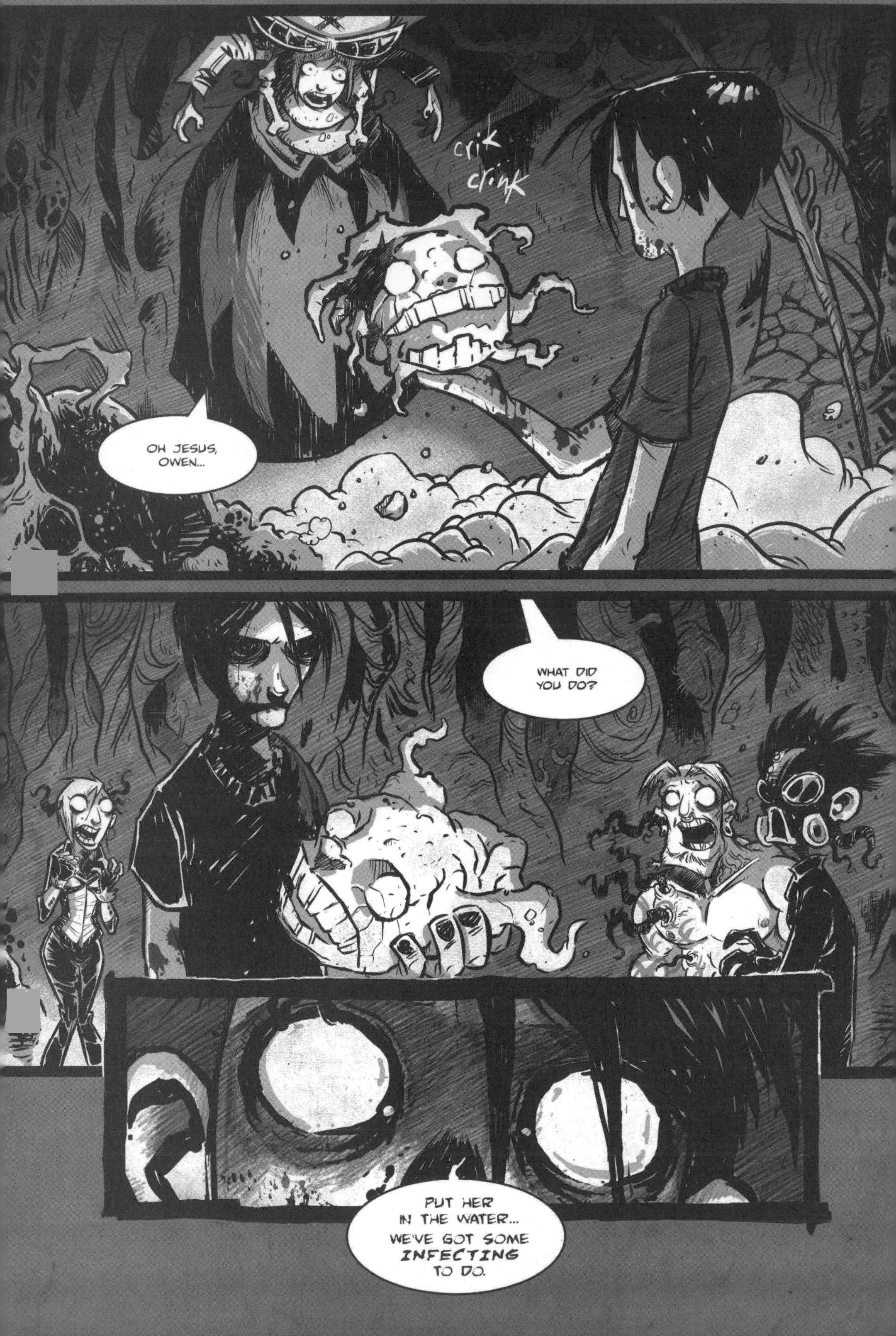
crik
crink
OH JESUS, OWEN...
WHAT DID YOU DO?
PUT HER IN THE WATER... WE'VE GOT SOME INFECTING TO DO.

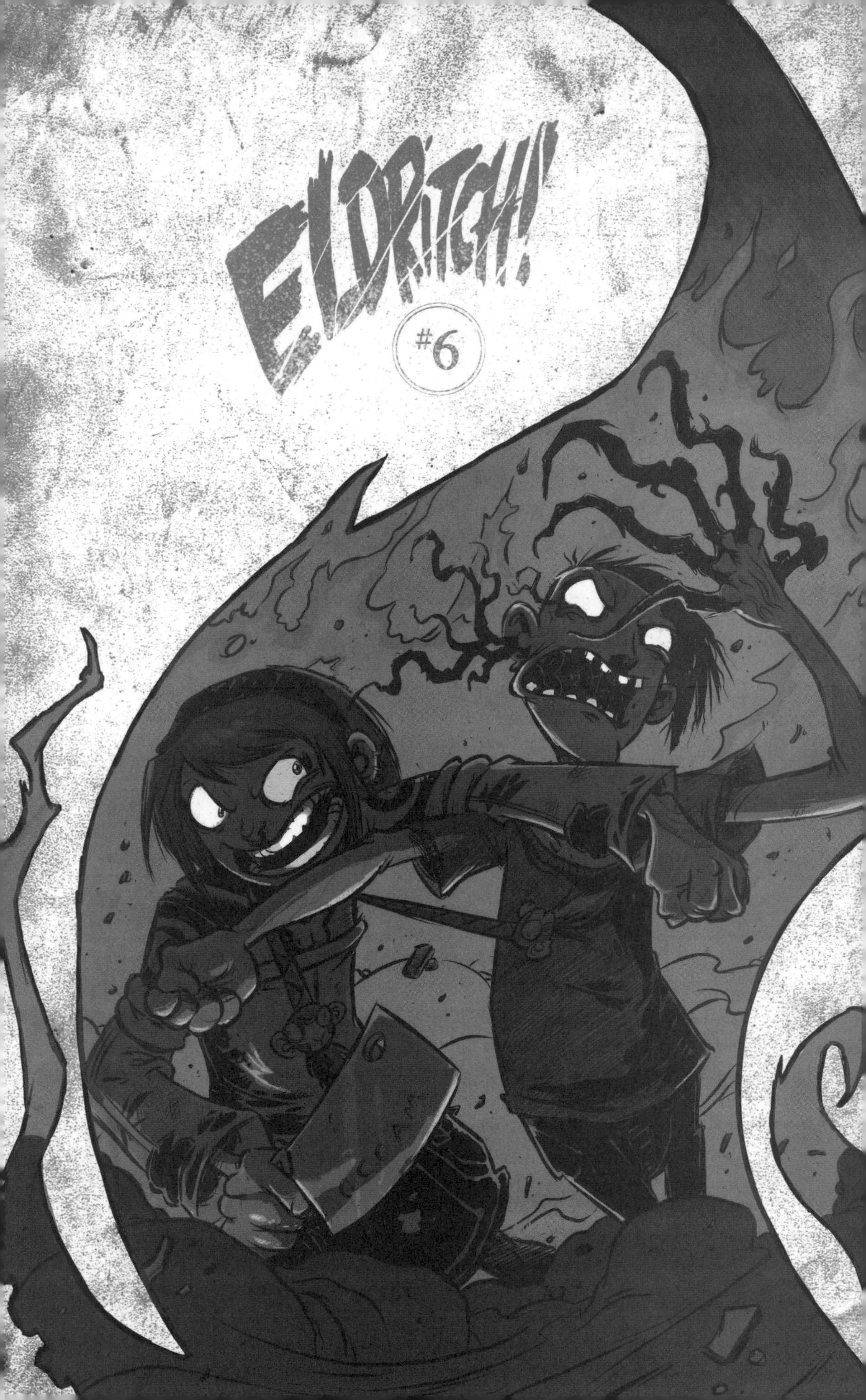
ELDRITCH!
#6

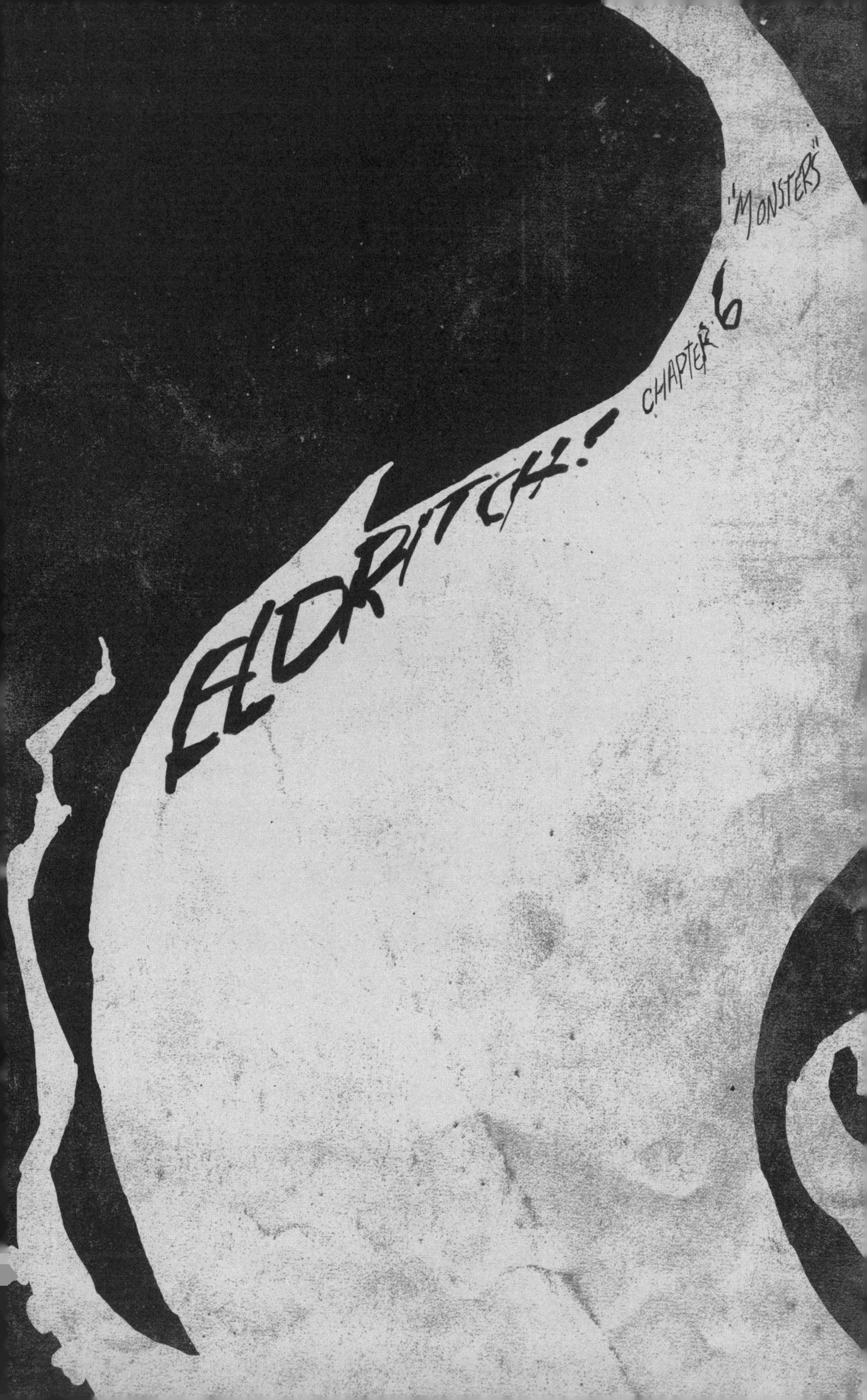
ELDRITCH! - CHAPTER 6
"MONSTERS"

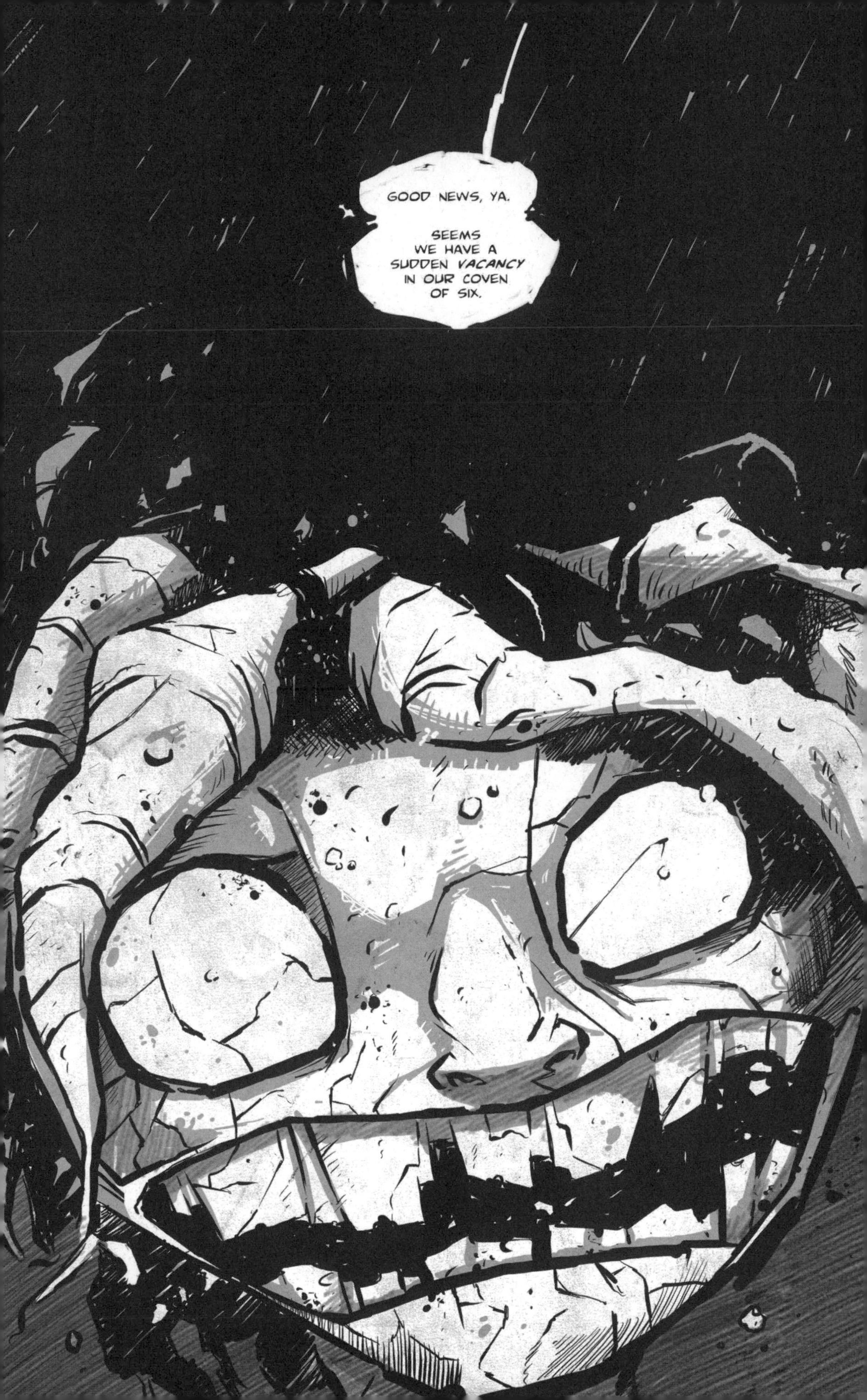
GOOD NEWS, YA.
SEEMS WE HAVE A SUDDEN *VACANCY* IN OUR COVEN OF SIX.

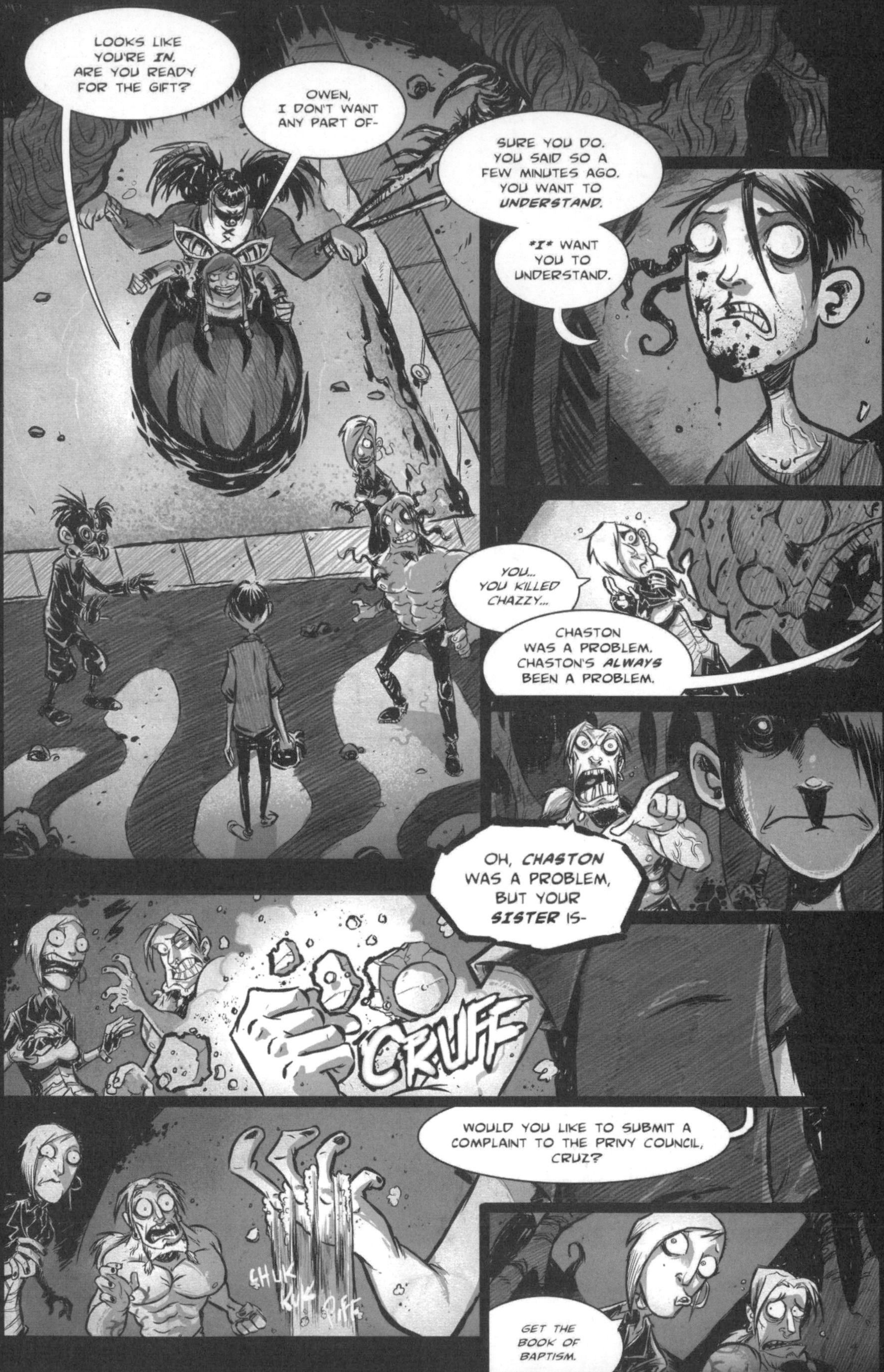
LOOKS LIKE YOU'RE IN. ARE YOU READY FOR THE GIFT?
OWEN, I DON'T WANT ANY PART OF-
SURE YOU DO. YOU SAID SO A FEW MINUTES AGO. YOU WANT TO UNDERSTAND.
I WANT YOU TO UNDERSTAND.
YOU... YOU KILLED CHAZZY...
CHASTON WAS A PROBLEM. CHASTON'S ALWAYS BEEN A PROBLEM.
OH, CHASTON WAS A PROBLEM, BUT YOUR SISTER IS-
CRUFF
WOULD YOU LIKE TO SUBMIT A COMPLAINT TO THE PRIVY COUNCIL, CRUZ?
SHUK KUK PIFF
GET THE BOOK OF BAPTISM.

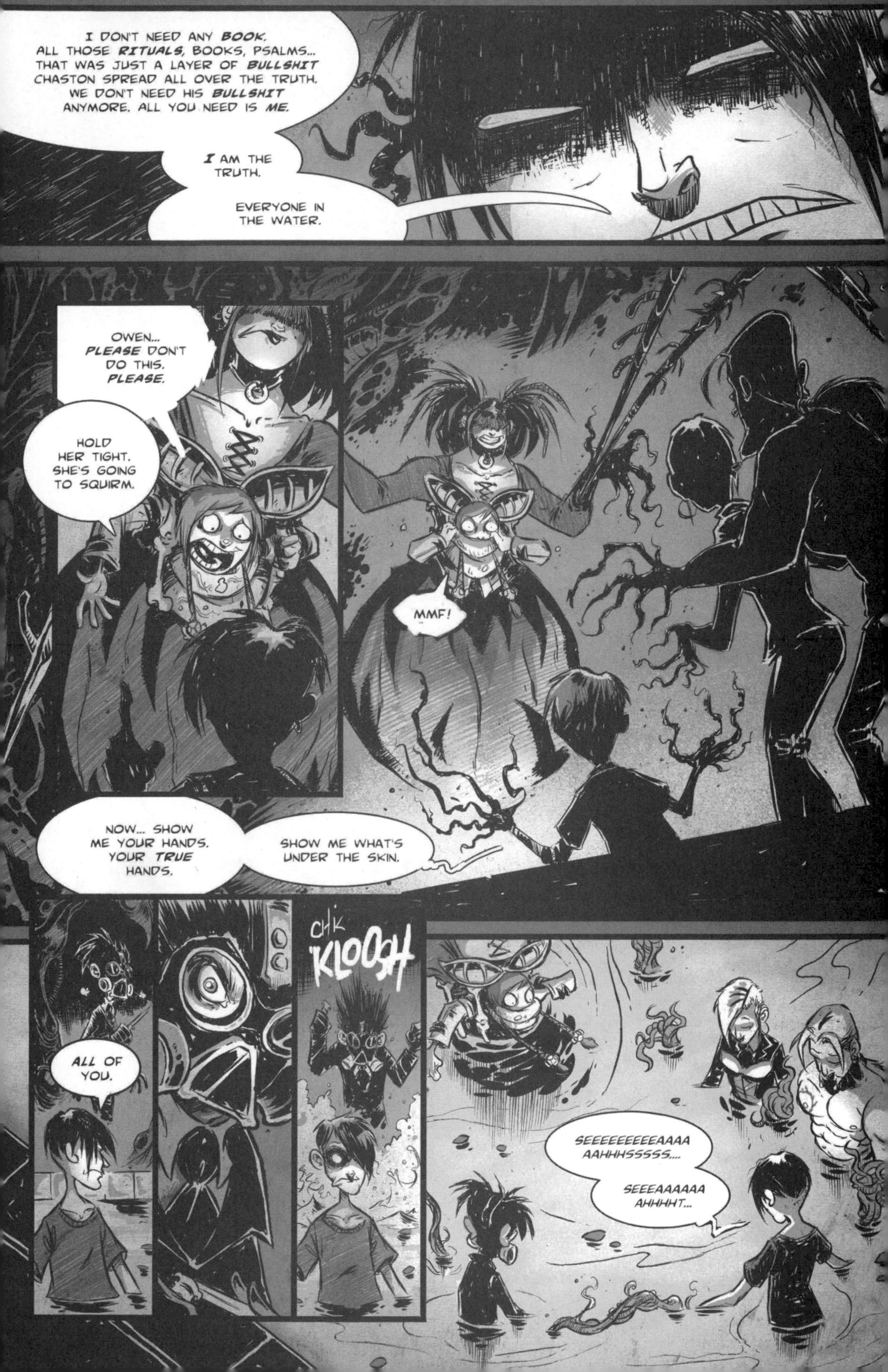
I DON'T NEED ANY BOOK. ALL THOSE RITUALS, BOOKS, PSALMS... THAT WAS JUST A LAYER OF BULLSHIT CHASTON SPREAD ALL OVER THE TRUTH. WE DON'T NEED HIS BULLSHIT ANYMORE. ALL YOU NEED IS ME.
I AM THE TRUTH.
EVERYONE IN THE WATER.
OWEN... PLEASE DON'T DO THIS. PLEASE.
HOLD HER TIGHT. SHE'S GOING TO SQUIRM.
MMF!
NOW... SHOW ME YOUR HANDS. YOUR TRUE HANDS.
SHOW ME WHAT'S UNDER THE SKIN.
ALL OF YOU.
CHK
KLOOSH
SEEEEEEEEEAAAA AAHHHSSSSS....
SEEEAAAAAAA AHHHHT...

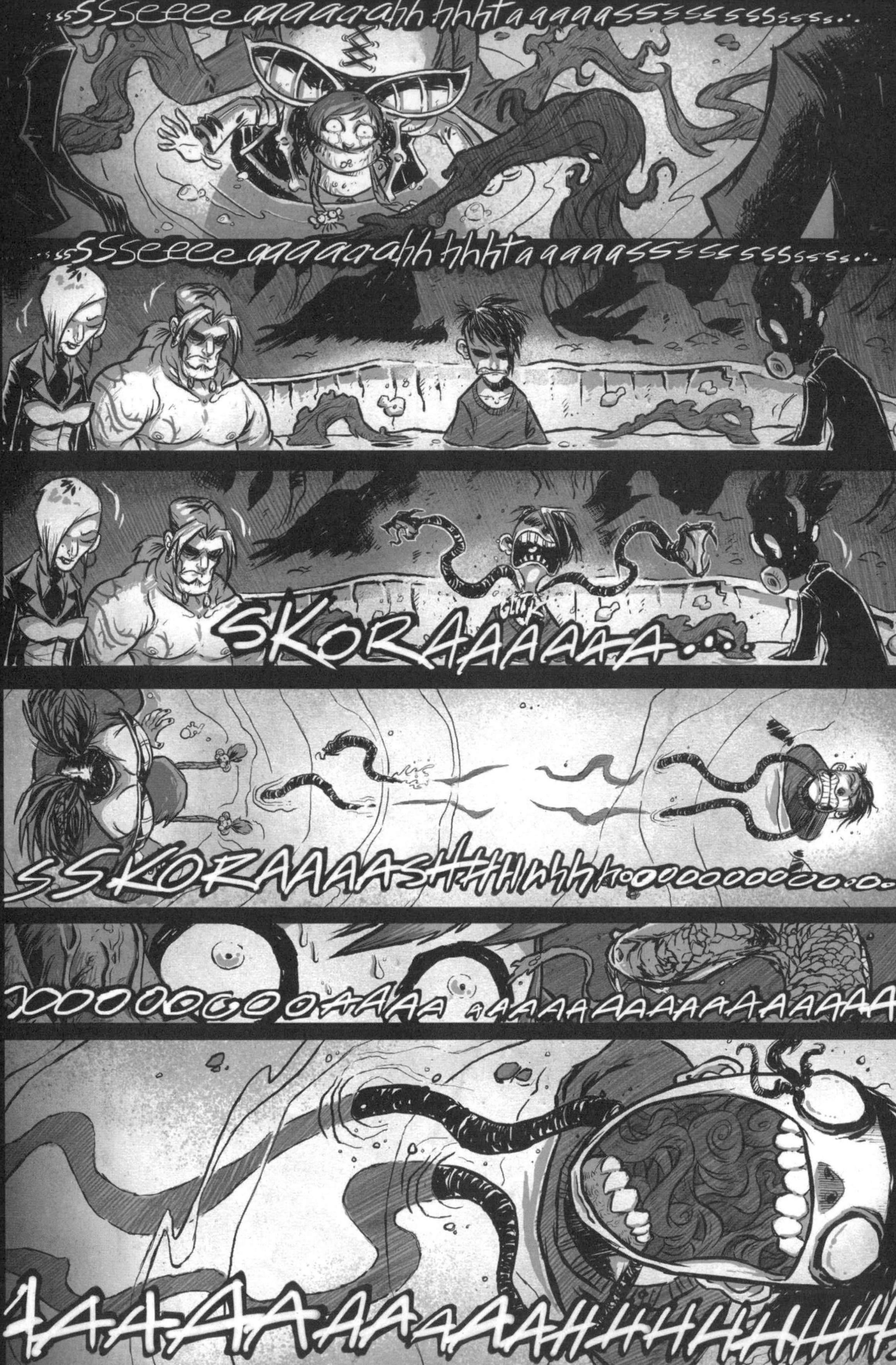

...ssSSSeeeee aaaaaaahh hhhhtaaaaaassssssssssssss...
...ssSSSeeeee aaaaaaahh hhhhtaaaaaassssssssssssss...
SKORAAAAAAA....
SSKORAAAASHHHHhhhhoooooooooooo...
OOOOOOOOOOAAAA AAAAAAAAAAAAAAAAA
AAAAAAAAAAHHHHHHHHH!

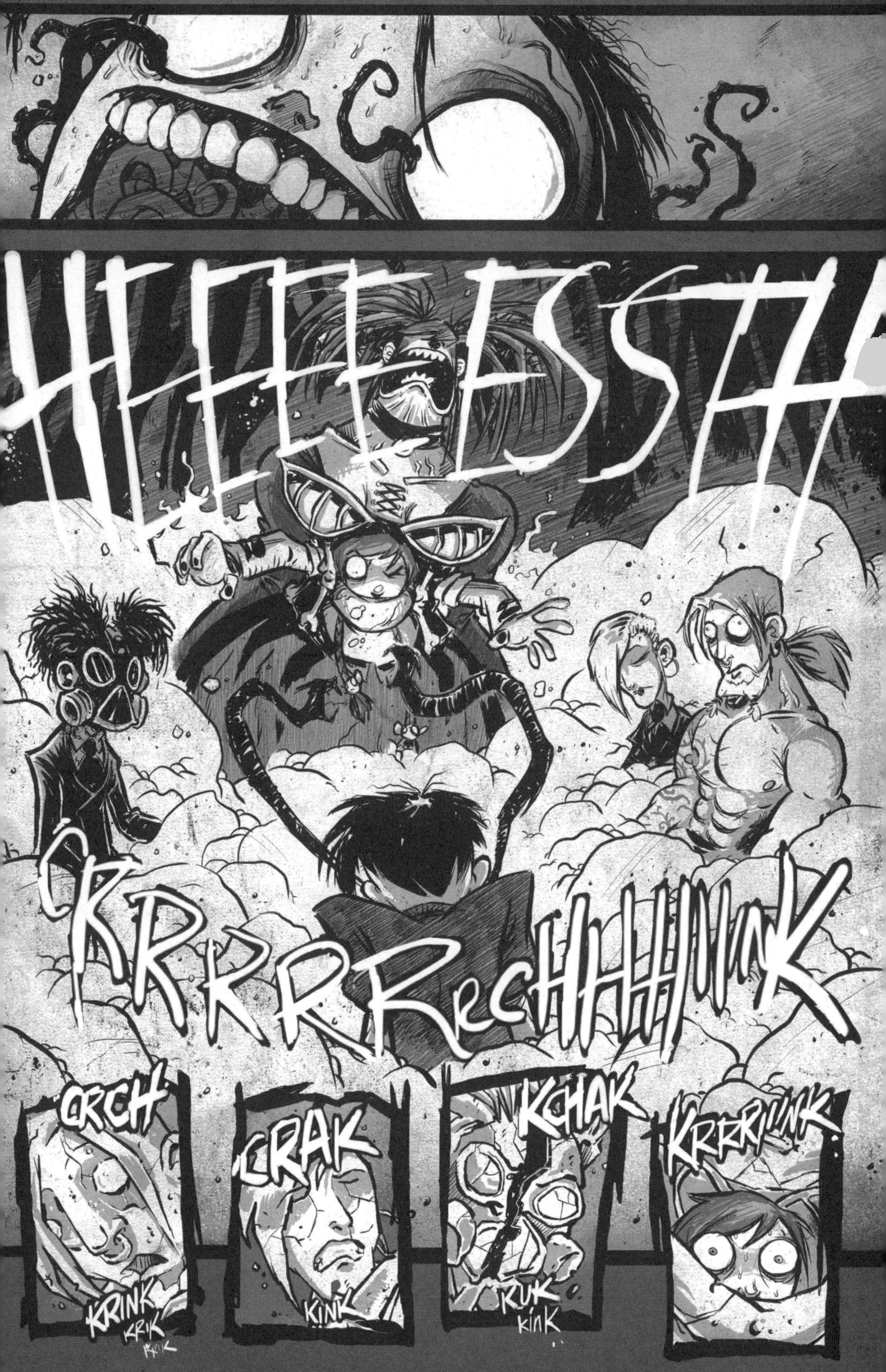
HEEEESSZA
CRRRRRechHHHNK
CRCH
KRINK
KRIK
KRIK
CRAK
KINK
KCHAK
KUK
kink
KRRRINK

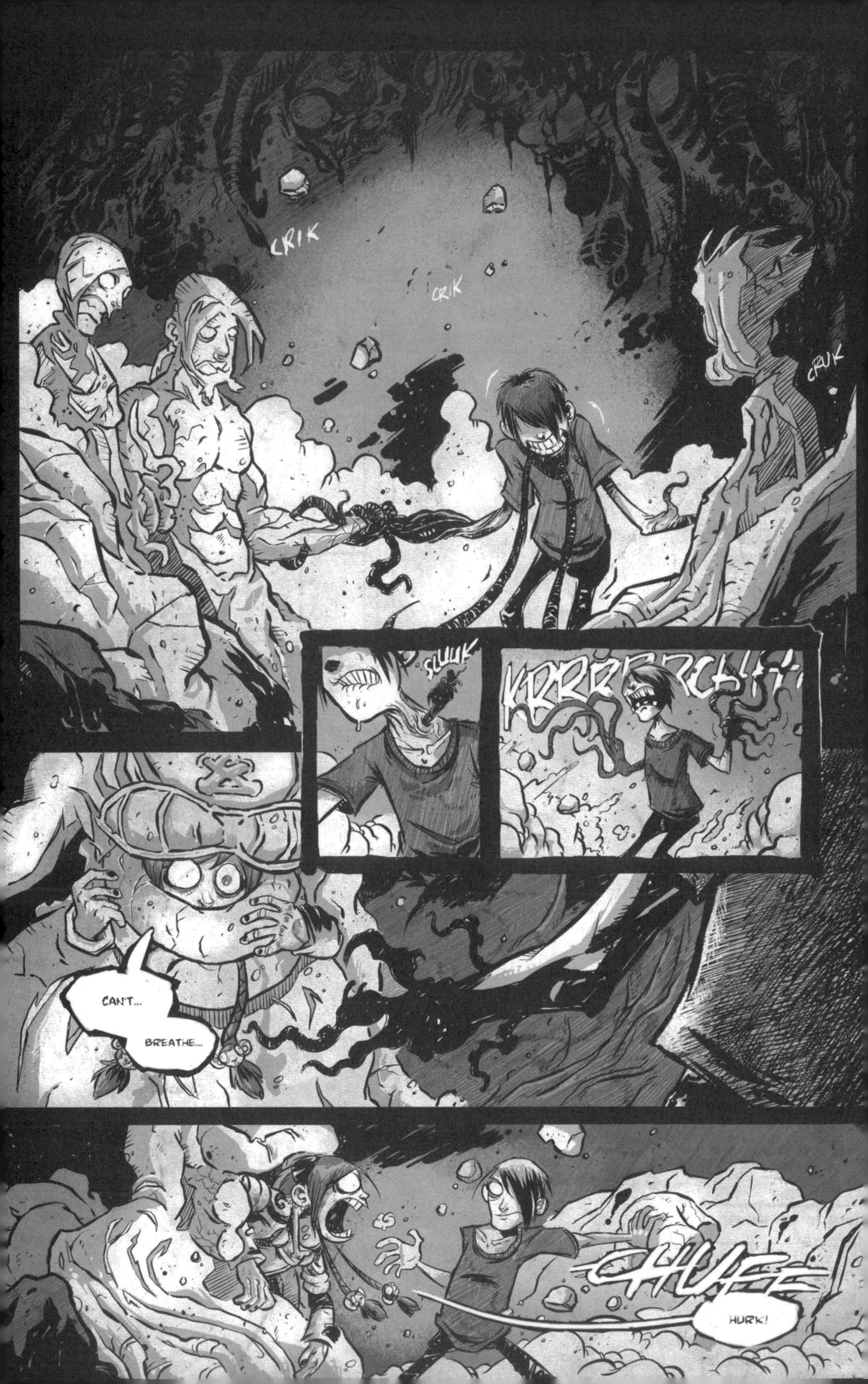
CRIK
CRIK
CRUK
SLUUK
KRRRRRCH!!
CAN'T...
BREATHE...
CHUFF
HURK!

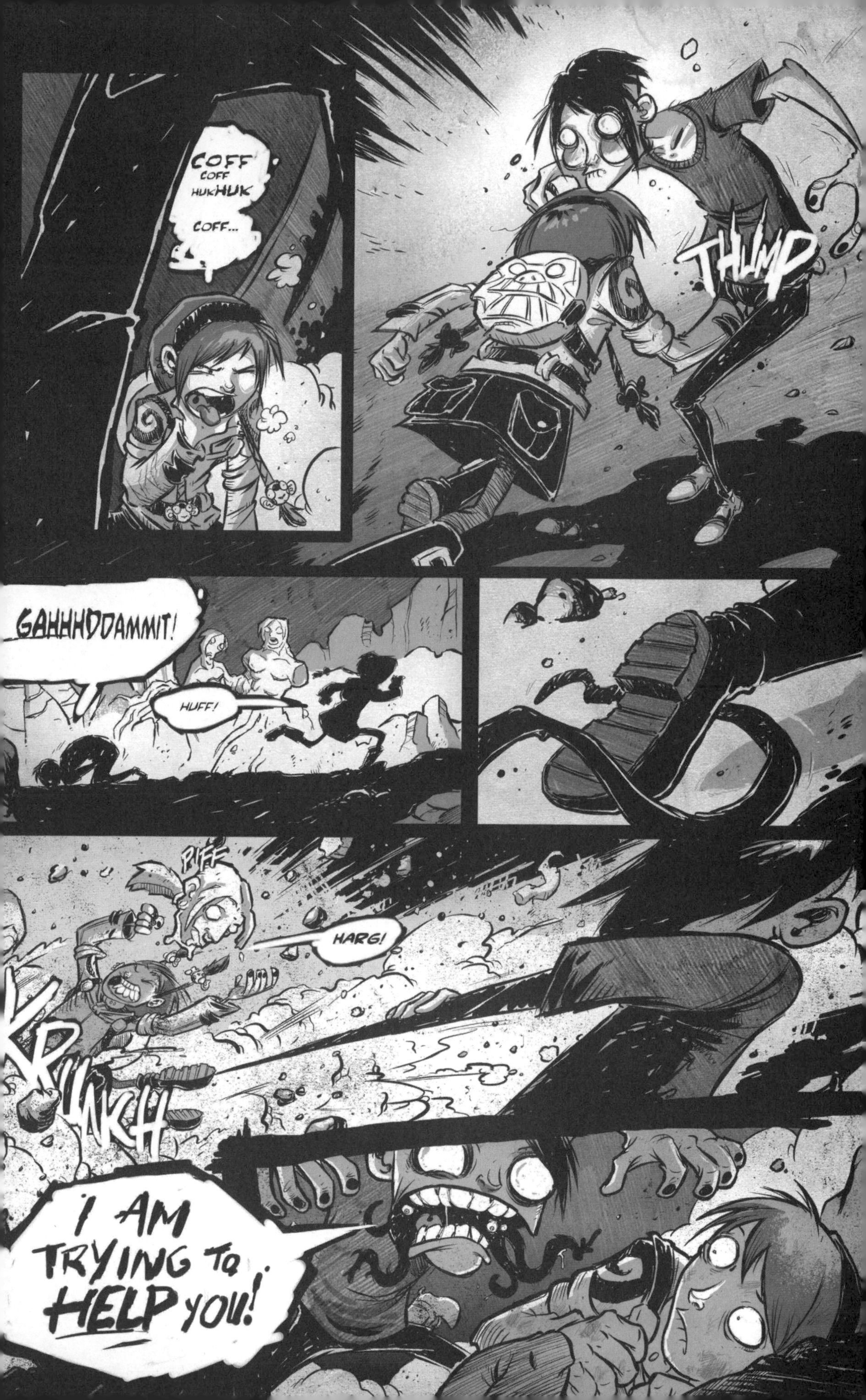
COFF
COFF
HUKHUK
COFF...
THUMP
GAHHHDDAMMIT!
HUFF!
PIFF
HARG!
KRUNKH
I AM TRYING TO HELP YOU!

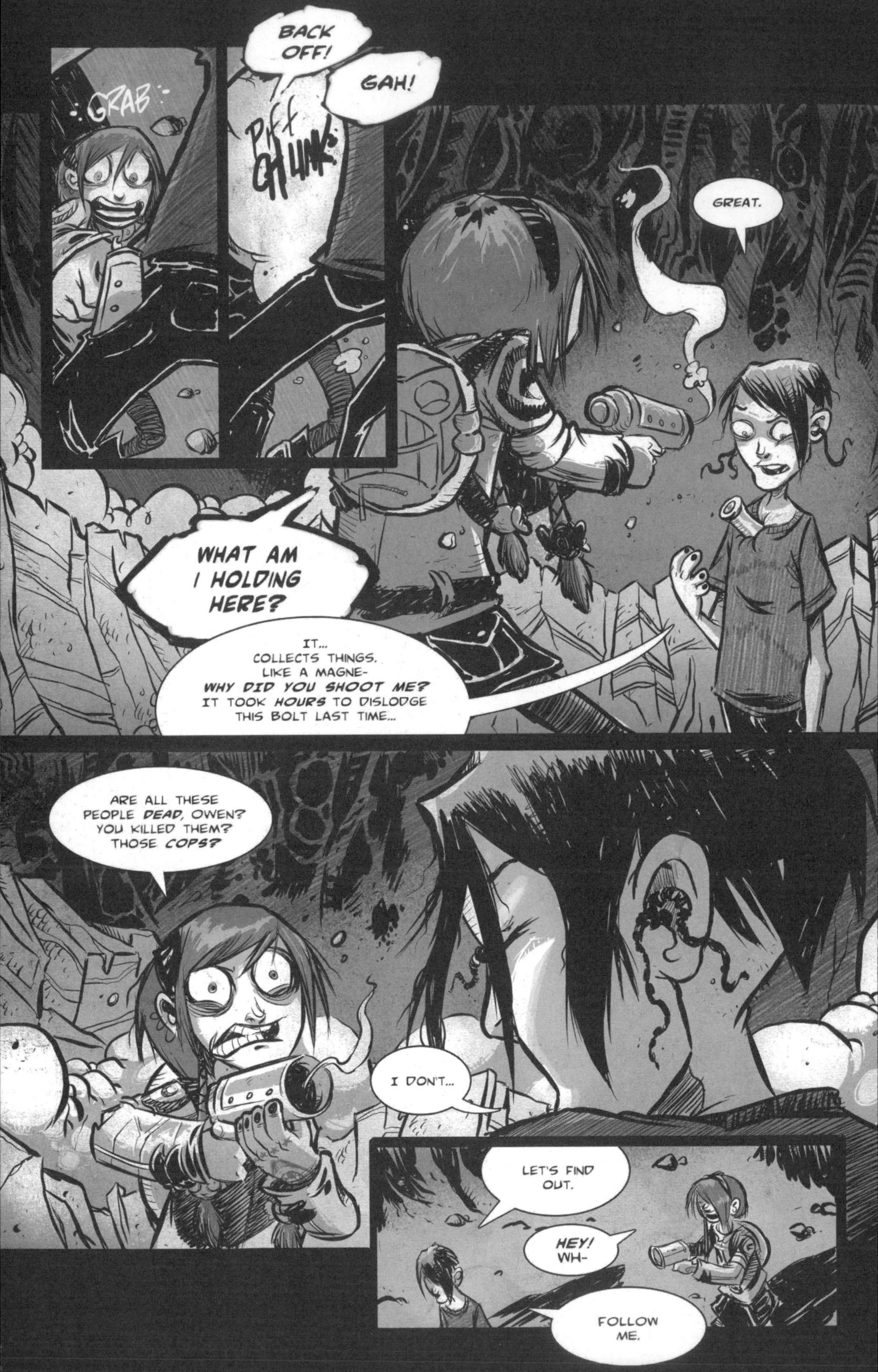

GRAB
BACK OFF!
GAH!
PFFT
CHUNK
GREAT.
WHAT AM I HOLDING HERE?
IT... COLLECTS THINGS. LIKE A MAGNE- WHY DID YOU SHOOT ME? IT TOOK HOURS TO DISLODGE THIS BOLT LAST TIME...
ARE ALL THESE PEOPLE DEAD, OWEN? YOU KILLED THEM? THOSE COPS?
I DON'T...
LET'S FIND OUT.
HEY! WH-
FOLLOW ME.

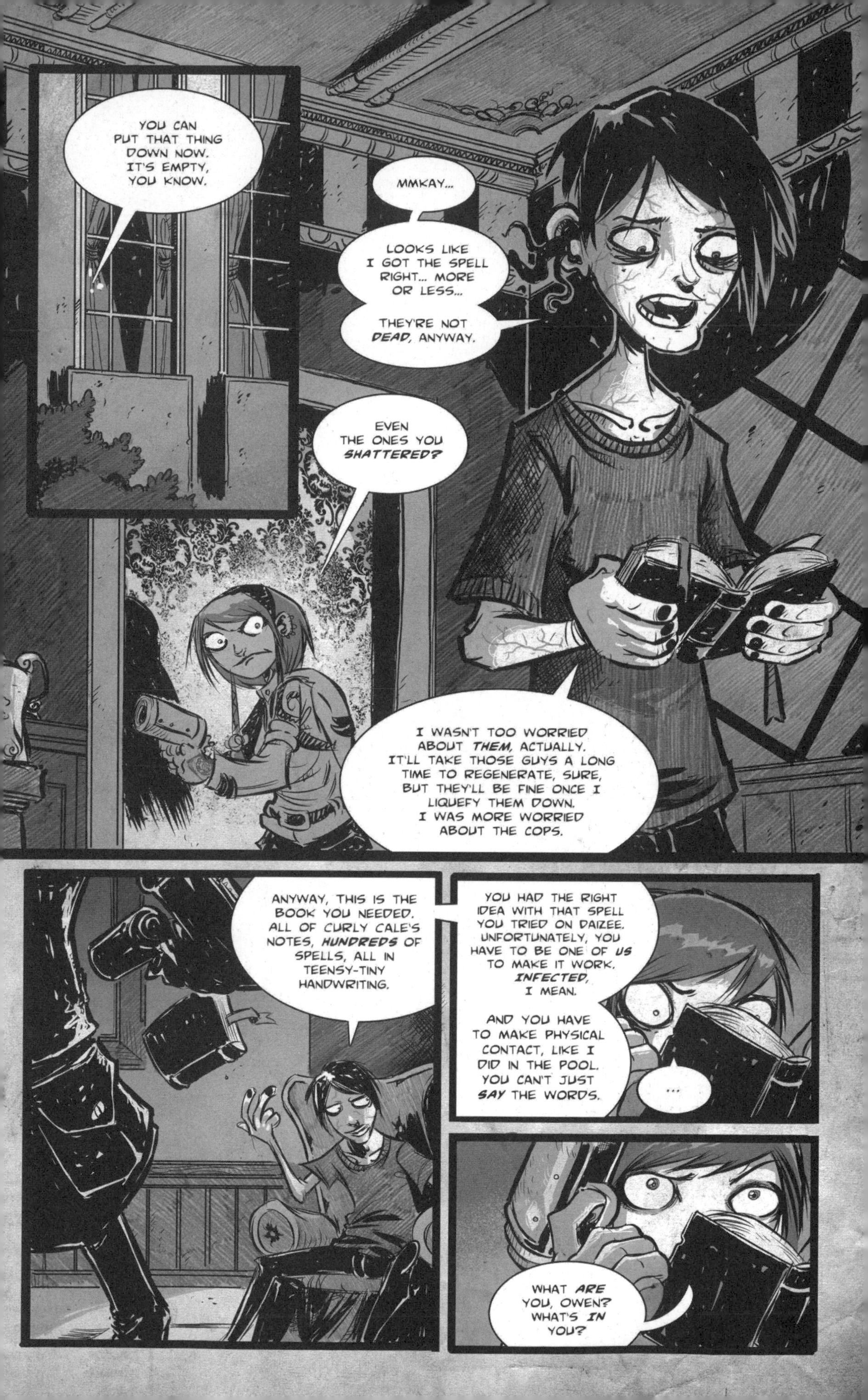
YOU CAN PUT THAT THING DOWN NOW. IT'S EMPTY, YOU KNOW.
MMKAY...
LOOKS LIKE I GOT THE SPELL RIGHT... MORE OR LESS...
THEY'RE NOT *DEAD*, ANYWAY.
EVEN THE ONES YOU *SHATTERED?*
I WASN'T TOO WORRIED ABOUT *THEM*, ACTUALLY. IT'LL TAKE THOSE GUYS A LONG TIME TO REGENERATE, SURE, BUT THEY'LL BE FINE ONCE I LIQUEFY THEM DOWN. I WAS MORE WORRIED ABOUT THE COPS.
ANYWAY, THIS IS THE BOOK YOU NEEDED. ALL OF CURLY CALE'S NOTES, *HUNDREDS* OF SPELLS, ALL IN TEENSY-TINY HANDWRITING.
YOU HAD THE RIGHT IDEA WITH THAT SPELL YOU TRIED ON DAIZEE. UNFORTUNATELY, YOU HAVE TO BE ONE OF *US* TO MAKE IT WORK. *INFECTED*, I MEAN.
AND YOU HAVE TO MAKE PHYSICAL CONTACT, LIKE I DID IN THE POOL. YOU CAN'T JUST *SAY* THE WORDS.
...
WHAT *ARE* YOU, OWEN? WHAT'S *IN* YOU?

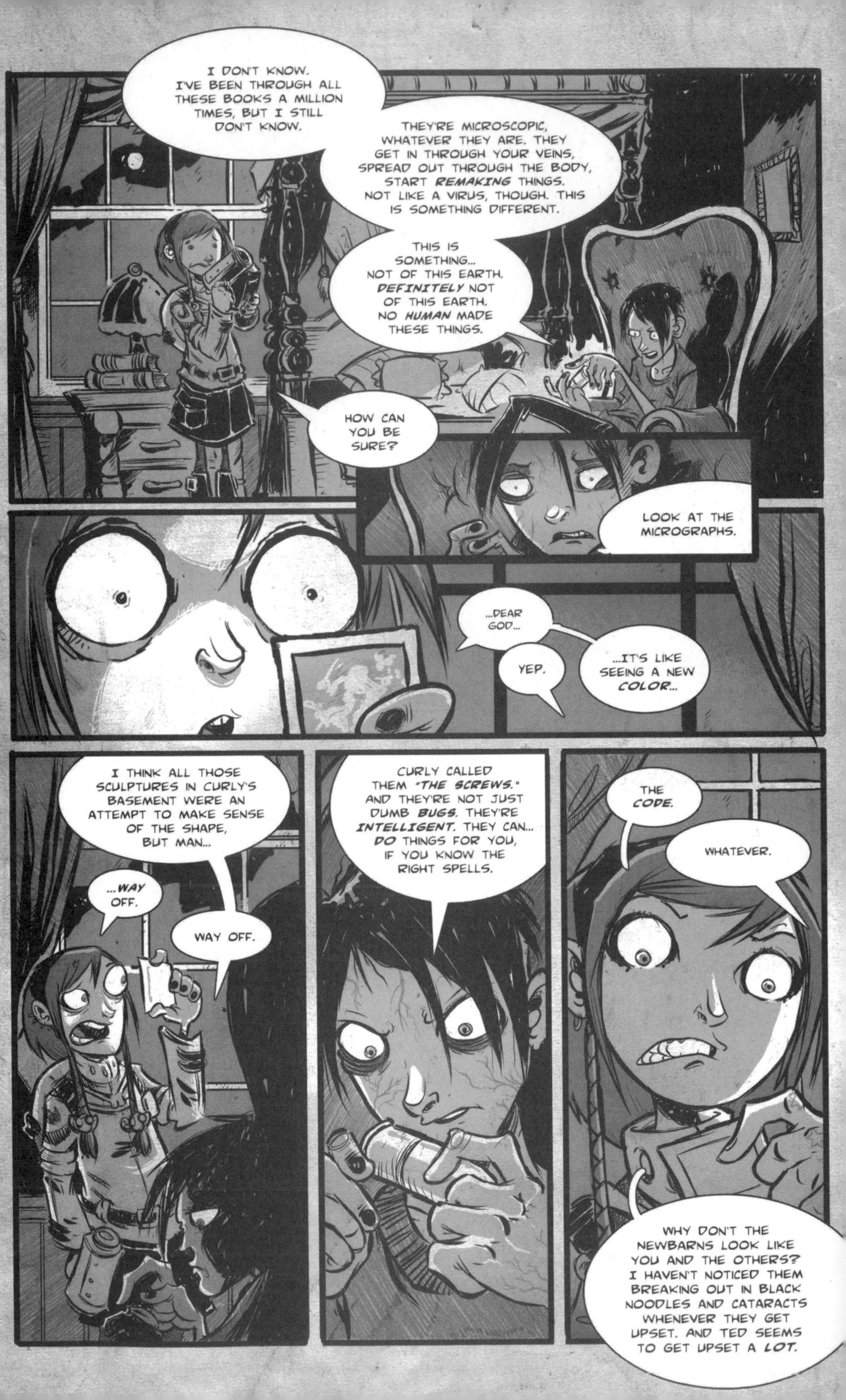

I DON'T KNOW. I'VE BEEN THROUGH ALL THESE BOOKS A MILLION TIMES, BUT I STILL DON'T KNOW.
THEY'RE MICROSCOPIC, WHATEVER THEY ARE. THEY GET IN THROUGH YOUR VEINS, SPREAD OUT THROUGH THE BODY, START *REMAKING* THINGS. NOT LIKE A VIRUS, THOUGH. THIS IS SOMETHING DIFFERENT.
THIS IS SOMETHING... NOT OF THIS EARTH. *DEFINITELY* NOT OF THIS EARTH. NO *HUMAN* MADE THESE THINGS.
HOW CAN YOU BE SURE?
LOOK AT THE MICROGRAPHS.
...DEAR GOD...
YEP.
...IT'S LIKE SEEING A NEW *COLOR*...
I THINK ALL THOSE SCULPTURES IN CURLY'S BASEMENT WERE AN ATTEMPT TO MAKE SENSE OF THE SHAPE, BUT MAN...
...WAY OFF.
WAY OFF.
CURLY CALLED THEM *"THE SCREWS."* AND THEY'RE NOT JUST DUMB *BUGS*. THEY'RE *INTELLIGENT*. THEY CAN... *DO* THINGS FOR YOU, IF YOU KNOW THE RIGHT SPELLS.
THE *CODE*.
WHATEVER.
WHY DON'T THE NEWBARNS LOOK LIKE YOU AND THE OTHERS? I HAVEN'T NOTICED THEM BREAKING OUT IN BLACK NOODLES AND CATARACTS WHENEVER THEY GET UPSET. AND TED SEEMS TO GET UPSET A *LOT*.

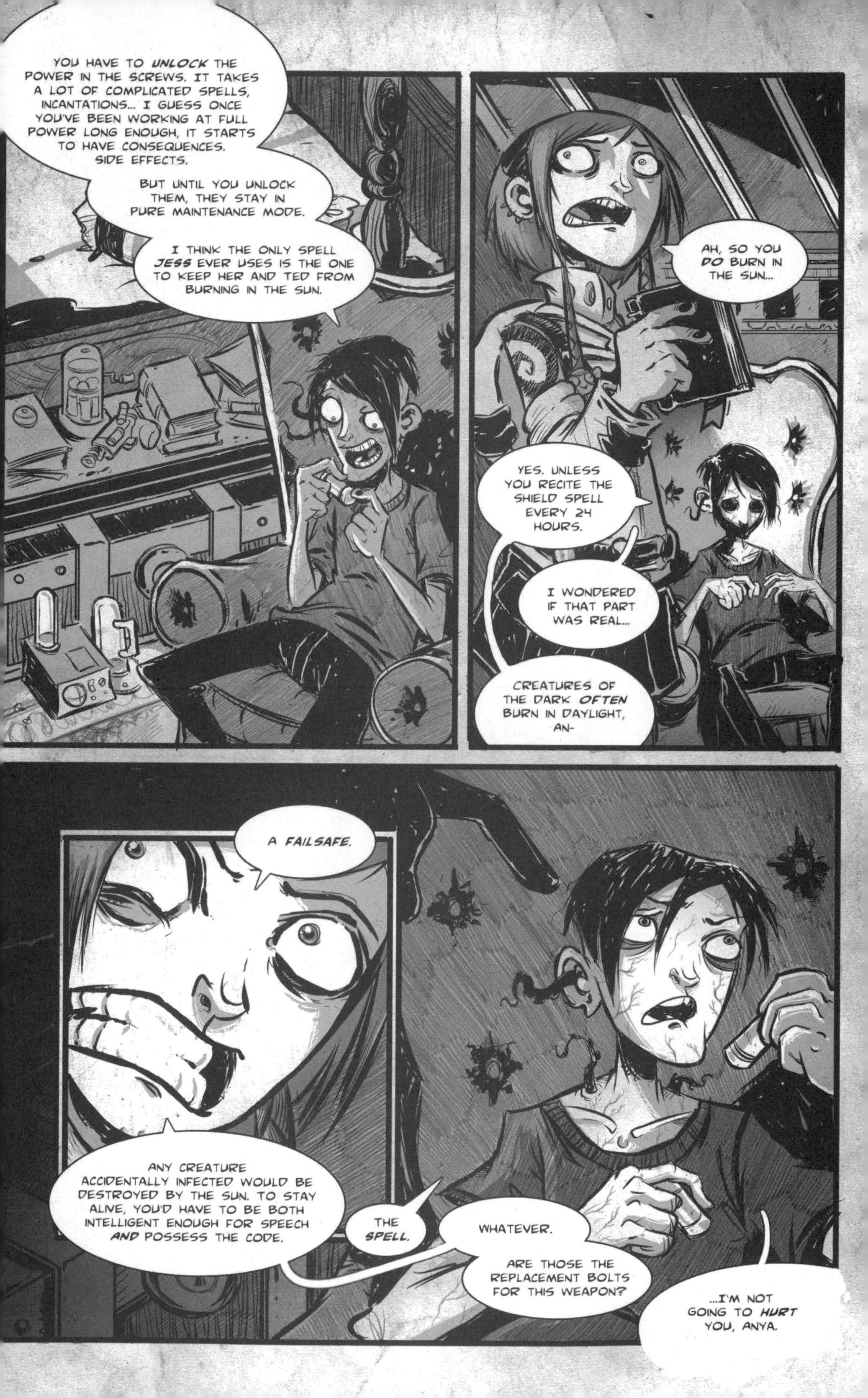
YOU HAVE TO *UNLOCK* THE POWER IN THE SCREWS. IT TAKES A LOT OF COMPLICATED SPELLS, INCANTATIONS... I GUESS ONCE YOU'VE BEEN WORKING AT FULL POWER LONG ENOUGH, IT STARTS TO HAVE CONSEQUENCES. SIDE EFFECTS.
BUT UNTIL YOU UNLOCK THEM, THEY STAY IN PURE MAINTENANCE MODE.
I THINK THE ONLY SPELL *JESS* EVER USES IS THE ONE TO KEEP HER AND TED FROM BURNING IN THE SUN.
AH, SO YOU *DO* BURN IN THE SUN...
YES. UNLESS YOU RECITE THE SHIELD SPELL EVERY 24 HOURS.
I WONDERED IF THAT PART WAS REAL...
CREATURES OF THE DARK *OFTEN* BURN IN DAYLIGHT, AN-
A *FAILSAFE*.
ANY CREATURE ACCIDENTALLY INFECTED WOULD BE DESTROYED BY THE SUN. TO STAY ALIVE, YOU'D HAVE TO BE BOTH INTELLIGENT ENOUGH FOR SPEECH *AND* POSSESS THE CODE.
THE *SPELL*.
WHATEVER.
ARE THOSE THE REPLACEMENT BOLTS FOR THIS WEAPON?
...I'M NOT GOING TO *HURT* YOU, ANYA.

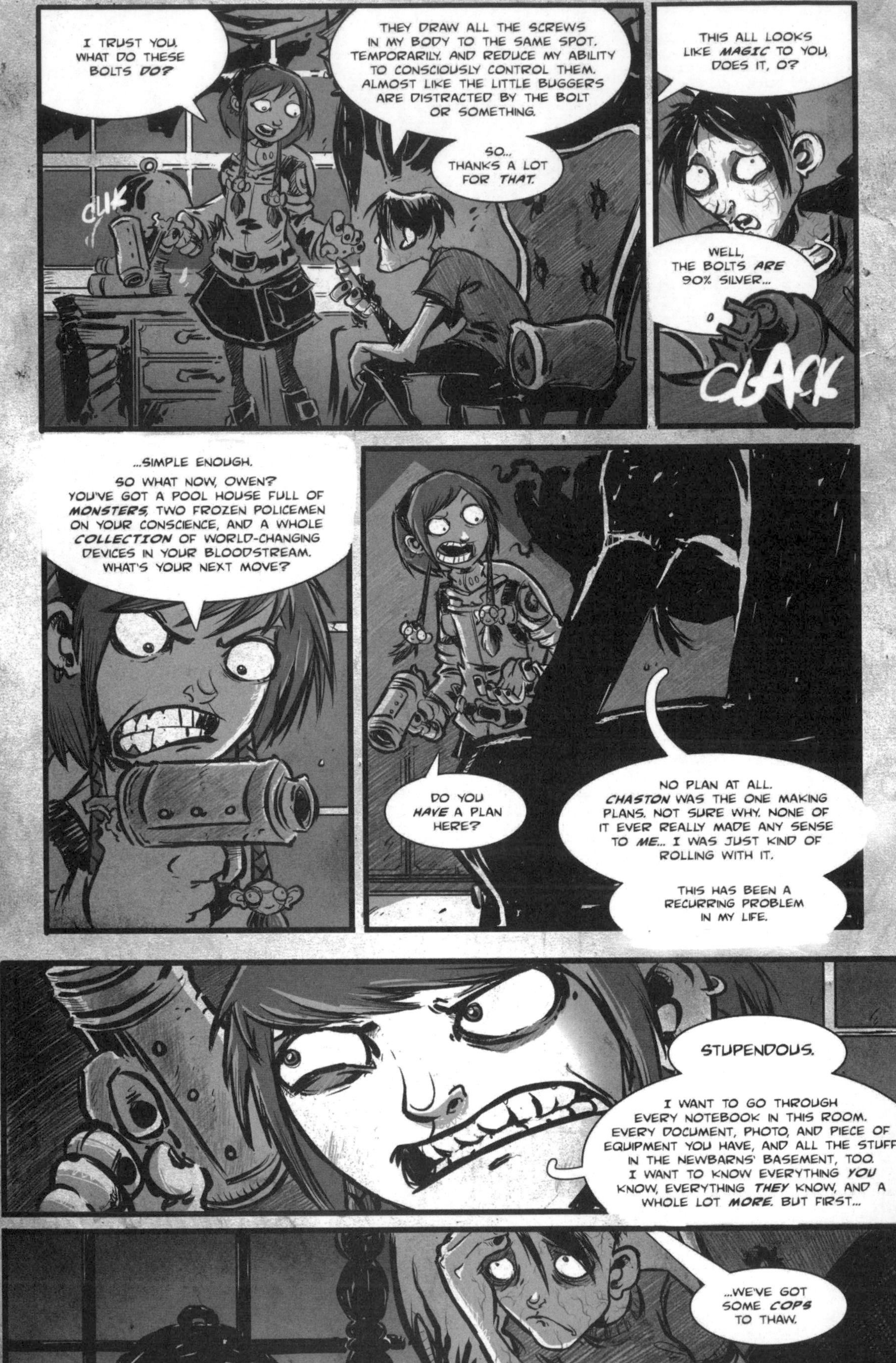
I TRUST YOU. WHAT DO THESE BOLTS *DO?*
THEY DRAW ALL THE SCREWS IN MY BODY TO THE SAME SPOT, TEMPORARILY, AND REDUCE MY ABILITY TO CONSCIOUSLY CONTROL THEM. ALMOST LIKE THE LITTLE BUGGERS ARE DISTRACTED BY THE BOLT OR SOMETHING.
SO... THANKS A LOT FOR *THAT.*
CLIK
THIS ALL LOOKS LIKE *MAGIC* TO YOU, DOES IT, O?
WELL, THE BOLTS *ARE* 90% SILVER...
CLACK
...SIMPLE ENOUGH.
SO WHAT NOW, OWEN? YOU'VE GOT A POOL HOUSE FULL OF *MONSTERS*, TWO FROZEN POLICEMEN ON YOUR CONSCIENCE, AND A WHOLE *COLLECTION* OF WORLD-CHANGING DEVICES IN YOUR BLOODSTREAM. WHAT'S YOUR NEXT MOVE?
DO YOU *HAVE* A PLAN HERE?
NO PLAN AT ALL. *CHASTON* WAS THE ONE MAKING PLANS. NOT SURE WHY. NONE OF IT EVER REALLY MADE ANY SENSE TO *ME*... I WAS JUST KIND OF ROLLING WITH IT.
THIS HAS BEEN A RECURRING PROBLEM IN MY LIFE.
STUPENDOUS.
I WANT TO GO THROUGH EVERY NOTEBOOK IN THIS ROOM. EVERY DOCUMENT, PHOTO, AND PIECE OF EQUIPMENT YOU HAVE, AND ALL THE STUFF IN THE NEWBARNS' BASEMENT, TOO. I WANT TO KNOW EVERYTHING *YOU* KNOW, EVERYTHING *THEY* KNOW, AND A WHOLE LOT *MORE*. BUT FIRST...
...WE'VE GOT SOME *COPS* TO THAW.

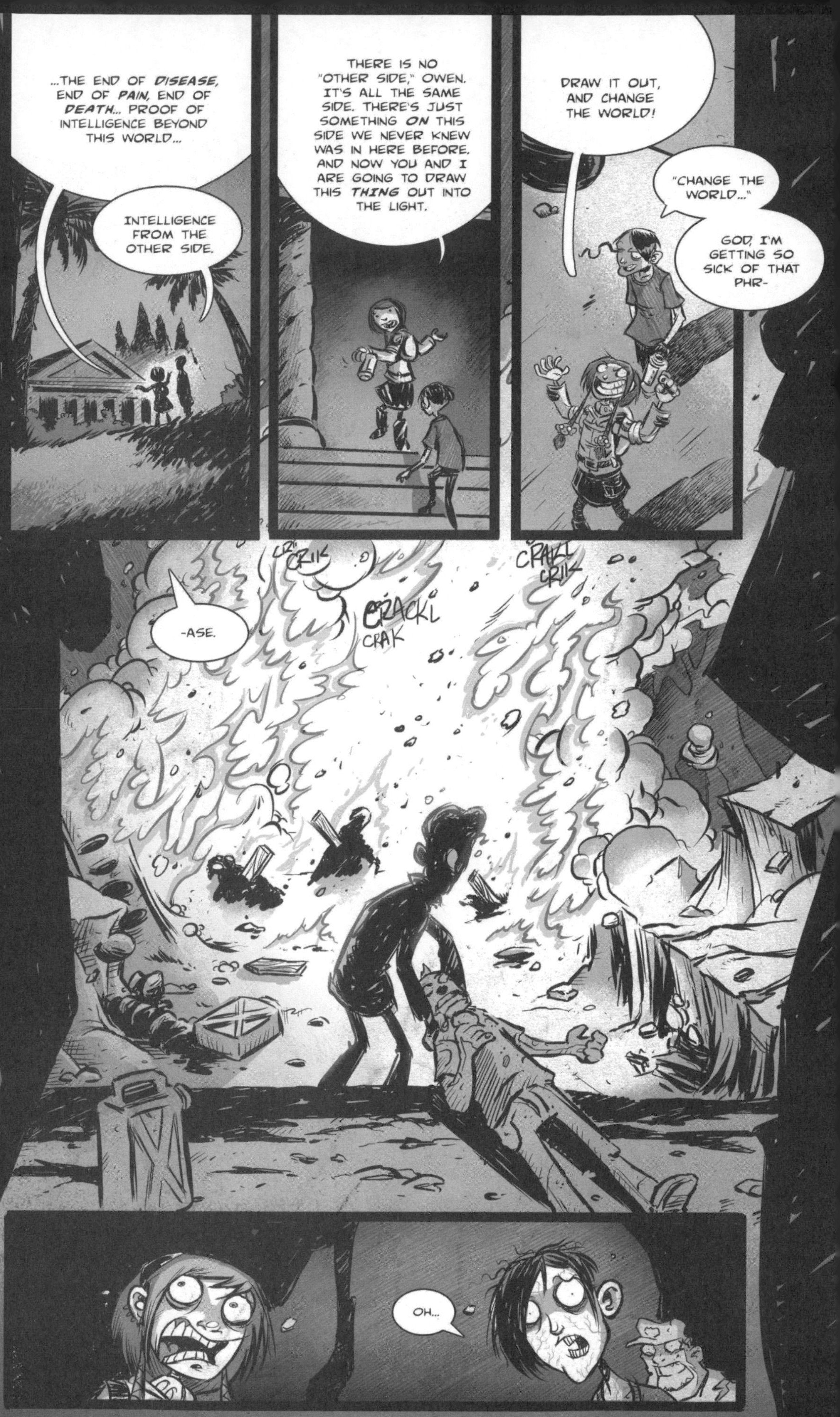
...THE END OF DISEASE, END OF PAIN, END OF DEATH... PROOF OF INTELLIGENCE BEYOND THIS WORLD...
INTELLIGENCE FROM THE OTHER SIDE.
THERE IS NO "OTHER SIDE," OWEN. IT'S ALL THE SAME SIDE. THERE'S JUST SOMETHING ON THIS SIDE WE NEVER KNEW WAS IN HERE BEFORE. AND NOW YOU AND I ARE GOING TO DRAW THIS THING OUT INTO THE LIGHT.
DRAW IT OUT, AND CHANGE THE WORLD!
"CHANGE THE WORLD..."
GOD, I'M GETTING SO SICK OF THAT PHR-
CRIK
CRAKL
CRIK
CRACKL
CRAK
-ASE.
OH...

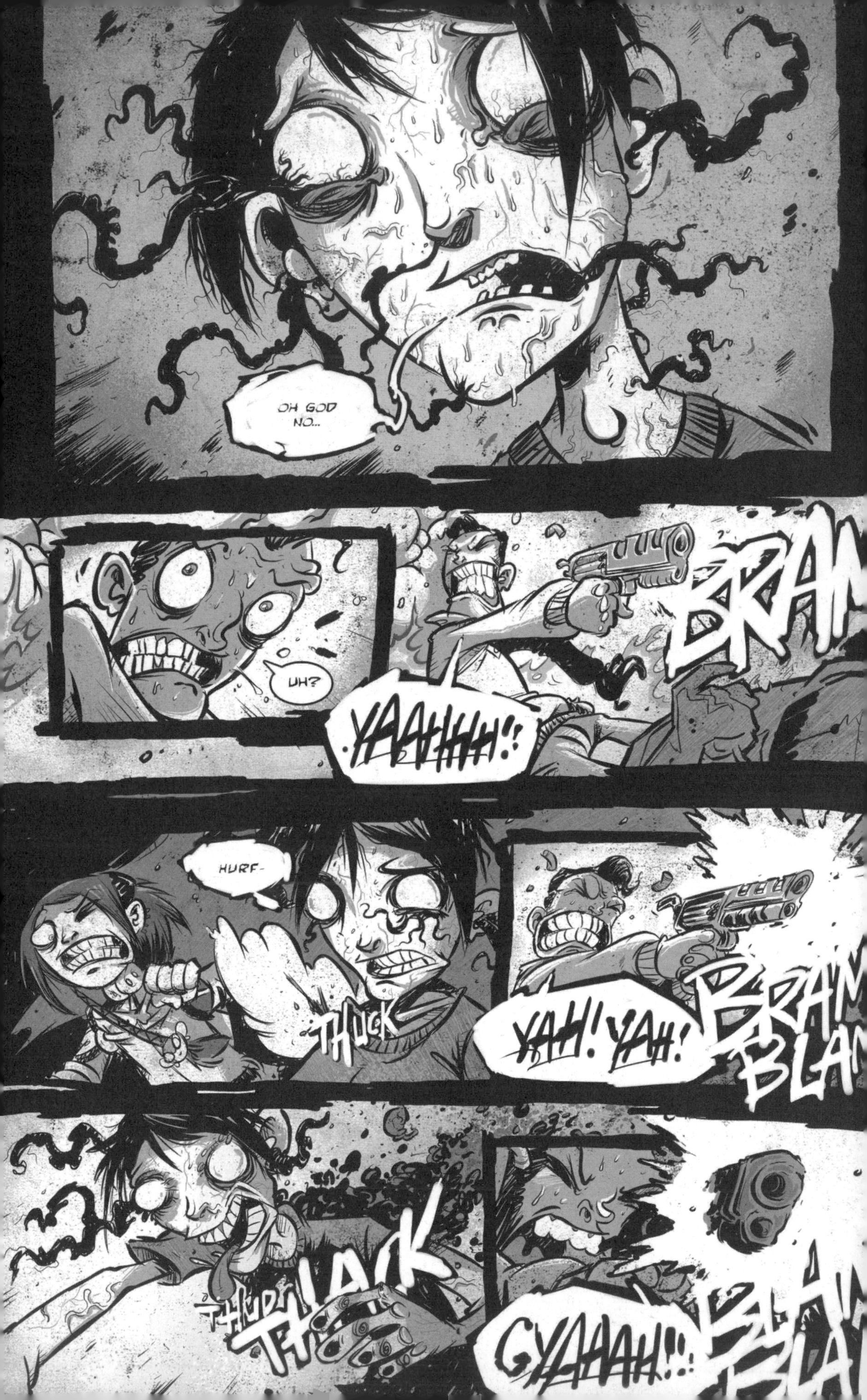
OH GOD NO...
UH?
YAAHHH!?
BRAM
HURF-
THUCK
YAH! YAH!
BRAM
BLAM
THUD
THACK
GYAAAH!!
BLAM

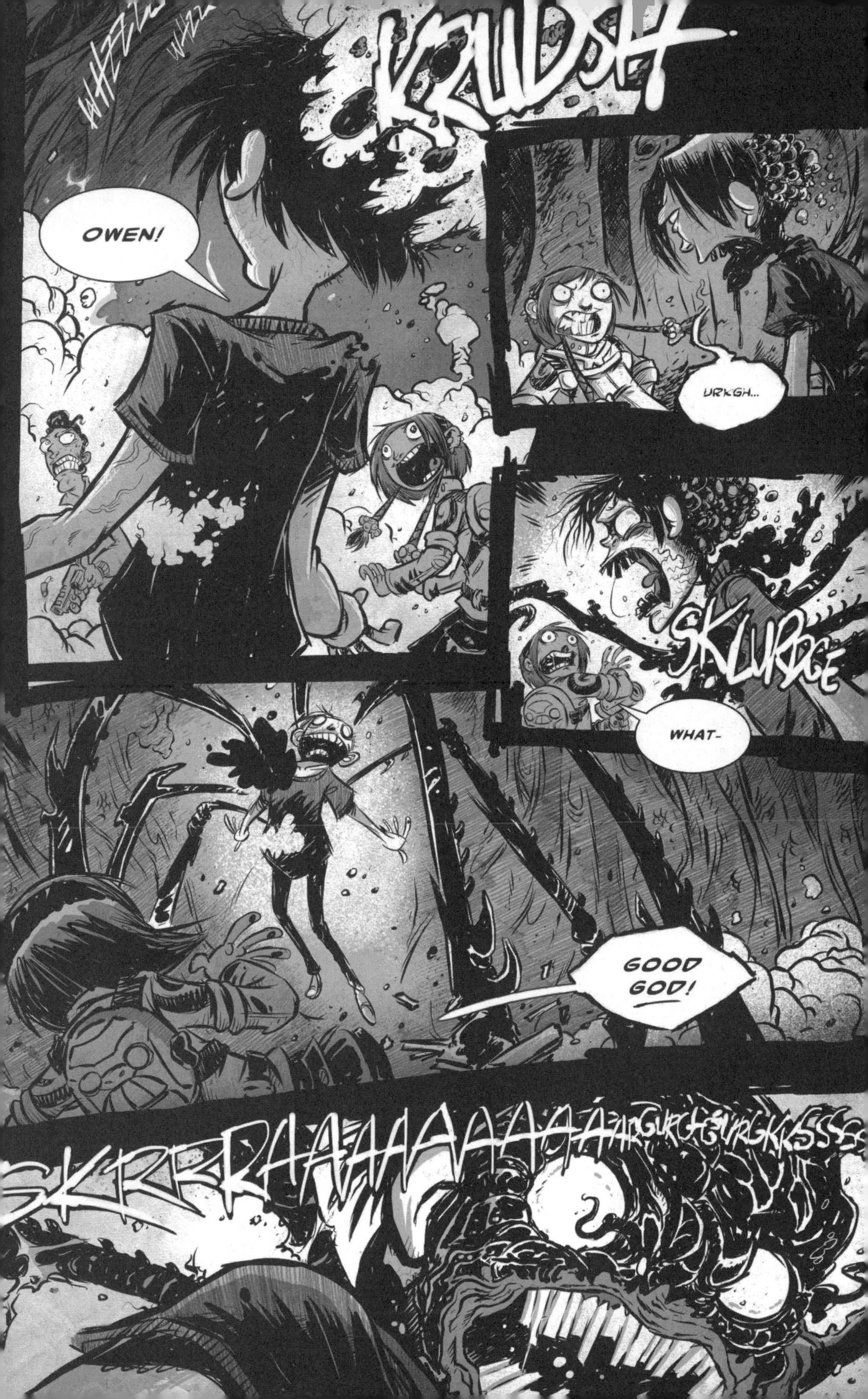
WHZZZ
WHZZZ
KRUDSH
OWEN!
URKGH...
SKLURDGE
WHAT-
GOOD GOD!
SKRRRAAAAAAAAARGURGHGURGKKSSSS

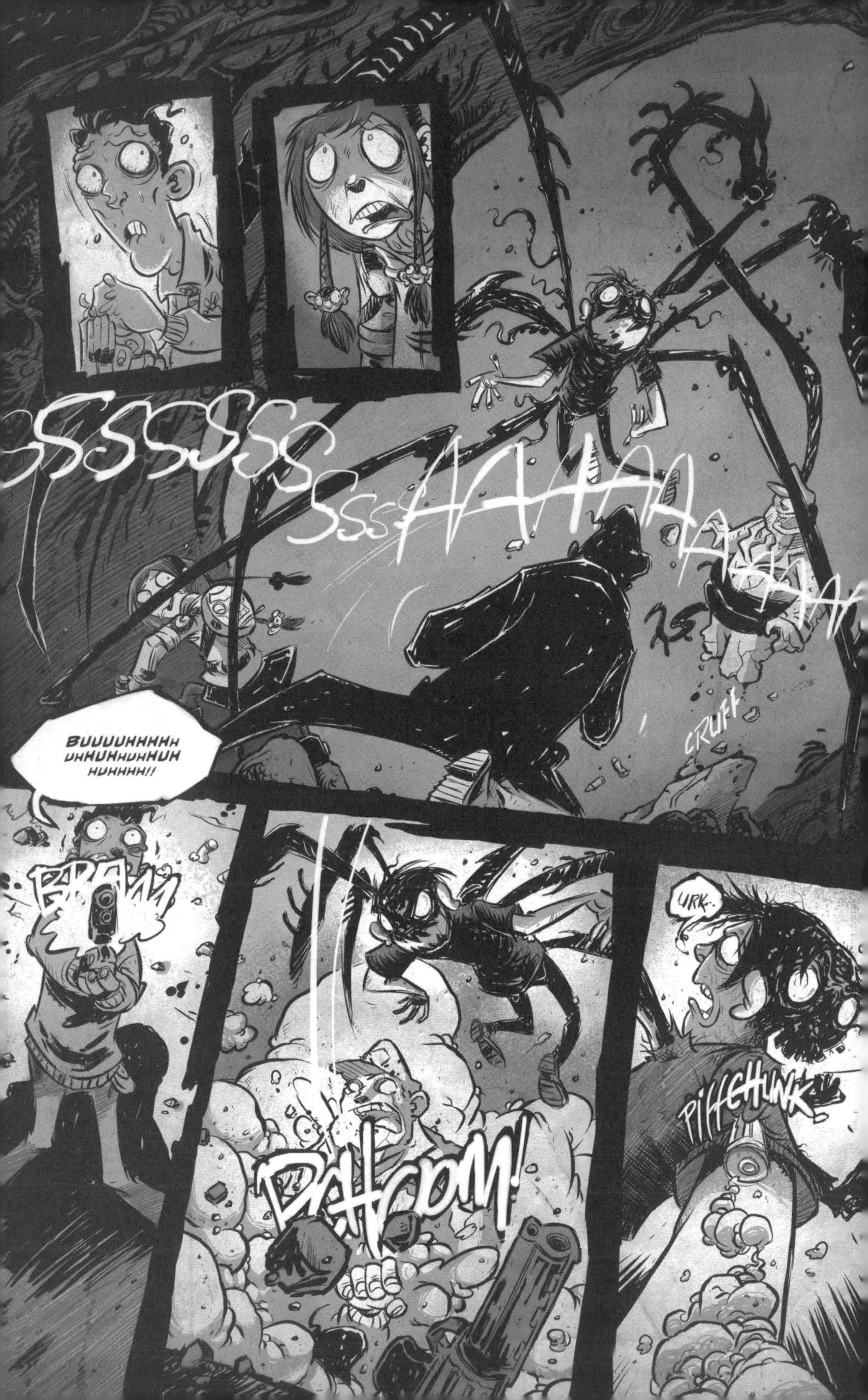
SSSSSSSSSSS
AAAAAAAAAAAAH
CRUFF
BUUUUHHHHH UHHUHHUHHUH HUHHHH!!
URK..
PITCHUNK

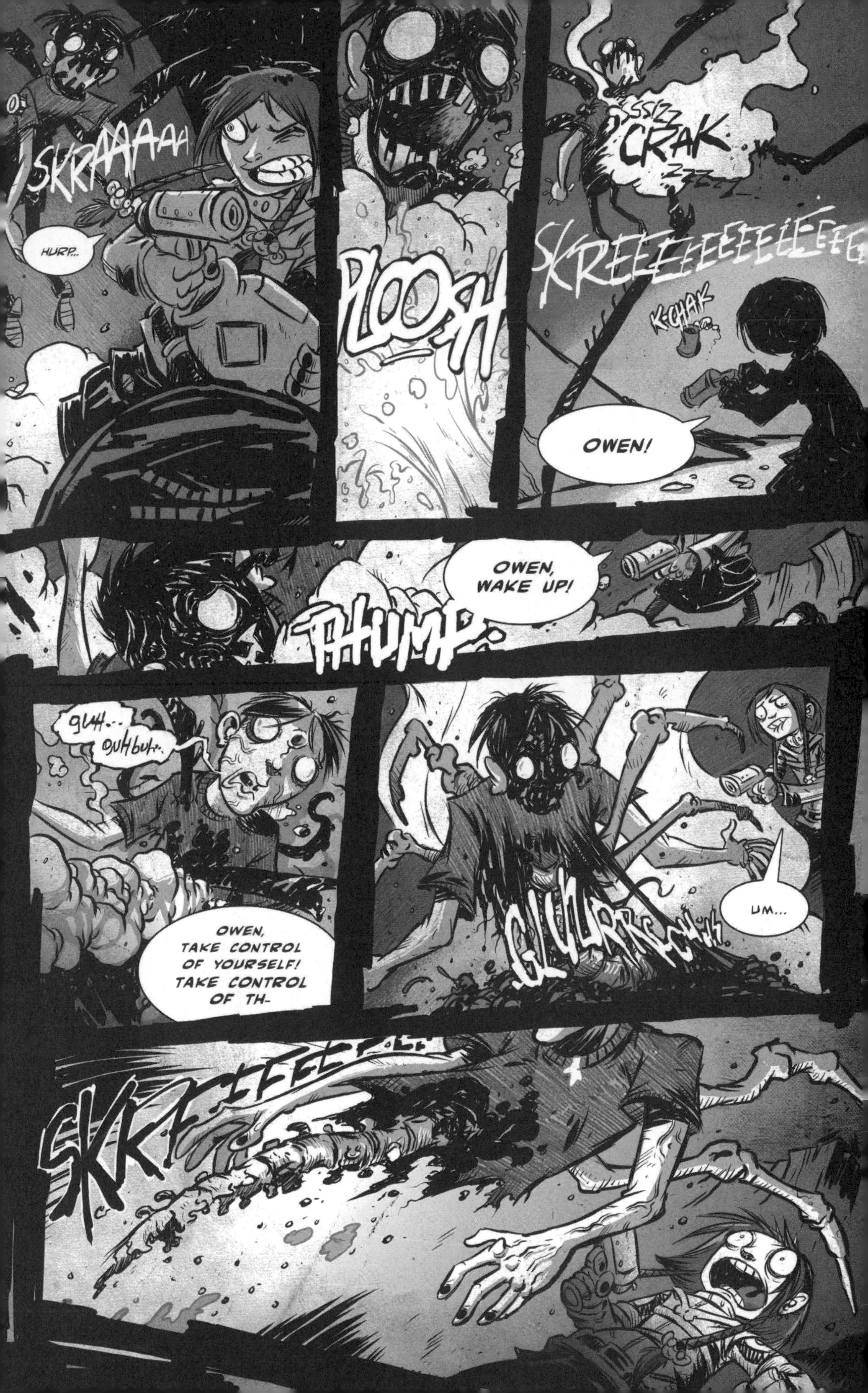
SKRAAAAAH
HURP...
PLOOSH
SSSIZZ CRAK ZZZ
SKREEEEEEEEEEEEG
K-CHAK
OWEN!
OWEN, WAKE UP!
THUMP
GUH... GUHBUH...
OWEN, TAKE CONTROL OF YOURSELF! TAKE CONTROL OF TH-
UM...
SKRIEEE

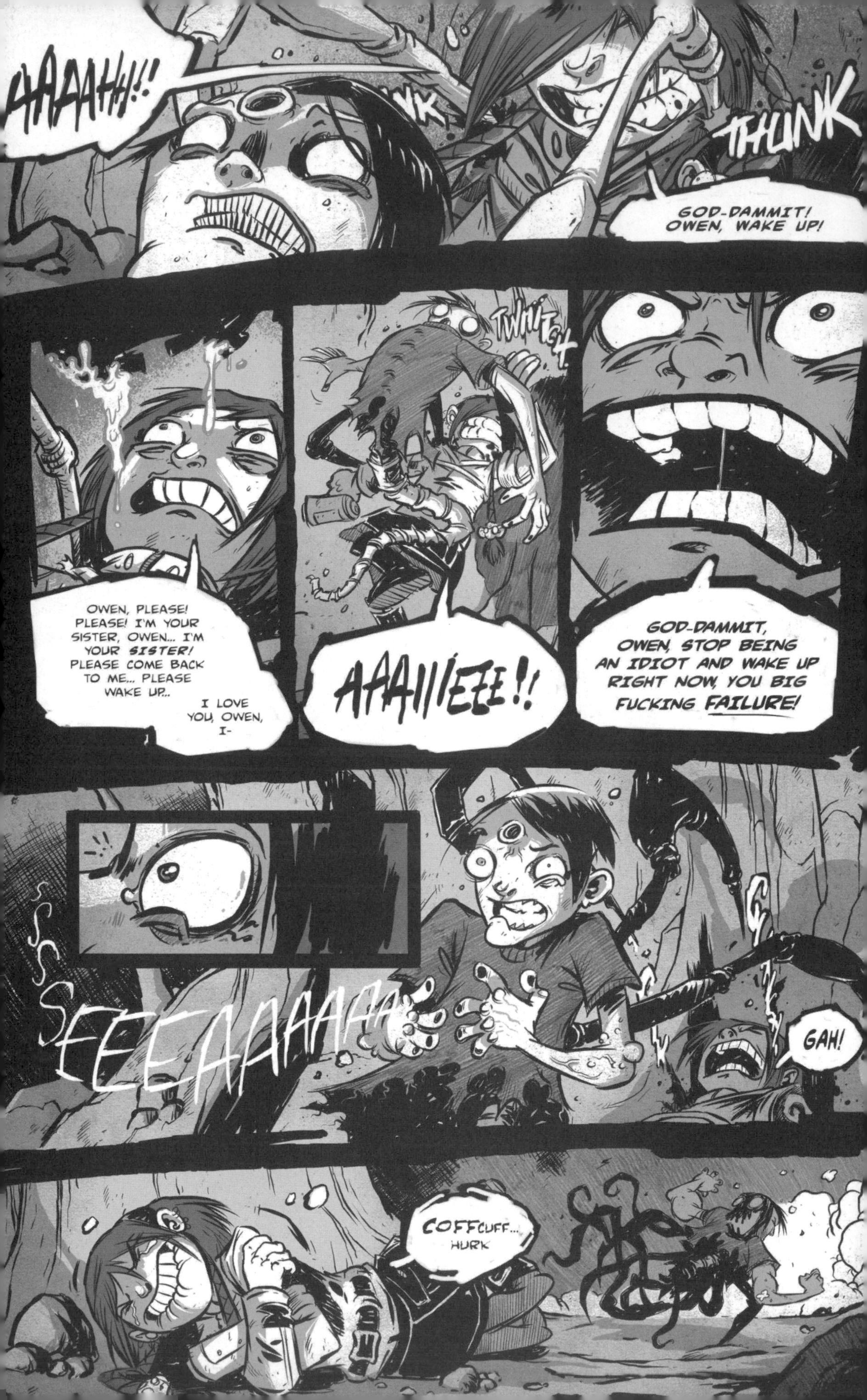
AAAAHH!!
THUNK
THUNK
GOD-DAMMIT! OWEN, WAKE UP!
OWEN, PLEASE! PLEASE! I'M YOUR SISTER, OWEN... I'M YOUR SISTER! PLEASE COME BACK TO ME... PLEASE WAKE UP..
I LOVE YOU, OWEN, I-
TWITCH
AAAIIIEEE!!
GOD-DAMMIT, OWEN, STOP BEING AN IDIOT AND WAKE UP RIGHT NOW, YOU BIG FUCKING FAILURE!
SSSEEEAAAAAAA
GAH!
COFFCUFF... HURK

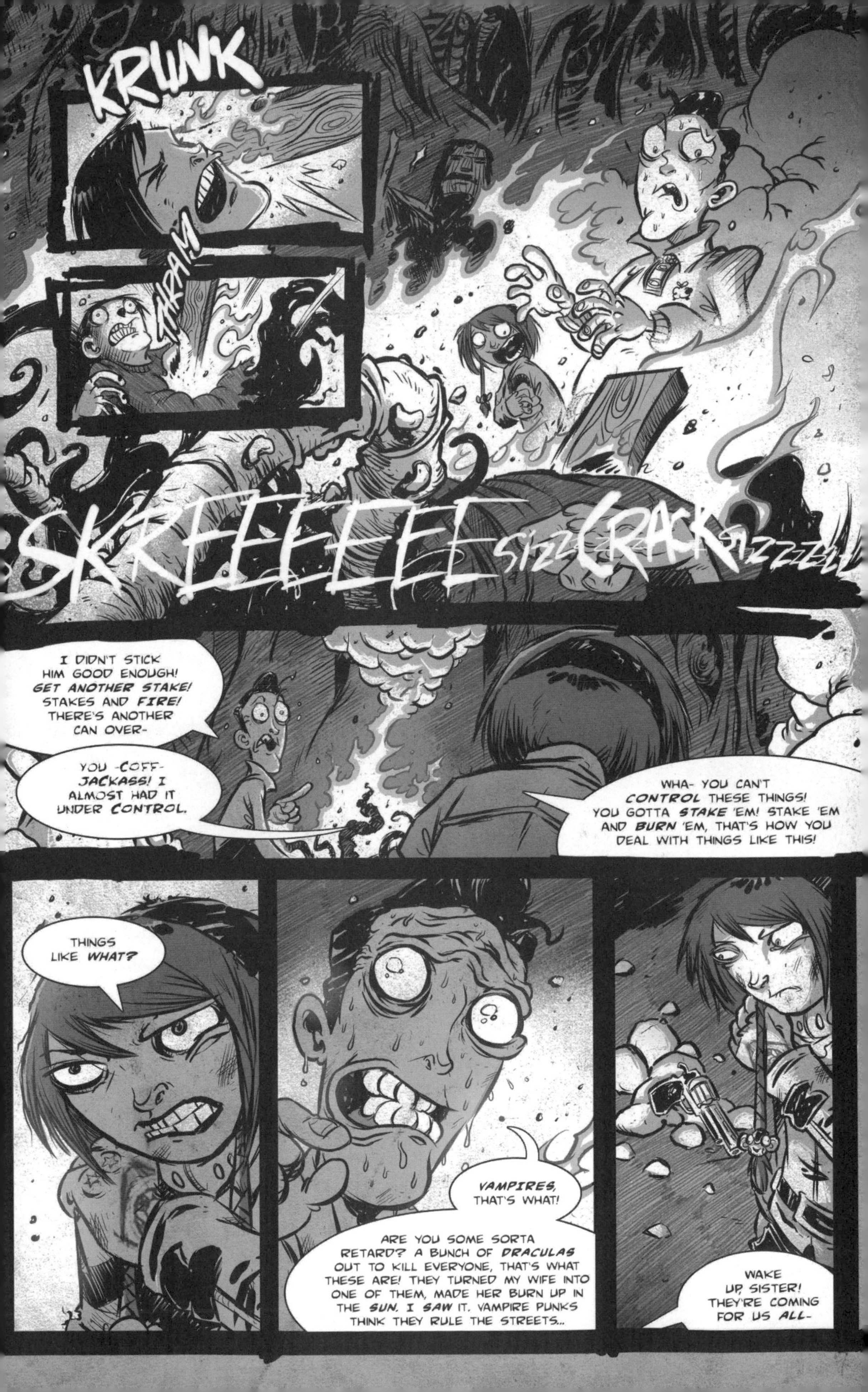
KRUNK
THRAM
SKREEEEEEE SIZZ CRACK SIZZZZL
I DIDN'T STICK HIM GOOD ENOUGH! GET ANOTHER STAKE! STAKES AND FIRE! THERE'S ANOTHER CAN OVER-
YOU -COFF- JACKASS! I ALMOST HAD IT UNDER CONTROL.
WHA- YOU CAN'T CONTROL THESE THINGS! YOU GOTTA STAKE 'EM! STAKE 'EM AND BURN 'EM, THAT'S HOW YOU DEAL WITH THINGS LIKE THIS!
THINGS LIKE WHAT?
VAMPIRES, THAT'S WHAT!
ARE YOU SOME SORTA RETARD? A BUNCH OF DRACULAS OUT TO KILL EVERYONE, THAT'S WHAT THESE ARE! THEY TURNED MY WIFE INTO ONE OF THEM, MADE HER BURN UP IN THE SUN. I SAW IT. VAMPIRE PUNKS THINK THEY RULE THE STREETS...
WAKE UP, SISTER! THEY'RE COMING FOR US ALL-

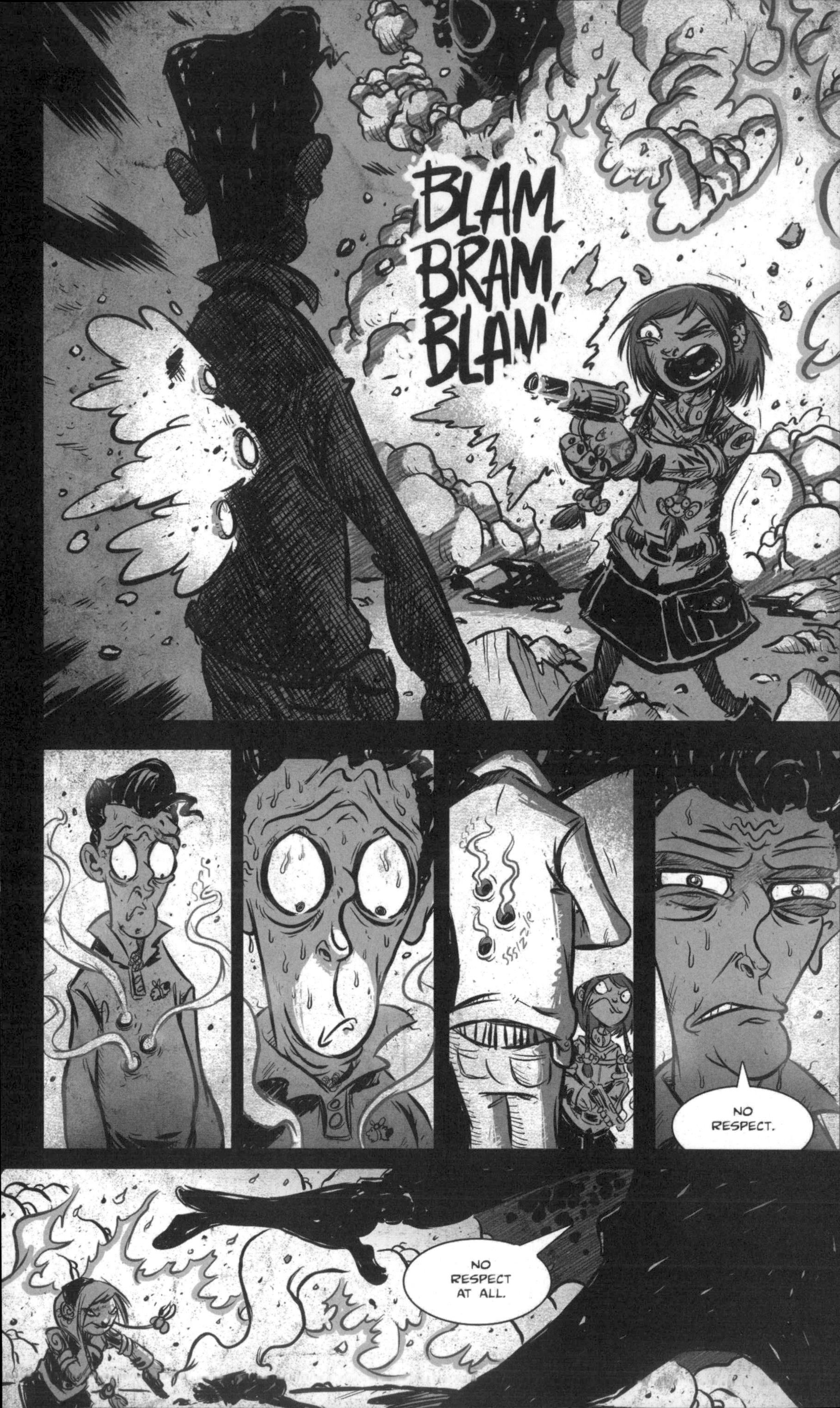
BLAM BRAM BLAM
NO RESPECT.
NO RESPECT AT ALL.

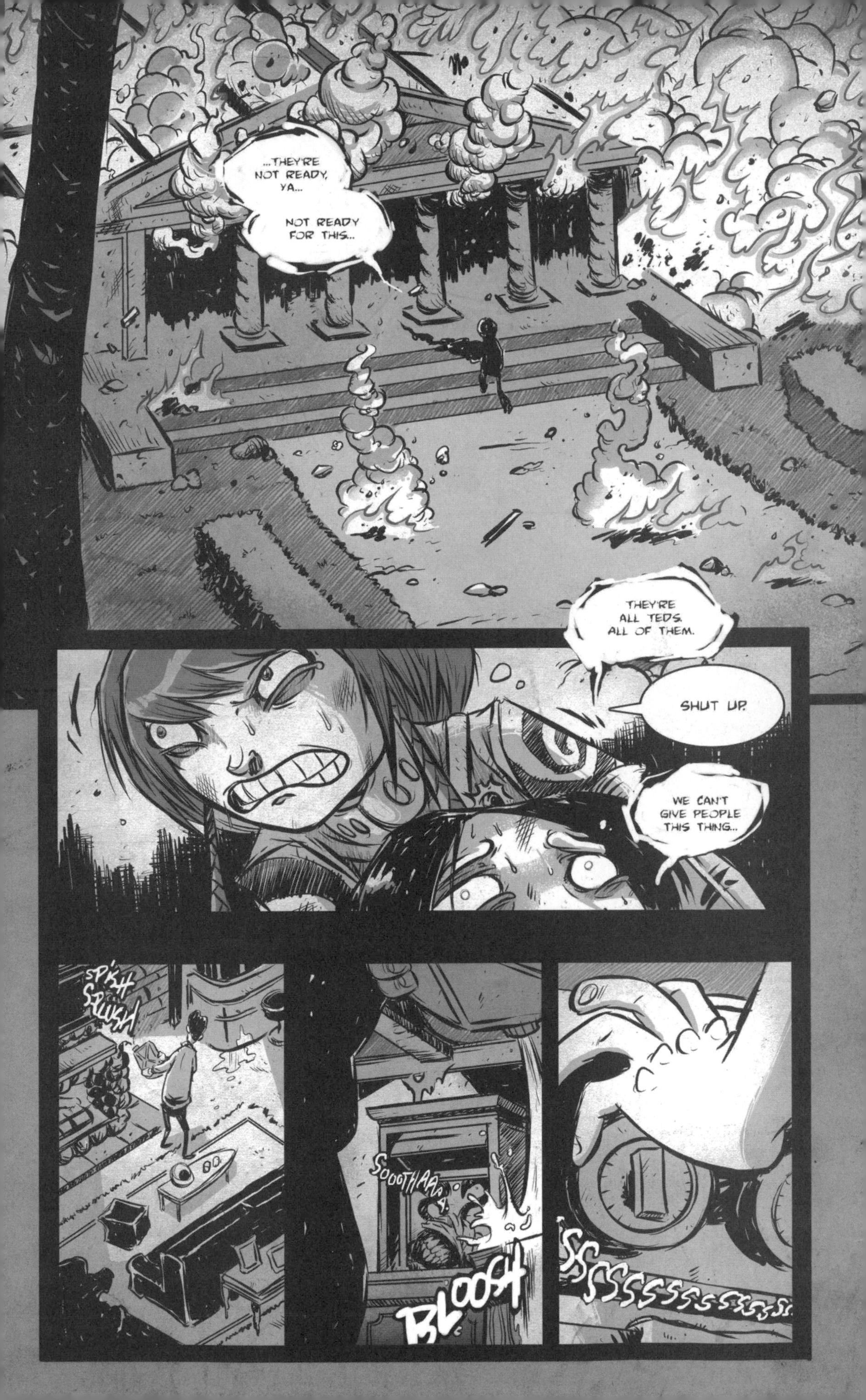
...THEY'RE NOT READY, YA...
NOT READY FOR THIS...
THEY'RE ALL TEDS. ALL OF THEM.
SHUT UP.
WE CAN'T GIVE PEOPLE THIS THING...
SPKH SPLUSH
SOOOTHAAA
BLOOSH
SSSSSSSSSSSSSSSSS

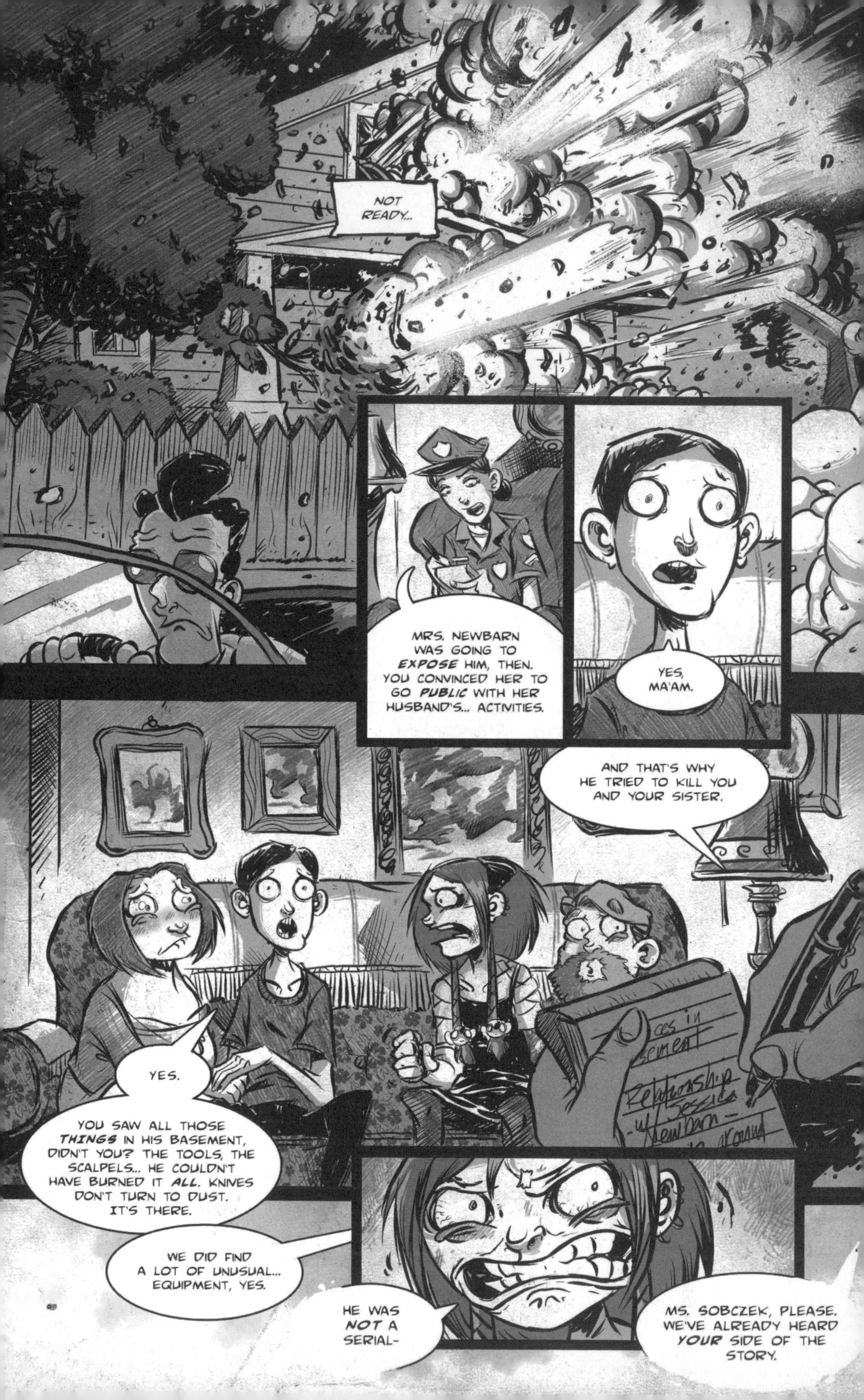
NOT READY...
MRS. NEWBARN WAS GOING TO EXPOSE HIM, THEN. YOU CONVINCED HER TO GO PUBLIC WITH HER HUSBAND'S... ACTIVITIES.
YES, MA'AM.
AND THAT'S WHY HE TRIED TO KILL YOU AND YOUR SISTER.
YES.
YOU SAW ALL THOSE THINGS IN HIS BASEMENT, DIDN'T YOU? THE TOOLS, THE SCALPELS... HE COULDN'T HAVE BURNED IT ALL. KNIVES DON'T TURN TO DUST. IT'S THERE.
WE DID FIND A LOT OF UNUSUAL... EQUIPMENT, YES.
HE WAS NOT A SERIAL-
MS. SOBCZEK, PLEASE. WE'VE ALREADY HEARD YOUR SIDE OF THE STORY.

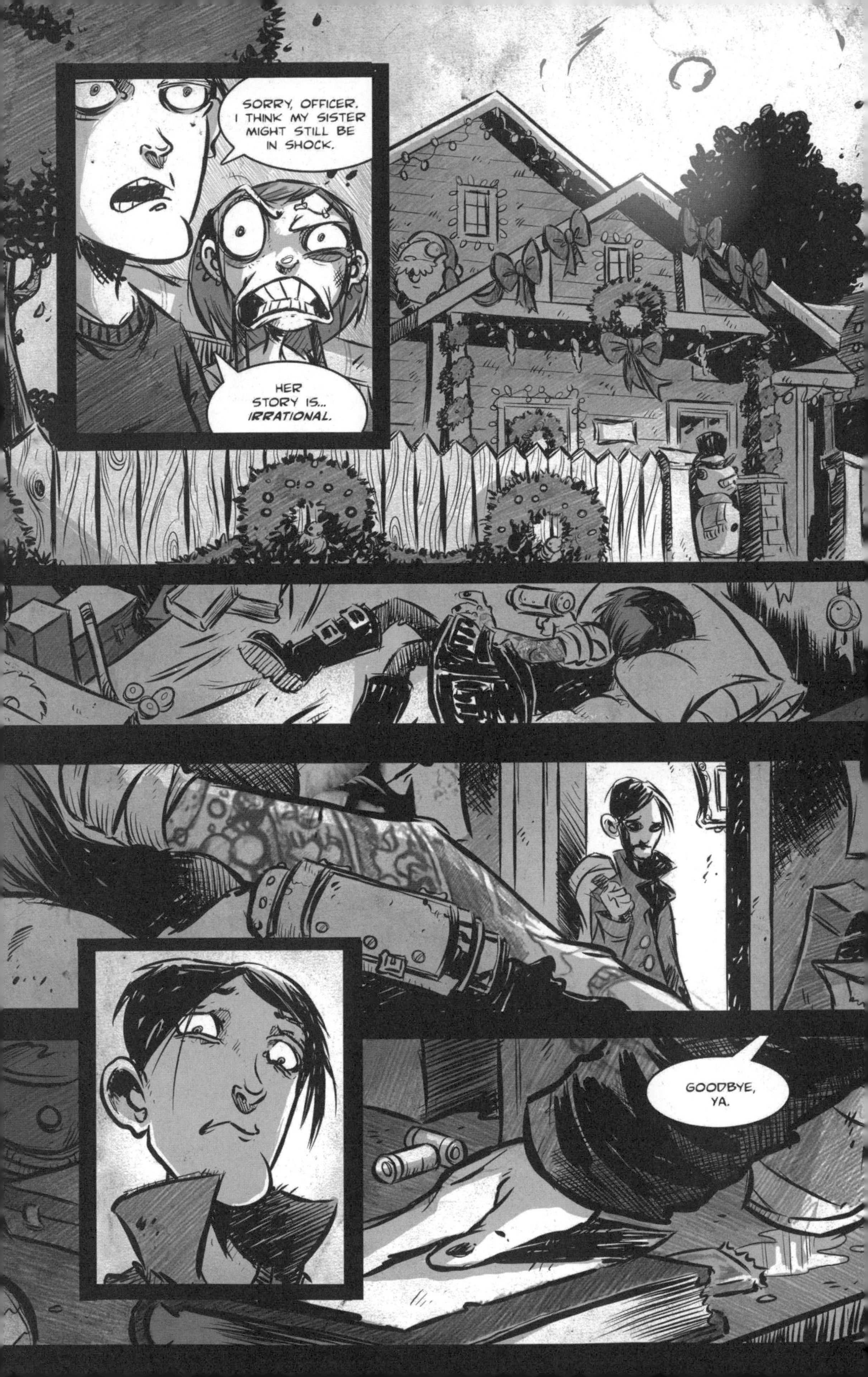
SORRY, OFFICER. I THINK MY SISTER MIGHT STILL BE IN SHOCK.
HER STORY IS... IRRATIONAL.
GOODBYE, YA.

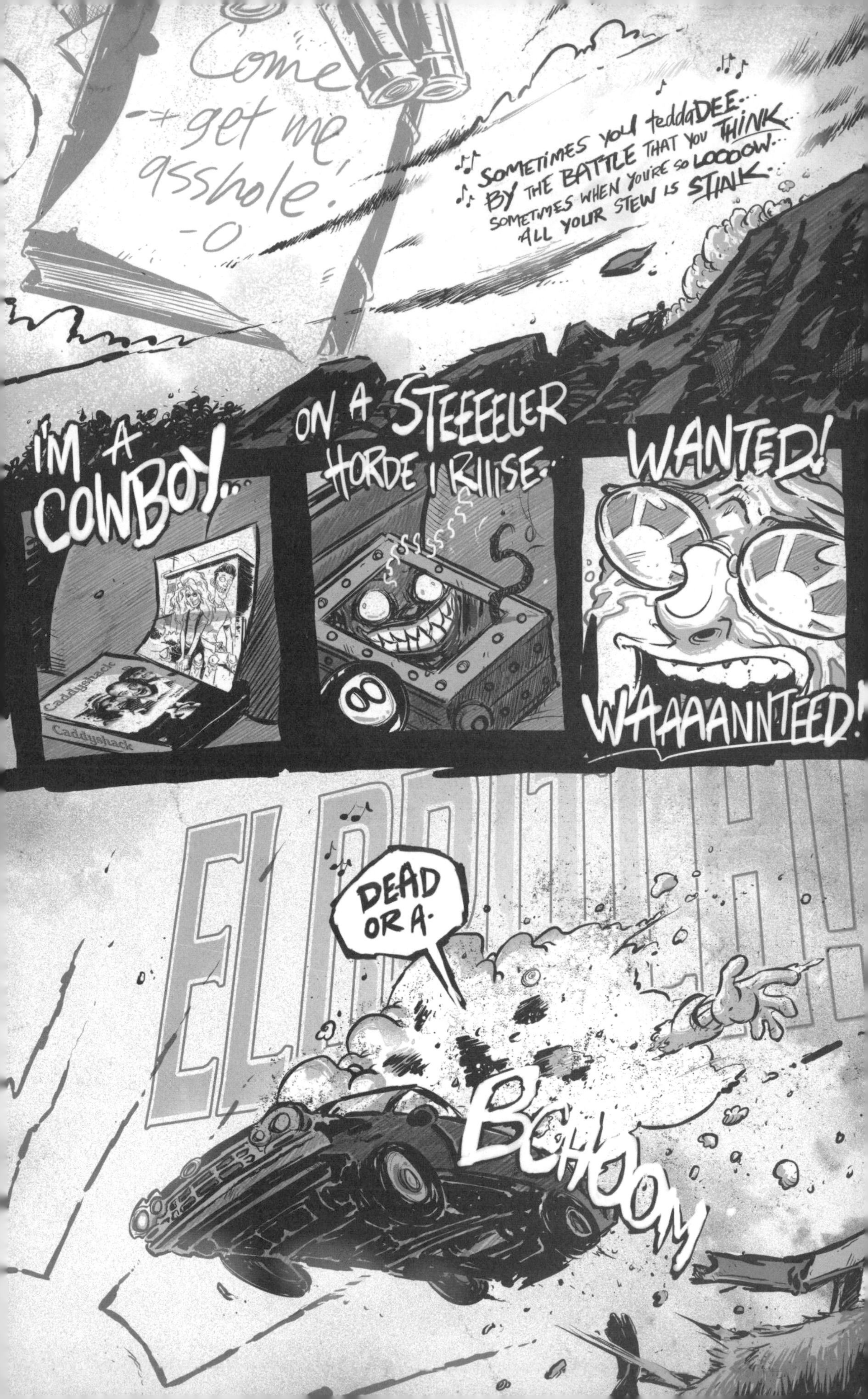
Come + get me asshole! -O
Sometimes you teddaDEE... By the battle that you THINK... Sometimes when you're so LOOOOW... All your stew is STINK...
I'M A COWBOY...
ON A STEEEEELER HORDE I RIIISE...
WANTED! WAAAAANNTEED!
Caddyshack
Caddyshack
DEAD OR A-
BCHOOOM

It's still Spreading

guest
art

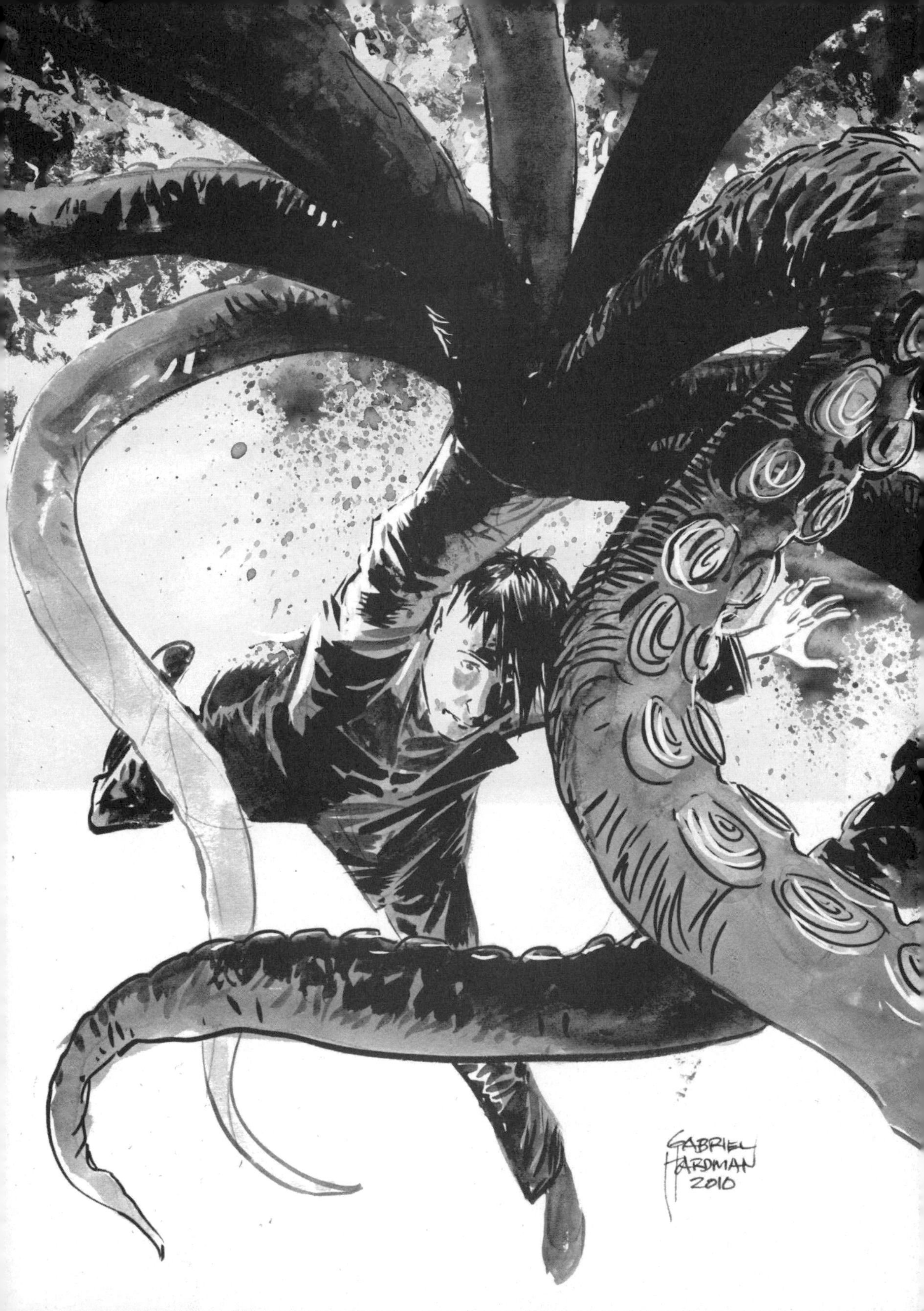
GABRIEL HARDMAN 2010

GABRIEL HARDMAN.

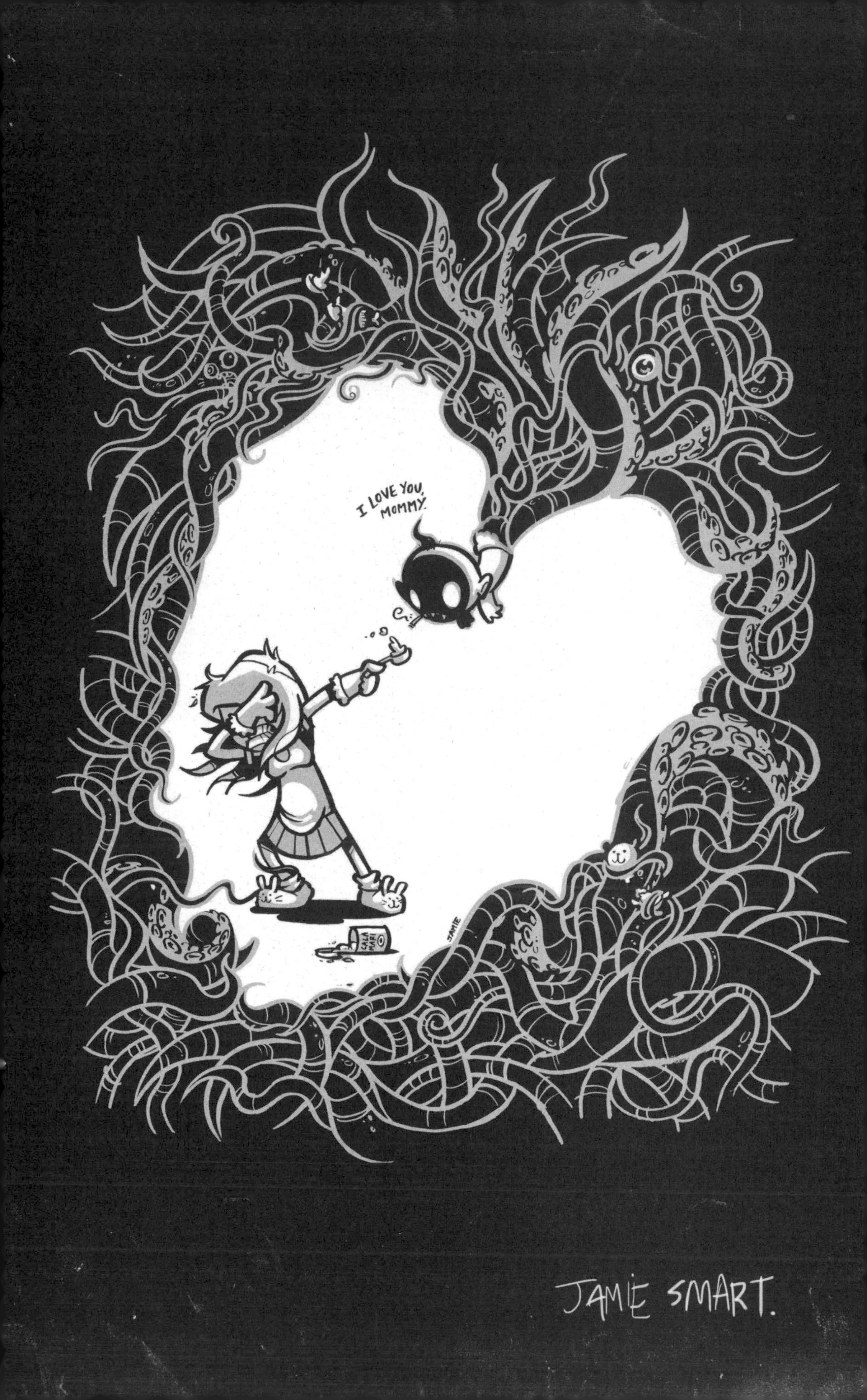
I LOVE YOU, MOMMY.
CALA MARI
JAMIE

JAMIE SMART.

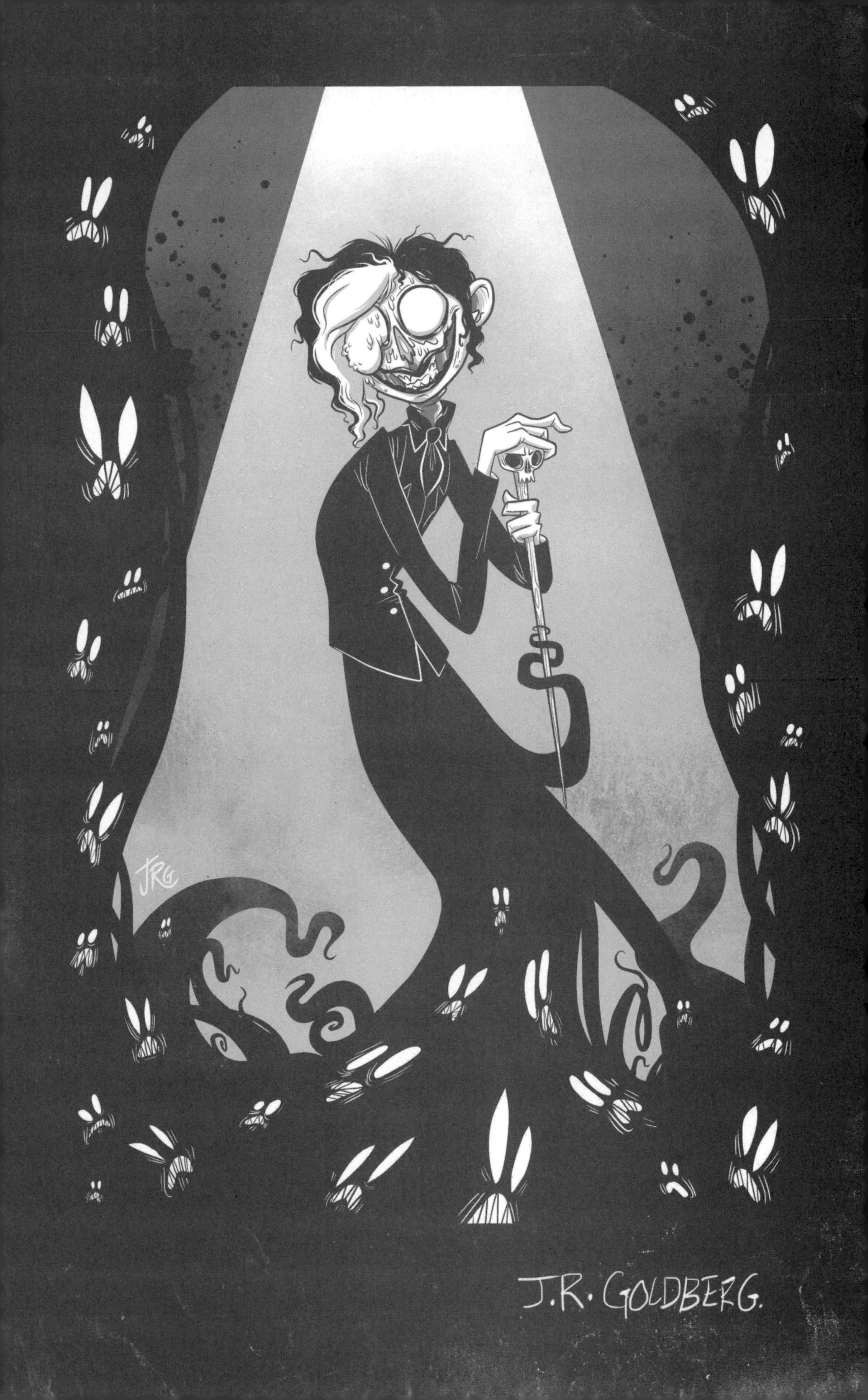
JRG
J.R. GOLDBERG.

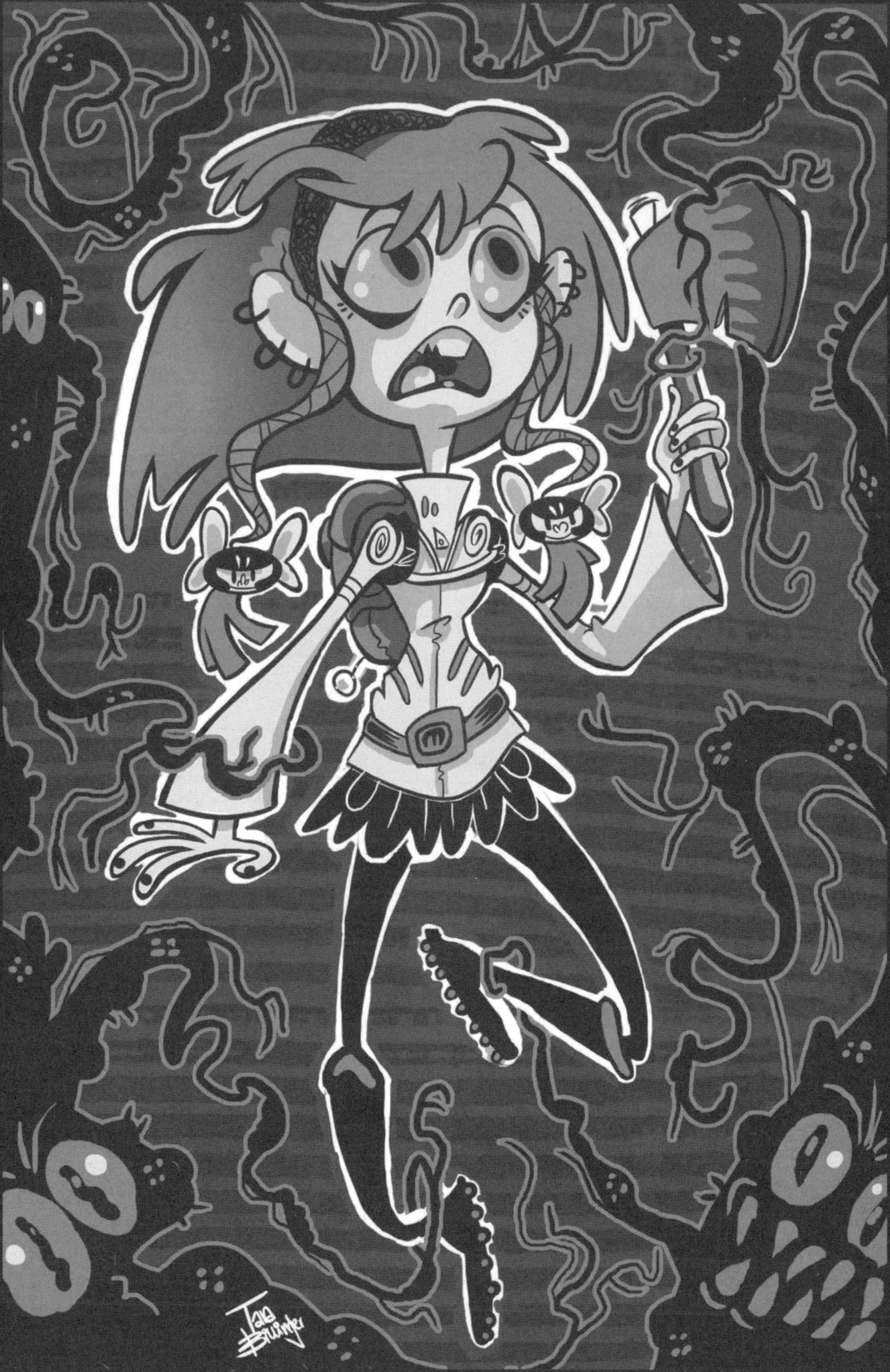

TARA BILLINGER

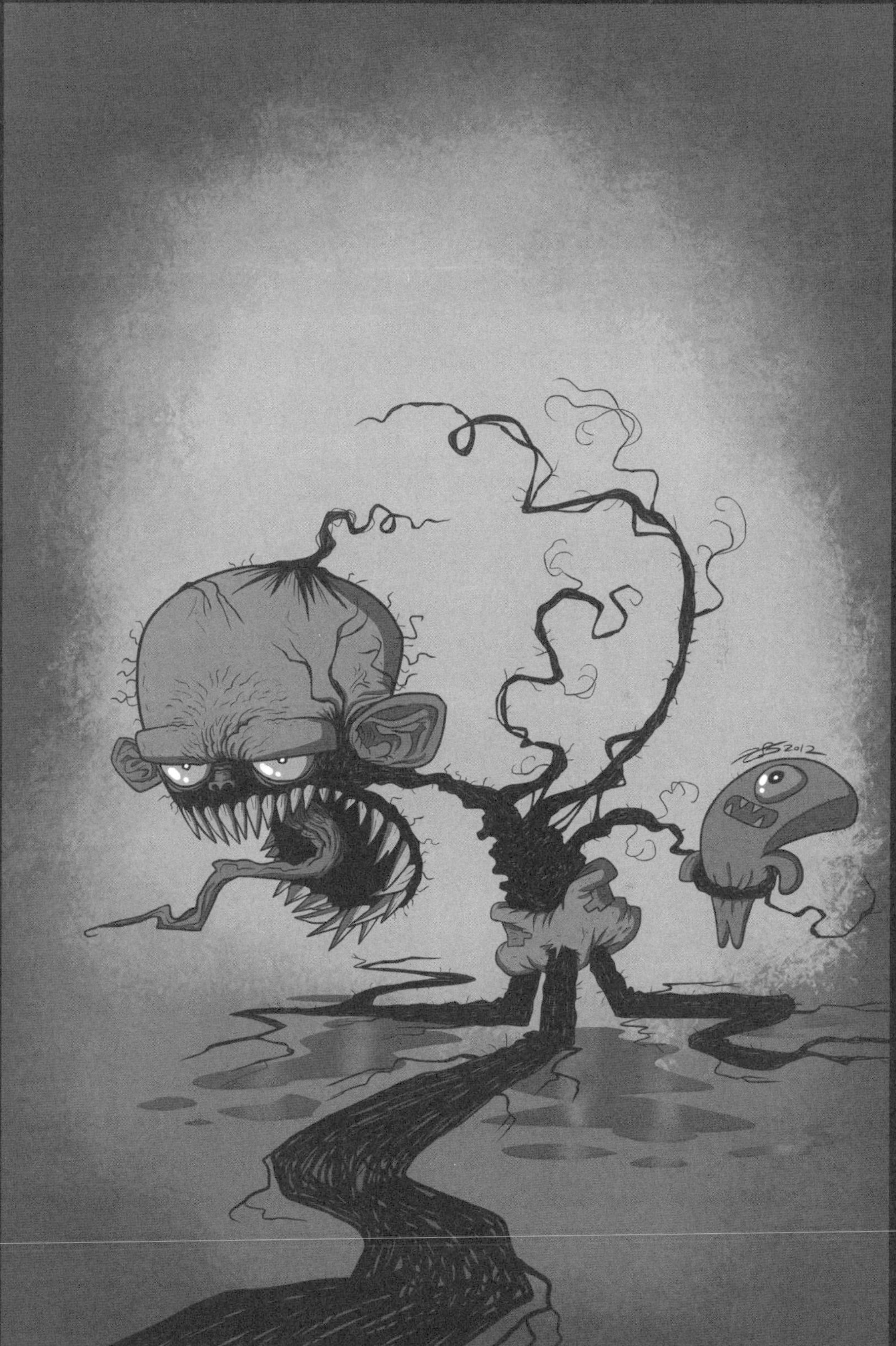

ZACH BELLISSIMO.

DANIEL BRADFORD.

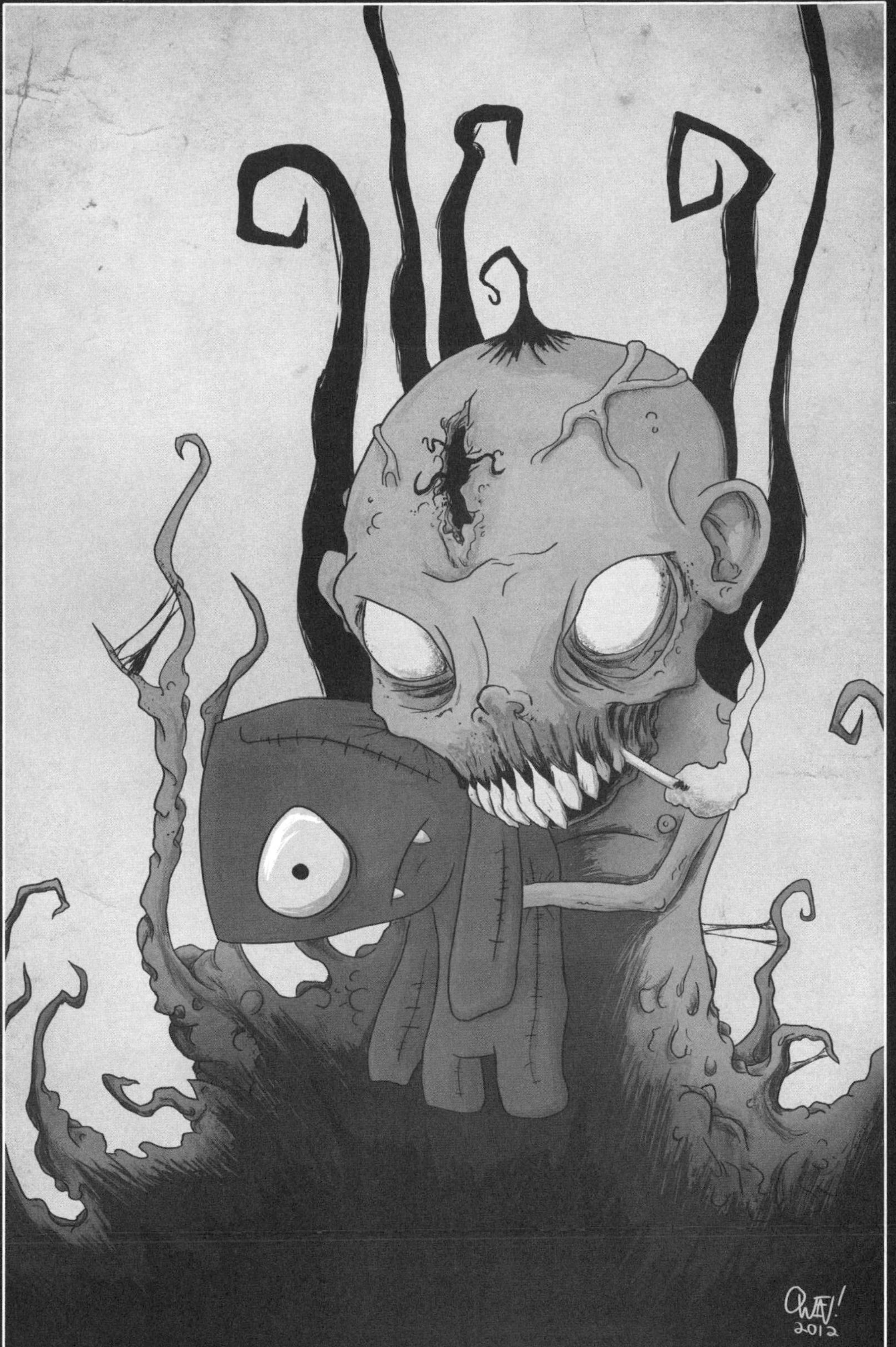
OWEN!
2012

OWEN MACKINDER.

LIVIN' ON A PRAYER

THE MAKING OF ELDRITCH!

CHARACTER DESIGNS

FELLOW CATECHISTS...

THIS IS AARON TYPING AT YOU, WITH A LOOK INTO THE BLACK HEART OF THE *ELDRITCH ARCHIVES!*

BELIEVE IT OR NOT, *ELDRITCH!* BEGAN AS A STORY CALLED *"FESTER"* I PITCHED FOR DC COMICS' "MINX" LINE OF TEEN GIRL GRAPHIC NOVELS.

(YES. REALLY.)

THIS PAGE HAS SOME OF MY FIRST DESIGNS FOR THAT PITCH.

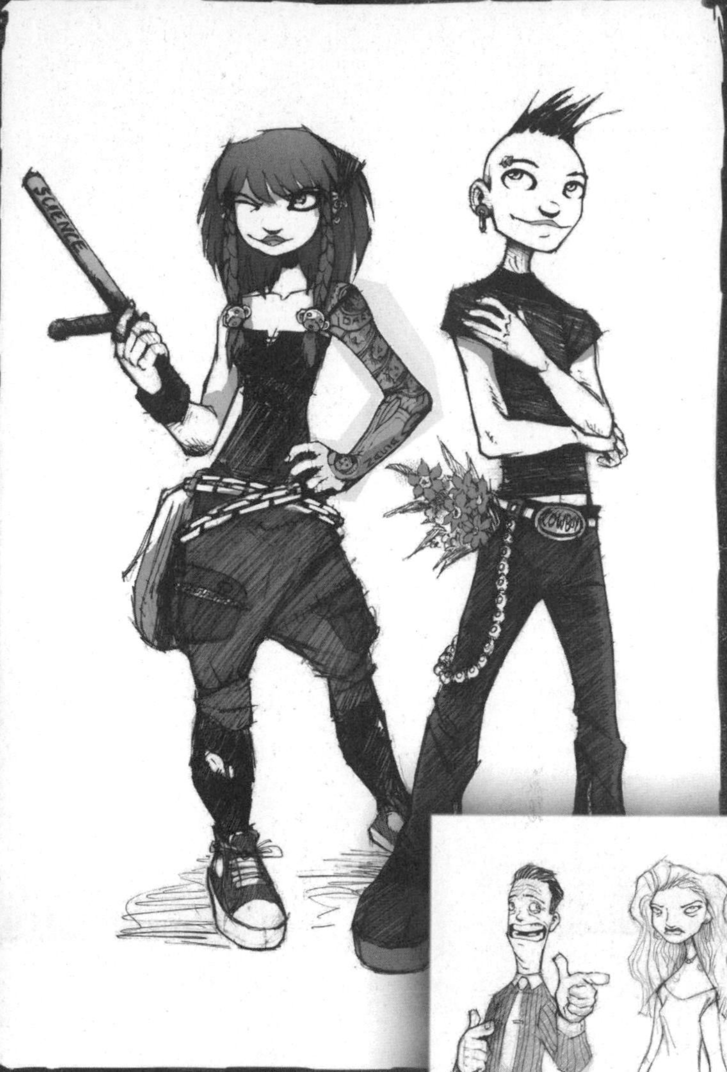
SCIENCE

AS YOU CAN SEE, MY ORIGINAL IDEA WAS TO MAKE OWEN AS DIFFICULT TO LOOK AT AS HUMANLY POSSIBLE. (SUCCESS!)

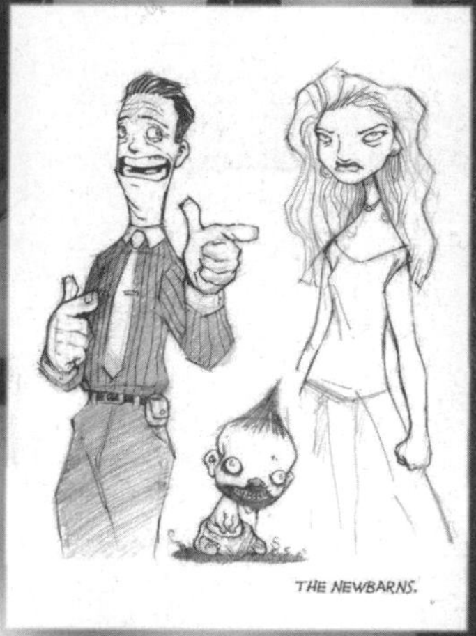
THE NEWBARNS.

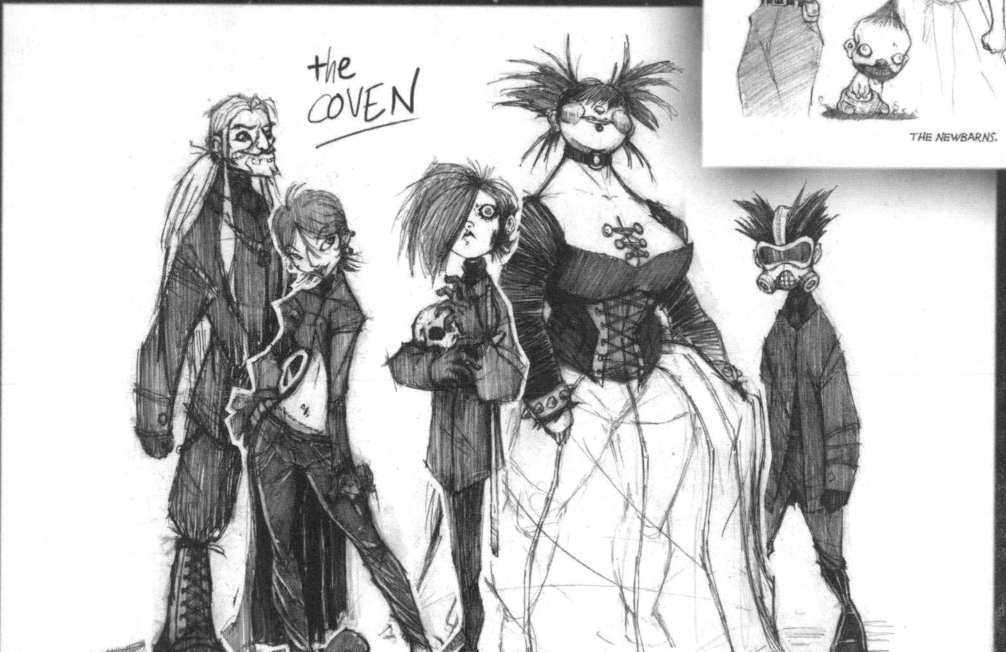
the COVEN

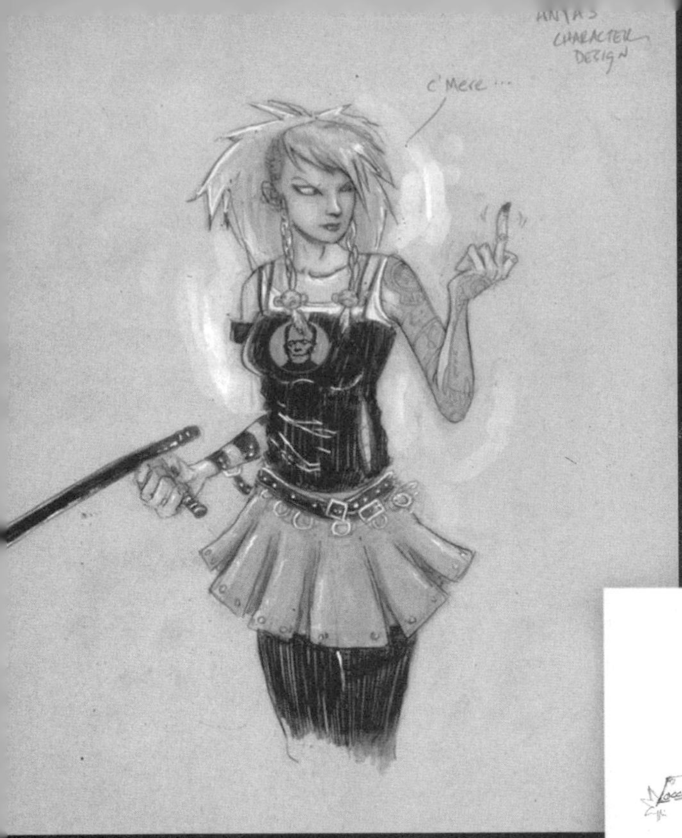
ANYA'S CHARACTER DESIGN
C'Mere...

ANYA

ONCE DREW SIGNED THE BLOOD OATH AND WAS INDUCTED INTO THE COVEN OF *ELDRITCH!*, WE REWORKED ALL THE OLD *FESTER* DESIGNS FOR DC'S "ZUDA" WEBCOMIC COMPETITION. AT THIS POINT, ANYA HAD MORE OF A PUNKY MAD MAX LOOK... THE IDEA WAS THAT SHE'D BE THE "WARRIOR QUEEN BOUDICA OF SCIENCE," DEFIANT AND READY FOR A FIGHT.

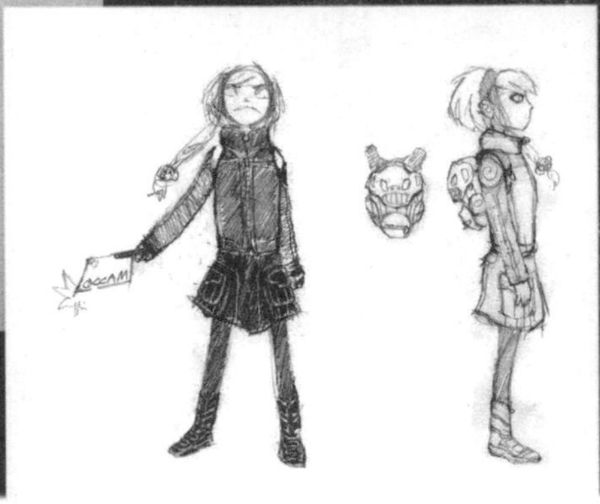

HER LOOK GOT UPDATED A BIT BETWEEN ZUDA AND THIS BOOK. HERE'S MY LITTLE SCRIBBLE... →

DREW'S FINAL DESIGN. WITH HER UTILITY SKIRT, FORM-FITTING MOTORCYCLE JACKET, AND HIGH-TECHIE BACKPACK, SHE LOOKS LESS LIKE A PUNK BARBARIAN AND MORE LIKE SOME STRANGE TRAVELLER FROM A DISTANT FUTURE. (OR, AT LEAST, THAT'S HOW SHE'D *LIKE* PEOPLE TO SEE HER.)

LIKE ALL THE OTHER CHARACTERS, ANYA GOT SLIGHTLY MORE CARTOONY BETWEEN ZUDA AND NOW. GIGANTIC EMOTIONAL TIRADES ARE A *LOT* MORE FUN IN A CARTOONY UNIVERSE.

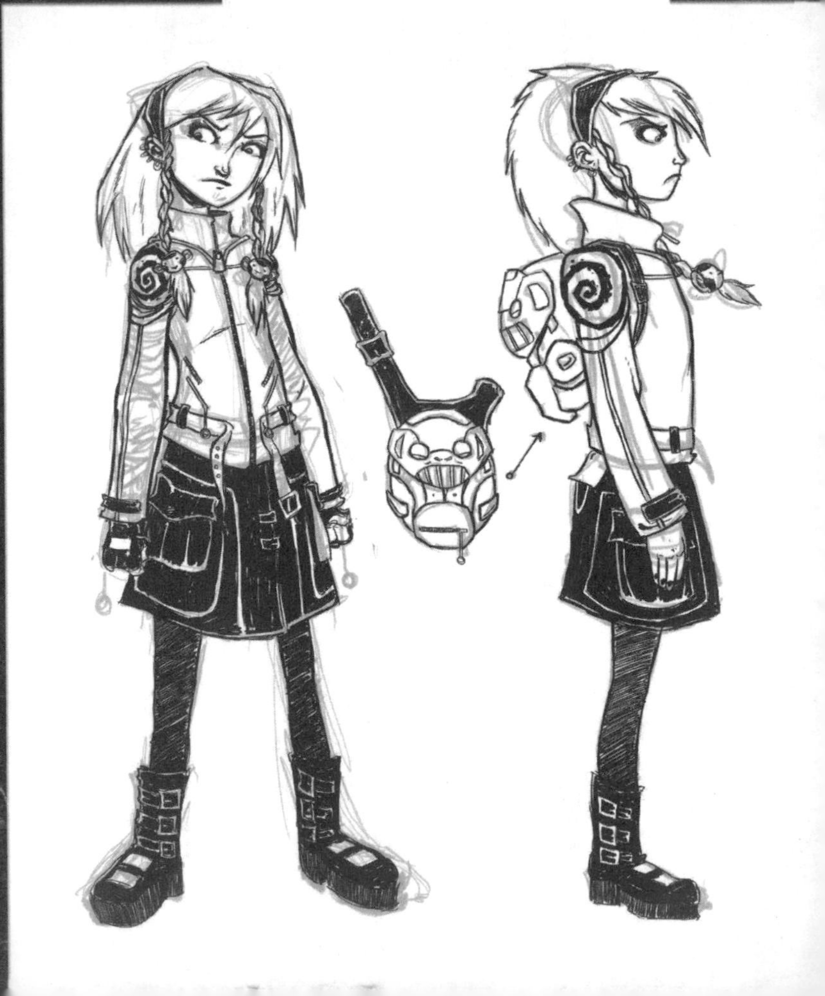

OWEN

DREW'S REDESIGN OF OWEN FOR THE ZUDA SUBMISSION.

THE LIVING EMBODIMENT OF ***SLUMP.*** I LOVED DREW'S IDEA TO PUT HIM IN THIS BIG, OVERSIZED PEACOAT. MAKES HIM LOOK REALLY SMALL, LIKE SOME TINY, FRAGILE CREATURE THAT JUST WANTS TO CRAWL DEEP INSIDE ITS SHELL AND ESCAPE THE WORLD FOREVER.

SORT OF A PERFECT "INNSMOUTH" LOOK, ISN'T IT?

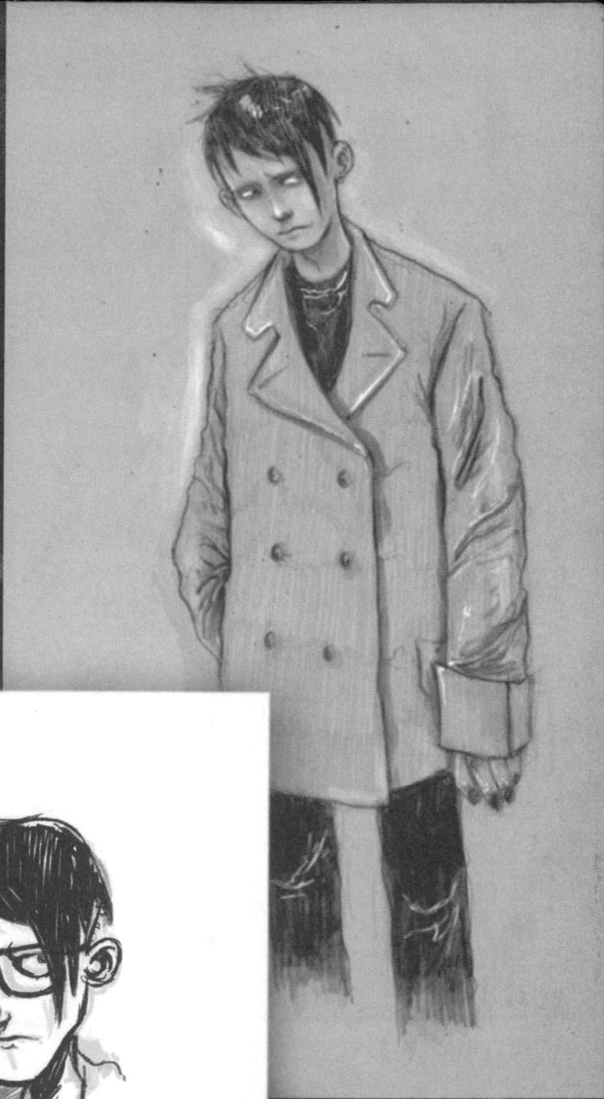

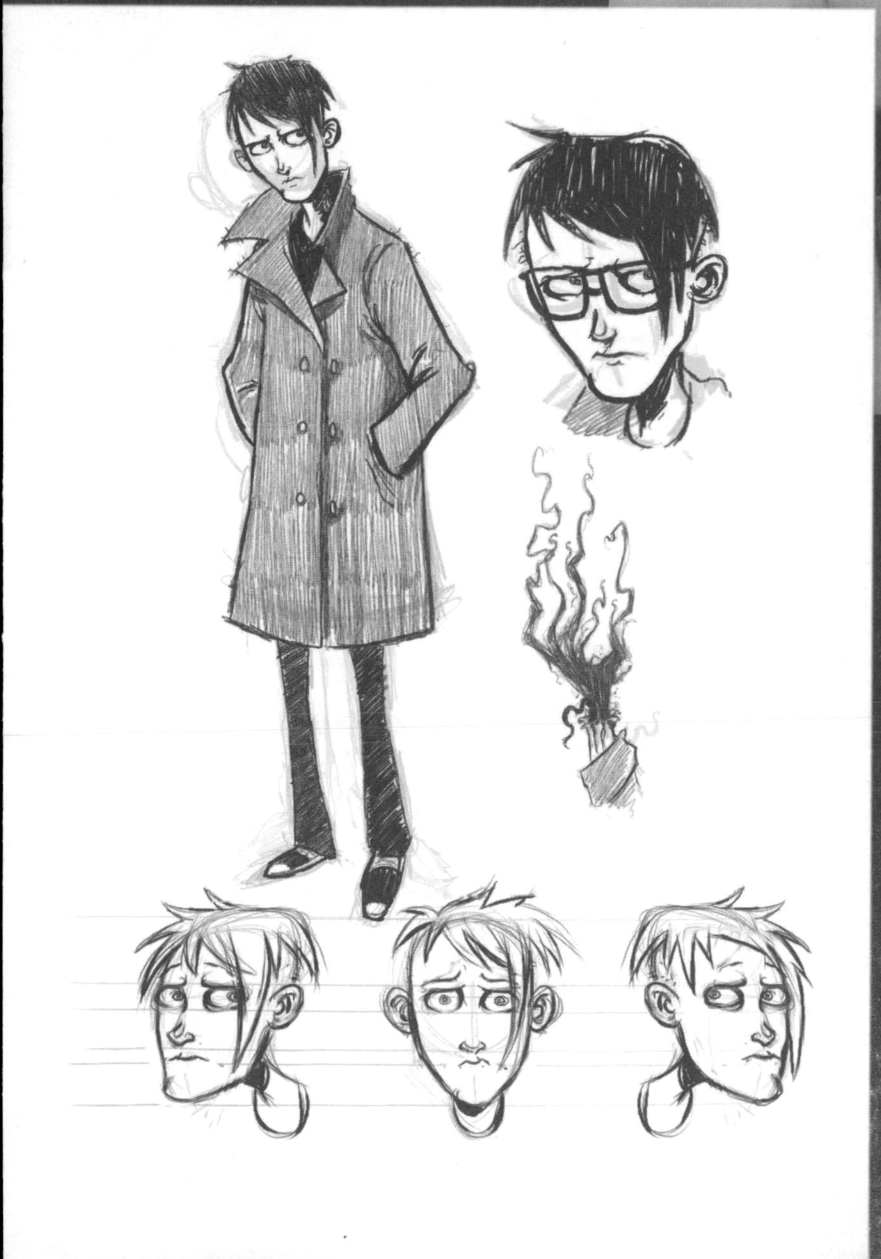

DREW'S FINAL DESIGN.

OWEN IS SUCH A LOW-KEY, INWARDLY-FOCUSED CHARACTER, HE'D PROBABLY WORK JUST AS WELL EITHER "REALISITC" OR "CARTOONY," BUT STYLISTIC CONSISTENCY IS IMPORTANT.

COOL EITHER WAY!

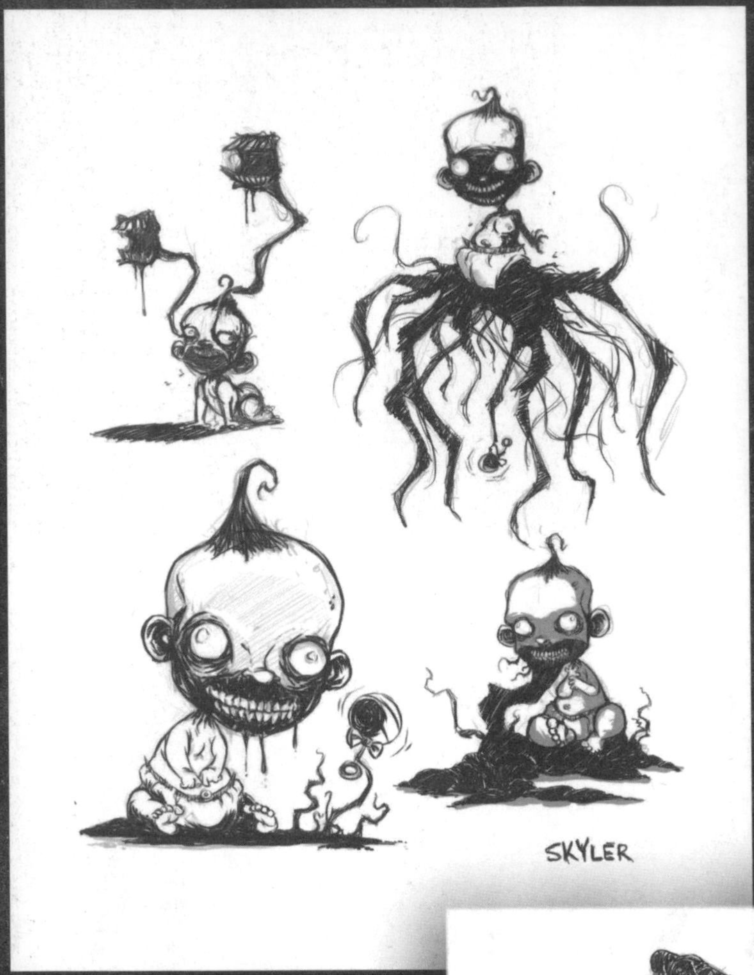
SKYLER

THE NEWBARNS

DREW'S FINAL DESIGNS FOR TED, JESS, AND POOR, MONSTROUS BABY SKYLER.

TED WAS DREW'S FAVORITE CHARACTER TO DRAW BECAUSE, WELL, HOW COULD HE ***NOT*** BE?

UGH... TEARING UP AGAIN JUST THINKING ABOUT TED'S FINAL MOMENTS HERE, MAN...

THE LOOK OF SKYLER'S TENTACLES WAS BASED ON VIDEO OF ***FERROFLUIDS*** (BASICALLY MAGNETIZED BLACK GOOP) IN ACTION.

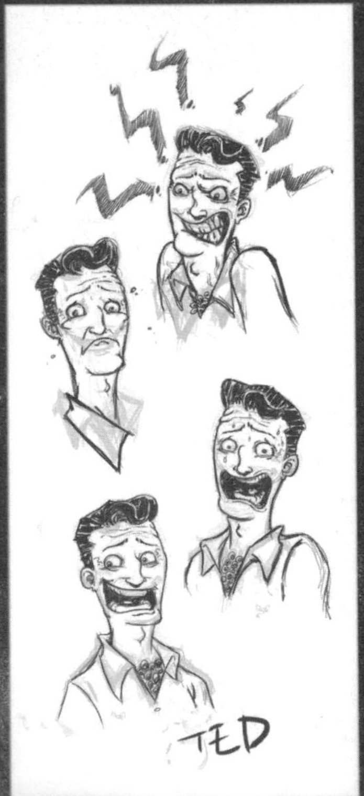
TED

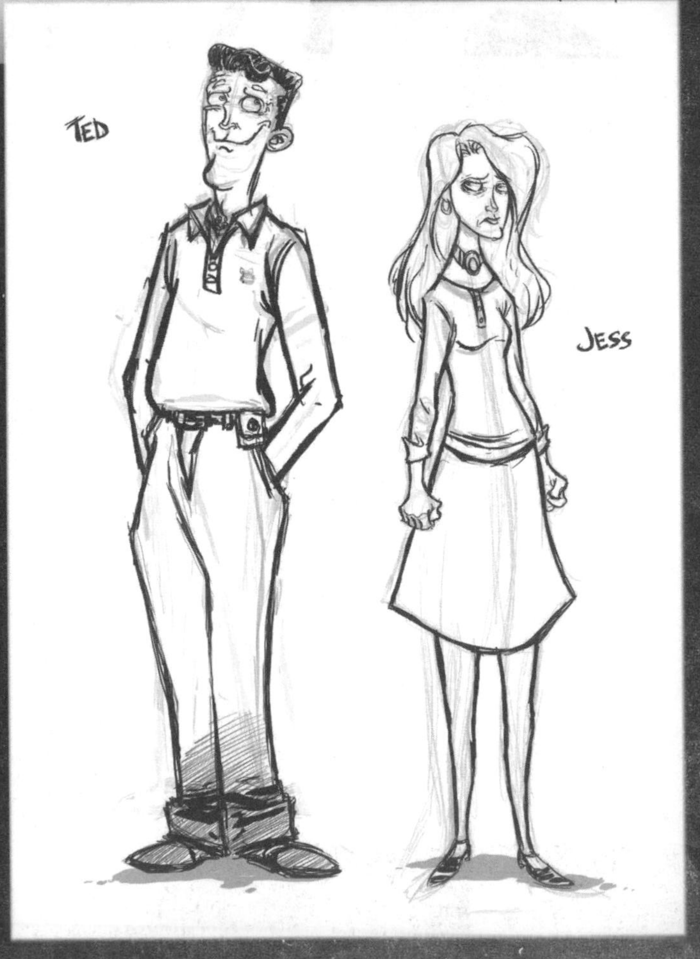
TED
JESS

THE SOBCZEK'S

FINAL PARENT DESIGNS BY DREW.
(PLEASE NOTE ARM HAIR DETAIL...)

THE COVEN

FINAL DESIGNS BY DREW.
ISN'T DAIZEE JUST THE *BEST*?

PHELIA.

CRUZ.

SKREW
TAPE.

RELIC?

CONTACT.

CHASTON

DAIZEE.

ELDRITCH! - Aaron Alexovich - ISSUE 05

How to build an ELDRITCH!

STEP #1: SCRIPT.

WHERE THE MAGIC BEGINS!

(I TOTALLY STOLE THIS SCRIPT FORMAT FROM MIKE CAREY.)

PAGE 9 PANEL 1

Anya looking down on Cruz, eyebrow arched. Cruz is lying facedown on the floor, all bunched up and shaking with rage.

ANYA: Wow, you are uniquely horrible at this...

PAGE 9 PANEL 2

Cruz leaps to his feet and spins toward Anya, smacking her hard in the head. His mouth has torn open so wide it's exposed the entire front of his torso, revealing a ribcage and abdomen writhing with oily black tentacles. His eyes have gone milky white and teary, his arms positively HULKED OUT, massive, sinewy, veins practically bursting from the skin. He lets out an awful roar of frustrated male pride. Tears in his eyes.

CRUZ: GREEEEAAAAARRRRRRGGGGHHH!!

SFX: THWOP!

PAGE 9 PANEL 3

CU Anya, hitting the ground, wincing.

OWEN (off-panel): ANYA!

PAGE 9 PANEL 4

Wide shot. In the background, Owen tries to calm the raging Cruz-monster. In the foreground, Anya groggily rolls onto her side and reaches behind her for a metal tube connected to her backpack.

CRUZ: GYAAAHGGGALLLÀAAH!

OWEN: CRUZ! GET IT TOGETHER! GET IT- SSSSSSSOOOO.... SSSOOOQ-

STEP #2: THUMBNAIL

I SCRIBBLE OUT A TINY LITTLE MESS OF LINES AS A WAY OF ANTAGONIZING DREW.

3. PENCILS

DREW MAKES SENSE OF IT ALL, ADDS THE DETAIL, STYLE, AND PERSONALITY...

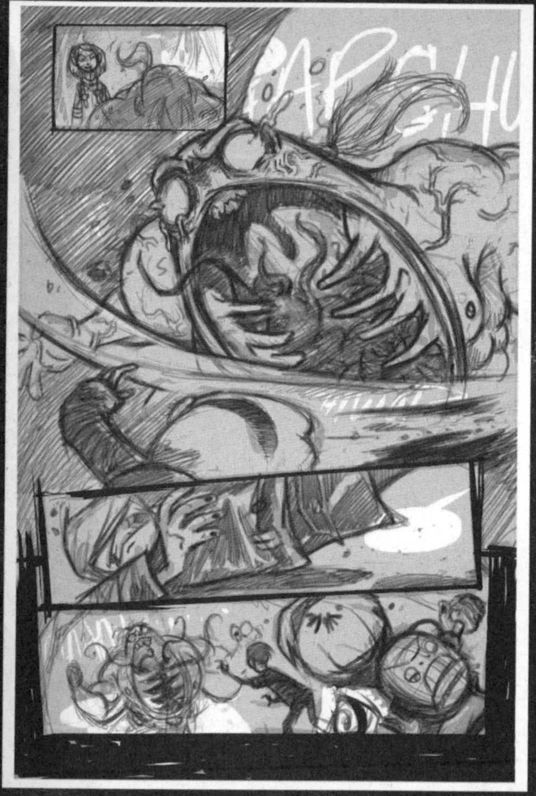

4. INKS

DREW PRETTIES IT UP WITH SOME LOVELY INK LINES...

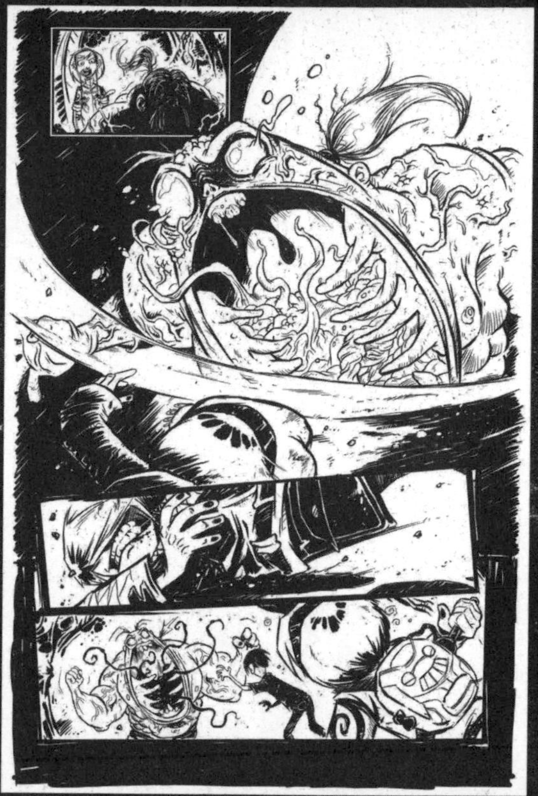

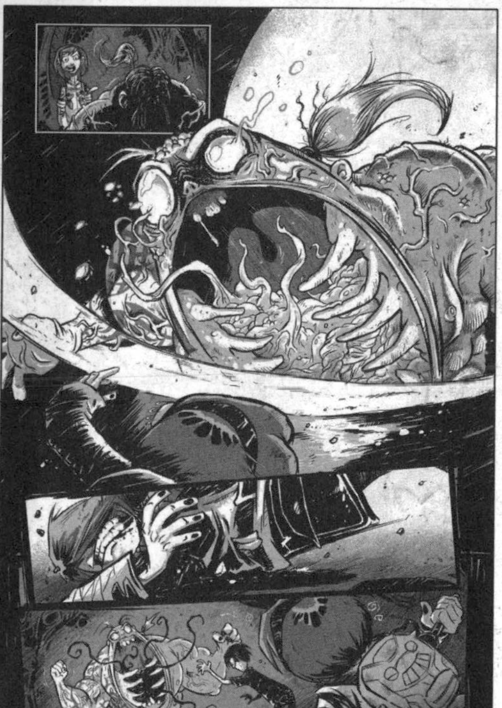

5. TONES

DREW PRETTIES IT UP EVEN *MORE* WITH SOME NICE, ATMOSPHERIC TONES...

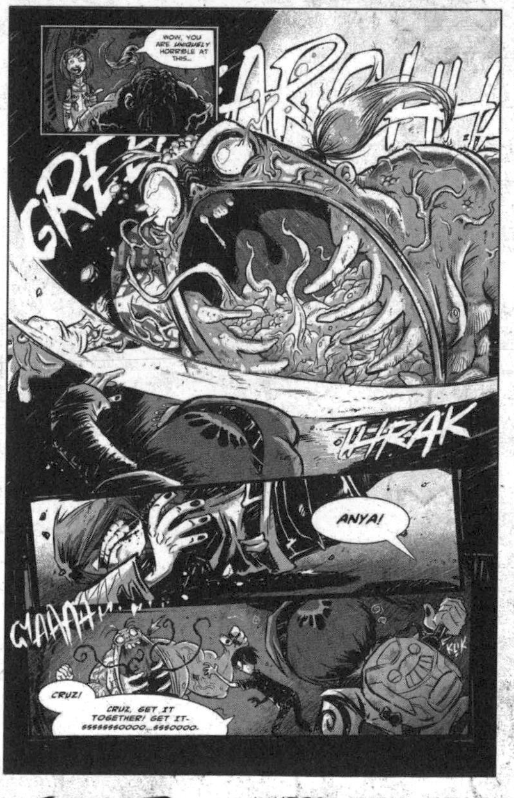
WOW, YOU ARE *UNIQUELY* HORRIBLE AT THIS...
THRAK
ANYA!
CRUZ!
CRUZ, GET IT TOGETHER! GET IT-SSSSSSSOOOO...SSSOOOO.

6. LETTERS

I WRECK IT ALL WITH SOME CRUMMY BALLOONS AND SOUND EFFECTS!

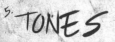

DREW RAUSCH

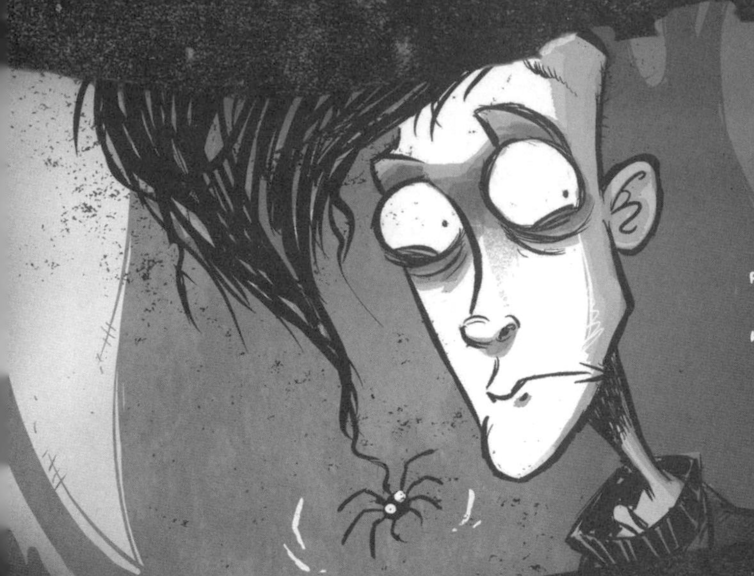

DREW RAUSCH IS CO-CREATOR OF THE SUBCULTURE HIT *SULLENGREY* (WITH JOCELYN GAJEWAY). PROOF OF HIS ARTISTRY CAN BE ALSO BE SEEN IN THE PAGES OF BOOM STUDIOS' *CTHULHU TALES* AND *ZOMBIE TALES*, AND SLG'S *HAUNTED MANSION* AND *THE SECRETS OF SARAH WINCHESTER*. WHILE WAITING FOR THE ELDER GODS TO RISE FROM THE DEEP, HE ENJOYS CLASSIC HORROR MOVIES (THE CABINET OF DR. CALIGARI BEING HIS FAVORITE) AND CUPCAKES. HE CURRENTLY HAUNTS A DUSTY APARTMENT IN SOUTHERN CALIFORNIA WITH HIS BRIDE AND 3 CATS.

AARON ALEXOVICH

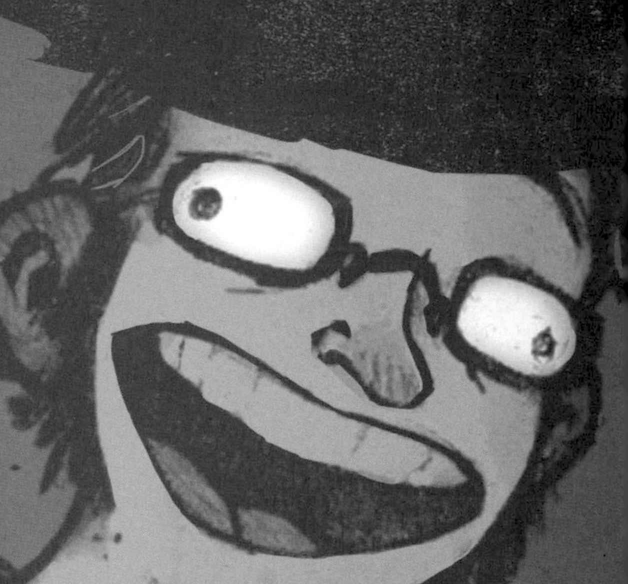

AARON'S FIRST PROFESSIONAL ART JOB WAS DRAWING DEFORMED CHILDREN ON NICKELODEON'S INVADER ZIM. SINCE THEN HE'S BEEN DEFORMING CHILDREN FOR VARIOUS ANIMATION AND COMIC PROJECTS, INCLUDING AVATAR: THE LAST AIRBENDER, SLG'S *HAUNTED MANSION*, DC'S *FABLES*, *KIMMIE66*, AND THREE VOLUMES OF HIS OWN HORROR/COMEDY WITCH SERIES *SERENITY ROSE*. AARON CURRENTLY LIVES IN SOUTHERN CALIFORNIA, WHERE THE BRIGHT LIGHT MAKES HIM SNEEZE FOR MYSTERIOUS REASONS.